GRASSROO
THE ARTS F... ...CHANGE

During these highly conflicted times, this book of essays is most welcome. What is most exciting is the wide range of topics and approaches to understanding the world-wide implications of appreciating the arts and social change. The authors bring diverse backgrounds and approaches to their very fresh subjects. I believe that their insights and perspectives will reach a wide international audience, that is thirsting for such understandings during these times of struggle, exploitation, but also hope. I am pleased to add my congratulations to the editors and all of the authors for this most stimulating book.

—*Ronald D. Cohen, Professor Emeritus of History, Indiana University Northwest, Gary, Indiana*

Grassroots Leadership and the Arts for Social Change is an important book, for it not only validates artistry as a vehicle for activism, but also shows how the myriad components of culture are integral to movements for social justice. While discussing specific projects, all over the globe, that have used art and popular education to effect positive change, this book is also a guidebook, a how-to for implementing such techniques within organizations and communities. I hope that activists at the base will read it widely. Doing so will make their activism more effective still.'

—*Marie-Claire Picher, Ph.D, Co-founder (1990) and Artistic Director of the Theater of the Oppressed Laboratory (TOPLAB), New York City*

This extraordinary book provides a platform for displaying how a broad array of artistic mediums – dance, theater, songs, murals, graffiti, photography, and more – are essential to social change movements. While the rich experiences shared have strong historical roots, in the current era of political turmoil and resistance, there are powerful lessons to be learned by activists today. What a great contribution Erenrich's and Wergin's collection offers, by demonstrating the deep power of the arts to provoke, to inspire, and to move us forward.

—*Marcy Fink Campos, Director, Center for Community Engagement & Service, Adjunct Professor, American University*

This timely and compelling book shines a spotlight on the creative cultural work of artists, musicians, performers and scholar-activists who spark and unleash the catalytic and transformative power of art to mobilize grassroots citizen action for meaningful social change. This wide ranging collection of essays focuses on the roles that artists and cultural activists play in inspiring people to take action. By providing valuable principles and practices, this work ultimately offers hope for a world in need of guideposts for human liberation, justice and peace. This book is an invaluable resource for fellow artists, performers, scholar-activists and practitioners of conscience who are committed to renewing the spirit of community from the local to the global level.

—*James V. Riker, Director, Beyond the Classroom Living & Learning Program, University of Maryland, College Park*

In this fine compilation, enhanced by Juan Gabriel Valdés' foreword of loss and resilience, activist scholar, Susan J. Erenrich and Antioch professor, Jon F. Wergin demonstrate the well-worn wisdom that is carved into the entrance hall of Chicago's Fine Art building, "Art Alone Endures."

Together, the editors have assembled herein an inspiring mosaic of such art – poetry and plays, portraits and photos – all of which illustrate how art and culture inform the struggle for social change.'

—*Thomas M. Grace, Ph.D., Assistant Professor of History, Erie Community College and author of Kent State: Death and Dissent in the Long Sixties*

As a survivor of the Kent State shootings in 1970, I can say with authority that we need this book. As co-editor Jon Wergin notes, from beginning to end the chapters in *Grassroots Leadership & the Arts for Social Change* provide "compelling evidence of the power of the arts to create disquiet; and ultimately to inspire." As lifelong civil rights activists and member of the U.S. House of Representatives said to the Kent State community during the 40th commemoration, we must all find a way to "get in the way." This book moves us to do just that with illustrations from the arts – stories from around the world. In each example, we find the particulars of a certain time, place, and people that each act as a timeless affirmation of the injustices we suffer and the principles that must be upheld – *and can be*, the stories show us.

Educators, scholars, students, citizens will benefit by reading *Grassroots Leadership & The Arts*. Wars have not stopped. Governments, systems remain corrupt, imperfect. We the people want the world to be a better place, for *everyone*. The arts – through appropriation and turning things around, by rousing our spirit, by affronting us and pulling us in – reveal the work to be done. In narrative and theory, these essays show the way. Susie Erenrich and Jon Wergin bring a perfect combination of experience, pedagogy, and spirit to *Grassroots Leadership & The Arts*. Together they have created a book that reaches people through both the mind and heart.

—*Laura L. Davis, Professor Emeritus, English, and Founding Director (ret.), May 4 Visitors Center, Kent State University*

GRASSROOTS LEADERSHIP AND THE ARTS FOR SOCIAL CHANGE

Edited by

Susan J. Erenrich
American University and New York University, USA

Jon F. Wergin
Antioch University, USA

United Kingdom – North America – Japan – India – Malaysia – China

Emerald Publishing Limited
Howard House, Wagon Lane, Bingley BD16 1WA, UK

First edition 2017

British Library Cataloguing in Publication Data
A catalogue record for this book is available from the British Library

ISBN: 978-1-78635-688-8 (Print)
ISBN: 978-1-78635-687-1 (Online)
ISBN: 978-1-78714-632-7 (Epub)

ISSN: 2058-8801 (Series)

ISOQAR certified
Management System,
awarded to Emerald
for adherence to
Environmental
standard
ISO 14001:2004.

Certificate Number 1985
ISO 14001

INVESTOR IN PEOPLE

Contents

Foreword

In Chile in 1973, General Augusto Pinochet and members of the armed forces and police overthrew the government of democratically elected President Salvador Allende. After the coup, my father Orlando Letelier, the former ambassador to the United States, was incarcerated in a concentration camp on a remote island in Patagonia, close to the Antarctic circle. A place of majestic volcanoes and lakes, where condors and pumas still roam, it became a harsh site of torture and imprisonment. After my father was released, our family went into exile like thousands of others.

In the United States, he worked to restore democracy in Chile denouncing the Pinochet regime for its abuse of human rights. On September 21, 1976, my father and coworkers, 23-year-old Ronnie Karpen Moffitt and her husband Michael Moffitt, were driving to work along embassy row in Washington DC when a C2 bomb attached to the undercarriage of our family car was detonated. My father and Ronnie were both killed. Agents working under orders from Pinochet collaborated with Cuban-American terrorists to carry out the act.

On the anniversary of the crime in 1977, burdened with the numbing darkness of the murders, people gathered in Washington DC and painted a collective mural in the Chilean tradition in honor of my father and Ronnie. Working together we found a way to care for our loss while imagining and creating our future. "Chilean" murals were characterized by their collective and participatory nature. In Chile, working class youth organized in squads had once hit the streets to write the names of candidates on walls. During the Allende campaign and government these politicized artists joined the graffiti squads leading to the creation of a visual vocabulary characterized by simple forms, bright colors, and black outlines. After the coup, murals were outlawed and whitewashed.

The **Brigada Orlando Letelier,** a muralist brigade grew out of that first mural.

The "Brigade" travelled across the United States painting Chilean solidarity murals in 11 cities while incorporating hundreds of participants. With an emphasis on human rights and creating sites of memory, the work encompassed the common experiences of Chileans, other Latinos, and the many other global communities we came into contact with.

40 years later, based in Venice, California, I continue the creation of murals, public artworks, and exhibitions throughout the United States and Latin America as well as in Europe, India, and Palestine. The projects develop inter-disciplinary curriculums in the arts, explore issues in human rights, cultural identity, and memory, and emphasize dialogues between nations, individuals, and communities.

In August 2016, I returned to Washington DC to create **Todas Las Manos**, a public art project commemorating the 40th Anniversary of the deaths of my father Orlando Letelier and Ronni Karpen Moffitt on September 21, 1976.

Chilean Ambassador Juan Gabriel Valdés was a young man working with my father at the time, if not for a slight change in plans he might have been in the car with him on that tragic morning. The project was conceived in consultation with the Chilean Embassy, the Institute for Policy Studies, the Latin American Youth Center and the National Security Archives, as well as with documentary film maker Aviva Kempner and others whose lives were impacted by the assassinations and events in Chile. Director Jack Rasmussen of the American University Museum at the Katzen Arts Center invited us to create our large-scale mural installation in the sculpture garden of the museum with the participation of youth from the Latin American Youth Center as well as scholars, students, activist, and others. It was an ideal moment for a public art project that could provide a space for the complex layers of history and memory that came together for the 40th anniversary.

The murders and subsequent FBI investigation into the crime led to a re-examination of United States policy in Chile and Latin America. The struggle for justice in the murders contributed directly to the downfall of the Pinochet dictatorship and although Pinochet was never directly indicted for his role in the crime, others were prosecuted and measures of justice achieved. The case continues to play an important role in creating transparency about the role of US policy concerning the murders. Through the Freedom of Information Act, and the release of previously classified documents, more is known about the activities of the Pinochet regime as well the role of the United States in Chile.

Following the assassinations, the Institute for Policy Studies established the Letelier-Moffitt Human Rights Awards to honor their fallen colleagues and recognize individuals and groups in the United States and elsewhere in the Americas most dedicated to the struggle for human rights. Nearing its 40th year, the prestigious award has been received by an outstanding list of individuals and organizations dedicated to human rights and social justice.

In honoring the legacy of Orlando and Ronnie after four decades, **Todas Las Manos** looks back at the events of September 21, 1976 and celebrates the initiatives for justice and human rights that were inspired by the tragedy. Early in the design process, declassified documents were integrated into the mural as I planned to work with youth to examine narratives about memory and identity while exploring issues of international human rights and justice. As in other projects, **Todas Las Manos** aimed to create a process where advocacy and art could coincide so we could experience the potential of cultural action and social practice.

When I arrived in Washington to begin the project, I learned that Chilean President Michelle Bachelet was scheduled to attend an unveiling of the mural.

I was also informed that the State Department had decided to declassify a new set of documents concerning my fathers' murder and they would be given to President Bachelet at the memorial event conducted yearly at the site of the murders, Sheridan Circle on Massachusetts Avenue.

When received, the documents confirmed what we had known with certainty all along; Augusto Pinochet ordered the murders. This contributed to the attention given to the mural after its unveiling and added to the impact the project had on all those involved. When the *Washington Post* published images of declassified documents taken from the mural the meaning of the work deepened. Tied to the 40th anniversary of the murders and the cultural memory of Chile, the mural allowed a broad community to recognize and acknowledge the solidarity work they had carried out for decades. **Todas Las Manos** serves as a strong example of arts for social change, providing a template for collaborative efforts that connect grassroots efforts with organizations, political movements, and initiatives for international cooperation for global justice.

This project would not have been possible without the increasingly interconnected global arts community. There have

always been artists that enact the power of imagination and creativity for the social good, serving as an inspiration and model for
the efforts of many others.

I learned about the publication of *Grassroots Leadership and
the Arts for Social Change* when Susan J. Erenrich visited the
Todas Las Manos site during its creation. I was impressed by the
inclusion of so many important creative voices from global movements for social justice. Broader understandings of the vital role
cultural action can play at key moments of history are essential
as our work continues, evolves, and grows. The volume can be
considered essential reading for those who seek models and further understanding of how cultural leaders are essential contributors to the creation of a better world.

Francisco Letelier

Foreword: September

September is for Chileans the most eventful month of the year. It is the month of our Independence, the beginning of the spring time, in which we dance and rejoice to celebrate the beauty of our nature and the life of the heroes that built the country in which we were born. But September is also the cruelest month of the year. It was on a Tuesday the 11th of that month in 1973 when we suffered the most brutal historical blow against our long-standing democratic institutions: the military coup that overthrew the government of President Salvador Allende. And three years later, on 21 September in Washington, DC, we were shaken by the murder by agents of Pinochet, of one of our most remarkable leaders in exile, Orlando Letelier, and also of Orlando's colleague at the Institute for Policy Studies, Ronnie Moffitt.

For 40 years, united by the same memories and ideals, Chileans and Americans have seen September 21 as a symbol of their strong and always-renewed commitment to human rights and democracy. During all this time, all those who have attended Sheridan Circle bringing flowers have dedicated a part of their lives to combat the Chilean military dictatorship, to denounce its violation of human rights, to put pressure on those in this country who helped to sustain the military in power during almost two decades and later, when democracy was recuperated, to keep alive the memory of these terrible and dramatic events.

This extraordinary community of Americans and Chileans, and everything that was done to change the history of the relationship between Chile and the United States, would not have been possible without the artists from both countries that were at the forefront of the movement of resistance and then of liberation from the military dictatorship. Since the beginning, the music of the Quilapayún, the Inti-Illimani, Aparcoa, and other Chilean folk groups joined Joan Baez, Pete Seeger, and Bob Dylan singing in memory of two Chilean giants' death at the hands of the military or immediately after the coup: Víctor Jara and Pablo

Neruda. Chilean Poets like Fernando Alegría in California, or writers like Ariel Dorfman in New York became deeply involved in the resistance movement. American writers such as William Styron and Saul Landau, and journalists like John Dinges dedicated their work to denounce the brutalities committed against the Chilean people.

Dore Ashton, the writer, professor, and critic of modern and contemporary art worked incessantly to protect the art works that had been donated by American painters to the Chilean Museum of Solidarity. This collection of world painters closed by the dictatorship in Santiago resurged in Mexico after the coup and is today – back in the capital of Chile – one of the most important museums of modern art in Latin America. One American painter in the collection, the world famous Robert Rauschenberg, produced *the Copperheads*, a series in which he used copper as a sign of solidarity with the Chilean people. And when the dictatorship was coming to a close, Christopher Reeve, the American actor that played Superman, visited Chile giving support to the democratic forces that were preparing the campaign for the plebiscite that defeated Pinochet. During the campaign, artists like Jane Fonda, Richard Dreyfuss, and Susan Sarandon became representatives of the American Solidarity Movement with Chile, calling Chileans to vote NO.

This is the inherited context in which Francisco Letelier, the artist son of Orlando, painted his mural *"Todas las Manos"* in commemoration of the 40th anniversary of the death of his father and of Ronnie Moffitt. The mural, exhibited at the American University Museum at the Katzen Arts Center in Washington since September, summarizes the extraordinary journey made by Chileans and Americans united to defend peace, human rights, and democracy, and of all those artists here and there, who with their creativity were able to mobilize the spirit of Chileans and Americans toward a higher and more humane future. It underlines the importance of artistic work in keeping memory alive, especially in the education of new generations who did not go through these dramatic events.

I bring these topics and ideas to the fore as a preface to this extraordinary book by Susan J. Erenrich and Jon F. Wergin: "Grassroots Leadership and the Arts for Social Change." Its chapters address different cases in which artists have led, connected, and inspired grassroots movements, and confirm once again that no social movement can advance to prominence without the presence of artistic production. Artists become leaders as part of the inevitable need of any social movement to transcend immediacy and project universality. This book responds to the essential task to underline the role of artists as teachers and guides in a world subject to the enormous transformation of the technological revolution and the confusing mushrooming of differing social movements.

Juan Gabriel Valdés
Ambassador of Chile

Preface

Dear Friends,

In the summer of 2005, I enrolled in Antioch University's doctoral program in Leadership and Change. I was excited about the social change portion of the curriculum, but the field of leadership didn't interest me. The top-down paradigms, pioneered by predominantly middle-aged white men, didn't speak to me. The concept of followership offended me. And quite frankly, it was antithetical to everything that I believed in.

So why was I there? I wasn't able to adequately answer this question until I advanced to candidacy. As I embarked on the most crucial leg of my journey, I knew I had to find a way or make one, otherwise I would be another ABD (All but Dissertation) statistic.

Thanks to Albert Camus, the 1957 literary Nobel Laureate, I forged a path to discover what it meant for artists to create dangerously. Camus challenged the creative class during his Nobel lecture to defy the status quo. To instigate. To make a difference with their craft. He knew that the road to victory might be treacherous and long. That the odds might be stacked against them. Nevertheless, Camus summoned artists to rise up and to speak out. Camus, however, never defined what was implied by his charge, or laid out a course of action. That was my job. To attempt to make sense out of Camus' provocation.

I established benchmarks for studying the create dangerously phenomenon and tried to shed light on the topic through an interdisciplinary theoretical framework. At the heart of my sojourn were the writings of scholars, organizers, and artists, who impacted my life in a profound way. Folks like Paulo Freire, Augusto Boal, Ella Baker, Howard Zinn, Myles and Zilphia Horton, to name a few. The scholarship on social movements, revolution, rebellion, resistance, dissent, protests, revolts and liberation was vast and it helped shape my understanding of grassroots leadership and the arts for social change. It was an eye-opening experience.

Jon F. Wergin, the co-editor of this book, was the perfect chair for my committee. We were equal partners in my quest for knowledge, working collaboratively to pave the way for a more inclusive, equitable, and accessible field of inquiry.

During my personal reconnaissance mission and after my rite of passage from student to "scholar," I became a leadership convert. For the first time, I saw that there was something here for me and I wanted to share it with others. I asked Jon to team up with me again to expand the leadership footprint. I wrote the proposal for this special BLB volume, and once accepted, invited fellow travelers from around the globe to participate in this new platform. The response was stunning. Ninety-eight prospective authors from six continents submitted abstracts. The top 20 were encouraged to craft a chapter for the book.

The invitees were welcomed to tell stories about cultural activists, the role of the arts in social movements, people power, and community building, in a nonconventional way. They were instructed to write for the masses. The language had to be accessible and engaging in spite of an author's affiliation with an academic institution.

The authors were also introduced to the notion of people's scholarship and were emboldened to talk about horizontal and collaboratively based leadership models, and show how art, as a weapon of choice, can have a real impact on society from the bottom-up. And that concepts, like grassroots leadership and the arts for social change, for the first time, have a front-row seat.

It is my wish that the leadership pioneers, who have yet to go beyond the classical thinking in this field, finally expand the boundaries, build bridges, and invite other stakeholders to the table. This is the new frontier. There is unexplored territory just waiting to be probed.

For everyone else, I hope you are inspired by the narratives spotlighted throughout this publication, reflect on the content, and continue to dream a better world full of possibility.

Susan J. Erenrich
Editor

Introduction One

PVC to BLB: An Intimate Portrait and Behind the Scenes Glance at Grassroots Leadership and the Arts for Social Change

Overcast skies and drizzle couldn't dampen my mood. I was home. New York City. It had been four years since I left the familiar sights and sounds of the urban jungle. Nevertheless, on May 21, 2016, as I briskly walked toward my destination, it felt routine. A path I traveled hundreds of times before.

I clumsily dodged the raindrops as I turned the corner onto East 35th Street. I was overcome with emotion. I was at my journey's end. Or was it the beginning?

I nervously glanced at my watch. It was 6:50 PM Eastern Standard Time. Approximately one hour before the commencement of the evening's program. I raced down the empty staircase, yanked open the door, and sashayed into the bustling room.

I was warmly greeted by my colleagues with cheerful hellos and affectionate embraces. After a split second of chit chat the all-volunteer army continued to equip the stage for the Saturday weekly performance. Three members of the engineering crew were on-hand meticulously installing cables, carefully assembling microphones, and prepping the board. Sound check was moments away. Other enlistees were diligently tidying the space, organizing the product table, methodically arranging chairs, and sprucing up the corridor.

In the midst of the commotion, my singer-songwriter compatriots, eagerly entered the scene with a truck load of instruments.

They gently unpacked their gear while I provided instructions for the team. There wasn't a moment to spare. Folks were already trickling in.

As sound check finally got underway, at approximately 7:15, I turned my attention to the gate. I started fretting about the weather impacting attendance for the show. This wasn't unexpected. I agonized over audience participation since I joined the booking committee at the all-volunteer collective in 2004. So this night, producing, *A Toast to Those Who Are Gone: Celebrating the Lives & Music of Two Troubadours of Topical Songs, Matt Jones & Phil Ochs*, brought on the regular stress and excitement that was a matter of course.

My deliberation and consternation was politely interrupted by a voice beckoning me to the right side of the wooden platform. "Testing Testing-This is a test." The booming sound permeated the space. Perfect.

My musical collaborators and long-time friends also monitored and evaluated the quality of their instrumental and vocal transmissions. Also splendid.

Shortly thereafter, the lights dimmed. Customary announcements were dispatched and I took my place at the microphone. *Good Evening Everyone.*

The Peoples Voice Café

As I continued my introductory remarks, welcoming fellow travelers to the last show of the season, I took a moment to reflect upon my 12-year history with the group. It certainly wasn't my first experience with horizontal leadership and participatory democracy. It was, however, a special transformational one.

I initially discovered the Peoples' Voice Café by accident. I had been living in Manhattan for two years when I saw an ad for a performance with Charlie King, a veteran of the contemporary topical song movement, and his partner Karen Brandow. Charlie was an acquaintance from my days at Kent State University. I was a member of an anti-nuclear community task force and he was a musician in Bright Morning Star. My associates and I sponsored the visit. It had been decades since our last face-to-face encounter. So I enthusiastically went to the gig. It was a marvelous reunion and an enlightening Café debut. I was hooked. The following Saturday was the 25th anniversary jubilee, featuring one of the café's founding members, Pete Seeger. I dropped in again and never looked back.

Peoples' Voice Café was right up my alley. It is an all-volunteer collective that has produced quality entertainment for New York City since the late 1970s. Every Saturday night from September through May, the Café provides space for the artistic expression of a wide variety of humanitarian issues and concerns. The concert that I produced the night of May 21, 2016, was just one link in the long history of the cultural activist chain. As I basked in the bright lights and relished the moment, I was acutely aware of the immense shoulders I stood upon, not only here, but throughout my life.

I turned my attention to the honorees. *Thank you for coming out to salute the lives and music of two troubadours of topical songs, Matt Jones and Phil Ochs. Both men have significantly made their mark and have touched our hearts.*

Matt was family. For 20 years we were musical co-conspirators. After our first rocky exchange in 1992, where he abruptly slammed down the phone, we cemented a bond that lasted until his death. For those of you unfamiliar with this incredible singer-songwriter, I'll provide a bit of background. Matt or Matthew to some, was one of the leaders of the Nashville student movement while enrolled at Tennessee State University in 1960. He wrote his first freedom song in 1961, and in 1963 developed the Danville Voices. The group would go into the tobacco fields of Virginia using freedom songs as an organiz-ing tool. In Danville, he wrote many anthems including the Ballad of Medgar Evers. In the fall of 1963, Matt went to Atlanta to reorganize the SNCC Freedom Singers. He remained with them until 1967. Matt was arrested 29 times while in the Civil Rights Movement. For more than five decades, he dedicated his life to the ongoing struggles for social change. Matt com-posed more than 500 songs during his lifetime. He will have turned 80 on September 17, 2016.

Phil was next. My inner voice was nudging me along and chastising me for being loquacious. Get on with it. The other part of my brain thought it was meaningful and essential to say something about the honorees. So I continued:

Phil Ochs, on the other hand was an ally to many social movements. Sadly, I never met him. Only vicariously through his sister, Sonny, who has been a contributor to many of the docu-mentarian projects that I've launched over the decades. Some of you may have been lucky enough to frequent a Phil Ochs performance or caught a glimpse of him at demonstrations and rallies prior to his suicide in 1976. For those like me, who only encountered him through his albums – yes vinyl, or not at all, he was lauded as a musical spokesman of the 1960s. His song, I Ain't Marchin' Anymore was one of the anthems of the anti-Vietnam War Movement. He was a committed activist who never compromised. In 1964, Phil joined the Mississippi Caravan of Music to help break the back of Jim Crow. He went South to support the domestic warriors on the front lines and then used his songs to educate those who were unaware of southern racial injustice or were unable to make the journey. Throughout his life he traveled the world, lending his voice to many causes and organizing significant concerts like the 1973 "Evening with Salvador Allende," to raise money for the Chilean people after the 9/11/1973 coup. Phil's friend, Chilean folksinger Victor Jara, was tortured and executed during the early days of the dictatorship, so the show took on special meaning. This tribute concert marks the 40th anniversary of Phil's death.

By this point, I was a little self-conscious. This was an extensive kickoff to the show. I gazed around the room to make certain the audience was still with me. They were. It was a good thing because I had amassed a number of testimonials from former colleagues, family members and associates to deliver in between the selected songs for the program. The first one was about to be shared:

Before I welcome this evening's musical guests, I'd like to read a note penned by Sonny Ochs: It has been 40 years since my brother Phil chose to end his own life. Amazingly, his songs continue to resonate and are sadly still relevant. Many artists are still recording his songs all these years later. I can think of no better tribute than that!

I am in my 33rd year of Phil Ochs Song Nights which have taken place all around the country and even in Australia. It is wonderful to see the young people starting to appear in the audiences.

I would like to thank the folks who came out tonight to hear Phil's music. Like tonight, there are many Phil Ochs Song Nights springing up everywhere. I hope you will make the effort to get your children to hear and adopt the music and share it with their friends. It's too important to let it be forgotten.

Enjoy the show!!
Sonny Ochs

I took a breath and waited for the spirited clapping to stop. Finally, the musical lineup of the program would commence. I joyfully welcomed Magpie (Terry Leonino and Greg Artzner) to the stage:

Tonight, all of the songs for this extraordinary tribute will be showcased by my dear comrades, Magpie. I first met this husband and wife duo at Boulder Junction, an intimate folk club in Uniontown, Ohio in 1976. I was with my former housemates, Dean Kahler and his partner Valerie Manning. Dean was one of the wounded students from the May 4, 1970 shootings where the Ohio National Guard opened fire on the Kent State University campus. Four students died that day and nine others were wounded. Dean was paralyzed from the waste-down. Terry was an eyewitness to the massacre and Greg was a Kent community resident. The incident impacted all of our lives so we bonded instantaneously. Since that first encounter, Terry and Greg have traveled the globe, bringing their unique sound and breathtaking versatility to audiences everywhere. From traditional tunes to vintage blues, swing and country to folk classics to contemporary and stirring original compositions, they cover a lot of musical ground. Much of it you will experience tonight. With their powerful voices and harmonies and their excellent instrumental arrangements on guitars, mandolin, harmonica, dulcimer, and concertina, their sound is much bigger than just two people. Terry and Greg are award-winning recording artists, songwriters, musical historians, and social activists, Tonight, they will honor two movers and shakers whom transformed their lives. Please give a warm welcome to Magpie ...

A Toast to Those Who Are Gone

Terry and Greg kicked off the evening with a beautiful rendition of *A Toast To Those Who Are Gone*, a Phil Ochs tune. It was a fitting and eloquent start for a commemoratory occasion. And notably, the title of the show. The room was still.

As I surveyed the crowd, I noticed that many of the folks gathered for the tribute were newcomers. There were returning Café devotees as well. Some of the veterans had been around since the early days. The Café was initially a response to the changing political climate of the times. Artists involved in social change campaigns or community and movement building activities were experiencing a backlash. Many of the balladeers were unable to secure paying gigs unless they altered or toned down their rhetoric. Others had to find alternative ways to convey their message. After numerous discussions between singers-songwriters, who had been shunned, or had to find alternative employment, performers from the New York City area, along with Pete Seeger, decided to take matters into their own hands. Judy Gorman, a singer-songwriter who was spearheading the charge, held the first meeting in her Manhattan apartment. A collective was formed and the artists searched for an appropriate space. Peoples' Voice Café was born.

The heightened applause at the end of the tune jarred me back to the present. I moved from my unobtrusive station beside the piano to the microphone. I invited Shelly Jones, Matt's widow to the stage. It was the first time since Matt's passing when she garnered enough strength to eulogize her late husband in public. Shelly was welcomed with open arms. I could feel the compassion in the room. She read a heartfelt remembrance from her nephew, smiled at the assembled concert goers and sat down.

I reappeared to show my appreciation for Shelly and to memorialize another Movement warrior who recently transitioned, Willie, Wazir Peacock. Wazir was one of the many brave unsung foot soldiers involved in the Southern Freedom Movement in Mississippi. He was born in Tallahatchie County, the same locality where Emmett Till, a 14-year-old Black adolescent from Chicago, was lynched in 1955. In 1962, Wazir became a full-time Field Secretary for the Student Nonviolent Coordinating Committee (SNCC) and one of the early song leaders, organizing in the Magnolia State. He was also the brainchild for the Community Cultural Revival, which was the forerunner to the Delta Blues Festival. I slowly spoke into the mic: *Sadly, I've been attending too many commemoratory programs for Civil Rights Movement veterans. I'd love to salute them all, but regrettably time is a factor. I do want to read a short tribute for Wazir Peacock, however, because for more than fifty years he was part of an extraordinary group of balladeers whom assembled to carry forward the mission of the Movement for equality and justice. This note of recognition is from the great blues singer Barbara Dane:*

Hello Susie,

Thank you so much for announcing this sad news. Otherwise, so many people would not know of Wazir's passing, just as we didn't know of his fading months or years. He was a good man, an upright man, a creative man, a generous man, and a fine singer too. His kind are hard to find, and he will be missed.

Barbara

Without further ado, I brought Magpie back to the stage to do a full musical set.

Matt Jones: SNCC Field Secretary

Matt was a prolific lyricist and an incredible performer. Throughout our 20-year alliance he frequently sang his latest creation over the phone so I had some indication where to place it in the lineup for some upcoming event. *When I Was Young* was one of those tunes. He wrote it specifically for a 1996-reunion concert I produced in Bethesda, MD. It was the first time that many of the Movement trail blazers gathered together in more than 30 years. It was a special moment and a reflective time for all of those assembled on-stage and off. The year before, Matt and his brother Marshall were inducted into the National Voting Rights Hall of Fame in Selma, AL. It was sobering for him to realize that after three decades, he was still fighting for some of the same things. The verses coalesced and he unveiled the beautiful lament during that particular show. He was no longer around, so Terry and Greg commenced the early part of the program with that song.

Four additional numbers followed. *Oginga Odinga*, a whimsical tune about a Kenyan Diplomat who visited the United States in 1963; *Ballad of Medgar Evers*, written for an assassinated Civil Rights Movement icon; *Legend of Danville*, where Matt was organizing during his earliest days in the campaign for equality and justice; and *Avon Rollins*, for his best friend who was on the Executive Committee of SNCC.

By the time Terry and Greg finished their set, the hall was filled with onlookers. It wasn't a standing room only crowd, but it was a respectable house. Full-capacity audiences at the Café are rare occurrences, but they do happen on occasion.

The Café can easily seat 150 people. There were about 60 enthusiastic fans on-hand for the 21st. The makeshift theater isn't permanent. Since 2008, the Café has rented space from The Community Church of New York Unitarian Universalist, which is located at 40 East 35th Street between Park Avenue & Madison Avenue. Prior to moving to the current location, the Café occupied a room at the Workmen's Circle two blocks away on East 33rd Street. Not having a stable, ever-present location has impacted turnout to a certain extent. Other factors prevail, including the absence of a solid publicity committee, and fierce competition amongst the hundreds of other venues in Manhattan offering quality productions at the exact same time.

The chairs are notably hard and uncomfortable, and the stage isn't raised, so the artists and spectators are on the same level making it difficult to see with the exception of the front row. There are no advanced ticket sales, so when artists commit, they have no idea how much they will earn. Every so often, a major leaguer, like Roberta Flack, will perform. In those instances, the Café can offer a small guarantee. The standard practice, however, is 60% of the gate goes to the performers; 40% goes to the Café to cover the organization's expenses.

In spite of the challenges of keeping an all-volunteer collective together for more than three decades, Peoples' Voice Café offers something that no other site provides. It is the last bastion for topical music in the Big Apple. The Greenwich Village heyday has long passed and the commercial establishments, so prevalent in the 1960s, have all disappeared. Hot spots like the Gaslight, Gerdes Folk City, Café Wha?, the Village Gate, and The Bottom Line, have been swallowed up by neighborhood gentrification. The Café is in a unique position to make this the premier venue for artists engaged in social change initiatives, but it hasn't arrived quite yet.

Another positive aspect of the Café is its healthy egalitarian spirit. There are no headliners on the bill. Every performer is treated equally regardless of status.

Café concerts are also reasonably priced. The suggested gate is $18 – more if you choose, less you can't; no one is turned away. If the theater goer is a member of the collective, then the recommended contribution is $12. The entrance fees are going up to $20 in September 2016, which is a modest increase compared to other venues in the area. Money is certainly not an issue for the public. The deep-rooted practice of equitability, however, can be problematic for the artists. From a political standpoint, Café performers believe that music should be accessible in spite of financial status. On the other hand, a small door greatly impacts the purse strings of the artists preventing some from accepting a gig. On the bright side, however, most of the balladeers welcome the opportunity to play. Peoples' Voice Café is a cause and many of the performers that I have booked have wanted to support its mission.

Like most meeting places, nowadays, the Cafe entrance is wheelchair accessible. The bathrooms are also unrestricted and in accordance with the Americans with Disabilities Act. Structural issues prohibiting wide chairs from being able to maneuver in the space were a predicament in past locations, especially with an aging baby boomer crowd, but these obstacles don't exist at the Community Church of New York.

And, after much discussion, in 2014, the Café finally incorporated and became a nonprofit opposed to a membership organization. In spite of changing its legal positioning, it continues to depend on its associates for financial support. A basic subscription is $20 per year. The subscription rate for two people at one address is $30. Supporters receive discounts to shows, and a monthly schedule of events. The Café has also obtained some small grants to help subsidize its efforts. Being able to secure tax deductible donations is a huge plus and will help sustain the group.

Most essential to the Café, however, is its on-the-ground enlistees and grassroots style of horizontal leadership. Every member in the collective has a job and everyone leads. It is an example of participatory democracy at its best and it has served the community well for more than 30 years. Tasks include collecting money at the door, staffing the refreshment table, setting up and breaking down chairs, assisting with mailings, running the sound, booking the artists, publicizing the shows, selling product for the performers, doing the accounting, and baking.

All shows start at 8:00 PM and end at 10:30 PM. The doors supposedly open at 7:30, but attendees tend to dribble in prior to the suggested arrival time. There really isn't any place for them to wait except outside the church. And no one wants to hang around on a blistery cold snowy night or in a torrential rainstorm while the Café properly prepares to greet its public. Early entry tends to interfere with the sound check, but the singers-songwriters and the crew have adapted to this unusual set of circumstances.

My meandering introspective thoughts were interrupted by thunderous applause following Magpie's opening set for Matt Jones. I casually walked back to the microphone to read another tribute. It was from Phil Ochs' long-time friend, Eric Andersen.

Phil Ochs: A Songsmith for a Generation

I have a note of gratitude from across the pond from the great Song Poet of Greenwich Village, Eric Andersen: Ohhhhhhhhhh. Clap clap clap. Phil was my older brother in the Village when I first arrived in Feb. 1964. He showed me around and introduced me to everybody who was anybody. I still look up to him as the best topical songwriter and ballad writer. His songs rang true and maybe even truer today. We miss him and I was thankful to know him. – Eric Andersen

Eric sent along an MP3 to play on this special occasion. The tune is Plains of Nebrasky-O. The words and music are by Eric Andersen. The backup vocals are Phil. It was recorded on October 29, 1964, for Broadside Volume 3 and published in Broadside #40, 1964. According to Eric, after leaving college, he wrote this song as "an impression when I was hitchin' West to San Francisco, I guess in a Woody Guthrie mode." Here it is. There was a minor glitch. The player froze. Disappointed murmurs emanated from the floor. The sound crew provided a quick fix and started the audio from the beginning. A sigh of relief. It came off without a hitch. The audience mindfully listened. The room was still. Then a wild burst of energy enveloped the space. It was one of the many highlights of the evening.

When the ovation came to a halt, I brought Magpie back to do a Phil Ochs Civil Rights Movement set. They performed two previously unrecorded basement tapes, *You Should Have Been Down In Mississippi*, and *How Long*. Both of these tunes were eventually introduced to the public, when Terry and Greg provided studio recordings for *Freedom Is a Constant Struggle: Songs of the Mississippi Civil Rights Movement*. The 2-CD collection, that I produced, was released during the 30th anniversary of the Freedom Summer Project of 1964. Those numbers were followed by two more, *Power & Glory*, and *What's That I Hear?* That concluded the first half of the show.

Intermission

Intermission at the Café is a time to mingle, gobble up some fresh baked goodies, purchase product, stretch your legs, and refresh.

It is also the point in the program where some folks make their exit. I crossed my fingers hoping that there would be a respectable house when we regrouped for the second half. Lucky for us, only a few people left the scene. The tireless majority stuck around.

Terry, Greg, and I utilized the interlude wisely. They geared up for 11 more songs while I did a quick meet and greet, sold a few CDs, and assembled the crew to kick off the last portion of the show.

It had been a whirl wind day for the three of us. Earlier that afternoon, we presented at the Global Left Forum, one of the biggest annual gatherings of activists, scholars, progressive thinkers, academics, and cultural workers, in North America. Terry and Greg are contributing authors to this groundbreaking volume of the Building Leadership Bridges series. So the 3:30 panel presentation at the conference served as an unofficial book launch and a great way to drum up support for this special publication.

And the evening performance, celebrating the lives and music of two troubadours of topical songs, was the perfect capstone to the day. The carefully coordinated itinerary was an illustration of how grassroots leadership is a viable model that has deep historical roots. In a matter of hours, the three of us managed to showcase three different examples of horizontal, collaborative leadership that spanned time and geographical location. Starting with our panel presentation of the Industrial Workers of the World (IWW), otherwise known as the Wobblies, an international labor union established in 1905, that believed in the collective ownership of production, and one of its singing balladeers, Joe Hill, who was executed on trumped up murder charges more than 100 years ago, Terry, Greg, and I painted a portrait of what participatory democracy looks like. From there, we moved on to a community-based organization, founded upon the "We Are All Leaders" principle, established to provide space to artists involved in humanitarian causes. And we finished the night by honoring two icons of the 1960s, each connected to the Ella Baker school of grassroots egalitarian leadership – "Give light and people will find the way." Ella Baker was one of the most influential unsung movers and shakers of the Civil Rights Movement. She strongly believed that ordinary folks could break their chains of oppression and work in solidarity to create a better world.

I took a moment to deeply reflect upon the intersection of the various prototypes of grassroots leadership and the arts for social change. Then the lights dimmed and it was time to carry us all home.

The Second Half of the Celebratory Evening for Matt Jones and Phil Ochs

Welcome back. We are going to kick off the second half with a beautiful testimonial from one of Matt's sons, Gerald Jones: A Tribute to my Father (Matthew A. Jones Jr).

I am thankful to all of you today for the remembrance of my father "Matt Jones." This musical tribute is special, because a lot of my father's life is in his music. Music was therapeutic for him, and a big part of his upbringing. Music was his diary, and he took the world on a ride through his music.

I want to thank Susie Erenrich for her devoted love for his music, and managing not only this tribute, but his memorial celebration after his passing.

To my best friend and step mom, Shelly Jones, you were and are the rock, and bridge of my father's life. He would not have made it as far as he did without you, and I love you for all you did for him and are doing. You are and will always be: Mrs. Matthew A. Jones Jr.

To the musical guests: Thank you for the love you put into my father's music, you help keep him alive.

I remember growing up not knowing what my father actually did for a living. All I did know was he traveled a lot. Then one day I heard him singing a song he wrote on a .45 record called: (Hell no, I ain't gonna go). It had a rock and roll beat to it, and I said Wow that's my daddy? I knew at that moment my dad was something special.

My father was a giant warrior, with a king's spirit, and he fought for freedom, justice, and equality for all people. He walked the line in the struggle for civil rights, and human rights. He wrote songs in the midst of every struggle, and is noted in history not only nationally, but international for his work and music.

Some say money is prosperity, but I say a good name is above any tangible thing you can touch. The Bible gives the name Jesus. After Jesus I say: (Matt Jones) a Freedom Singer, and Freedom Fighter for all people.

Son of a Freedom Fighter
Gerald Jones

I choked back tears as I welcomed Terry and Greg back to the stage. It had been five years since Matt passed away, but the feelings were still raw. The heart-to-heart talks ceased. The collaborations vanished. The regular sharing of songs came to a complete halt. All that was left was the hole in my soul and the responsibility to persevere.

Matt routinely reminded me that I had an obligation to carry on. With a prolonged hardy chuckle and twinkle in his eye he would say, "We will all be gone — you are younger than us — it will be up to you to keep the music alive." I took this charge seriously, even though I never wanted to think about death and loss. As a social movement history documentarian, who spent decades chronically the Southern Freedom Struggle, I had made a conscious commitment to do right by my adopted family. It was not only the ethical thing to do, it was a joy to do it.

Terry and Greg commenced the top of the set with *Demonstrating GI*. Matt wrote this song while he was in prison during the summer of 1963. He had been placed in a cell with a soldier by the name of Buford Holt. The recruit had attended a protest in his military uniform, which was illegal, so he was thrown in jail. After Matt heard the young man's story, he wrote the tune out on toilet paper. It was the only material he had at his disposal during his incarceration.

Three more tunes followed. *Tree of Life*, an introspective rumination about mindfulness and our capacity as human beings to actively engage in the world. *Hell No, I Ain't Gonna Go*, a topical anti-Vietnam War number, co-authored with Elaine Laron. And *Brother That Ain't Good*, another Elaine Laron collaboration. Elaine was a lyricist for Sesame Street and Captain Kangaroo. The song, penned in the late 1960s, focused on the plight of Black people in the United States.

Terry and Greg knocked all of the songs out of the park. They have a rare skillset as instrumentalists and vocalists, and a powerful delivery, that has the ability to captivate audiences in multifarious settings. Their previous association with Matt strengthened their resolve and provided the necessary emotional energy to transmit their message. In some ways they appeared to be channeling Matt. It was mesmerizing.

Interlude

I glanced at the clock above the collection table. It was ticking. I tried to be in the moment, but was acutely aware of our time constraints. It is essential that the last chord is struck no later than 10:30. That is the Café's agreement with the Church. At that time, all of the volunteers spring into action. Cleanup ensues to ready the space for Sunday morning services. At 11:30 the alarm goes off so the premises must be vacated to eliminate any potential problems that may arise with the Café's contract.

I took a deep breath and walked back to the microphone: *I have greetings from four of the surviving SNCC Freedom Singers. I saw them at Ivanhoe Donaldson's memorial service in Washington, DC. Ivanhoe was a SNCC Field Secretary during the Movement and he lived a consequential life. The Singers, who shared the podium with other dignitaries, raised their voices once again to honor one of their own. When I told Chuck Neblett, one of the original Freedom Singers, about this gathering, he said, "Matt was Matt. He was our brother. We loved him."* An unidentified, unified, acoustic sound of approval encompassed the room. I paused. Then I put in motion the final tribute for Matt. It was from my long-time partner and it was personal: *What happens when two tough, strong-willed, uncompromising individuals lock horns for the first time? A few missteps by Susie in her initial phone conversation with Matt Jones led to his hanging up on her in the early 1990s. It could have been the end and not a beginning.*

Persistence and a passion for preserving and presenting songs of the Mississippi Civil Rights Movement soon displaced distrust and initial misunderstandings and their relationship blossomed.

Susie and I first heard Matt's voice in the acclaimed television documentary "Eyes on the Prize." One verse of "Ballad of Medgar Evers" was played in the episode "Mississippi: Is This America?" (1962–1964). We knew instantly that this song, along with his brother's "In the Mississippi River" must be part of Susie's CD project: Freedom Is A Constant Struggle: Songs of the Mississippi Civil Rights Movement. All she had to do was make a call. The call was made. She referred to Matt as Marshall – his brother's name, at least once.

Matt already had doubts about Susie's intentions, so calling him Marshall didn't help. But that wasn't the end of a beautiful relationship.

For the next 20 years, Matt Jones would be an integral and willing participant in every project Susie created. The phone was their meeting place to work out the details of every venture.

It is likely that Susie spent more time on the phone with Matt over a 10-year period, than anyone else prior to her move to New York City. Often, Matt would sing songs over the phone to get Susie's take on them. Their lives were intertwined until the day Matt moved on in 2011.

I am fortunate to have known Matt Jones and I treasure my time with him and his music. If you don't think that you know Matt well enough, then listen to some of his 500 songs. There's a history lesson in his music, for everyone. – Brad McKelvey

Following the tributes, Terry and Greg immediately continued with a melodious rendition of one of Matt's signature songs, *We Won't Turn Back*, superseded by *Long Kesh*. Long Kesh was a prison in Northern Ireland. Matt composed the song in the early 1980s after a human rights expedition. On his way to Belfast, Matt and his contingent, which included the Reverend Frederick Kirkpatrick, Professor Jim Dunn, civil rights activists, and family members of imprisoned revolutionaries, who were in the middle of a hunger strike, had been detained by a British tank. They sat in the snow for hours. When Matt wrote the song, he wanted to show the universal connectivity of struggle. After Matt succumbed to his long illness, Terry and Greg penned a verse for him. It was an eloquent final toast for the long-serving Civil Rights Movement veteran. Rest in peace Matt Jones.

The Home Stretch

This is the last tribute of the evening. It is from Carolyn Hester. For those of you who don't recognize the name, you should. Carolyn is a folksinger/songwriter who burst on the scene through an unusual path – the rock n' roll icon Buddy Holly. In turn, she gave Bob Dylan a break, who played harmonica on her first album. Carolyn was involved in the 1964 Mississippi Caravan of Music and she performs at the Café when she gets the chance. In fact, I'll be producing Carolyn's 80th birthday bash here in September 2017 so stay tuned. Here's her parting words for Phil Ochs:

Dear Phil: We all wish you were not gone from us so soon, so terribly soon. There is the fact of your death, which haunts us.

You took your own life. For someone like me, who shared some stages with you, bought your albums, because I was your fan, and recorded your song, "What's That I Hear" at Town Hall on February 13, 1965, there is grief that still tugs at us all. Your death is one of the reminders that the glory of the sixties included the excitement of creating songs of protest and peace, as well as the connections we had with each other and our audience. There seemed to be tangible proof that we really were affecting our world. Yet your death reminds us that there were pressures on us to be in show business and to regard each other as competitors. We were contemporaries, not competitors. And so in that spirit of brotherhood, which you and I and all the sixties generation believed in, we sing your songs forever. We are so grateful for your sister, Sonny Ochs, who creates events we can participate in. And, we are beholden to Susie and to the Peoples' Voice Café for another evening spent enjoying the treasures in your song bag, Phil. We heard you then. We hear you now. Much love, Carolyn Hester

And with that, the music carried us home. Terry and Greg concluded the night with four of Phil's tunes from the anti-Vietnam War era: *Draft Dodger Rag, Is There Anybody Here, Cops of the World,* and *I Ain't Marchin' Anymore.*

It was 10:32. We missed the cutoff and there was still one very important number to go, *When I'm Gone.* It was a regular closer during Phil Ochs Song Nights. It was a haunting composition, given the circumstances surrounding Phil's death. It conveyed a cautionary message for those of us still working for social change — to keep on keeping on. It was Phil's rallying cry to all of the foot soldiers in the movement.

The collective granted the additional time. Everyone tunefully sang along on the chorus. When the music came to a halt, the audience jumped to their feet for a prolonged, enthusiastic standing ovation. The show was a hit. I was relieved. I thanked the sound crew, individual members of the collective, and of course those in attendance. Then everyone vigorously sprang into action.

A Meditative Moment

I gathered my belongings and helped Terry and Greg cart their gear outside. We made our breakfast plans for our Sunday morning debriefing session at Candle West, one of our favorite vegan New York City restaurants. After a few hugs and farewells I slowly walked back to the hotel. I was all alone in my thoughts. Post-performance heavyheartedness began to settle in. It is an affliction experienced by many artists following a high energy show.

When I reached East 33rd Street, I slowly turned the corner. My deliberations were abruptly interrupted by honking vehicles and raucous interchanges. Once inside my room, my musings refocused and I set my sights on next year's show. The one scheduled for the launch of this book.

As I put my head on my pillow, I thought about how lucky I was to have crossed paths with so many extraordinary folks. Up to this point, I have lived an interesting and remarkable life. The road ahead looks bright.

The brain chatter continued for a while. Eventually, I wore myself out. Then I calmly and gradually drifted off to sleep.

Susan J. Erenrich
Editor

Acknowledgments

Where does this story begin? Where does it end? Like most narratives, it has a beginning, middle, and end, but they are artificial boundaries. In actuality, *Grassroots Leadership & The Arts For Social Change* was launched long before I wrote the Building Leadership Bridges proposal. The journey will continue beyond the publication of the book.

Even so, there were many people who assisted me along the way. Too many to include now; but you know who you are. I would like to take a moment, however, to express my gratitude to the ones who played prominent roles during this scholarly exploration.

First and foremost, I would like to thank my incredible co-editor, Jon F. Wergin. Jon and I forged a meaningful alliance during my days at Antioch University. He chaired my dissertation committee. Jon supported me and trusted me as I pushed through traditional academic boundaries trying to create a more inclusive path for cultural activists and grassroots agents of social change in the leadership field. He enthusiastically joined me again on this newest venture.

Debra Deruyver, the International Leadership Association, and Emerald deserve a major shout out. Without them, this collection would never see the light of day.

Words can never adequately express my gratitude to the authors in this compilation. I am indebted to each and every one of them. Their contribution to this groundbreaking book accentuates the salient role artists play in helping to shape our world.

My heartfelt thanks to the countless Civil Rights Movement veterans, volunteers, and artists who welcomed me into their lives, entrusted me with their most precious thoughts, and showed me how horizontal leadership and participatory democracy is a viable and necessary model. I am indebted to each and every one of you.

I am beholden to Augusto Boal for his extraordinary Theatre of the Oppressed annual spring gatherings at the Brecht Forum in New York City. His workshops transformed my life. During those sessions I learned important lessons about community and movement building from the ground-up. Sadly, Augusto passed away on May 2, 2009. I was not ready to say goodbye.

The Highlander Research and Education Center, formally known as the Highlander Folk School, also contributed to my growth in a major way. I'd especially like to express my appreciation to Guy and Candie Carawan, who spearheaded the cultural program several years after Zilphia Horton died in 1956. Decades of communiques and a few visits to the leadership training institution strengthened my resolve and convinced me that grassroots leadership and the arts for social change is uncharted territory worth examination.

I'm forever indebted to the teachings of Paulo Freire. I became a popular education practitioner long ago and never turned back.

I'd like to take a moment to recognize the Peoples' Voice Café and the Wallflower Order Dance Collective. My experience with both of these groups were life-changing. I saw first-hand how horizontal leadership is a feasible approach to running organizations.

My lengthy association with the May 4th Movement has been eye-opening. For more than 40 years my participation in that campaign for social justice has led me to this point.

Brad McKelvey, my long-time partner, best friend, and accomplice, was always by my side. For 32 years, he has been my rock.

Last, but certainly not least, I want to thank my mom and dad. I miss you. I love you.

Susan J. Erenrich
Editor

Introduction Two

Unlike Susie, I've come to an interest in the arts and grass-roots leadership for social change in a roundabout way. Like many of my generation who attended college during the turbulent years of the 1960s, I took part in various anti-war protests and even dabbled for a while with Students for a Democratic Society (SDS), spending Saturday nights in the kitchens and living rooms of fellow students, engaging in earnest discussions about the immorality of the Vietnam War, usually surrounded by giant maps of Southeast Asia and a haze of marijuana smoke. But I have to admit now, half a century later, that my "activism," if you can call it that, was based less on commitment to principle than a fear of getting drafted.

I did however retain a passion for politics. I was able to avoid the draft through a medical deferment, and so continued my education in graduate school, writing my dissertation – a political model for evaluating organizational policymaking – while keeping one ear tuned to the Watergate hearings. The day it was revealed that the president had a taping system that recorded every conversation in the Oval Office, I stopped what I was doing, hopped on my bicycle and sped to campus, where I burst into my advisor's office and blurted, "Larry, you'll never believe what I just heard!" I remain a news junkie to this day: "News Junkie" is literally on the front of a t-shirt I bought at the Newseum in Washington, DC.

After getting my PhD in 1973, I spent the next 30 years in academic life at Virginia Commonwealth University in Richmond, a city I still call home. My doctoral background in educational psychology with a specialty in psychometrics and a cognate in organizational behavior led to a lot of program evaluation projects; but an increasing focus of my work in faculty and organization development led to the discovery of what I am truly passionate about: how people and organizations develop, and in particular what cognitive science tells us about what *retards* that development. I have learned through experience that people and organizations are amazingly resistant to anything that competes with their existing mental models of how the world works. I have learned that belief comes first and learning comes second. In my own case, for years I believed in the power of evidence that facts matter, only to have to finally admit that no, often only *certain*, facts matter, those that support an already-held belief. I'll have more to say about this phenomenon in a bit.

Enter Susan J. Erenrich. In 2003, I left VCU to join Antioch University's PhD program in Leadership & Change as a core faculty member, and in 2005 Susie was a member of the incoming student cohort. We didn't know each other well in the first couple of years; because she is a dancer and activist and I am a psychologist and methodologist we didn't seem to have much in common. I remember fondly now how surprised she seemed when she discovered that I was a huge fan of Paulo Freire, the great emancipatory educator cited frequently in this book and author of the classic *Pedagogy of the Oppressed* (1970). As we began to know each other better she slowly persuaded me that hidden inside my middle-of-the-road, centrist persona was a radical educator. Because of Susie I started to dive more deeply into Freire's work, to re-discover Myles Horton and the Highlander Folk School, and to re-read John Dewey, including his *Art as Experience* (1934). Still, I was surprised – pleasantly – when Susie asked me to chair her dissertation committee. Her dissertation, *Rhythms of Rebellion: Creating Dangerously for Social Change* (2009), foresaw the key theme of this book, that creating energy for social change is not just about persuasion through rational argument, as necessary as that might be; it is also about connecting to others in extra-rational ways, through the heart, which of course is what the arts do. In the years since completing her dissertation, Susie and I have looked for a way to continue our work, not as professor and student but as committed academic activists working in collaboration. We found that way in the book you're now reading.

In writing about the People's Voice Café, Susie's perspective as an artist/activist/scholar is clear. In my own Introduction, I have a complementary perspective to present, that of a scholar and teacher of current and future agents of social change. I have already alluded to elements of that perspective; now I'd like to elaborate on one of these elements, namely how the arts can break through existing worldviews and cause people to see things differently, in ways not available through other means.

How People Change

Earlier I noted that strongly held beliefs are rarely changed with strictly rational arguments. When John Adams wrote that "facts are stubborn things," he neglected to mention that beliefs are more stubborn still. When I studied learning theory nearly 50 years ago cognitive science was still in its infancy. Most of what we know today about how learning happens has been discovered since then. Today we know that the brain is not like a computer; it is infinitely more complex than that, with interlocking webs of billions of synapses connecting our roughly two billion neurons, creating thousands of mental models that help us make sense of an otherwise chaotic and intimidating world. Stimuli dissonant with these mental models threaten our comfort level and so we tend to dismiss them, leading to what Michael Shermer (2011) and others have called "confirmation bias," accepting information that conforms to mental models – including stereotypes – and rejecting that which does not.

What does this have to do with the arts and social change, you may ask? The answer is, *plenty*. Two giants in the field of learning and behavior change are Jack Mezirow and Mihalyi Csikszentmihalyi, the former in cognition (thinking), the latter in motivation (feeling). Both thinking and feeling are essential for deep learning in adults.

Mezirow is the father of *transformative learning* (cf. Mezirow & Associates, 2000), a theory that has revolutionized how we think about adult learning. Briefly, the theory looks like this: in order for adults to learn deeply they have to be presented with a stimulus that disrupts their web of mental models, one too powerful to be dismissed and ignored. Mezirow called this a "disorienting dilemma." Disorienting dilemmas may be small – having one's GPS fail in a strange city – or large, a personal crisis caused by devastating illness or loss of a spouse (or, something positive such as a new romantic relationship). The disorientation forces us to step back and reconsider, to see things differently, and to try on new perspectives – most powerfully, Mezirow suggests, in the presence of others. Adopting new ways of viewing the world is the essence of transformative learning.

What is the ideal level of disorientation leading to transformative learning? Csikszentmihalyi's theory of *flow* (1990) offers some insight. Most of us have experienced flow, the sense that one is completely engaged in an experience, so much so that one's focus is sharper and narrower and the sense of time is lost. As a teacher and writer, I have experienced flow often in my work. Artists, I suspect, experience flow all the time. It is the single most intrinsically motivating experience there is. So here is the connection to transformative learning: flow is most likely when the challenge of an experience is just slightly more than one's sense of competence in dealing with the experience – in other words, when one has a slight sense of disorientation, but not too much. An imbalance of challenge over competence leads to anxiety and dismissal; an imbalance the other way leads to complacency and boredom. Individuals change when they experience cognitive disorientation *and* are motivated to follow it.

In his book *Art as Experience*, John Dewey (1934) recognized the power of the arts in human learning. Art, according to Dewey, should reflect "the emotions and ideas that are associated with the chief institutions of social life" (p. 7). "The artist does not shun moments of resistance and tension. He rather cultivates them, not for their own sake but because of their potentialities, [to] bring to living consciousness an experience that is unified and total" (p. 15). The key phrase here is "bring to consciousness." The artist – visual, literary, or performing – invites the observer to have a conscious experience that reveals a latent truth. The truth may be confirming or, as Dewey suggests, unsettling. One goes to a museum, ballet, or theater to have an esthetic experience that connects with larger human experience. When that esthetic experience creates disorientation – as when, for example, one sees and hears a solitary cellist creating beautiful music in the very spot in a public square in Sarajevo that was hit by a mortar shell the day before – the observer is invited to engage in some fresh thinking about how to deal with oppression and the worst instincts of humanity.

Artists as Provocateurs and Agents of Social Conscience: An Introduction to the Chapters

In an op-ed piece titled "How Artists Change the World," David Brooks (2016) noted how Frederick Douglass, the most-photographed American of the 19th century, used his portraits – as a serious and dignified African-American – to deliberately challenge the image white Americans had of black people. "He was using art to *reteach people how to see*" (para. 12, italics added). "This is where artists make their mark," Brooks wrote, "by implanting pictures in the underwater processing that is upstream from conscious cognition. Those pictures assign weights and values to what the eyes take in" (para. 16). Therefore, instead of involving themselves directly in political life, artists' "*real* power lies in the ability to recode the mental maps that people project into the world" (para. 17, italics added).

The effect can be subliminal, as with the Frederick Douglass example, when the re-coding takes place at a thoroughly subconscious level; or the effect can be so arresting as to stop people in their tracks, as did the cellist of Sarajevo, the subject of this book's first chapter.

Other chapters in this book provide similarly compelling evidence of the power of the arts to provoke; to create disquiet; and ultimately to inspire.

A master of provocation was Fela Kuti, the subject of Chapter 2. By singing about real people, those in Nigeria's corrupt power structure, he was able to galvanize grassroots support for change, even as "an underpants-wearing, marijuana smoking, and womanizing social misfit" (p. 39).

Václav Havel, the subject of Chapter 3, was a provocateur of a very different sort. The future leader of the Czech Republic was a poet and playwright who used the power of the absurdist tradition in theater – not to lay out a vision for the country, but to "unmask, raise concerns, and carefully diagnose" the essence of political oppression (p. 49).

Havel used theater as a social experience that led to a collective consciousness. Armand Gatti (Chapter 4) went further, raising consciousness both in spectators and in *the performers themselves*: "the truth behind the words that are being spoken is the first step away from passive understanding, because to embody a text – to own it in a public moment – is a move toward leading others instead of being led" (p. 73).

The profile of Kenyan photo-journalist Boniface Mwangi (Chapter 5) reveals the importance of calibrating artistic provocation: how does the artist create disquiet by showing examples of injustice, while also protecting the dignity of his subjects? The anti-war images shown in his traveling photographic displays — images not otherwise published in the media — forced Mwangi to make "a tough choice to be sensitive, considering the harrowing experiences of the victims and their families" (p. 90).

Chapter 6, a study of the "benevolent subversion" of graffiti and street artists, offers a contrast between the reality of photo-journalism and "tricksters," like the notorious street artist Banksy, who "inject a small dose of disorder into the system" (p. 98). Thus, as with Havel's absurdist theater, tricksters force attention to social problems but in a more liminal way. "Without the trickster and the independent public artist," the authors note, "we may never think to question how we define terms like good, evil, normal, weird, decent, or fair" (p. 106).

French photographer JR, the subject of Chapter 7, creates disorientation in an entirely different way, using his photographs to "deal with serious conflict through the emotional strategy of humor and connection" (p. 112). "Subjects are not viewed as victim or aggressor; rather, the similarities among people divided by ideology are shown to be striking enough to begin a conversa-tion on how we may come together as a socially viable force" (p. 116). JR thus seeks to break down stereotypes: "To change the way you see things is already to change things themselves," he is quoted as saying.

Filmmaker Peter Young is described as an "agent provoca-teur" in Chapter 8. "His intention is not primarily to entertain, but rather to provoke and stir, to illustrate injustice and provide a platform for reflective thinking about important issues that could otherwise remain buried and forgotten" (p. 128). A cata-strophic earthquake hit Christchurch, New Zealand, in 2011, destroying most of the oldest part of the city, and Young's film The Art of Recovery demonstrates how grassroots artistic endea-vors, in this case a self-organized group calling themselves the "Gap Fillers," can successfully challenge moneyed interests and centralized urban planning.

The book then moves to another key role of artists, not just to provoke or unsettle as outsiders, but also to be integral to social movements themselves. In Chapter 9, the authors show how the Industrial Workers of the World (IWW, also known as "Wobblies"), used well-known songs in the early part of the 20th century with new lyrics to energize the struggle against oppres-sion, establishing a precedent for the Civil Rights Movement in the United States 50 years later. The authors quote the late Pete Seeger, who noted that if the world is going to survive, "one of the reasons would be that we learned to sing together, to raise awareness, and to unify us to fight against our common enemies which have always been hatred, fear, prejudice, violence and injustice" (p. 159).

In Chapter 10, composer and singer Holly Near further explores how music can be more than a source of entertainment but a powerful agent for social change. She writes about how Women's Music emboldened women to face their days in a "man's world": "Ranging from bold love songs to tender lullabies to rallying cries for change to electric condemnations of oppression, Women's Music gave voice and visibility to feminism" (p. 170).

The case study of ACT UP (Chapter 11), organized by AIDS activists in the late 1980s and 1990s, shows how works of art can move audiences in ways that arguing and brow-beating could never do – a lesson learned the hard way by activists Larry Kramer and Michael Callen. The chapter underscores the power of art to recode mental maps: artists can "do more to raise consciousness through their creative work than through polemics alone" (p. 181).

The book returns to theater in Section IV, with three chapters devoted to variations on Theatre of the Oppressed, now used all over the world as a way to raise collective consciousness through participative performance. Chapter 12 provides an overview of Theatre of the Oppressed and shows how it was applied successfully in Kenya. "Theatre brings dissenting voices, emotions and motivations into an 'as-if' world," the authors write. "This artistic frame provides freedom from harm; because violence is represented within the aesthetic space, none get hurt – and all get heard" (p. 190).

Chapter 13 picks up this theme in a very different context, Ukraine at a time of social upheaval: "Theatre of the Oppressed in Ukraine … has shown its potential in both social and esthetic plays, demonstrating how the formation of civil consciousness can emerge through the self-reveal of a person as an actor or spectator" (p. 213). Including stories from actual participants, the chapter shows how requiring people to take positions other than their own helps conflicting parties come into contact and, aligning with theories of transformative learning, try on the perspectives of others.

Chapter 14 returns to Africa, specifically South Africa and Theatre for Development (TFD). Especially noteworthy is the authors' analysis of the early failures of TFD projects: "their intention to create critical awareness among participants on the one hand, and to disseminate dominant ideologies that tend to domesticate participants on the other" (p. 225). The authors show how combining the qualities of TFD with an Asset-Based Community Development (ABCD) model created an endogenous, inside-out approach to grassroots intervention.

Section V contains four chapters on the power of the arts to create bridges and build community. Chapter 15 is a fascinating look at how a symbol of "establishment" art, the Kennedy Center in Washington, DC, became transformed by erecting a music-fueled skateboard complex right on its grounds. It was a "project [that took] the improvisational act at the core of skateboarding — finding a line through physical space — and [applied] it to the process of transforming community space" (p. 243). This combination of improvisation and grassroots energy recalls the "Gap Fillers" profiled in Chapter 8.

Just as Chapter 15 shows how artists can design creative projects to bring disparate groups together, artists involved in the Tikondwe Teachers Project in Domasi, Malawi (Chapter 16) used the African philosophy of Ubuntu, a worldview in which the one exists only through the others, to form a collaboration of art and schooling, showing once again the importance of grassroots answers to address long-standing community problems. "In the side-by-side of *being with* each other and worrying together over time as global teachers and learners," the authors write, "freedom is realized and power gets generated, often and most delightfully, in ways we cannot foresee" (pp. 278-9).

Chapter 17 focuses on dance as an agent for grassroots change. Just as Theatre of the Oppressed uses words to focus on political differences, dance uses movement to scrutinize sociopolitical "assumptions and values ... revealing that differences not only exist, but are also rationalized from different sociopolitical standpoints" (p. 283). The authors describe how they used intercultural projects to stimulate "the collaborative generation of ideas, a consensual method of composition, and the production of artwork that has clear social relevance" (p. 295).

The final chapter of the book looks at the role of public museums, often the embodiment of the dominant, established culture. But when seen as "pedagogic contact zones," spaces "where diverse cultures meet, clash and struggle" (p. 300), museums can have a major impact on society. Museums, in fact, have the capacity to embody all art forms: "A key part of cultural practice, and the work of museums, is telling stories through visuals, objects, narratives, and even theater to engage their audiences" (p. 304).

What a wonderful buffet these chapters offer! I have a running joke with my students about how two-tired clichés, "amazing" and "awesome," are never to be used when referring to one another's work. I am breaking my own rule here. This amazing set of essays collectively demonstrates the awesome power of the arts in the service of grassroots leadership and social change. Anyone who doubts the power of the arts to provoke, disturb, and ultimately to inspire social change will feel differently after reading these wonderful stories. Enjoy them.

Jon F. Wergin
Editor

References

Brooks, D. (2016). How artists change the world. *The New York Times*, August 2. Retrieved from www.nytimes.com. August 3, 2016.

Csikszentmihalyi, M. (1990). *Flow: The psychology of optimal experience*. New York, NY: Harper and Row.

Dewey, J. (1934). *Art as experience*. New York, NY: Minton, Balch & Co.

Erenrich, S. (2009). *Rhythms of rebellion: Creating dangerously for social change*. Unpublished doctoral dissertation, Antioch University.

Freire, P. (1970/2000). *Pedagogy of the oppressed* (30th Anniversary Edition). New York, NY: Bloomsbury.

Mezirow, J., & Associates (2000). *Learning as transformation*. San Francisco, CA: Jossey-Bass.

Shermer, M. (2011). *The believing brain: How we construct beliefs and reinforce them as truths*. New York, NY: Henry Holt.

SECTION I
Grassroots Leadership and Cultural Activists Part 1: Performance Art

1

The Cellist of Sarajevo: Courage and Defiance through Music as Inspirations for Social Change

Randal Joy Thompson and
Edin Ibrahimefendic

You ask me am I crazy for playing the cello?

Why do you not ask if they are not crazy for shelling Sarajevo?

Vedran Smailović (Keuss, 2011, p. 125)

On May 27, 1992, a grenade was thrown into a crowd waiting for bread at a bakery in Sarajevo, Bosnia–Herzegovina, killing 22 people and injuring many more. Bosnian cellist Vedran Smailović lived nearby and was horrified at the senseless slaughter as he helped the wounded and moved the dead. Still in shock, the next morning, Smailović dressed in a tuxedo, took his cello, walked to the crater created by the grenade, and played Tomaso Albinoni's *Adagio in G Minor* in the rubble, despite gunfire and grenades exploding around him. He performed his musical vigil for 22 days to honor each of the victims. Then, for two years, he continued to play his cello in the streets, in bombed out buildings, at funerals, and in cemeteries. Smailović's act of courage and defiance helped change the mood of Sarajevo from fear to determination; inspired at least three classical music pieces, a Christmas medley, several folk songs, a children's book, several paintings and poems, and two novels; and secured his place among world peacemakers (Buttry, 2011). Smailović became a grassroots leader whose actions, along with those of other artists trapped in the siege, illustrated how art can catalyze social change.

In this chapter, we explore how the blend of music and intentionality manifested in Smailović's leadership, together with the cultural productions of other artists, served to build a transformational global community that took a stand against the war. His and other artists' defiance of the existing ideology of power and war helped to promote the international dialog of peace. We speak from the perspective of having lived through the war, either actually, in the case of one of the authors, or vicariously, in the case of the other. Our spirits hence resonate with the spirits of the grassroots artist leaders of the siege.

We argue that grassroots artist leaders trapped in war are unique in that their identity is that of performer–victim. The identity of the audience is, at the same time, that of spectator–victim. Such unusual blurred identities bring performer and audience into a merged unity so that they all become grassroots leaders defying the brutality of the reality around them and promulgating culture and civilization. Their actions as performers and spectators manifest courage and defiance. They magnify their chances of being targeted by participating in public, thus acting courageously, and defy the powers-that-be whose intent is to dehumanize and annihilate them. They speak a language distinct from the ongoing political narrative and it is this language that has the power to catalyze social change. Irony and surreal twists of the war reality through various artistic expressions are essential aspects of this language. They reveal truths hidden in situations and catalyze the global response that the world does not have to be this way after all. It is this realization that is the beginning of building a new more civilized world.

Bosnian War and the Siege of Sarajevo

Following the death of Tito in 1980, nationalist leaders who had been restrained during Tito's rule began filling the leadership vacuum and making moves to declare their republics' independence. Being a multiethnic state comprised of Muslim Bosniaks, Croatian Catholics, and Orthodox Serbs, Bosnia–Herzegovina was split about whether to declare independence. Fearful that they would become a minority and hence be marginalized in an independent Bosnia, the Bosnian Serbs wanted to remain in Yugoslavia. On October 24, 1991, Bosnian Serb members of parliament formed the Assembly of the Serb People of Bosnia and Herzegovina. On January 9, 1992 the Assembly established the Serbian Republic of Bosnia and Herzegovina, which they renamed *Republika Srpska* in August 1992 (Donia, 2006).

Despite the actions of the Bosnian Serbs, Bosnia declared its sovereignty on October 15, 1991; held a referendum for independence on February 29 and March 1, 1992; and declared independence on March 3, 1992 (Donia, 2006). Twelve European Communities and the United States recognized Bosnia–Herzegovina's independence in early April 1992. Serbs responded violently and by the end of April, the siege of Sarajevo, which is officially said to have commenced on April 5, 1992, was in full force (Donia, 2006).

An estimated 13,000 Serbs surrounded Sarajevo (Donia, 2006). They cut off the water and electricity supplies to the city and took key positions around Sarajevo. Serb snipers began terrorizing the inhabitants of Sarajevo and killing people randomly while they were searching for scarce water and scarcer food, trying to survive by whatever means they could. Snipers were paid for each "hit" and paid more for killing children (Dizderevic, 2012). Being the longest siege of a capital city in modern warfare history, 13,962 people were killed, including 5,434 civilians. Almost all of the buildings in Sarajevo were damaged and 35,000 were completely destroyed (Dizderevic, 2012; Donia, 2006).

The Cellist of Sarajevo

The siege was in its infancy on May 27, 1992 when the grenade killed the 22 people waiting in line for bread and stirred Vedran Smailović into spontaneous action. Smailović was a cellist in the Sarajevo String Quartet and had also played for the Sarajevo Opera, the National Theater, and the Symphony Philharmonic Orchestra RTV Sarajevo. Born on November 11, 1956, the fourth of five children, he was born into a celebrated Sarajevan musical family (Gateway Baptist Church, n.d.). He was a colorful character, using the 'Fijaker" traditional use of horses and traps as transportation and "creating a fiesta wherever he went" (Gateway Baptist Church, n.d., para. 1).

Smailović described the scene after the attack and his response in the children's book *Echoes from the Square* (Wellburn, 1998):

> In the first instant there was utter silence ... shock ... and then chaos! ... Fearful screams, yelling, shouting, blood ... People lay about ... dead ... and wounded. From my home I heard the cries for help. I dashed out and saw ... intermingled masses of bodies ... blood everywhere. Everyone was in shock. Some ran away, agony on their faces ... some ran towards the massacre, trying to help the wounded. Then cars arrived with rescuers ... to help those who were injured. ... even some of the rescuers were hit by sniper fire ....
>
> The whole town was filled with pain. I didn't sleep that night, wondering why this had happened to these innocent people, my good neighbors and friends.

The next morning, I went out to look again ... the area was adorned with flowers and wreaths. I had brought my cello, but I didn't know what to play. Tears just slid down my cheeks as I thought about the people who had died. I opened the cello case and somehow ... something guided me to begin playing. Part way through, I recognized what I was playing — Albioni's "Adagio." It had emerged as my musical prayer for peace.

When I finished I noticed that people had stopped to listen and cry with me. As I talked with them I realized that this healing music helped us all to feel better. It provided us with hope ... I was afraid ... Everybody who's sane is afraid when there are bullets and shells in the air. But when I play, the darkness is lifted and I am able to show the world my other feelings. Music is love that connects people. My wish is for everybody to be able to share this. (pp. 27–29)

Smailović played the Adagio in G Minor (SukiChaos, 2009) as a tribute for each of the 22 victims on 22 sequential days and then went on to play for two years as the war worsened. As one source recounted (Gateway Baptist Church, n.d.), Smailović

would place a little campstool in the middle of the bombcraters, and play a concert to the abandoned streets, while bombs dropped and bullets flew all around him. Day after day he made his unimaginably courageous stand for human dignity, for civilization, for compassion, and for peace. When this vigil had ended, he would go to the infamous "Lion Cemetery," infamous, because of the snipers who would lurk there and pick off civilians as they came to bury or mourn their dead. In an act of fearless defiance bordering on madness, Mr. Smailović, beautifully dressed, braved sniper fire, to play for the dead, as though he could reach them; as though he could comfort them. As though protected by a divine shield, he was never hurt, though his darkest hour came when, taking a walk to stretch his legs; his cello was shelled and destroyed where he had been sitting. The news wires picked up the story of the extraordinary man, sitting in his white tie and tails on a camp stool in the center of a raging, hellish war zone — playing his cello to the empty air. (para. 6)

Adagio in G minor

Smailović's choice of Adagio in G Minor was a likely piece to express his shock, grief, and bewilderment and to pay tribute to the 22 who had been killed at the bakery. Often attributed to the 18th century Venetian master Tomaso Albioni (1671–1751), the adagio was composed in its entirety by 20th century musicologist Remo Giazotto (1910–1998). Giazotto copyrighted and published the adagio in 1958 as "Adagio in G Minor for Strings and Organ on Two Thematic Ideas and on a Figured Bass by Tomaso Albinoni" (Perrottet, 2013). Giazotto claimed to have obtained a tiny manuscript fragment from one of Albinoni's trio sonatas shortly after the end of World War II from the Saxon State Library in Dresden, which had preserved most of its collection despite being firebombed. Giazotto said he developed the work based on the theme he discovered (Perrottet, 2013). The Adagio's slow tempo and majestic sounds have served as the theme or background music in movies and television shows, and has been adapted to pop music by popular singers. The Adagio accompanied the tributes to British pop singer/songwriter Amy Winehouse who died in 2011 of alcohol abuse at the age of 27 (Stambeccuccio, 2011); and American rock singer/songwriter Jim Morrison of the famous 1960s rock band, the Doors, who died in 1971 in Paris in mysterious circumstances at 27 (Ama Lia, 2010). Also played at British Princess Diana's funeral, as well as at the 2011 commemoration of 911 in the Catholic Church of the Holy Rosary in Manhattan, New York, the adagio elicits stalwartness and triumph in its languorous tones.

Artistic Response to the Cellist

MUSICAL RESPONSE

Broadcast on television and written about by several journalists covering the siege, Smailović's story resonated around the world. In Seattle, a conceptual artist called Beliz Brother arranged a tribute to Smailović and Sarajevo. Twenty-two different cellists performed Albinoni's Adagio on 22 successive days on a street in the city's university district (Bock, 1992).

English pianist and composer David Wilde heard about Smailović's action soon after. As Wilde wrote (n.d.), the report by John Burns in the *New York Times* of his heroic musical declaration made an impact more immediate than any political statement up to that time. I first read about it on a train from Nuremberg to Hannover. As I sat in the train, deeply move, I listened; and somewhere deep within me a cello began to play a circular melody like a lament without end. (para. 1)

World-renowned cellist Yo Yo Ma played the composition on his solo album for Sony Classical (pelodelperro, 2009). Ma called Smailović "a real present-day hero whose spirit I greatly admire. His spontaneous act of courage can be an inspiration to us all. It shows that an individual can make a difference in the world" (Wellburn, 1998, n.p.).

British composer David Heath wrote a string quartet called "The Cellist of Sarajevo," often played by Cilo Gould, Steve Morris, Gillianne Haddow, and Diane Clark (Heath, 2014). Both Wilde's and Heath's compositions are slow, languorous, and dark, expressing great sorrow and grief and the pain and horror that the victims of war must feel as transmitted to these composers. Heath's composition is also dissonant with sounds similar to sirens and phrases from Albinoni's Adagio in G Minor.

The band Savatage released an album *Dead Winter Dead* in 1995 that focused on the Bosnian war and a love story between a Serb boy and a Muslim girl. This love story was likely based on the true tale of the young lovers Serb Bosko Brkic and Bosniak Admira Ismic who were shot and killed on May 19, 1993, as they were trying to escape Sarajevo over a bridge now dubbed the Romeo-Juliet Bridge. The song on the album called *Christmas Eve Sarajevo* 12/24 was based on the story of Smailović. The song was rereleased in 1996 on the album *Christmas Eve and Other Stories* by the Trans-Siberian Orchestra, comprised of some of the members of Savatage (HeliasValinti, 2010). The band had heard an erroneous version of the cellist's story that depicted him as an old, white-haired man who played Christmas carols in the rubble every night of the siege (Breimeier, 2003). As the band's founder Paul O'Neill told a reporter (Breimeier, 2003):

It was just such a powerful image — a white-haired man silhouetted against the cannon fire, playing timeless melodies to both sides of the conflict amid the rubble and devastation of the city he loves. Some time later, a reporter traced him down to ask why he did this insanely stupid thing. The old man said that it was his way of proving that despite all evidence to the contrary, the spirit of humanity was still alive in that place. (para. 11)

In 2001, American folk singer-songwriter John McCutcheon wrote and sang "The Streets of Sarajevo" in honor of Smailović. McCutcheon wondered in his lyrics where Smailović could have found music in the middle of the madness of the siege and how he could be so kind while under attack (McCutcheon, 2009). Smailović eventually moved from Sarajevo to Ireland and began to collaborate with Irish folk sing-songwriter Tommy Sands. Together, they wrote "Ode to Sarajevo," which is featured on their album *Sarajevo/Belfast*. Sands and Joan Baez sang the ode and Smailović played the cello accompaniment. The song's refrain spoke of the global impact of the cellist's action and how he inspired people everywhere who heard his story (Smailović, 2014a, 2014b).

The story of the Cellist of Sarajevo has long endured. Fourteen-year-old Canadian cellist Rylan Gayek wrote a duet for Remembrance Day in 2007 entitled "In the Streets of Sarajevo," in honor of Smailović (Rylan Gayek Leonard, 2009). In 2009, the pop group The Light Company wrote "The Cellist of Sarajevo," inspired by the novel *The Cellist of Sarajevo* written by Steve Galloway, which is discussed below. The lyrics laud the resolve of Sarajevans as they proclaim their pride and the fact that they will never forget each other's names (Mlangiewicz, 2011).

POETRY AND MEMORIAL SCULPTURES

Ten-year-old Jason Crowe from Indiana heard about Smailović's actions and the cellist became Jason's hero. As Jason said (Jewell, 2004),

> ... it ... dawned on me how symbolic his response has been ... I realized all of a sudden that the only reasonable response to war is harmony ... I came face to face with a profound truth: if you answer violence with violence, you create a vicious, unending cycle. The answer to violence has to be creative energy, not more destructive energy. (para. 3)

Jason wrote a poem about Vedran Smailović for a memorial and vigil he organized in Evansville, Indiana on the 5th anniversary of the breadline massacre. In his poem, Jason called on the people of the world to wake up, get out of their comfort zone, and share responsibility for this atrocity (Jewell, 2004).

Jason was also inspired by Smailović to write two books. His historical novel told the story of three boys, one, a Bosnian Muslim, one, a Bosnian Croat, and one, a Bosnian Serb who were close friends before the war but whose friendship was destroyed by the war. By faith, they were eventually reunited (Jewell, 2014). The other talked about the courage of Bosnian and other children in war (Jewell, 2014). In addition, Jason started a fund called "The Cello Cries On" that pop star Bono, folk singer Joan Baez, folk singer Pete Seeger, folk singer Tommy Sands, cellist Yo Yo Ma, and other famous artists contributed. With the donated funds, Jason commissioned American artist David Kocka to design a sculpture to commemorate all the children killed in the siege, the Children's International Peace and Harmony Statue (Jewell, 2014). The bronze sculpture depicts several life-sized children and it was installed in the Woodwynn Peace Garden in British Columbia, Canada in 2014 (Woodwynn Peace Garden, n.d.). According to Jason, the 3 "Spirits" of the statue were meant to honor (Jewell, 2004):

> 1. The spirit of all Bosnians who have lived through or died in the madness of ethnic cleansing; 2. The spirit of harmony that cries on like a lone cello in a world full of violence, which refuses to listen; and 3. The spirit of children around the world who want peace and harmony, not war and genocide, as their legacy in the new millennium. (para. 6)

Bosnian poet Admiral Mahic also wrote a poem about Smailović. Born in Banja Luka in 1948, Mahic was the leader of the literary program in "Napredak" during the siege of Sarajevo. In his poem, Mahic seemed to decry the destruction of unity of Bosnians and his inability to disappear from such unity. He likened the situation of Bosnians with that of Palestinians and Kurds whose voices fell on deaf ears. Even the music of Smailović was silent because the world stood by, doing nothing (Mahic, n.d.).

CELLO

To Vedran Smailović*

We all drink one dish:

blood off a lily!

That cello of Vedran's —

is the most distressing silence!

After the Palestinians, Bosnians, and Kurds,

who will

coo like a clay pigeon

on the bare branch of absurdity?

The ever-same soul

says to the sweet soul:

I do not know how to disappear from Unity,

like that cad wishes.

We all drink one dish:

blood off a lily!

That cello of Vedran's,

is the most distressing silence!

*The cello player who gave a concert in burnt-down Sarajevo City Hall.

(Translated by Ana Ilievska, 2016)

BOOKS AND BOOK COVERS

Smailović's act inspired literature and his photo has been seen in a variety of literary contexts. A photograph of Smailović playing his cello in the ruins of the National Theater was on the cover of *The Impossible Country: A Journey through the Last Days of Yugoslavia* by Brian Hall (Jurich, 2005). His photo also appears on the September 2015 issue of the *Forced Migration Review* that discussed the Dayton Peace Accords' 20-year anniversary and the political challenges that continue to plague Bosnia–Herzegovina (Forced Migration Review, 2015).

Canadian author Elizabeth Wellburn wrote a children's story, *Echoes from the Square*, in 1998 in collaboration with Smailović. The book told the story of a young boy named Alen who loved to play the violin and whose family lived in the cellar of his house. Alen had to go outside every day to gather water for the family and lived in terror each time he ventured out. One day he came across the cellist and was so captivated by the music that he forgot his fears. Alen noticed that many people had gathered around the cellist and that his music "fills their hearts and reminds them all of happier days. It stirs in them the hope that these forlorn times can pass" (Wellburn, 1998, p. 18).

In 2008, Canadian author Steven Galloway wrote *The Cellist of Sarajevo*, a novel that explored the impact of war on Sarajevo and the novel's three main characters, Arrow, a young female Bosniak sniper; Dragan, a 60-year-old baker; and Kenan, a middle-aged man with a wife and children he needed to keep safe. Arrow was assigned the task of keeping the cellist alive, given that the Serbs planned to send a sniper to kill him. The cellist remained mostly in the background of the novel, but he exercised a tremendous impact on each of the characters. Each of them wondered why the cellist was playing and what he hoped to accomplish, concluding that he was trying to stop things from getting worse. The characters were all mesmerized and somehow transformed by the cellist's music. Even the Serb sniper targeting the cellist was transfixed by the music and hesitated to pull the trigger, giving Arrow time to kill him. The need to maintain an ongoing effort to build civilization, along with the redemptive role of music in this task, are resonating themes of the novel. Dragan reflected, "Civilization isn't a thing that you build and then there it is, you have it forever. It needs to be built constantly, recreated daily. It vanishes far more quickly than anyone ever would have thought possible" (p. 248).

The story of the Cellist still reverberates and people are still discussing it. Montgomery College as recently as 2013 held a discussion of the Cellist of Sarajevo at which a music student played Wilde's "The Cellist of Sarajevo" and Albinoni's Adagio in G Minor (Montgomery College, 2013).

DANCE AND FILMS

Choreographer Shannon Hobbes created "Sarajevo Requiem," as a tribute to Smailović. Dancer Jennifer Pollack performed the dance at the Dance Space in New York on November 21, 1992. Danced to an original score by Kevin Lawson, the dance juxtaposed ordinary life with the brutality of war and disintegration and expressed this contrast in movement (Kisselgoff, 1992).

Michael Winterbottom's 1997 film, *Welcome to Sarajevo*, based on the novel written by British journalist Michael Nicholson's *Natasha's Story*, included a character based on

Smailović. The final scene of the movie showed this character playing the Adagio in G Minor at a concert to save Sarajevo (AnirbanMitra, 2010). His performance sent the message that Sarajevans would overcome despite the power games of Bosnian and superpower politicians and their indifference toward the people suffering in the war.

THE BROADER ARTISTIC RESPONSE TO THE SIEGE

The siege catalyzed a massive cultural response of which Smailović was a highly visible symbol. Both international and local artists together formed a powerful counterpoint to the violence. Arriving in Sarajevo in 1993, American journalist Bill Carter covered the siege and provided humanitarian assistance. He interested pop singer Bono in shooting a documentary together, *Miss Sarajevo*, covering a 1993 beauty pageant "Miss Besieged Sarajevo." The contestants famously carried a large banner blazed in huge letters "PLEASE DON'T KILL US." Seventeen-year-old Inela Nogic won the pageant and her photo splashed the cover of U2's vinyl single *Miss Sarajevo*, a song that also was included in the U2 album *Original Soundtracks 1*. Bono and Luciano Pavarotti sang the main song in the documentary, "Miss Sarajevo" (Alexander Pavlides, 2010).

Joan Baez came to Sarajevo in 1992 and 1993 (Baez, 1993). She encountered Smailović where he was playing in the street and cemented an immediate bond with him, spontaneously sitting on his chair and singing "Amazing Grace" (Baez, 2014). Author/Photographer Susan Sontag visited Sarajevo on numerous occasions and, in collaboration with theater director Haris Pasovic, directed *Waiting for Godot* with Croatian, Bosniak, and Serb actors (Burns, 1993; Hadzic, 2011). Folk singer Judy Collins wrote and sang "Song for Sarajevo" in 1995. She sang of dreams of seeing one's mother's eyes and of peace in the midst of the chaos and destruction (JudyCollinsForever, 2012). Zubin Mehta played the Mozart's *Requiem* in the ruins of the National Theater (Visionaria Art Group, 2012). Actress Vanessa Redgrave (AP Archive, 2015) and photographer Annie Leibowitz (Hadzic, 2011) also became involved. All of these artists and others encouraged world leaders to intervene to end the siege.

Bosnian artists thrived during the siege of Sarajevo in contradiction to what people would assume would normally happen during a war. A rich cultural life was expressed in plays, poems, paintings, writings, filmmaking, creative posters, and other artistic endeavors. Estimated performances during the siege included 148 plays, 170 art exhibits, and 48 concerts (Kurtovic, n.d.). The world-famous Sarajevo Film Festival began during the siege, as did The Sarajevo War Theater (SARTR). *Kamerni Theater* was also active during the siege staging over 1,000 performances (Bilic, n.d.; Hadzic, 2011; McRobie, 2014). Radio ZID played a significant role by playing music and sponsoring concerts that bolstered the cosmopolitan culture of Sarajevo. A number of rock bands comprised of mixed ethnic musicians were formed (Kurtovic, n.d.). Bosnian artists also performed plays and concerts, and organized exhibitions internationally (Bilic, n.d.).

Grassroots Leadership

Grassroots leadership is a bottom-up, horizontal, collective, collaborative, social change model grounded in community and movement building. Grassroots leaders generally organize to solve community challenges that the government or private corporations are not willing to solve at best, or have caused, at worse. These leaders often organize to change what they see as dangerous societal practices such as for-profit prisons, inequality, poverty, lack of access to quality education and medical care, marginalization (Andert, Platt, & Alexakis, 2011). They generally uphold the values of democracy, equity, fairness, representativeness, and inclusion. Grassroots organizations and movements are built on trust and mutual accountability.

Grassroots leadership is transformational leadership. Like grassroots leadership, transformational leadership is horizontal and inclusive such that everyone involved in a particular leadership situation is also a leader. Transformational leaders motivate and inspire each other to embrace change (Burns, 2004). As Burns (2004) pointed out, transformational leaders encourage "a sense of collective identity and collective efficacy, which in turn brings stronger feelings of self-worth and self-efficacy ... By pursuing transformational change, people can transform themselves" (pp. 25–26). Further, transformational leaders facilitate the recognition among fellow leaders that what they are doing responds to a higher calling and achieves a higher social good (Burns, 2004).

Grassroots leadership during times of war and conflict poses a special case. Certainly, pacifists who refuse to go to war and who march against wars comprise grassroots leaders' intent on ending the violent approach to solving political, religious, and ethnic conflicts. Yet, for those victimized by war, grassroots leadership takes a special form. Refusing to engage in an ongoing war or staging marches or demonstrations to end the war are sterile attempts when the bullets and bombs are already flying and people are dying. Efforts to change policy or laws like other grassroots efforts are also futile. Rather, grassroots leadership through art is an appropriate response and approach to alter the situation and push social change because art speaks through a distinctly different language, a different aesthetic than the political discourse that currently characterizes the world. The narrative of art resists the brutality defining reality during war. Courage, defiance, irony, and surreal twists on the war reality are essential elements of the artistic response to ongoing war.

Further, grassroots artist leaders trapped in a war zone have a merged identity as performer–victim. They perform for spectator–victims. Such a shared identity as victim brings artists and spectators closer together so that they all become grassroots leaders standing up for civilization while mired in a barbaric drama. In so doing, they distort the reality of this barbarism and live a reality based on aesthetics and creative expression.

Grassroots artist leaders in war are also transformational leaders because their intent goes beyond that of survival. As they stand against the onslaught of the enemy, they encourage fellow victims to stand up and not lose hope. They uphold the higher values of society, continuing to believe that they can help move society a bit more toward a just and equalitarian world where war is not the most common weapon of solving disputes and gaining power.

The documentary *Miss Sarajevo* described previously is an example of an artistic event that combined the elements of courage, defiance, irony, and surreal twists of the war reality. The row of tall beautiful young contestants in the Miss Besieged Sarajevo pageant with svelte bodies in bathing suits holding the gigantic banner "PLEASE DON'T KILL US" created a surreal vision that distorted the audience's current reality. American pop star Barry McGuire's 1965 song "Eve of Destruction" accompanied the women as they walked along the stage (Cerkez & Niksic, 2012). The lives of the young women had no doubt been shattered. They had all probably lost loved ones or friends. Some of them stood on stage with shrapnel in their legs (Cerkez & Niksic, 2012). Yet, they acted as if they were living in a normal situation with a banner that did not belong to their prewar reality. As Bono wrote on the sleeve notes to U2's *Original Soundracks I* album, "the film captures the dark humor of the Sarajevans, their stubborn refusal to be demoralized and suggests that surrealism and Dadism are appropriate responses to fanaticism" (Alexander Pavlides, 2010, para. 1).

Noteworthy productions of the musical *Hair: Sarajevo AD 1992, Bomb Shelter*, Jean Paul Sartre's *The Wall*, Eugene Ionesco's *Rhinoceros*, and Sławomir Mrożek's *On Foot* and *The Greatest Hits of the Surrealists*, illustrated how artists used irony and dark humor to both satirize the war and defy its brutality (Bilic, n.d.; Hadzic, 2011; Kutovic, n.d.). Critic Gradimir Gojer, who attended the opening of *Hair* wrote "we all dressed up, our best suits, some wore ties ... everyone was dancing and the room fell into a collective trance, one against evil. To beat that evil through art" (Bilic, n.d., p. 4). Bilic (n.d.) argued that the pretense of dressing up provided a "sense of metaphysical freedom" (p. 5). *The Greatest Hits of the Surrealists*, comedy sketches, used black humor to ridicule the horrors of the siege. For example, one of the sketches featured races across "sniper alley," the street in Sarajevo where snipers most actively targeted civilians (Bilic, n.d.). Comic news reports were also broadcast in an effort "to undermine those who were bombing the city in a witty and powerful way" (Bilic, n.d., p. 8).

Irony more effectively catalyzes social change than simply portraying the horror of war. People watch war movies for entertainment. Violence is ever present on television and in the news. Showing the horrors of war might upset the audience but does not always move spectators to action, while seeing the irony of war and people's courage and defiance of war shows the audience that war makes no sense and that there may be an alternative. The difference between the impact of a movie such as Angelina Jolie's *In the Land of Blood and Honey* versus Danis Tanovic's *No Man's Land* is illustrative. The former movie depicts the horrors of the Bosnian war and the decline into insanity of a Serbian Commander who ultimately confesses that he is a war criminal. The audience reaction to her movie is no doubt sorrow because the war reality depicted is so terrible. Yet, there is nothing they can do to change it. There is no hope. Tanovic's movie uses dark humor and buffoonery to depict the absurdity of the war and the incompetence of the United Nations. Scenes like the Bosniak and Serb in their underwear waving white cloths to get help; the Bosniak left to die on the mine because the German "mine expert" does not know how to defuse it; and the throngs of reporters trying to get "the big story" while people are dying around them, speak louder than showing the gore of battle. The audience response to such irony is typically "This is ridiculous. Things don't have to be this way." Such a thought is the beginning of action, of change, of having the power to reconstruct reality.

SMAILOVIĆ AS A GRASSROOTS LEADER

Smailović's spontaneous action took place early in the siege and this fact contributed largely to his role as a grassroots leader. The inhabitants of Sarajevo were still in shock and in denial that war had besieged them. As Smailović later said, the confidence of Sarajevans in their unity and plurality as Bosniaks, Croats, and Serbs was so secure that when they watched the wars in Slovenia and Croatia, they were certain that this destruction could never occur in Sarajevo. They soon realized they were naïve and dreaming. By 1992, "Sarajevo was the capital of hell" (Gateway Baptist Church, n.d., para. 3).

Smailović was one of the first "regular citizens" who also happened to be an artist to step out and challenge the war status quo and publically show that Sarajevans were not going to allow the war to defeat them. He personified the courage and defiance that Sarajevans expressed during the siege and a form of resistance, not resistance in a military sense but a cultural one, one that is much more interior, an act of individuals trying to keep at least fragments of normal life (Kurtovic, n.d.; Bilic, n.d.).

His outrageous actions brought international attention to the siege because he was a highly visible symbol that photographers and journalists could highlight to make noteworthy news. Motivated out of horror and pain, his action of playing his cello in ruins projected an ironic and surrealistic vision, causing people to question whether he had gone mad. His story began attracting artists from around the world who responded by coming to Sarajevo to support the people or create artistic expressions in their personal mediums. Bosnian artists also began to more actively organize to produce artistic events to improve the morale of the people. As evidenced in the global response to his actions, Smailović was also a transformational leader, in that he inspired people around the world to take actions to focus the world's attention on the siege and to work toward a resolution of the conflict.

Smailović's spontaneous performances as an artist in his familiar musical language honored each of the 22 victims. His courage to face the shells and grenades and his defiance of the barbarity around him expressed his grassroots and transformational leadership. Smailović, who became known as the "soul of Sarajevo," represented the "triumphant, cultured city whose spirit could not be crushed" (Jurich, 2005, para. 6). He was "a man of the metropolis, a man of the multiethnic, multicultural world … the act of cello playing effectively transformed Smailović into a front-line soldier fighting the war of culture against barbarism, and life against death" (Jurich, 2005, para. 9). Some artists called Smailović's and other artists' performances during the siege part of the "cultural front" against the war, in language harkening back to socialist days (Kurtovic, n.d.).

Music teacher Angelina Papp, who continued to teach at the Conservatory of Music during the siege, told a reporter that "Musicians … are people who see war as something very strange to them. All musicians of the world speak the same language: the language of their scores. Moreover, music has no limits and so it poses the question, why must we live in this cage?"(Cohen, 1994, para. 26). It is this question that challenges the current political narrative that justifies war. It is this question that begins the dialog about recreating a more civilized world.

That more civilized world would be void of ethnic divisiveness. Smailović, like most Sarajevans, eschewed the effort of outsiders to cement ethnic divisions. He, like others, saw the war as the onslaught of the traditional rural against the cosmopolitan urban (Hadzic, 2011). As he abruptly told a reporter (Burns, 1992):

> My mother is a Muslim and my father is a Muslim but I don't care. I am a Sarajevan. I am a cosmopolitan. I am a pacifist. I am nothing special. I am a musician, I am part of the town. Like everyone else, I do what I can. (para 12)

Smailović never aspired to be a leader. He wanted to be considered an individual who, in an extraordinary situation, did what he considered to be morally right. When asked whether he would repeat the same act, Smailović replied: "Who knows. That was a spontaneous reaction. Instinct. Defense mechanism." Smailović saw playing his cello in a war zone as something normal. He refused to give it give any symbolic meaning. As he further explained (Pavlovic, 2010):

> Sarajevo and Sarajevans are one beauty, and in that time it was somehow normal what I was doing. That was instinctively showing of love and despair. That was a cry for help that lasted a few years, not the f*****g defiance as the media with high respect was showing. They were making a bigger drama than it was ... That was the absolute spontaneous reaction of one individual that deserves respect and the question that arose was are all in Sarajevo that 'crazy.' I didn't fit in with the scheme. I was breaking a conception, but not only me. After the first shock and first grenades, very soon, Sarajevo artists reorganized themselves. And they went on attack. The soul of the city and its inhabitants had to be saved. And we succeeded. (para. 1)

Smailović was not pleased that he was depicted in Galloway's novel *The Cellist of Sarajevo* several years after the siege without being contacted. He felt that his image was being used in a manner that did not truly represent him or his actions (Sharrock, 2008). The cellist desired to disappear in anonymity by the time the novel was written and no longer wanted to be considered a peacemaker nor to return to the limelight. Eventually reconciled with Galloway, Smailović's attitude reflected the fact that he did not consider himself a hero, but rather a normal Sarajevan who did what he thought was right during traumatic times (Houston, 2012).

Smailović, together with other artists and spectators, were grassroots leaders who questioned the status quo by speaking an aesthetic language, strikingly different than that spoken by the ongoing political narrative. Ordinary citizens of Sarajevo joined the artists in undertaking heroic acts and in continuing the dialog that artists proclaimed (Donia, 2006). Many of the actors in the theater productions were soldiers who would put down their weapons to perform (Bilic, n.d.). These citizens also were grass-roots and transformational leaders whose actions transformed a desperate situation into one that upheld cosmopolitanism and the tenants of civilization.

THE ROLE OF ART IN WAR AND DISASTER

Hadzic (2011) argued that the use of art as a weapon during the Sarajevo siege was a political act in the sense that Jacques Ranciere used the term when describing how the plebeians violated the dominant order, set up a parallel order, and learned a language, gaining recognition as legitimate speaking beings from the patricians on the Aventine Hill. Hadzic quoted Ranciere who contended that in politics, "subjects act to create a stage on which problems can be made visible" (p. 5). Hadzic argued that through art, "rejecting … the position of either the 'other' or the 'sub-human other,' they [Sarajevans] re-invented and re-presented themselves" (p. 15).

Paul Chan, who produced *Waiting for Godot* in New Orleans in the aftermath of Hurricaine Katrina wrote that art has the potential to interrogate and rival the prevailing "reason" in society (Bates, n.d.):

> Art is the reason that makes reason ridiculous … To rail against the inactivity, inertia, or apathy of politicians using the language of politics, to my mind, is clearly ineffective. It is a blind alley, a cul-de-sac where the rationale in use is more often reified than challenged. (para. 28)

Julia Bates expanded on Chan's observation. For art to speak in the same language and using the same logic that led to the siege would not achieve social change. Art with its particular meaning-making renders the reason of the contemporary political narrative ridiculous and it does not speak to power or reaffirm authority but speaks a far deeper language of beauty and harmony (Bates, n.d., para. 28).

Kurtovic (n.d.) argued something similar. She argued that the power of the artists performing in Sarajevo

> lay in their ability to cultivate a set of sensibilities, dispositions, and structures of feeling, said to be constitutive of Sarajevo's self-professed cosmopolitan identity and in radical opposition to the agenda of nationalists. These dispositions, encoded in aesthetic preferences, tastes, and social norms, formed a core of a collective subjectivity that underlined a way of life, stretching outside any particular political or even anti-war program. (p. 198)

Methodist Pastor De Vega (2014) also contended that Smailović's music "embodied a bold confrontation to the powers at large, proclaiming that no act of violence and no evil deed, could thwart the spirit of a people determined to live in freedom" (para. 4). He compared the significance of Samilovic's act as the same as the mission of the church to sing against evil and thereby bring in a new more ethical and humane world.

ART AS A WEAPON IN CONTEMPORARY WARS

Artists continue to employ art as a weapon in the wars in Iraq and Syria in the same spirit as the Bosnian artists. For example, the "Cellist of Baghdad," Karim Wasfi, conductor of the Iraq Symphony Orchestra, explained that playing his cello on a bombed out site was (Malone, 2015)

> an action to try to equalize things, to reach the equilibrium between ugliness, insanity, and grotesque, indecent acts of terror — to equalize it or to overcome it by acts of beauty creativity, and refinement ... The act of playing the cello was the opposite to the act of detonating a bomb. It created life ... When things are insane and abnormal like that, I have the obligation of inspiring people, sharing hope, perseverance, dedication, and preserving the momentum of life. People love it. Soldiers cried, they kissed, they clapped, they felt alive, they felt human and they felt appreciated and respected ... Music refines and cultivates. It inspires people ... It has a positive impact on the psychology of mankind. You can breathe better. You can think better and clearer. You can find more talent within yourself. It's an international language of mutual understanding. It's everything. (para. 1)

Chinese dissident artist Ai Weiwei said simply "Art defeats war" as he brought a white grand piano to the Idomeni Refugee Camp in Greece, inviting Syrian refugee Noor Alkhzam to play for the first time in months (Akbar, 2016).

THE CELLIST AND SOCIAL CHANGE

Jurich (2005) included the photograph of Smailović playing in the ruins of the National Theater as one of the three iconic photographs of the Bosnian War, the others being the photograph of the Bosniak prisoners of war in the Serbian concentration camp and the photograph of Bosniak Ferida Osmanovic hanging from a tree having committed suicide after the Srebrenica genocide that also murdered her husband. Although it took several years for a peace agreement to be signed after Smailović's initial "performance," it seems clear that his actions helped to move the peace dialog along by increasing awareness of the war and by involving influential artists and world leaders in the process. Further, as Jurich (2005) argued, "in the midst of uncontrollable destruction, the individual artist remakes the world, even if only briefly, even if it might cost him his life … It is the responsibility of the living to remember the killed and to embody a creative life force even in the midst of death" (para. 12).

Phillips (2004) contended that in order for music to be effectively engaged in the pursuit of peace it must "resist the subversive force of contemporary ideologies centered in commodification, control and power … through the negation of social phenomena infected by these ideologies" (p. 66). War is a central motif in these ideologies. Phillips (2004) argued that any attempt to promote peace through music must emerge out of human love, but not to soothe the human soul. Rather music should evoke "both the present horror and the hope of humanity. It must reveal to us the real possibility of human relationships able to stand 'above identity and above contradiction' … a togetherness of diversity" (p. 71). Certainly, Smailović's performance fulfilled these requirements. His performance also came from within the system not outside it and, as Phillips, believed social change is most effectively accomplished if it emerges from living in the world and "being part of its fabric," rather than being an outside agent (p. 72). Unfortunately, wars have not become an archaic approach to addressing conflict. Yet, as grassroots artist performer—spectator—victim leaders continue to employ art to reveal the absurdity of war and to counteract brutality with beauty, humanity may slowly move toward a new way to reconcile their differences.

Conclusion

Smailović's decision to play his cello in the rubble was a spontaneous action deriving from his pain and his artistic sensibilities, in the musical language he knew best. Not considering himself a leader but rather a regular citizen spontaneously doing what he thought he should do, he became a grassroots transformational leader. Joined by other artists and citizens, unified by being victims of war, Smailović initiated a global conversation about the war. He, along with other grassroots artist−spectator−victim leaders exercised courage and defiance and employed irony and surreal twists on the war reality to assuage fear, generate hope, preserve civilization, and help construct an alternative reality to war, one characterized by a different aesthetic of beauty, benevolence, and brotherhood. As Smailović said when he returned to Sarajevo in 2012 to play his own musical composition "Remembrance," "they [Sarajevan artists] held 250 concerts in bomb shelters, in schools. They were hungry, but still had soul" (Niksic, 2012, para. 5).

Smailović again played Albinoni's Adagio in G minor in the rebuilt National Library in Sarajevo in 2012. Two female modern dancers accompanied him, one dressed in white, representing Sarajevo, and the other dressed in black, representing the Serb enemies. Although the dancer dressed in black initially trampled the dancer dressed in white, by the end, the dancer dressed in white victoriously defeated the enemy and slung her to the ground (Dario Bourqui, 2014). Sarajevo had won. Art had won. Civilization had won. As grassroots leaders, all the artists and spectators in Sarajevo had successfully employed art to help engender peace, stand up for cosmopolitanism, and catalyze social change.

Acknowledgments

- Permission to publish the excerpt from Vedran Smailović was provided by: Wellburn, Elizabeth, *Echoes from the Square*. Paintings by Deryk Houston. Oakville, Ontario: Rubicon Publishing, Inc. @1998. All rights reserved.
- Permission to use the photographs of Vedran Smailović in this chapter was provided by photographer Michael Evstafiev under a Creative Commons license (https://commons.wikimedia.org/wiki/File:Evstafiev-bosnia-cello.jpg).

- Permission to publish the poem "The Cello" by Admiral Mahic was provided by the editor of Sarajevske Sveske.
- We would like to thank Ana Ilievska, PhD Candidate in Comparative Literature, University of Chicago, who graciously agreed to translate Admiral Mahic's poem "The Cello" from Serbo-Croatian into English.

References

Akbar, J. (2016). A song for the stranded: Chinese dissident artist Ai Weiwei drags white grand piano to squalid Idomeni camp where Syrian refugee woman serenades rain-soaked refugees. *Daily Mail*, March 12. Retrieved from http://www.dailymail.co.uk/news/article-3489495/A-song-stranded-Chinese-dissident-artist-Ai-Weiwei-drags-grand-white-piano-squalid-Idomeni-camp-Syrian-refugee-woman-serenades-rain-soaked-migrants.html

Alexander Pavlides. (2010, December 29). U2 and Pavarotti – *Miss Sarajevo* [video file]. Retrieved from https://www.youtube.com/watch?v=z7FM0zuuwBM

Ama Lia, (2010, April 5). *Jim Morrison tribute – Adagio in G minor* [video file]. Retrieved from https://www.youtube.com/watch?v=Yd6KpSSsPFc

Andert, D., Platt, A., & Alexakis, G. (2011). Alternative, grassroots, and rogue leadership: A case for alternating leaders in organizations. *Journal of Applied Business Research*, 27(2), 53–61.

AnirbanMitra. (2010, November 17). *Welcome to Sarajevo* [video file]. Retrieved from https://www.youtube.com/watch?v=vb6va1KXzHU

AP Archive. (2015, July). *US: Vanessa Redgrave and Susan Sontag Hand in Sarajevo Petition* [video file]. Retrieved from https://www.youtube.com/watch?v=GQ-D0LXf3Yw

Baez, J. (1993, April). *Joan Baez in Sarajevo* April 1993 [video file]. Retrieved from https://www.youtube.com/watch?v=AkTh_oxtcbk

Baez, J. (2014, December 23). *Amazing Grace* 1992 Sarajevo [video file]. Retrieved from https://www.youtube.com/watch?v=-v4Emv8Yl5o

Bates, J. (n.d.). *Autumn essay no. 4: Waiting for Godot in Sarajevo and New Orleans*. Retrieved from https://newmodestproposals.wordpress.com/2013/12/30/waiting-for-godot-in-sarajevo-and-new-orleans/

Bilic, A. (n.d.). Theater and performance as a means of survival and resistance during the siege of Sarajevo. *Academia*. Retrieved from https://www.academia.edu/10869586/Theatre_and_Performance_as_a_means_of_survival_and_resistance_during_the_Siege_of_Sarajevo

Bock, P. (1992). Music expresses Sarajevo's sorrow. *The Seattle Times*, September 10. Retrieved from http://community.seattletimes.nwsource.com/archive/?date=19920910&slug=1511983

Breimeier, R. (2003). A Christmas story. *Christianity Today*, December 22. Retrieved from http://www.christianitytoday.com/ct/2003/decemberweb-only/tso-1203.html

Burns, J. F. (1992). The death of a city: Elegy for Sarajevo – A special report; people under artillery fire manage to retain humanity. *New York Times*, June 8. Retrieved from http://www.nytimes.com/1992/06/08/world/death-city-elegy-for-sarajevo-special-report-people-under-artillery-fire-manage.html?pagewanted=all

Burns, J. F. (1993). To Sarajevo, writer brings good will and Godot. *New York Times*, August 19. Retrieved from http://www.nytimes.com/1993/08/19/world/to-sarajevo-writer-brings-good-will-and-godot.html

Burns, J. M. (2004). *Transforming leadership*. New York, NY: Grove/Atlantic Publishers.

Buttry, D. (2011). *Blessed are the peacemakers*. Canton, MI: David Crumm Media, LLC.

Cerkez, A., & Niksic, S. (2012). 1993 Bosnia queen stood up against the war. *CBS News*. Retrieved from http://cnsnews.com/news/article/1993-bosnian-beauty-queen-stood-against-war

Cohen, R. (1994). Music helps Sarajevo stay sane during war. *The New York Times*, October 23. Retrieved from http://www.nytimes.com/1994/10/23/world/music-helps-sarajevo-stay-sane-during-war.html?pagewanted=all

Dario Bourqui. (2014, May 10). *Vijenica//Vedran Smailović//Adagio* [video]. Retrieved from https://www.youtube.com/watch?v=1HgZnd5KZCY

De Vega, M. R. (2014). Midweek message. St Paul's Methodist Church. Retrieved from http://mdevega.blogspot.com/2014/10/the-cellist-of-sarajevo.html

Dizderevic, A. (2012). *Sarajevo War Journal*. Retrieved from http://kirkesque.blogspot.com/p/sarajevo-roses.html

Donia, R. (2006). *Sarajevo: A biography*. Ann Arbor, MI: University of Michigan Press.

Forced Migration Review. (2015). *Dayton +20: Bosnia and Herzegovina twenty years on from the Dayton Peace Agreement*. September. Retrieved from http://www.fmreview.org/dayton20.html

Galloway, S. (2008). *The cellist of Sarajevo*. New York, NY: Riverhead Books.

Gateway Baptist Church. (n.d.). Vedran Smailović – A brief biography. *Soundfaith*. Retrieved from https://soundfaith.com/sermons/108542-cellist-of-sarajevo-story

Hadzic, A. (2011). *The Plebs speak: Theater in besieged Sarajevo (1992–1995)*. Master of Arts Thesis. Retrieved from http://search.proquest.com.fgul.idm.oclc.org/docview/905561764?pq-origsite=summon (1501893).

Heath, D. (2014, May 14). *The cellist of Sarajevo* (string quartet) [video file]. Retrieved from https://www.youtube.com/watch?v=YHgq-fscmhY

HeliasValinti. (2010, December 24). *Savatage – Christmas Eve Sarajevo* 12-24 (HQ) [video file]. Retrieved from https://www.youtube.com/watch?v=yZSWKB1_o4E

Houston, D. (2012). Vedran Smailović: The Cellist of Sarajevo. *Economic Voice*, January 27. Retrieved from http://www.economicvoice.com/vedran-smailovic-the-cellist-of-sarajevo/50027558/

Jewell, W. (2004). *Hero's hero: Vedran Smailović*. Retrieved from http://myhero.com/hero.asp?hero=vedrans

Jewell, W. (2014). *Peacemaker hero: Jason Crowe*. Retrieved from http://myhero.com/hero.asp?hero=jasoncrowe

JudyCollinsForever. (2012, December 2). *Song for Sarajevo* [video]. Retrieved from https://www.youtube.com/watch?v=46ss5p3KSps

Jurich, J. (2005). Remembering to remember: Three photojournalism icons of the Bosnian war. *Afterimage online*. Retrieved from http://vsw.org/afterimage/ 2011/07/28/remembering-to-remember-three-photojournalism-icons-of-the-bos-nian-war-by-joscelyn-jurich/

Keuss, J. F. (2011). *Your neighbor's hymnal: What popular music teaches us about faith, hope, and love*. Eugene, OR: Cascade Books.

Kisselgoff, A. (1992). Dance in Review. *The New York Times*, November 29. Retrieved from http://www.nytimes.com/1993/11/29/arts/dancw-in-review-351393.html

Kurtovic, L. (n.d.). The paradoxes of wartime "freedom": Alternative culture during the siege of Sarajevo. *Academia*. Retrieved from https://www.academia.edu/ 2490901/Paradoxes_of_Wartime_Freedom_Alternative_Culture_during_the_Siege _of_Sarajevo

Mahic, A. (n.d.). *Poems*. Retrieved from http://sveske.ba/en/content/savremeno-pjesnistvo-bosne-i-hercegovine

Malone, B. (2015). Interview: Why I played the cello at a Baghdad bombsite. *Al Jazeera English*, May 28. Retrieved from: http://www.aljazeera.com/news/2015/ 04/omtervoew-played-cello-baghdad-bombsite-150429292916834.html

McCutcheon, J. (2009, March 1). *Streets of Sarajevo* [video file]. Retrieved from https://www.youtube.com/watch?v=b9LqVc8OSc8

McRobie, H. (2014). *Briefing notes: Culture on the frontline*. Retrieved from https://www.freewordcentre.com/blog/2014/08/briefing-notes-culture-war-heathe r-mcrobie/

Mlangiewicz (2011, February 11). *Light Company: The cellist of Sarajevo* [video file]. Retrieved from https://www.youtube.com/watch?v=geFNcPDglTk

Montgomery College. (2013, February 11). *One Maryland, One Book: The cellist of Sarajevo* [video file]. Retrieved from https://www.youtube.com/watch?v= e9ckYG7-SkM

Niksic, S. (2012). The cellist of Sarajevo plays in his city again. *Yahoo News*, April 5. Retrieved from https://www.yahoo.com/news/cellist-sarajevo-plays-city-again-184346177.html

Pavlovic, P. (2010). Sta je danas Sarajevo. *eNovine*, March 30. Retrieved from http://www.e-novine.com/intervju/intervju-kultura/41029-danas-Sarajevo.html

Pelodelperro. (2012, March 19). David Wilde. *The cellist of Sarajevo* [video file]. Retrieved from https://www.youtube.com/watch?v=HvsNU4eEt74

Perrottet, M. (2013, August 8). *Who wrote the Adagio in G Minor? – A musical mystery*. Retrieved from http://hubpages.com/entertainment/Who-Wrote-the-Adagio-in-G-Minor-A-Musical-Mystery

Phillips, G. L. (2004). Can there be music for peace?. *International Journal on World Peace*, 21(2), 63.

Rylan Gayek Leonard. (2009, March 19). *Echoes from the square: Remembering the cellist of Sarajevo* [video file]. Retrieved from https://www. youtube.com/watch?v=b8h7vPU2EAU

Sharrock, D. (2008). Out of the war and into a book and in a rage. *The Australian*. Retrieved from http://www.theaustralian.com.au/arts/out-of-the-war-into-a-book-and-in-a-rage/story-e6frg8n6-1111116651859

Smailović, V. (2014a, November 14). *Ode to Sarajevo* [video file]. Retrieved from https://www.youtube.com/watch?v=JcEA6pw9Y4A

Smailović, V. (2014b, November 8). *Momento mori — Albinoni Adagio* [video file]. Retrieved from https://www.youtube.com/watch?v=NlQVRXcLtZo

Stambeccuccio. (2011). *Tomaso Albionini-Adagio in G Minor Amy Winehouse Tribute* [video file]. Retrieved from https://www.youtube.com/watch?v=90jHwxGo4Jk

SukiChaos. (2009, November 30). *Sarajevo's adagio* [video file]. Retrieved from https://www.youtube.com/watch?v=u1eAykukI58

Vinajak Pal. (2014, January 17). *Cellist of Sarajevo Vedran Smailović* [video file]. Retrieved from https://www.youtube.com/watch?v=fj9BILgs3zo

Visionaria Art Group. (2012, November 19). *Zubin Mehta — Sarajevo 1994* [video file]. Retrieved from https://www.youtube.com/watch?v=KfTE_1wTrtQ

Wellburn, E. (1998). *Echoes from the square*. Oakville, ON, Canada: Rubicon Publishing.

Wilde, D. (n.d.). *The cellist of Sarajevo*. Retrieved from http://www.sccs.swarthmore.edu/users/03/hhsu1/music_articles/wilde_cellist.html

Woodwynn Peace Garden (n.d.). http://www.twoglassyladies.ca/peacesanctuary/

2 Fela Kuti: The Man, His Music, The Activist

Greg Chidi Obi

Who Is Fela Anikulapo Ransome-Kuti?

I was born into an Igbo Roman-Catholic middle-class family to college-educated parents. This meant that my siblings and I had privileges and exposure that many of our play/school mates did not have growing up in the late 1970s in the then East Central State of Nigeria. One such privilege was the joy of waking up Saturday and Sunday mornings to the tune of classical music: Handel, Mozart, and Beethoven being played from the family's LP player. There was also the music of American pop (or country) musicians, such as Jim Reeves, Pat Boone, and many others. We also listened to music by British pop singer Roger Whittaker, and in the evenings we heard some good old West African highlife music.

As much as my parents allowed my siblings and me to experiment with and enjoy all kinds of musical genres, the one artist we were banned from listening to was Fela! And as it has always been, when children are told not to do something, their curiosity is awakened.

The first Fela music I heard was "Alu jon jonki jon" when I was in primary school, 5th grade I believe, at a friend's house. And alas I discovered there was good rhythm in the music, but the lyrics I did not appreciate since I could not understand the Yoruba language then. For us, Fela was played only when our parents were out of the house or not within hearing distance. One began to appreciate the message in his music as one grew older and more mature.

Fela Anikulapo Ransome-Kuti was born in Abeokuta, Nigeria, in 1938 to a prominent Yoruba family. His music, which he named "Afrobeat," represents African originality in art. Afrobeat was also inspired agitation for social change, including resistance against military dictatorships (Dougan, 2015).

Fela used the privilege of his birth as well as his celebrity to stimulate social change from the grassroots level. Among ordinary workaday Nigerians, he created a desire for freedom, self-expression, and the yearning for a civil democratic government. Fela became a grassroots transformational leader who championed the cause of the "common man." Uzodinma Iweala (2012) noted that Fela's resistance and leadership gave courage to the otherwise silent and passive "common people" of Nigeria.

Writing in the online edition of the Nigerian news magazine *Newswatch Times*, columnist Tope Olukole stated:

> Fela recorded more than 70 albums in a tumultuous 30-year career rife with police arrests and unjust detentions. He wrote and performed songs highly critical of the (*various military*) governments. He was jailed more than a hundred times and severely beaten, but his resilient spirit remained unbroken. His house was broken into several times by soldiers, and its occupants violated. (2014, p. 23)

Agent for National Pride

Through the themes of his music, Fela sought to engender a sense of national pride among the people of Nigeria and indeed Africa. Fela stated that he wanted to create a musical careers in the mid-1960s, according to his biographer Carlos Moore (2009), he stated he wanted to create a musical sound and a genre that is distinct and different from the White Man's music:

> I have to be very original and clear myself from shit. I was still hustling. Hustling to make bread. I must clear myself from this mess. I must identify myself with Africa. Then I will have an identity .... I must give it [*his music*] a name-o, a real African name that is catchy. I've been looking for names to give it. And I've been thinking of calling it Afro-beat. (pp. 74–75)

And thus his signature tune and music genre "Afro-beat" was born. Fela never looked back from that point. Through his music he encouraged and advocated for his audience to be proud of their skin color, the way they spoke, their food, their clothes, their language, and culture. His songs "Colonial Mentality" and "Lady" addressed and condemned the idea of Africans giving their children "foreign" names, wearing foreign clothes and eating "foreign foods." "Lady" encouraged women to be proud of such natural gender ascribed duties and roles, advocating that such roles and duties do not make them any less a person or less important to society (Dougan, 2015).

The song "Yellow Fever" informed his audience of the dangers of using bleaching body cream (which was the fad from the 1970s to the early 1980s in Nigeria) to give the skin a lighter tone. Fela encouraged listeners to be proud of their skin tone/color. In the music, he noted that using bleaching cream will result in the discoloration of the skin, with different parts of the body having different skin color. He decried the error of educating young Nigerians with Western-oriented textbooks and materials in his song, "Teacher Don't Teach Me Nonsense." He observed that it was erroneous to teach African children about "White men" who "discovered" great African geographic landmarks (like the River Niger, etc.) since the Africans have always lived with these landmarks. Hence, to Africans such landmarks were never hidden to be discovered.

Other songs, such as "Why Black Man Dey Suffer," "Gentleman," as well as "Mr. Follow Follow," denounced Western-oriented behaviors and argued that the suffering of black people is a result of years of miseducation and oppression by the colonial masters. Fela's crusade for national pride encouraged his audience to be proud of who they are in all facets of life.

According to Michael Veal (2000), Fela articulated that the best way to transform a people and a nation was to control their head by altering their way of thinking, and therefore sought to use his music not just for entertainment but also to change the thought process of the minds of African people.

Fela's journey into becoming a grassroots activist was also a journey of self-discovery. His original purpose seems to have been to find his place in the world of music, but that journey led him through a path of a discovered mission, which was advocating for the unheard grassroots of Nigeria through his music.

Some may contend that Fela's use of music as a weapon for social behavioral transformation is nothing new or unique to Nigeria or African cultures in general. Kashope Handel (2000) observed that some Africanist authors (Isichei, 1983; Mazrui, 1986; Nkosi, 1981)

have opined that most African music, songs, crafts, paintings, literature dances are not just meant to be entertaining alone, but are
mainly themed toward teaching some valuable life lessons: the concept that African arts and literature are more utilitarian than just arts
for art's sake.

Fela's music is indeed an offshoot of the African utilitarian
approach to arts. His music was unique in that he did not create
fictitious characters and events but rather sang about real people
(mainly corrupt government officials, and the wealthy) and real
events, thus using his music to inform, educate, and articulate
change. He used his music as a vehicle to expose corrupt government leaders, their corrupt business associates, as well as those
social behaviors that seem to run counter to the well-being of the
general populace.

His music became the megaphone for carrying the complaints
of the otherwise-ignored mass grassroots audience; his music
became their channel to voice their desire for social change and
transformation. Fela's music themes focused on germane current (at
his time) issues facing the Nigerian nation and the world in general.

Fela's music and public speeches attacking the various military governments of Nigeria became a source of concern for each
successive ruling junta. Olusegun Obasanjo (former military head
of state and former civilian president), testified at the Justice
Oputa-led Human Rights Violations Investigation Commission
(HRVIC) that all top military officer in power, including himself,
were concerned and worried about the constant protests and
riots by university students inspired by Fela's rhetoric and music.
He, however, denied that neither he nor any of his immediate
lieutenants gave direct order for the burning of Fela's property
(The Nigerian Village Square, 2013).

Close observers of Nigeria's civil democracy history would
know that students of Nigerian universities and colleges as well
as trade union leaders played dominant roles in the demand for
civil government. These two groups have also been involved in
agitation for the demand for accountability of government officials to the citizens. Many of these "activist" student union leaders graduated to become avid human rights activists. One of
such is Mr. Femi Falana, now a Senior Advocate of Nigeria
(SAN) and was a past president of the Students' Union of the
then University of Ife (now Obafemi Awolowo University).

Falana in a 2003-interview with Nigerian Television
Authority's Channel 2 Lagos news program stated that Fela held
regular meetings with key students' union leaders (including

Falana) at which Fela encouraged the students to keep mounting pressures on the corrupt military government to relinquish power to the people (NTA 2 Lagos, 2013). According to Falana, Fela gave over 60 speeches across various universities most of which ended with protest march to the main government building of whichever city the university was located.

All through the mid-1970s to late 1990s the major cities of Nigeria witnessed constant public protests, riots and mass demonstrations either by university and college students backed by various trade union members or vice versa. Falana observed that Fela was the soul of such public demand for change and accountability.

Perhaps the biggest indicator of how much a threat the various military governments considered Fela's music was the successive outright ban of playing of his music on government owned radio stations, which for a long time in Nigeria meant all radio stations. Although the first time the ban was issued the Obasanjo-led junta explained that the ban was due to ongoing dispute over copyright payments (Herszenhorn, 1997). Irrespective of the radio-airing ban, Fela's music was the rave on the streets of any of the major cities and towns in Nigeria.

Anti-Corruption and Democratic-Rule Crusader

Fela's close friend and biographer Carlos Moore observed that Fela's transformation into an anti-corruption and civil democracy activist was a gradual process whose beginning could be traced back to his stay in Los Angeles, California from late 1969 to early 1970. In his own words Fela stated: "it was in America I saw I was making a mistake .... I had decided to change my music. And my music did start changing according to how I experienced the life and culture of my people" (Moore, 2009, p. 89).

Veal (2000) offers that several factors played together to help Fela emerge as a champion of anti-corruption and the megaphone of the masses. Among these factors was the need for a "voice for the growing underclass (in Nigeria), who were increasingly marginalized in the midst of the oil-boom prosperity".

Fela was a strong voice against "corruption in high places" (Iweala, 2012, p. 6) even in face of personal danger. He constantly spoke against the corrupt practices of the various military governments of Nigeria at the risk of his personal freedom.

A press kit issued by Amnesty International declaring Fela a Prisoner of Conscious (PoC) stated that Fela was imprisoned or detained by the Nigerian military government on at least five different occasions (Amnesty International, 2011).

The same amnesty report observed that "Fela Kuti was widely known as a critic of Nigeria's military government and a number of his songs included political elements" (Amnesty International, 2011, p. 1). In his song "Zombie," Fela encouraged the rank and file of the army to stop acting like zombies or puppets by carrying out every order given to them by their officers even when such commands are wrong.

In 1980, the current Nigerian President, Mr. Mohammadu Buhari, who was then the head of the ruling junta, orchestrated a military tribunal to sentence Fela to a five-year prison term for an alleged foreign currency-related offense, but many believed this was merely a way of silencing Fela's advocacy against the corrupt military government in Nigeria (Denselow, 2015).

On his release from prison, Fela quickly put out a new album, "Beast of No Nation" declaring the government leaders a bunch of crazy people for declaring a mass re-orientation movement termed "War Against Indiscipline." The song also labeled Western political leaders as animals in human skin for supporting the Apartheid government in the Republic of South Africa, while at the same time sanctioning third world nations for not granting their citizens basic human rights. The song was a strong criticism of the United Nations and the veto powers of the permanent members of its Security Council.

Fela's years in prison and detention at various times for confronting corrupt government officials as well as being at the forefront of mass protests did not mute Fela and his music. The themes and lyrics of Fela's music were aimed at exposing corruptions in the government that many at the grassroots level were otherwise unaware of. The album "Army Arrangement" highlighted how the then General Obasanjo-led dictatorship supposedly misappropriated over 2.8 billion Naira (Nigerian currency) from crude oil sales (The Cable, 2014). In his song "ITT" Fela exposed the alleged bribery of Nigerian top civil servants, and senior military officers by the New York based International Telephone and Telegraph Corp. (Berry, 1980).

The bribe was ostensibly given to help ensure that ITT's bid for the contract of providing and maintaining telecommunication satellites in Nigeria was won. Several years after the contract was awarded (to ITT) and executed, most parts of Nigeria still had telephone services that were by and large comatose. It is interesting to note that though ITT was at the time the sole company servicing the Nigerian Telecommunication Company, most Nigerians did not even know what the abbreviation ITT meant, nor were people aware of the services the firm provided until Fela through his song ITT exposed the suspected bribery scandal (Oduyela, 2004).

Around this same period in the 1980s, military dictatorships were rampant across African countries. Fela vehemently opposed these dictatorships in his song "ODOO (Overtake Don Overtake Overtake)," noting that each successive group of junta was as bad as the one they replaced, irrespective of whatever fancy names they may give to their regime. In the album, he lamented that the grass-roots populace of Africa have remained impoverished irrespective of these purported changes the new governments may claim to have brought. In the lyrics of the song, Fela sings that the soldier-leaders were simply leading their nations and people backward instead of creating progress. The songs also praised the resilient nature of the average African to improve her/his family's well-being, irrespective of the bad management of the economy by their governments.

Fela believed that public officials must be held accountable to the masses on how they conducted their duties. He openly spoke against military rule in Nigeria; his song "Coffin for Head of State" not only criticized the Obasanjo-led military administration but also decried the ostentatious lifestyle of religious leaders in Nigeria while the bulk of their congregants wallowed in poverty. The song's lyrics states that these religious leaders were in cahoots with the corrupt leaders in exploiting the poor masses who flock to the places of worship (Metrolyrics, n.d.).

In his song "C.B.B. (Confusion Break Bone)," Fela criticized the various wrong actions as well as the confusion the military government had created in Nigeria. Particularly the song noted how the federal government of Nigeria in a bid to protect local producers of fabrics and certain processed foods banned the importation of such items. However, the task force created to prevent the importation of such goods would send policemen/women and soldiers into the markets to confiscate these "illegally" imported goods from shop owners and set them (the goods) ablaze at public events. Fela advocated that instead of burning these goods the agency could have sold them at very cheap prices to the poor or donate the items to orphanages and destitute homes.

Fela's advocacy and crusade led him to declare his large family home a communal compound. He named it the Kalakuta Republic and declared it independent of the control of the

Nigeria military government. Kalakuta Republic was an all-are-welcome shelter for the homeless. It offered free food and free healthcare to the poor, beggars, and the street kids of Lagos (Icha, 2016). It also became a rallying ground for several human rights advocates and pro-democracy activists ranging from Fela's younger brother Beko Ransome-Kuti (a medical doctor), Femi Falana (a lawyer), students' union leaders of various Nigerian universities and colleges, as well as Fela's mother; Funmilayo Ransome-Kuti, a teacher, mostly known for being a long-term grassroots political campaigner and grassroots women rights advocate (Moore, 2009).

Fela held sway at his night club which he referred to and came to be known as the "Shrine." At the shrine Fela and his band held open rehearsals of his songs. As these open practices began to attract massive audience, Fela used them as an opportunity to educate and discuss the lyrics of his songs. This form of public speaking he termed "yabis." Lindsay Barrett (1998) writes that yabis, which became a consistent feature at Fela's shows, was used to berate government officials for their inefficiency and corruption.

One can conclude that Fela's purpose was to transform the common people of Nigeria into well-informed individuals that can take charge of their lives and determine the nature of the government they desired. Fela was a fearless critic of the various military governments in Nigeria, believing that they were all corrupt and that the very nature of military junta, who rule with intimidation and fear, was against progress. According to Veal (2000), Fela in a television interview called on the press to "tell the man with the gun that the people who teach our people fear, render the whole country defenseless".

At the dawn of Nigeria's Second Republic (1979–1983), and then again in the 1992 primaries leading to the 1993 presidential election, many encouraged Fela to run for one political office or the other, but he declined, preferring to educate the populace through his music rather than be involved in what he termed the "system." In an interview with the London *New African* magazine, Fela stated:

> I don't have to enter the mainstream of politics. I can have a program, which is much more productive than entering the system, which would mean that I agree with the system. We can never win, so I will educate instead.

> (Highet, 1989, pp. 41–42)

Fela believed that music is a strong weapon that can be used to transform society and its people; he therefore preferred to fight through his music.

Kalakuta Republic

One can argue that another of Fela's biggest impacts on the lives of the grassroots and common people of Nigeria was the opening of his large compound and home, renamed Kalakuta Republic (named after his cell at the Kirikiri Prisons in Lagos) to the general mass of homeless, poor, and desperate people in the sprawling city of Lagos. Kalakuta Republic has been described as akin to the American hippie communes (Olukole, 2014) where resources were shared among the inhabitants. The commune welcomed anyone who wished to enter as long as they lived in peace and contributed to the community. Kalakuta Republic was not only the home for Fela's personal family, but it also housed his large band members as well as all and everyone who could not find a roof over his/her head in the city of Lagos. Many taxi drivers, bus drivers and conductors, street traders, street laborers, and other menial job workers lived and went to their various work places from Kalakuta.

The home offered free food, medical care, basic reading, writing, and math classes for the children who could not afford to go to school (for lack of money) and even for the older people who were past school age. Fela was said to have believed in his heart that the true masses or grassroots were the homeless, the jobless, the prostitutes, the street urchins, and even the thieves. Noting that they deserved to have their voices and agitation heard by their leaders (Veal, 2000). Fela declared, "my sole aim is to fight the injustice in Africa particularly in Nigeria and I shall continue to do this …. I talk politics and the only avenue is through my music" (Denzer, 2003, p. 119).

Indeed Fela's Kalakuta Republic, until its sacking in February 1977 (Fela's album "Kalakuta Show" tells the story of the demolition from his viewpoint), was a refuge and rally ground for anti-corruption, anti-military rule advocates. It was not uncommon for university students, who were in the forefront of periodic street rallies and protests against the military government to begin or end their protest marches in Kalakuta Republic.

The government and law enforcement authorities often alleged that Kalakuta Republic was a refuge for armed robbers, thieves, and all sorts of miscreants, as well as political agitators running from the police and other law enforcement agencies.

It was not uncommon for anyone running from the authorities to find refuge in Kalakuta Republic (*Daily Times of Nigeria*, 1977).

Allegedly it was an incident between soldiers controlling traffic and some taxi drivers who ran to Kalakuta republic for safety that led to the raid of the compound. The attack began in the early morning of February 8, 1977 with supposedly over 1,000 soldiers involved. Purportedly the soldiers were acting on the direct order of the then military Head of State, General Olusegun Obasanjo, who incidentally comes from the same town as Fela.

The soldiers were said to have shot at unarmed civilians living within Kalakuta, some of the inhabitants were severely beaten, and the compound burned to the ground. The soldiers allegedly held back men of the fire service from quenching the fire.

In the melee, Fela's mother, Funmilayo Ransome-Kuti, MON, a decorated Nigeria national honor holder, who is also noted as the first Nigerian woman to drive a vehicle as well as a veteran grassroots political activist. She was reported to have been thrown down from the window of a story-building within the compound during the melee with the soldiers. As a result, she sustained life-threatening injuries which many believe contributed to her death a little over a year later in April of 1978.

In reaction to Fela's agitations as well as the continued public outcry of Madam Ransome-Kuti's death, the government of Lagos state later built the Funmilayo Ransome-Kuti Memorial Grammar School at the old site of Kalakuta public.

Fela's Message and Lifestyle: A Clash of Ethics

Perhaps one of the greatest hindrances of Fela's influence on the wider Nigerian audience, his critics say, was that his lifestyle ran contrary to his message. Beginning with his attire Fela was known to wear no more than a pair of pants and quite often only his underpants (Speedo). It is important to note that in Nigeria, especially in southern Nigeria, Christian moral values are often emphasized and social misbehavior was heavily frowned upon.

Fela's choice of language of communication posed another controversy between his messages of positive transformation of the grassroots versus the general quest for good western-oriented education by most Nigerian families. The issue is that Fela deliberately spoke and sang in Pidgin English contrary to the fact that, in Nigeria, especially at the grassroots level (at least mainly in the south) families spend hard-earned money to send their children to get good educations and avoid speaking Pidgin English.

Within the context of such social values it was easy for the upper lower-class, to the growing middle class and beyond to enjoy Fela's music, but dismiss the message contained therein as the rantings of an underpants-wearing, marijuana smoking, and womanizing social misfit. One of Fela's official biographers observed that "the perception of Fela as a social deviant held political consequences" (Veal, 2000, p. 250) for him to appear as a credible spokesperson for the urban elite. Veal (2000) cited an internet posting of one of Fela's critics, stating that Fela "contributed a lot to the current state of absolute moral decadence among the youths in Nigerian urban centers" (p. 250).

Veal (2000) opines that to the critical Western audience Fela's lifestyle made his "message of African empowerment become increasingly intertwined with dominant racist stereotypes of the African as vulgar, intoxicated, primitive, hypersexualized, and indigenous mystic".

Other critics such as Nkiru Nzegwu (2003) have argued that Fela's use of his "wives" dancing in skimpy patches of clothes did not match his rhetoric of upholding women values, and African culture. Nzegwu opines that Fela's image of a true African woman as portrayed in his Album "Lady" was more akin to the Western Judeo-Christian view of a good wife than that of an authentic economically independent African wife. She further explains that, historically, the precolonial African wife had carriers (traders, famers, craft-makers) outside of the home long before the introduction of the docile wife concept by the colonial masters.

To this author, one of Fela's weaknesses was finding the balance between his crusade for equality, freedom, and anti-corruption and his need for "showmanship" during his musical performances. The use of his "dancing queens" on stage wearing very skimpy clothes, and even once in a while these ladies appeared on stage wearing no tops except for some strands of coral bead necklaces. One can conclude that this objectification of women runs contrary to Fela's claim of being a grassroots leader.

On the other hand, Fela's supporters claim that Fela provided employment to these ladies who otherwise would have resorted to prostitution or other illegal activities in a city, like Lagos, where finding any form of job was a daunting challenge. Such supporters explain that the dancing queens' outfit (if it can be called that) and their sexually suggestive dance steps were simply a form of artistic expression which is common across music gen-res and common to most musicians all over the world.

But then those who understood Fela and his enthusiasts will argue that Fela was not the advocate of the Nigerian urban elite but that he advocated for the often unheard voices of the mass grassroots audience that were the unseen and passive majority that carried the burden of the oppressive elites and corrupt government officials in the Nigeria of his time. Tope Olukole (2014) writes that within his band and indeed within Kalakuta Republic, Fela encouraged learning, and reading to expose the mind. He discouraged misbehaviors such as the young ones not being respectful to older residents, lying, or stealing. Such misbehaviors, notes Olukole, were severely punished sometimes by flogging the culprit with Fela's approval of such.

Fela was a complex being who came from a family of professionals; his father was a pastor, his mom was a school teacher, his older sister was nurse, his older brother was a pediatrician, and his younger brother was a medical doctor too. He was sent to London, England, to study medicine, but he switched to music and ended up an activist musician. Fela understood his own complexity as he self-described himself in his native Yoruba language as "Abami Eda," loosely translated to mean the weird one or the mysterious one (Moore, 2009).

Unusual Leader: Conclusion

Unlike many artists and entertainers of his generation, Fela's music cut across generations and national boundaries. His message still resonates across the ages and nations. Fela sang and spoke about the plights and suffering of common folks, who had a voice, but whose voice did not speak as loudly as Fela's did for them.

From his music and interviews, Fela had a deep-seated belief that the best way to positively change a nation was from the ground up. He understood and advocated for civil democratic rule not just for Nigeria but for all other African countries. He condemned the various military juntas that ruled several African countries from the late 1960s to late 1990s (Olaniyan, 2004). He was a stalwart opponent of corruption as well as mistreatment of people by their leaders.

His home became a "hiding place" for many human rights and pro-democracy activists as well as the simple urban poor who could not afford a shelter in the city of Lagos. Fela's music and his person became a galvanizing force and made it possible for the Nigerian to openly begin to agitate for civil democratic rule. His music encouraged people at the grassroots level to oppose and resist soldiers who ruled with guns and to question the activity of their leaders.

According to a CBS News report, American businessman Stephen Hendel (creator of the Broadway musical "Fela") stated regarding Fela: "I was just totally floored .... I had never heard music like that, the great musician who had sacrificed everything to stand up for human dignity, and nobody knew who he was" (Mason, 2014). Mason, quoting Hendel, noted that Fela's music was about legacy and inspiration, and about "what a man can stand for, what a man leaves and how a man's legacy can inspire" generations after him. The Broadway musical "Fela," which portrays Fela's life, won three Tony Awards and was nominated as one of the top five candidates for the best musical category at the 64th Tony Awards in 2010.

Fela, as a transformative leader, tried to use his music to educate his listeners, to advocate civil democratic rule and wipe away corruption in Nigeria. He aimed at creating a proud African mentality in his audience as did other Pan-African thinking political leaders and writers, such as Leopold Sédar Senghor of Senegal (Negritude), Kwame Nkrumah of Ghana (African Personality), Mwalimu Julius Nyerere of Tanzania (Ujamaa), and Nnamdi Azikiwe of Nigeria (Pan Africanism).

Fela died in 1997 of HIV/AIDS-related complications. His family recognized the cause of his death as a teachable moment. His death occurred at a time when many people at the grassroots level across African nations believed that HIV/AIDS was not real but was a myth by the White Man and urban elites to stop procreation. In order to dispel the erroneous views of HIV/AIDS not being real, Fela's family led by his older brother, Dr. Olikoye Ransome-Kuti (a pediatrician), chose to turn their personal grief into public service by announcing the root cause of Fela's death so people would know that HIV/AIDS is real – thus working in line with Fela's desire to educate and transform the grassroots.

His family stated it was important for the public to know, so that those who had had sexual contact with him can seek medical care. This action, opined Chinweokwu Madubuike (2008), brought about a more open conversation of HIV/AIDS to the forefront of public discussion and government policy in Nigeria. Even on his death bed, Abami eda Fela Anikulapo Ransome-Kuti was bringing transformation to the grassroots of the Africa he declared he cared for.

Writing in the Melbourne, Australian online edition of the *Herald Sun*, Blanche Clark summarized Fela in what I consider an apt description: "imagine Che Guevara and Bob Marley rolled into one person and you get a sense of Nigerian musician and activist Fela Kuti" (Clark, 2011, p. 1).

Irrespective of how one may view Fela, one narrative remains constant and true: Fela was one of those leaders who helped transform Nigeria from a corrupt military dictatorship where intimidation of the common man held sway into a civil democracy where public servants are beginning to be held accountable to the common people who elected them.

Acknowledgments

I would like to dedicate this chapter to my son, Clive, whose imminent immigration to live with me here in the United States was a driving force to ensure I completed this work on schedule. And to my sister, Ekeoma Ezeibe, who has always been my number one and greatest cheerleader.

It would be impossible to have successfully completed this chapter without the knowledge gathered from prior books, articles, blogs, and internet posting by various authors on Fela done before this chapter. I acknowledge that these prior works made it quite easier for me to give substance to this chapter rather than relying on my personal experiences alone. I acknowledge the insights gathered from the Trevor Schoonmaker's edited text, *Fela: From West Africa to West Broadway*, 2003, Palgrave Macmillan. Quotations from it reproduced with permission of Palgrave Macmillan. I also acknowledge use of materials from Michael Veal's *Fela: The Life and Times of an African Musical Icon*, 2000, published by Temple University Press. Materials from it reproduced with the permission of Michael Veal and Temple University Press.

The first book I read on Fela was the Lawrence Hill Books' edition of Carlos Moore's *Fela: This Bitch of a Life* (2009); I acknowledge the use of quotations from the text. I also acknowledge Anthony Mason and CBS News for their detailed report on Fela. I also thank and acknowledge Henry Bainbridge of Partisan Records/Knitting Factory Records.

I owe a debt of gratitude to my brother, Felix, who did the basic research on Fela for the initial abstract submission for this chapter. I am thankful to my former classmate and friend; Dr. Joyce Parks, and my colleague here at Ohio University Chillicothe; Dr. Tony Vinci. Both painstakingly read though all my drafts and made copious corrections. My friend Kimberly Dawn Spraggins thanks for caring and being there for me.

References

Amnesty International. (2011, June). *Amnesty at 50 press kit*. Retrieved from http://www.amnestyusa.org/news/media-relations-contacts/amnesty-at-50-press-kit

Barrett, L. (1998). Fela Anikulapo-Kut. *The Wire* 169, March, pp. 34—40.

Berry, J. F. (1980). ITT allegedly spent millions to obtain contracts in Nigeria. *The Washington Post*, August 17. Retrieved from https://www.washingtonpost.com/archive/politics/1980/08/17/itt-allegedly-spent-millions-to-obtain-contracts-in-nigeria/e44ffce6-2b75-4fd8-bd7a-c1005cb15713/

Clark, B. (2011). Entertainment: Man of beats brings a message with him. *Herald Sun*, February 4. Retrieved from http://www.heraldsun.com.au/entertainment/man-of-beats-brings-a-message-with-him/story-e6frf96f-1225999739892

Daily Times of Nigeria. (1977). The raid at Kalakuta Republic. *Daily Times* of Nigeria, February 24.

Denselow, R. (2015). Nigeria's new president Muhammadu Buhari: The man who jailed Fela Kuti. *The Guardian*, April 1. Retrieved from http://www.theguardian.com/music/2015/apr/01/nigerias-new-president-muhammadu-buhari-is-the-man-who-put-fela-kuti-in-jail

Denzer, L. (2003). Fela, women, wives. In T. Schoonmaker, *Fela from West Africa to West Broadway* (p. 119). New York, NY: Palgrave Macmillian.

Dougan, J. (2015, November 26). *Fela Kuti*. Retrieved from http://www.allmusic.com/artist/fela-kuti-mn0000138833/biography

Handel, K. W. (2000). Not so strange bedfellows: Indigenous knowledge, literature studies, and African development. In G. J. Sefa Dei, B. L. Hall, & D. G. Rosenberg (Eds.), *Indigenous knowledges in global contexts: Multiple readings from our world* (pp. 184—201). Toronto: University of Toronto Press.

Herszenhorn, D. M. (1997). Arts: Fela, 58, dissident Nigerian musician, dies. *The New York Times* (U.S. edition), August 4. Retrieved from http://www.nytimes.com/1997/08/04/arts/fela-58-dissident-nigerian-musician-dies.html?pagewanted=all

Highet, J. (1989). When music becomes a weapon. *New African*, September, pp. 41—42.

Icha, E. (2016). Pioneers of change: Funmilayo Ransome-Kuti. *The Communicator*, March. Retrieved from http://www.ncc.gov.ng/thecommunicator/index.php?option=com_content&view=article&id=322&Itemid=22

Isichei, E. (1983). *A history of Nigeria*. New York, NY: Longman Inc.

Iweala, U. (2012). An unspoken part of Fela Kuti's legacy. *The Wall Street Journal*, June 28. Retrieved from http://blogs.wsj.com/speakeasy/2012/07/28/an-unspoken-part-of-fela-kutis-legacy/

Madubuike, C. U. (2008). The politics of women's empowerment in Nigerian HIV/AIDS Prevention Program: 2003–2007. *Doctoral dissertation*. London: Gender Institute, London School of Economics and Political Science.

Mason, A. (2014). Legacy of legendary Nigerian musician, activist gets fresh look. *CBS News*, August 16. Retrieved from http://www.cbsnews.com/news/legacy-of-fela-kuti-legendary-nigerian-musician-gets-fresh-look/

Mazrui, A. A. (1986). *The Africans: A triple heritage*. Boston, MA: Little, Brown and Company.

Metrolyrics. (n.d.). *Metro lyrics*. Retrieved from http://www.metrolyrics.com/coffin-head-of-state-lyrics-fela-kuti.html

Moore, C. (2009). *Fela: This bitch of a life*. Chicago, IL: Lawrence Hill Books.

Nkosi, L. (1981). *Tasks and masks: Themes and styles of African literature*. New York, NY: Longman Publishing Company.

NTA 2 Lagos. (2013, August 6). Retrieved from https://www.youtube.com/watch?v=brgFRiGqmR4

Nzegwu, N. (2003). School days in Lagos: Fela, Lady, and 'Acada' girls. In T. Schoonmaker (Ed.), *Fela: From West Africa to West Broadway*. New York, NY: Palgrave Macmillan.

Oduyela, S. (2004). Seyi's expose: Owners of Nigeria (V). *NigeriaWorld*, September 20. Retrieved from http://nigeriaworld.com/feature/publication/oduyela/092004.html

Olaniyan, T. (2004). *Arrest the music: Fela and his rebel art and politics*. Indianapolis, IN: Indiana University Press.

Olukole, T. (2014). Untold story of Fela's Kalakuta Republic and its neighbours. *Newswatch Times*, June 7. Retrieved from http://www.mynewswatchtimesng.com/untold-story-felas-kalakuta-republic-neighbours/

The Cable. (2014). NNPC asks Buhari: Was $2.8bn oil money truly missing when you were petroleum minister? *The Cable Nigeria*, December 14. Retrieved from https://www.thecable.ng/nnpc-asks-buhari-2-8bn-oil-money-truly-missing-petroleum-minister.

The Nigerian Village Square. (2013, November 7). *Former president Olusegun Obasanjo answers to Fela Kuti's petition*. Retrieved from http://nigeriavillagesquare.com/forum/main-square/79954-former-president-olusegun-obasanjo-answers-fela-kutis-petition.html

Veal, M. (2000). *Fela: The life and times of an African musical icon*. Philadelphia, PA: Temple University Press.

3

Václav Havel, the Playwright-Dissident: Theater as a Seismograph for Social Change

Joshua M. Hayden

O n August 21, 1968, Soviet tanks rolled into Czechoslovakia and ended a period of liberal reforms known as the Prague Spring. The result was devastating. After being taken to Moscow to sign a capitulation, the reform leader, Alexander Dubček, broke down and wept while addressing the nation on the radio. Reflecting on that moment, the dissident Edá Kriseová (1993) wrote, "we knew our cause was lost" (p. 74). For many others, optimism turned to despair. Over 20 years of oppressive communist "normalization" followed. During this tumultuous period in Czech history, a 32-year-old playwright emerged as a beacon of hope within a community of writers and artists. Václav Havel's absurdist plays were a conduit for his collaborative engagement that would culminate in the Velvet Revolution in 1989, peacefully uprooting the Communist regime. Because of his courageous leadership, Havel would become the President of a democratic Czechoslovakia in 1990.

Nearly a year after the 1968 Soviet invasion, Havel wrote a private letter to Dubček that would articulate the rationale behind Havel's persistent grassroots leadership as a banned playwright-dissident. He urged Dubček to speak the truth about the reforms and confront the injustice even if there would be no immediate results:

> Your act, therefore, will have no positive effect on the immediate situation; on the contrary, it will probably be exploited to justify further repression. But that is all negligible when set beside the immeasurable moral significance of your act for the social and political destiny of our two nations. People would realize that it is always possible to preserve one's ideals and backbone; that one can stand up to lies; that there are values worth struggling for; that there are still trustworthy leaders; and that no political defeat justifies complete historical skepticism as long as the victims manage to bear their defeat with dignity.
>
> (Havel, 1992, p. 43)

Havel would, throughout his career as a reluctant political dissident, embody the type of courage he was calling forth in Dubček. The cost would be over 20 years as an "exiled" playwright in his own country, many interrogations, searches by the secret police, and ultimately prison. Havel's significance as an artist and grassroots leader stems from his moral authority and articulation, through his plays and writing, of the struggle for human identity and responsibility within a repressive society. His plays were warnings, caricatured stirrings of the moral imagination, unveilings of the totalitarian system, and painful yet hilarious satires of modernity. Havel likened theater to "a seismograph of the times" (Havel, 1990, p. 40). His view of the role of the theater had everything to do with the way he led and why he was such an effective catalyst for social change. Havel defended and empowered other artists and writers to "live in truth," as he often said, and claim their human dignity by bearing witness to the conscience of a people through their art. The case of Václav Havel as a dissident leader is indispensable for a deeper understanding of the connection between effective grassroots leadership and the arts for social change.

This chapter will explore Havel's early role as a playwright-dissident in Communist Czechoslovakia through the lens of "Adaptive Leadership." Adaptive leadership is a theory advanced by Ronald Heifetz (1994), and further articulated in Heifetz, Grashow, and Linsky (2009) as a process of mobilizing others for change at the level of their fundamental priorities, beliefs, habits, and loyalties. As a nonhierarchical model that

distinguishes leadership from authority, it is especially condu-
cive to understanding the processes of grassroots leadership.
This analysis utilizes a case study methodology to provide a
detailed analysis and account for situational factors that
impacted the way Havel led. Over the course of three decades
(1960s through the 1980s), three of Havel's plays were
emblematic of his adaptive response to his changing situation
and cultural mood of his "audience" at three different stages of
enacting social change under communism. They each functioned
as a seismograph for mobilizing change: *The Memorandum*
(1965) during the cultural explosion that culminated in the
Prague Spring; *Audience* (1975) under the early communist
"normalization" period as a banned playwright; and *Largo
Desolato* (1984) after almost four years as an imprisoned dissident. The themes of each play mirror Havel's actions and writings as a grassroots leader and provide insights into how
theater can mobilize people for social change.

Theater and Social Change

To lay the groundwork for exploring Havel's plays and social
change, it is important to understand how he viewed the relationship between the two. First, Havel belonged to a rich legacy of
playwrights. Czech theater is world famous for its ability to critically reflect the events and life of its people; in many ways it was
the center of cultural life (Burian, 1984). In his early career as a
stagehand at the ABC Theatre Havel made an important discovery: theater was more than a factory producing plays for entertainment, it was "a living spiritual and intellectual focus, a place
of social self-awareness, a vanishing point where all the lines of
force of the age meet, a seismograph of the times, a space, an
area of freedom, an instrument of human liberation" (Havel,
1990, p. 40). As a "seismograph" and area of freedom theater
could increase urgency, broaden social awareness, liberate the
heart and mind. This insight was particularly important in light
of what would happen in the late 1960s, and the two decades following, when he worked as a banned playwright.

Second, Havel believed theater was a powerful place of self-
awareness and a call to action. He wrote in the late 1960s, "What
should theatre do, actually? According to my opinion, it should
awaken in man his authenticity; it should help him to become
aware of himself in the full span of his problems, to understand

the situation in which he lives, to provoke him to think about himself …. At most I can only help the spectator to formulate problems, which he must solve himself" (quoted in Burian, 2000, p. 110). Theater provides a diagnosis, perspective on the problems of man in society, and space for self-reflection. This is the critical part of adaptive leadership; as Heifetz (1994) argues, leadership often falters because of a failure to diagnose, see one's part in a system, and understand the problem's complexity.

Finally, just as "leadership" is a particular kind of relationship, Havel understood theater as a form of human relationship (Havel, 1989). He wrote, "theater cannot exist without an audience … even if it did it would still not be theater in the deepest sense of the word" (p. 256). Theater is a social experience, a reciprocal relationship between audience and actors and between audience members, forming new relationships. This kind of engagement created what Havel once called "a conspiratorial sense of togetherness" (Havel, 1990, p. 43). Under the social isolation manifested in the communist regime this sense of community was essential to the solidarity of the dissidents in the human rights movement that Havel led. As an art, he believed theater was like "playing with fire" because it transcends itself into the meaning-making of audience members as co-creators of the work and its consequences (Havel, 1989, p. 170). Theater's influence could mean a variety of creative responses germinating a readiness for change.

The Memorandum and the Cultural Explosion of the 1960s

A metaphor at the heart of Adaptive Leadership is "getting to the balcony as well as the dancefloor." This means being in a place of perspective, where one can distinguish between adaptive and technical issues. Heifetz et al. (2009) observed, "To practice adaptive leadership, you have to take time to think through your interpretation of what you observe before jumping into action" (p. 34). Adaptive challenges fundamentally involve shifting people's loyalties, values, and priorities, which requires raising difficult issues and anticipating others' loss and resistance. In adaptive change, leaders address their own contribution to the problem. Following a decade of purges, censorship, and the absence of intellectual freedom, the Czech cultural explosion started in the early 1960s and included the creative outpouring of small theaters, rock and roll clubs, and "the 1960's culture" emerging in the United States. Havel was in the middle of it all, but in a period of increased optimism, he looked beneath the surface. His job as a playwright at the Theatre of the Balustrade gave him the collaboration and experimental environment to work against illusion, pose questions, and explore provocative themes (Havel, 1990). With the cultural momentum behind him, Havel found creative expression in his plays to identify an adaptive challenge in the subtle dehumanization that the scientific bureaucracy of communism forced upon people. Yet rather than casting a vision with his plays, Havel used the absurdist tradition to unmask, raise concerns, and carefully diagnose.

Havel's "balcony" perspective had its roots partly in the influence of absurdist playwrights Franz Kafka and Eugene Ionesco, but more personally in his experience of seeing his society "from below," as he called it. His upper-middle class "bourgeois" background under communism disadvantaged him emotionally and socially keeping him out of academic opportunities and branding him with suspicion (Zantovsky, 2014). Yet Havel believed that being an outsider helped him escape from "eventual illusions and mystifications," and sensitized him to the absurd dimensions of the world (Havel, 1976, p. 4). Havel's poetic introspection and self-awareness gave him insight into the deeper human problems of living within the system.

The Memorandum was a 12-scene play, set in an office, about the imposition of a new scientifically precise language called Ptydepe designed to make communications more efficient. The central conflict of the play is between the Managing Director, Josef Gross, and the heavily absurd (and hilarious) vortex of the bureaucratic system in which Gross attempts to get a memorandum written in Ptydepe translated. In the course of his attempts, Gross discovers first that his Deputy, Jan Ballas, has introduced the language behind his back; second, that everyone else knew about it; third, that almost no one understood it; and finally, that there was no escape from it. Gross was caught in a vicious circle of protocols one must go through for translation. Language became the instrument of control, and bureaucracy its accessory. In a moment of realization Gross, exasperated, said, "the only way to learn what is in one's memo is to know it already. An extraordinary paradox, when you come to think of it. Ladies and Gentlemen, do you come to think of it?" (Havel, 1965/1994a, p. 95). That was a question as much to the audience as it was within the play.

The play was a seismograph warning that it is possible for humans to lose their dignity and freedom through the systems they create and serve. The critical tool Havel used to have his audience face this reality was humor. The audience humorously experienced with Gross the estrangement of suddenly being an outsider in one's familiar surroundings. According to Barnancizak (1999), a moralist needs humor in the arts because it implies an understanding of human motivation and self-deprecation. The audience laughed at how much Gross was a product of the system. As Goetz-Stankiewicz (1979) observed, "The absurd incident thus seems to have a rational explanation, but only for the non-thinking bureaucrat whose mechanical reaction to the new way of communication is simply that he shrugs his shoulders and gets down to his copy of *Ptydepe for Beginners*" (p. 55). Gross was subsequently demoted all the way down to Staff Watcher (allusion to Communist secret police), the lowest position with an office in between the walls, which he happily accepts. At several key moments the characters recognize that they are stuck in a ridiculous system, but they change nothing. It is through and after the laughter that the truth becomes palatable. At the end, Gross observes his and others' plight: "our life has lost a sort of higher axle, and we are irresistibly falling apart, more and more profoundly alienated from the world, from others, and from ourselves ... manipulated, automatized, made into a fetish, Man loses the experience of his own totality" (Havel, 1965/1994a, p. 129).

Havel's leadership from "the balcony" also challenged the passive participation and ritualized adherence to communist ideology, making people within the system accessories to its dehumanizing effects. The language of Ptydepe, like the ideology of the regime, existed for its own sake and thus was unthinkingly perpetuated. It does not take long in the play to discover that the language does not deliver on its promises, but yet it is propagated. According to Zantovsky (2014), "In *The Memorandum*, Havel for the first time posed the question of a passive participation in evil that he would return to again and again in the decades to come. In doing so, he shattered the moral complacency of many of his contemporaries, who were content to engage in criticism and reformist rhetoric only within carefully observed limits" (pp. 93–94). During the 1960s, Havel confronted this passive participation himself in his actions as part of the Writer's Union. His strong voice against subtle repression in his writing earned him a place on the editorial board of the Union publication Tvář. Havel's defense of Tvář as a vehicle for intellectual freedom with coalition-building and petitions was his own act against complacency even though the publication was shut down by the Party in the late 1960s.

Theater as a form of human relationship also must be assessed in terms of audience response. As Rocamora (2004) reported, "After the Memorandum in 1965, people were optimistic, enthusiastic. They felt better able to criticize Communism and the system; they felt freer" (p. 73). Havel found a way of articulating in dramatic form what people felt and sensed about their world. One review of the play praised Havel for his talent in helping society "to understand itself and straighten itself out"; another claimed that he was changing society by "satirizing the slogan-like phrases of the Communist party" uncovering their lack of meaning (quoted in Rocamora, 2004, pp. 66–67). Havel admitted that the 1960s was a favorable atmosphere for his plays and that his society was ready to accept them, that people were hungry for the type of self-knowledge that they engendered (Havel, 1977/1992). He had expanded people's field of awareness, for a more precise diagnosis, and broadened people's capacity for action. Yet everything was about to change.

Audience and Life under Normalization as a Banned Playwright

One of the challenges of grassroots leadership is resisting the temptation to continue operating from one's initial diagnosis of the social situation that first compelled one to action. Learning is critical and ongoing. In the 1970s, Havel struggled to find a new tactic for social change within his plays. Following the Soviet invasion in 1968, his plays were blacklisted, the Communist Party purged thousands, and almost three quarters of a million people lost their jobs (Rocamora, 2004). After his initial success as a playwright and spokesman for intellectual freedom, the ground had radically shifted. Havel observed, "Once people's spines were bent the lying, cheating, and betrayal became common – the theme of human identity and existential schizophrenia was everywhere ... human existence itself was at stake. Suddenly, instead of laughing, one felt like shouting" (Havel, 1977/1992, p. 9). Havel faced a new adaptive challenge, and the quality of his leadership depended on learning new ways, getting new perspective, and understanding where others were in response to new problems. It was a time of incredible isolation, but a testament to how a grassroots movement of an underground intellectual community can be a sphere of freedom and moral authority.

Havel's response to the new adaptive challenge was first to reach out of his social isolation to a community of artists and invent an enduring character that would speak to people's new experiences. Havel wrote his one-act play, *Audience*, in a couple of hours to entertain friends that were coming to his country home called Hrádeček (little castle). Just prior, Havel worked at Trutnov Brewery, which fascinated him. Many in the cultural and intellectual elite in those days were demoted to manual labor jobs. Havel's central character and brewery worker in *Audience*, Vaněk, appeared in two more of his subsequent plays and was adopted by four other playwrights: Pavel Kohout, Pavel Landovský, Jiří Dienstbier, and Tom Stoppard. In Vaněk, Havel created a character that was not necessarily a hero, but that would highlight the struggle for authenticity against the moral void of fear and paralysis. He was a polite, gentle, reserved, and banned playwright, just like Havel. Although the play was not performed in a Czech theater until the 1990s, it made its way to an audience in 1975 as Havel read the play to his playwright friends in his living room; circulated in "samizdat" underground publication; was performed for friends in his neighbor, Andrej Krob's, barn; was produced around the world; and made into an audio dramatic recording on cassette tape smuggled out of the country by two Swedish hockey players (Zantovsky, 2014).

Audience was a humorous play with two actors, the Foreman and Vaněk, set in the Foreman's office. Havel again used humor to smuggle in truth. During the course of the play, the Foreman drinks 12 bottles of beer, cajoles Vaněk to drink, repeats himself over and over with lines like "don't be depressed," "don't keep thanking me," and "I don't trust a soul," only to tell Vaněk the real reason for their conversation: he wants Vaněk to inform on himself to the secret police. Vaněk is offered a promotion if he does it, but he refuses:

> Vaněk: ... I can't inform on myself.
>
> Foreman: Inform? ... Inform? Who's talking about informing?
>
> Vaněk: It's not myself I am worried about ... It wouldn't do me any harm ... but there's a principle involved. How can I be expected to participate in ...

Foreman: In what? Go on, just say it! What can't you participate in?

Vaněk: In something I have always found repugnant …

(*a short, tense silence*)

(Havel, 1975/1994b, p. 208)

The Foreman shows his indifference to the cost to human identity in sarcasm like, "I can soil my hands as much as I like, as long as the gentleman stays clean. The gentleman has principles. Everything else can just go hang. Just so he keeps his lilywhite soul. Putting principles before people" (Havel, 1975/1994b, p. 208). The play was one of Havel's "islands of authenticity" which he believed was an enduring part of the role of the theater (Havel, 1994c, p. 163). *Audience* exposed the regime's way of trapping people in its workings and for its purposes, but now Havel had a troubled protagonist to call people to authenticity.

In the same year, Havel wrote *Audience*, he initiated something both courageous and unprecedented. His friends called it political suicide (Rocamora, 2004). Havel wrote a public letter directly to the General Secretary of the Czechoslovak Communist Party, Dr. Gustav Husák. The reasons that Havel gave for writing it were that he wanted to openly contribute to the process of social self-awareness and his personal need to break out of his isolation by means of direct confrontation (Havel, 1975a/1992, pp. 84–85). His confrontation was polite, but unambiguously described what the regime was doing: inducing fear, contaminating the moral climate, destroying the rich culture of the Czech people. Havel diagnosed who the system advantaged: "people willing to support anything as long as it brings them some advantage; to unprincipled and spineless men, prepared to do anything in their craving for power and personal gain; to born lackeys, ready for any humiliation and willing at all times to sacrifice their neighbors' and their own honor for a chance to ingratiate themselves to those in power" (Havel, 1975b/1992, p. 55). One can easily see this type of man Havel caricatures in The Foreman in *Audience*. This was a new tactic for a new adaptive challenge – an awakening through a display of authenticity. Rocamora (2004) stresses the open letter as a turning point, "With this first expression of protest, a new era in Czech history began" (p. 147).

Audience lacks the aggressiveness and confrontation of Havel's letter to Husák, but it did expose the weak solidarity of the regime. The Foreman states, "We are all in this together" as well as "I don't trust a soul" on a number of occasions. Pontuso (2005) pointed out, "It was ironic that late totalitarian social cohesion was based on opposition to a state apparatus whose principal reason for existence was to represent the communal aspiration to mankind" (p. 10). What kind of social cohesion can there be if everyone is out for themselves, if we are all just consumers? Havel uses references to "they" to describe the ambiguous fear of the regime and the secret police who need information on Vaněk. Says the Foreman: "They come here and ask about you ..." "... They're scared of you" (pp. 199, 203). The common ground depends on "them."

In contrast to this oppositional solidarity, the essential work of leadership for social change is shifting from resistance to common purpose. Here again, Havel's writings and actions mirror the play's theme. Charter 77, drafted in 1977 as a human rights document about breaching the human rights protections under the Helsinki Conference, challenged the integrity of the regime and acknowledged the dissidents' co-responsibility for the state of society. The latter was controversial because the Communist Party claimed to be the sole arbiter of the state of society (Zantovsky, 2014). A year later, Havel wrote his devastating manifesto, "The Power of the Powerless." In "Power of the Powerless," Havel exposed the illusions of a system based on ideology. He demonstrated that the totalitarian ideology was a weak way of living in the world because it offered people a false sense of identity, a mask of dignity, and a fake morality while making it easier for people to part with their own sense of transcendence over the world (Havel, 1978/1992). Havel emboldened people to "live in truth," for principles that transcend their situation, by no longer supporting the prevailing ideology and claiming their authentic identity. This is how the powerless can claim power. It was a manifesto for oppressed peoples that also found widespread resonance in other solidarity movements in the Soviet Bloc.

Largo Desolato and the Release of an Imprisoned Dissident

From 1979 to 1983, Václav Havel was tried, convicted, and imprisoned for subversion of the regime. There were two incidents around this time that tested Havel's ability to model his message of "living within truth." The first, just after drafting Charter 77 and while held in secret police custody, was when Havel offered a promise not to engage in further public political activities in exchange for his release (Zantovsky, 2014). It was a failure Havel deeply regretted and it humbled him mightily because he hypocritically denied his authenticity. The second incident, while imprisoned, was when Havel declined an offer by the regime of a year-long theatrical fellowship in the United States. Havel believed saying "yes" would be tantamount to giving up his cause and denying the significance of what he and other dissidents were fighting for (Rocamora, 2004). These two incidents form an important backdrop for Václav Havel's most autobiographical play, *Largo Desolato*.

Heifetz et al. (2009) stress that an essential aspect of addressing an adaptive challenge is giving the work back to the people with the problem. Grassroots leadership without formal authority allows for more creative deviance, a deeper understanding of the struggle for change, and a broader influence beyond a primary supportive group (Heifetz, 1994). To build capacity in others to lead, Havel had to prepare the way by disappointing expectations for answers, stepping back from action, and directing attention to the moral issues still at hand. The danger in leadership is becoming over-identified with the problem and shouldering the work that belongs to others (Heifetz et al., 2009). Building a shared identity, getting differing factions to work together, and intentionally stepping back are all parts of the process of giving the work back. Havel's success in the theater and Writer's Union of the 1960s during the cultural boom and his outright dissidence emerging from his plays in the 1970s now posed as threats to his leadership after his release from prison. In this third stage of Havel's work as a playwright-dissident, he prepared the way for others to shoulder the work of confronting the regime through his own vulnerability in *Largo Desolato*, keeping the critical link between identity, responsibility, and action at center stage. Adaptive leadership in his context meant that the final answer to communist oppression in Czechoslovakia could not be "Havel's answer."

For Havel, reentry back into everyday life from prison was marked by depression, anxiety, and anguish. Many people now avoided him, except for a core group of dissidents. One year after he was released, he wrote *Largo Desolato* in just four days – in what some speculate as an anxious rush in a time of increased police surveillance and possession seizures (Kriseová, 1993).

The play features an intellectual dissident, Leopold Nettles, who is awaiting a prison sentence for his subversive writings. In the opening and closing scenes, Leopold stares at the front door and looks through a peephole in the door, waiting to be arrested. His friends express concern for him throughout the play while his wife, Suzana, stands aloof coming and going to the store, the theater, and the cinema. One could easily imagine that the audience felt the vulnerability and isolation of Leopold. At two separate points, generically named paper mill workers, "First Sydney" and "Second Sydney," treated him as a hero for his writings and encouraged him to get back in the movement. They repeated phrases like "we're your fans" and admonitions like "The main thing is that you mustn't weaken – we need you and we believe in you" (Havel, 1985, pp. 6–9). The second time they returned, they carried writing materials urging him to compose another essay. The crux of the conflict comes when two secret policemen, called "First Chap" and "Second Chap," want Leopold to sign a document stating that he is not himself, nor is he the author of the paper he wrote, in order for charges to be dropped. In the end, Leopold refuses to sign the document, but discovers that even though the charges were finally dropped, he had already lost his identity. Numbed to the care of others and the courage of his convictions, his identity disintegrates with his denial of proactive responsibility to live in truth.

The play offers some deep insight into Havel's own self-awareness and struggle to come to terms with the adaptive challenge at hand. There were people depending on him, telling him he was a hero, yet he was collapsing inside, immobilized by fear and spiritual darkness. Though caricatured, his inner struggle and alienation, his isolation and lack of meaningful connections with people were tragic and comedic at the same time. At the end of Scene Five, his wife, his friends, and the Sydneys were all around him repeating their disappointment in the line "some hero" and Leopold shouted, "GET OUT!" (Havel, 1985, p. 46). For many dissidents, the play captured their inner struggle better than any piece of writing. Jan Grossman, Havel's old artistic collaborator at the Balustrade, said of the play, "there is something self-critical about it. You might even say that it is a caricature of a dissident" (quoted in Rocamora, 2004).

The extravagance of the demands combined with the inner struggle of Leopold mark Havel's deployment of humor in the play to deliver the hard truth of the audiences' notion of looking to a hero to fight their battles for them. According to Soderberg (1999), "For Havel, Leopold represents the corpselike apathy and ennui of the Czech people after the Soviet invasion. His country's morale disheartened Havel so much so that he created Leopold as a comic character, not a tragic one" (p. 225). That people could see themselves and not just a prominent dissident in the main character was essential for them to prepare to shoulder the work. Both had to come to terms with their failure and approach the present situation with much more humility, recognizing their limitations and vulnerability. A few years later Havel showed a mix of humility and determination as he brought together students and artists in public protests, declarations, and negotiations that would culminate in the Velvet (nonviolent) Revolution. He played a pivotal role in mobilizing widespread participation, creating a space for people to voice their anger, and building a growing confidence that "truth and love must prevail over lies and hatred!" (Zantovsky, 2014). They together toppled the Communist regime.

Conclusion

The case of Václav Havel as a playwright-dissident powerfully shows that grassroots leadership can emerge from theater as a seismograph of consciousness for social change, even in the most despairing of conditions. In *The Memorandum*, Havel exposed the bureaucratic system and helped his audience see that their own identity was threatened within it. In *Audience*, Havel modeled in Vaněk a character that exemplified authenticity and the call to "live in truth" as the way for the powerless to claim their power. In *Largo Desolato*, Havel laid bare, in an autobiographical way, both the dissident struggle to galvanize the public and the apathy of the public to face its own responsibility. These plays used humor to usher in truth, moral ambiguity to pose critical questions, and an absurd environment to expose reality.

As a grassroots leader, Havel placed the question of what it means to be fully human at the center of adaptive change. Theater was the instrument to whet his audience's appetite for a full humanity based in freedom, dignity, responsibility, and hope. His art called for action — it lit a spark that would eventually rage into a fire. In November 1989, 20 years after Havel had written to him about the "immeasurable moral significance" of telling the truth about the regime, Václav Havel stood with once-ousted reform leader Alexander Dubček in Prague's Wenceslas Square in the midst of the Velvet Revolution. Havel's hopeful and trustworthy moral leadership, in the end, had finally prevailed.

58 JOSHUA M. HAYDEN

References

Barnancizak, S. (1999). All the president's plays. In M. Goetz-Stankiewicz & P. Carey (Eds.), *Critical essays on Václav Havel* (pp. 173–183). New York, NY: G.K. Hall.

Burian, J. M. (1984). High points of theatre in the first Czechoslovak Republic. *Modern Drama*, 27(1), 98–111.

Burian, J. M. (2000). *Modern Czech theatre: Reflector and conscience of a nation.* Iowa City, IA: University of Iowa Press.

Goetz-Stankiewicz, M. (1979). *The silenced theatre: Czech playwrights without a stage.* Toronto: University of Toronto Press.

Havel, V. (1985). *Largo desolato: A play in seven scenes* (T. Stoppard, Trans., English version). New York, NY: Grove Press.

Havel, V. (1989). *Letters to Olga.* New York, NY: Henry Holt and Company.

Havel, V. (1990). *Disturbing the peace: A conversation with Karel Hvížďala.* New York, NY: Alfred A. Knopf.

Havel, V. (1977/1992). Second wind. In *Open letters: Selected writings, 1965–1990* (pp. 3–9). New York, NY: Vintage.

Havel, V. (1975a/1992). It always makes sense to tell the truth: An interview with Jiří Lederer. In *Open letters: Selected writings, 1965–1990* (pp. 84–101). New York, NY: Vintage.

Havel, V. (1975b/1992). Dear Dr. Husák. In *Open letters: Selected writings, 1965–1990* (pp. 50–83). New York, NY: Vintage.

Havel, V. (1978/1992). The power of the powerless. In *Open letters: Selected writings, 1965–1990* (pp. 125–214). New York, NY: Vintage.

Havel, V. (1965/1994a). The memorandum. In *The garden party: And other plays.* New York, NY: Grove Press.

Havel, V. (1975/1994b). Audience. In *The garden party: And other plays.* New York, NY: Grove Press.

Havel, V. (1994c). International theater day. In *The art of the impossible: Politics as morality in practice* (pp. 162–164). New York, NY: Fromm International.

Heifetz, R. (1994) *Leadership without easy answers.* Cambridge, MA: Harvard University Press.

Heifetz, R., Grashow, A., & Linsky, M. (2009) *The practice of adaptive leadership: Tools and tactics for changing your organization and the world.* Cambridge, MA: Harvard Business Review Press.

Kriseová, E. (1993). *Václav Havel.* New York, NY: St. Martin's Press.

Rocamora, C. (2004). *Acts of courage: Václav Havel's life in the theater.* Hanover, NH: Smith and Kraus.

Soderberg, D. (1999). Life under absurdity: Václav Havel's Largo Desolato. In M. Goetz-Stankiewicz & P. Carey (Eds.), *Critical essays on Václav Havel* (pp. 173–183). New York, NY: G.K. Hall.

Zantovsky, M. (2014). *Havel: A life.* New York, NY: Grove Press.

4 Armand Gatti's *L'Inconnu N°5*: Theater as a Catalyst for Resistance

Suzanne Epstein

> My world is the world of road sweepers, deportations
> and escapes. Shakespeare's universe, with its kings and
> princes, rings hollow for me. My kings lived in shanty-
> towns. They are of more consequence for me than the
> kings in great literary works.
>
> Knowles (1989)

France's best-known contributions to post-World World II culture may be the Theater of the Absurd, as championed and practiced by the likes of Jean Cocteau, Jean Genet, and Antonin Artaud in the 1950s, and the New Wave Cinema (think Chabrol, Godard, and Truffaut) in the 1960s. Deriving influence from both is perhaps a lesser-known master of theater and filmmaking: French playwright, poet, and director Armand Gatti (b. 1924), who has throughout his life used theater as a means of raising social consciousness among those he terms the "*exclus*," or victims of social exclusion. The nature of the change Gatti seeks to bring about is one of independent thought, consciousness, or a heightened awareness that recognizes and subsequently comes to own the role language plays in defining an individual's position in society. His theater achieves this goal primarily through his use of immersive experimentation with language and words, a method that this chapter seeks to explore. It will also look at the similarities between the work of Gatti and that of Brazilian educator and philosopher Paolo Freire (1921–1997). The awareness participants gain in performing Gatti's plays is akin to and is perhaps another aspect of educator and philosopher Paulo Freire's concept of critical consciousness, wherein individuals develop consciousness of the social and political contradictions that surround them.

Both men use language, even specific words, to launch journeys toward an understanding of the historical and social factors that influence a person's life. Another shared facet of Gatti's and Freire's concepts is the strong representation of authentic leadership in their respective work. Ilies, Morganson, and Nahrang (2005) suggested that authentic leaders, as opposed to traditional ones, develop their own level of authenticity while inspiring supporters to achieve a similar goal. Gatti, through his theater, and Freire, through his pedagogy, both sought the empowerment of those they worked with. For Gatti, the aim is to initiate liberation and consciousness in both participant and spectator, and for Freire it was to engender social consciousness and emancipation for the poor. In keeping with the concept of authentic leadership, both men felt that they were not the leaders but rather humble participants in work that belonged to those who came to them and engaged in the process.

Armand Gatti

Armand Gatti, is a French poet, playwright, and filmmaker who has made a career of working with amateurs and individuals outside the mainstream, bringing the complexity of his theater to communities struggling with questions of unemployment, racism, and violence. He is committed to the theatrical spectacle as a place where language and words are front and center. Vocabulary and numbers are given dramatic life, and the action on stage is the full and complex world created by that language. Gatti's theater is meant to stimulate action rather than entertainment (Banu, 2012; Knapp, 1969). His fascination with science and math are echoed in the construction of his plays, which refuse traditional notions of time and space. Knapp defines Gatti's plays as "designed to liberate audiences from established notions, enabling them, thereby, to acquire new insights and meaningful experiences" (Knapp, 1969, p. 57). Its characters live in different worlds, eras, and geographical places, all at the same time, on stage. The past, present, and future coexist and merge; under Gatti's direction time and space are not linear but rather are lived and experienced as one continuum (Gatti, 1987; Knapp, 1969).

Gatti was born on January 26, 1924. His father was a street cleaner in the Principality of Monaco. He grew up poor, and felt the cruel sting of social injustice early on in life. He went to school hungry as a child, though he recounts that his father's ability to describe the marvelous imaginary meal they were having took much of his hunger away. In 1940, when Germany invaded France during the Second World War, Gatti joined the French Resistance at age 16 and was captured by the Germans a year later. He was forced into a labor camp in Germany but later escaped to England and joined the parachutist special services. After the war he became a journalist and traveled through Asia, the United States, and South and Central America, where he observed various forms of tyranny and the devastation it had on the world's innocent and poor (Knowles, 1989; Kravetz, n.d.).

In the 1950s, Gatti wrote and edited for *Le Parisien Libéré*, a radical newspaper that had been a prominent voice for the popular theater movements at the turn of the century. He continued to travel the world, observing the hard struggles of people fighting for social justice and waging war against dictators. Gradually, he became interested in theater that engaged the working-man and reflected his or her views of the world. He began to write and perform his plays in Paris. It was also around this time that Gatti began to experiment with language and spectacle, writing poetry, plays, and screenplays.

One of Gatti's early plays, *The Passion of General Franco*, was censored and forbidden in France. But in 1959 Jean Vilar defended the work and produced it with his Théatre National Populaire (TNP) theater company (Fisher, 1977). However, Gatti felt that his work was suited neither to the bourgeois theater nor to the popular theater of the time in France, so he moved his theater away from these particular genres, setting his work instead in locations that he defined as much closer to the realities of everyday life – factories, prisons, hospitals, and low-income neighborhoods (Gatti, as cited in Friexe, 2013). His chosen subject matter has centered on the horrific historical acts of destruction and devastation modern man has inflicted on the innocent or those whose voices are unheard. His plays have been about worker strikes, Mayan revolt against Spanish soldiers, revolt in feudal China, American Labor Union battles, the devastation of fascism — the list goes on. These plays are themselves historical acts of resistance, written in a style that removes the traditional theatrics of a great historical play. Deconstructing time, space, and language to create complex, almost philosophical spectacles, Gatti's works explore the relationship between the history of mankind and visions of utopia (Bouillaguet & Lenin, 1982). He has a very strong suspicion of government and says that political discourse is as much a form of tyranny as the actual dictators themselves. Gatti has stated that the language of politics is one of "annexation, whereas the language of creativity is slightly different. Its basic characteristic is not to colonize people" (Gatti as quoted in Bouillaguet & Lenin, 1982). This notion is fundamental to Gatti's writing and to his theatrical work. He believes that in moving his productions out of the traditional theater, the force of the words themselves creates a space for freedom and liberty. "It is words that create things, not things that give birth to words" (Gatti, as quoted in Friexe, 2013, p. 428).

Gatti's plays explore the human spirit and its ability to resist the types of authoritarian narrative that dictate destruction. Gatti's engagement with words is a constant assessment of whether language aids in creating devastation or resists it. One of the best explanations of Gatti's experimentation with words, and why repositioning them is so important, comes from the playwright himself.

> What seemed false to us... was the language of the author, the given author, his age, his experience, which becomes the majority language, the priority language. Now, a twelve-year-old boy has a limited vocabulary. If he is from an immigrant family, he's even more limited as far as words are concerned, but his is language full of its own truth, which doesn't need the enrichment of other experiences or other ways of seeing the world. He has his own world, so why shouldn't he express himself in his own way.
>
> (Gatti, 1987)

During the 1970s, when Gatti began working with individuals living on the fringes of society (Knowles, 1992, 1993), experimentation with language and words became a dominant feature of his theatrical work. "When I am working with the *exclus* I do not try to inculcate them into the theatrical technique, nor am I trying to do anything in the sociocultural field. The work is done elsewhere, in the words, in the language" (Gatti as quoted by Knowles, 1992). Knowles describes Gatti's work as inviting his volunteers to write along with him, not to entertain but to prove themselves to themselves. Gatti describes himself as a catalyst of the creativity of others, and therefore a public scribe (Knowles, 1993). This idea of being a catalyst to others' creative expression and self-actualization aligns Gatti's work to that of Paulo Freire and his role as an educator and a leader for social justice. In *The Pedagogy of Freedom*, Paulo Freire speaks at length about how the role of an educator is to liberate, encourage, assist, and give witness to the creativity of the student, thus encouraging critical consciousness (Freire, 1998). This connection between Freire and Gatti is further explored later in the chapter.

La Traversée des langages (The Traversal of Languages)

Gatti's long-term project *La Traversée des langages* (*The Traversal of Languages*) encompassed the development and performance of 15 plays over a period of 12 years, with his notion of language, writing, and vocabulary at its heart. The centrality of language leads the performers on a journey toward a certain form of awareness and an empowerment of the individual. Throughout the series *La Traversée des langages*, the lived experience of the performers and the written/spoken word is a step toward individual self-reliance and Gatti's concept of liberty. There is change, and one cannot go back.

Many of the works in this decade-long series explore and condemn the world of disastrous scientific discourse and its effects on the human condition (Leterrier, 2012). Several confront the science behind such atrocities as Nazi Germany's theory of racial superiority and the use of atomic bombs in Hiroshima and Nagasaki. His heroes are real-life mathematicians, physicists, and philosophers who were victims of a world seemingly gone mad: Évariste Gallois, a mathematician and founder of the theory of groups, who died in a duel; Werner Heisenberg, whose field was quantic physics; and Jean Cavailles, a philosopher of mathematics and French Resistance fighter who was executed and buried in a grave marked simply "5." In his plays, there is a constant struggle between the world of logic that demands obedience and the well of human resistance, which not only questions obedience but the reality and logic it stems from.

LInconnu N°5 du fossé des fusillés du pentagone dArras

Gatti created a play about Jean Cavailles, *L'Inconnu N°5 du fossé des fusillés du pentagone d'Arras* (*The Unknown No. 5 from the Arras Prison Mass Grave*), for the 50th anniversary of the end of the Second World War. It was based on the story of the aforementioned philosopher and mathematician, who fought with the French Resistance during the war and was captured by the Germans. Cavailles was shot to death at the Arras Prison in northern France, where the Nazis were holding him. The play examines the nature of mathematics, the dynamics of tyranny, and the reality of existence by destructing time and space and exploring how consciousness is in equal measure dangerous and vitally important during a reign of fear and political tyranny.

The operatic play was produced in Sarcelles, a northern suburb of Paris, a working-class town with sprawling housing complexes that is a 40-minute train ride from the city. The unemployment rate is high and so is crime. At the time of the performance in 1995, unemployment was 27 percent. Duflo and Quenet (2006) describe Sarcelles and other northern suburbs of Paris in the following terms.

> The French suburban bus stop is an image of diversity. Muslim headscarves, Jewish kipas and the bold primary colors of African garb offer a kaleidoscope of diverse cultural images. But the world's fashion capital hides harrowing hardships in its suburbs, its residents bound for the usual destinations: job discrimination in the workplace, poor living conditions, and institutional oppression by the "real" France. These hardships surround a complex net of identities based on community, ethnicity, religion, race, and gender.
>
> (Duflo & Quenet, 2006)

Sixty participants were drawn from the Solidarité Jeunes Travailleurs (SJT), a long-term unemployment reinsertion program in Sarcelles, to work on this complex and demanding production.

When I was a student in Paris, I went to see the Gatti production in Sarcelles and found it to be like no theater I had experienced before. I was fascinated by the energy and engagement of
the nonprofessional actors who were performing before a live
audience for the first time. To this day, I remember being deeply
moved by the quality and skill of the performers, who brought a
sense of timelessness and urgency to the spectacle. I have always
wondered what it was like for these amateur players to reach such
a high level of artistic and intellectual expression. This chapter is
part of my research into that question. I reached out to Gatti, now
92 years old, and his company suggested I speak with Mohamed
Melhaa, a longtime associate of Gatti. Mr. Melhaa is one of many
who changed his direction in life after working with Gatti in one
of his plays. Having struggled through his studies and life, he met
Gatti and worked in several of his theater projects, including
L'Inconnu N°5. He went back to theater school, became an actor,
an assistant director and is now a professor of theater in the
University of Strasbourg, France. Much of the following is sourced
from my conversations with Mr. Melhaa.

Over a period of ten months, Gatti and the participant-
performers worked daily on developing and rehearsing *L'Inconnu
N°5*. Four performances were held during the month of January
in Sarcelles. The play was performed in a large gymnasium, with
the audience seated on all four sides of the arena. The players
spread out across the space and performed facing different directions. Some of them moved through the space from one side to
the other, while others performed intimate scenes in different set
spots. There were often congruent scenes happening, and as is
typical of Gatti, the action of these scenes took place in different
eras. Past, present, and future were acted out at the same time
and intermingled. The spectator had to make choices as to which
scenes they would focus on. There were synchronized movements, loosely based on martial arts, for each group of performers, including more intimate duos and trios. The performers
worked with highly stylized choreographic movements and
choral structures; at times they were solo and still in the silent,
vast space of the gymnasium. Their monologues were long and
complex, with high-energy performers depicting everything from
the importance of numbers and math to the very existence of
mankind. "And we, issued from calculated probabilities, we
correct our definition of origins … belonging to a spectacle that
holds the infinite possibility of both the grand and the infinitely
small" (Gatti, 2012, p. 679). As a spectator, one shifted back

and forth between understanding the complexity of the play and taking in the poignancy of the performers, all seemingly engaged in a battle to resist any tyrannical narrative that might assert their invalidity or nonexistence.

L'Inconnu N°5 du fossé des fusillés du pentagone d'Arras.
Rehearsal Sarcelles, France 1996 © Stephan ZAUBITZER.

One of the particularities of Gatti's direction is that he often organizes the performers into different choral groups who symbolically represent aspects of the play. For example, in *L'Inconnu N°5*, a few of the groups are *Les cycliques* (The cyclical group), *Le groupe des hypothétiques* (The hypothetical group), and *Le groupe des associatifs* (The associative group). This last group represents the participants who hail from the associations in the community, the long-term unemployed and disenfranchised youth. In this way, participants interrogate the themes of the play and their own participation in its structure while at the same time confronting the spectators' understanding of their roles as performers and members of society. "As you can see, we came to see how a group that obviously owes its likelihood to mathematics can claim to have structure … as in this very moment, in such a place, that is always reinventing itself" (*Gatti*, 2012, p. 663). The very notion of whether what is seen on stage is performance or reality is a constant question for both the audience and the performers. The performers use the play, its structure, even mathematics to reinvent themselves, their community, and perhaps a certain reality.

At no point during the performance does Gatti give the participants or the spectators an opportunity to relax. The work is rigorous, and intellectually demanding. "You think you have to learn and explain something like transfinite numbers to the whole group, and then perform it. But it's all about the text. You have to cultivate the text, the words, make them your own" (M. Melhaa, personal communication, May 5, 2016). The performers have long and intricate monologues, as well as songs, that convey Cavailles' theories of quantitative math, the loneliness of prison, and the terror of a firing squad. "Your name is Pentagone d'Arras, forest of trees, tribunal of the storm, one white tree around the pole of execution, one white tree, interrogation every day and a lack of light … Dancers around the wall of execution" (Gatti, 2012, p. 689). Seemingly endless passages depict what a number means and question how the language of mathematics can possibly be used to prove our existence. The narrative of a hero who was killed and buried in absolute anonymity is the play's incredibly poignant core. It is also pertinent for the many long-term unemployed, who are often listed as statistical numbers and products of inevitable economic realities, with little regard to who they are and whether or not they even exist. "There is a feeling early on [with the participants] of what is the sense to all of this? They have been hit hard by life, beaten down: 'I can't do anything else.' But as they engage with the passion, the text, they find another way to see things" (M. Melhaa, personal communication, May 5, 2016).

L'Inconnu N°5 du fossé des fusillés du pentagone d'Arras.
Rehearsal, Sarcelles, France 1996 © Stephan ZAUBITZER.

Freire and Gatti

Paulo Freire grew up in a middle-class Brazilian family, but the economy faltered and he and his family fell into poverty. As a boy he realized that the primary aspects of his situation, being poor and hungry most of the time, were severe drawbacks on his ability to do well in school or secure his place among his better-performing peers. As a young man he began to develop his views on education and the poor. He described the hunger so painfully felt by the poor as also, metaphorically, a hunger for learning, knowledge, and the ability to shape one's own future (Freire, 1998; Watkins, 2012). Freire also had a strong understanding of how words and societal or oppressive narratives influenced and victimized the weaker members of society. Freire's theory of critical consciousness first derived from his understanding that dialogue is "a way of knowing" (Freire & Macedo, 1995, p. 379). Freire recognized that the process of knowing involved dialogue of both an individual and a social nature, rather than learning cookie-cutter definitions without question. Gatti's view of dialogue was also based on an understanding of the disempowering influence words can have when left unquestioned or unexamined. As Watkins states, Freire saw that dialogue is not to be used for the sake of a revolution; it *is* the revolution (Watkins, 2012). This relates to Gatti's work in that the playwright constantly questioned the use of words and their meaning when coming from figures or institutions of authority. Gatti's look at historical abuses of power engineered through the use of oppressive and tyrannical language echoes Freire's views about who resists and how they are able to visualize and create their own narrative.

Another view that Freire and Gatti share is the notion of presence. Presence is one of the fundamental concepts behind Freire's theory of critical consciousness. Freire theorized that being in the world is "a presence that is relational to the world and to others" (Freire, 1998, p. 26). For Freire, presence not only allows the individual to self-reflect or intervene but also to transgress that which has been determined or dictated by others. One is "conditioned not determined" (p. 26). It is also an important part of performing and the lived experience of language found in Gatti's work. It is through language and the participant-performer's presence that Gatti is able to explore and transgress language, to deconstruct words, playing with syntax, and distort time and space. For Gatti, this process allows one to counteract determinism, and conditions dictated by tyrannical authority. Freire is also a strong proponent of the autonomy of individuals (students, in his view) and the constant importance of searching for knowledge or meaning (Freire, 1998, 2005). Progressive education needs to "create possibilities for the construction and the production of knowledge" (Freire, 1998, p. 123). Every stage in the education process has the goal of "adding a capacity for growth." Gatti, however, throws even this notion on its head, as he sees all meaning as circumstantial and even demagogic. He deconstructs language, time, and space and questions what is really happening at any given moment, what the essence is of what is said or experienced. Freire thought that education was the fundamental way a future citizen could shape his own destiny and participate in society at large (Freire, 1970). Both Freire and Dewey wrote that education must respect the individual and recognize his or her identity. They argued for a progressive form of education that develops the critical-thinking skills students need to engage in their own learning process as well as to socially and intellectually take part in the community around them (Dewey, 2007; Freire, 2005).

Throughout Gatti's work, there is an understanding that resistance is central to much of mankind's relationship with power and the tyranny of "civilized society," one in which the individual who does not submit to brainwashing or to relinquishing their individuality is denied liberty. Similarly, Freire states that human existence is a "radical and profound tension between good and evil" (Freire, 1998, p. 53). He believes that throughout human history, "freedom, choice, decision, and possibility are only possible because they can also be denied, despised, or refused" (Freire, 1998, p. 57).

Math and the Spoken Word

It is not without interest that Gatti chose to do a play about a mathematician, though his choice was probably linked to the tragic yet fascinating story of Jean Cavailles. However, Gatti sees math and science as a central means of examining power. It is "an important part of gaining real popular, democratic control over the economic, political and social structures of our society" (Frankenstein, 1983, p. 315). This is significant, as the members of Gatti's amateur troupe are considered outsiders in a numbers-based economy. The rate of unemployment is often measured through mathematical calculations that are hard to grasp for most people. Much of the economic decision-making in the national and local administrations that govern the lower-income banlieues (suburbs) is left to the experts. Or as Frankenstein argues, "This knowledge is also considered value-free, it is rarely questioned. Attempting to create an approach to mathematics education can lead both to greater control over knowledge and to critical consciousness" (Frankenstein, 1983, p. 315). In working on a piece that involves complex mathematics, most performers had one or two monologues about different mathematical theories, such that the philosophy of math and its potential as a tool for resistance became integral to the play. The participants' engagement with Cavailles' mathematical work allowed them to reflect on and perform different concepts of political and philosophical thought. In this way, Gatti brought Freire's critical consciousness to the forefront of the participant-performers' experience. Gatti often challenged the participants, saying, "If you say it is too difficult, you leave knowledge to others" (J. Hocquard, personal communication, April 29, 2016). As the performers learned the text, then performed it, their lived experience gave them ownership over these concepts, shifting their consciousness by lending them a critical understanding of the math that had been used for decades to define unemployment and opportunity in their town of Sarcelles. "Even though I have a hard time stating it, I know it is in me" (M. Melhaa personal communication, May 5, 2016).

As Freire states in *Pedagogy of the Oppressed*, every fact must be understood in its historical, social, economic, and political context. To understand a particular moment of history or a fact of the world in which we live, it is important to examine causal relationships and how they impact our humanization or dehumanization (Freire, 2005). The play's hero is a man who was killed and buried in obscurity with only the number five ascribed to his cell to indicate that he was at one point a human being with an identity. Freire goes on to state that depending on the questions that are posed, the answers can have an impact on social structures, class structures, and even our individual relationships (Freire, 2005). By performing a collective work based on a historical figure and the mathematical theories to which he devoted his professional life, the participant-performers confront the historical, political, and social connections between the hero, Jean Cavailles, and themselves.

In its own particular way, Freire's philosophy of critical consciousness is a form of theatrical and historical thinking. Looking at the past in the context of a new awareness and consciousness not only opens up the opportunity to see things in a different way but also allows for a much more rigorous and critical approach (Freire, 1998; Kaak, 2011). Freire's concept of critical consciousness "implies seeing angles that were not perceived before. Thus, a posterior view of the world can be done in a more critical, less naïve, and more rigorous way" (Freire, 1998, p. 38). By looking at both the historical context of the Nazi occupation of France and the story of Jean Cavailles' death in obscurity, Gatti demands reflection and engagement from the participant-performers as they seek to make sense of a senseless death and connect the story's narrative to their own lives. In this way, Gatti's 12-year-long project, *La Traversée des langages*, creates a space where critical consciousness can develop within different socially excluded groups, over and over again, as each group makes the story their own in performing it. In a sense, the project builds community and engenders an empowering social consciousness one performance at a time.

Theater and Leadership

Today there is a growing interest in theater as an important lens through which to study and understand leadership (Biehl-Missal, 2010; Taylor & Ladkin, 2009). Much of this scholarship correlates theater, performing, and acting with the knowledge and development of charismatic leadership (Shamir, Dayan-Horesh, & Adler, 2005). Biehl-Missal argues that it is the very nature of theater to function as a platform from which to learn about and experience the antihero, conflict, and the idea that appearances can be deceiving (Biehl-Missal, 2010). There is a correlation between the performance aspect of theater and the conception of leadership as charismatic, performative, and contextual, possessing the ability to improvise and to role-play. However, it is in its ability to overturn traditional notions of the status quo, hero status, and the power of authority that theater also introduces questions of social justice. For Gatti, the roles of leader and follower, director and actor, are irrelevant. He is interested in the language of domination and the individual's ability to resist it. The hero model is central to his work, especially that of the hero who has taken up resistance. But his primary fascination is with the actual words themselves and how they form or subvert a narrative.

The idea of theater as a collaborative experience relates to many theories in the field of relational and collaborative leadership. Gagnon, Vough, and Nickerson (2012) see an emerging trend away from the paradigm of dominant leadership and posit that the relational aspects of leadership are a much more success-ful model for organizations in today's world. Leadership that is co-created finds a strong example in the theater, particularly in its use of improvisation, and in the dynamic between director and performer (Gagnon et al., 2012). Improvisation in theater aligns with relational theories of leadership in that there is a move away from introspection toward a model that values the ability to adapt quickly to change, express curiosity, and be responsive (Gagnon et al., 2012). Another key concept in theater is being present in the moment. In Gatti's plays, there is a com-plex and powerful relationship between being present and *"sans temps"* (without time), as the performers experience the words and the nonlinear construct of Gatti's script. The participant-performers are also developing a critical sense of the relationship between what is being said and how it is actually experienced by those on stage and those in the audience – the ability to observe and recognize both sides of an event, is the paramount trait of collaborative leadership. Gatti's scripts demand a critical con-sciousness that derives from these relational and collaborative methods, and that allows performers and audience members alike to experience words and their meaning not as passive receivers but as collaborators who define their own meaning.

Gatti offers a different twist on this paradigm of theater as col-laboration; it is not his use of collaborative play creation but the deep engagement and collaborative experience that comes from immersion in the text of the play. Participants search individually and with the director for what the word and the performance of the word signify. The exchange between Gatti and the performers is not a chaotic experience of trying everything and then choosing; rather it is thoughtful and precise research into the essence of the text. Gatti's theatrical process does embody a concept of leader-ship, and that is what the participants carry into the world after the performance: a consciousness of how words create status quos, and how this affects them and the world around them – the beginning steps in the development of critical consciousness.

Gatti and Authentic Leadership

Gatti is far from having an interest in reflections on leadership. On the contrary. Though he is a charismatic director of his plays and performers, he rejects any power or decision-making rules in working with the participants. The goal of the play and much of

Gatti's directorial work is the embodiment of the text and *"les paroles,"* the words themselves. His stipulation is only that a participant must find the truth behind the words in order to truly enact and embody the work. At this moment, the participant becomes an actor and lives an authentic experience. "This is not acting as pretending to be something or someone you're not, it is not acting as faking it − it is acting as producing real, authentic behavior on stage" (Ladkin & Taylor, 2010, p. 13). There is no room in Gatti's direction for a participant to remain aloof or far from the authentic moment. It is also at this moment that the individual experiences a moment of leadership. Understanding the truth behind the words that are being spoken is the first step away from passive understanding, because to embody a text − to own it in a public moment − is a move toward leading others instead of being led. As Ladkin and Taylor state, "the demonstration of emotion can be subtly expressed, as long as it connects with a resonating truth of one's own experience" (Ladkin & Taylor, 2010). Theories of authentic leadership emphasize this connection between emotion and the event or task at hand. Reaching a level of true authenticity closely mirrors the reality of theater. And in the case of Gatti, it is a complex yet stimulating search for the expression of the authentic word or the authentic speech and the performance or lived experience of it.

Gatti has been used as an example by many in the social justice movement for his genius at coalescing creative communities around his theatrical productions. He hires and works with non-professionals who often have an outsider's perspective: prisoners, disenfranchised youth, and, as in *L'Inconnu N°5*, the long-term unemployed. But Gatti was always clear about his decision not to prolong his engagement with the community, allowing it to grow or dissolve after he and the production are over and gone. This particular decision was problematic for him, and he was often criticized for not understanding the needs of developing social justice outcomes (Banu, 2012). Gatti himself said that his charismatic leadership was limited in time. But in keeping with authentic leadership principles, he also saw that it was necessary to transfer responsibility to the participants (Banu, 2012). In Gatti's theater, the transformation is individual and participatory. It is up to the individual to engage in change through the rehearsals, the performances, and the engagement with language. However, collective change is not up to him or any leader. Those who came, who worked, who watched are those who decide what change or liberty of their own making comes next.

L'Inconnu N°5 du fossé des fusillés du pentagone d'Arras.
Performance, Sarcelles, France 1996 © Stephan ZAUBITZER.

Language and Individual Agency

In both Gatti's and Freire's work, language is seen as a tool that can lead to awareness and critical thought. Through Gatti's theatrical process and the concepts outlined in Freire's *Pedagogy of the Oppressed*, individuals attain a sense of identity and can begin to critically engage in the world around them through the very words they or those in power use. Gatti's project *La Traversée des langages* is, in effect, a decades-long examination of how language constructs or hinders society's collective morality. Gatti is also fascinated with the eternal quest of the individual to confront, through language, both historical and present-day status quos. Freire and Gatti consider language and its power to be fundamental aspects of both domination and emancipation. Freire saw language as necessary to an individual's ability to construct his or her own identity and to navigate his or her participation as a member of different groups. Whether those groups are family, work-related, religious, or symbolic, the individual uses the language of the group to increase his/her right to membership and to enhance his/her position in the group. Sterling (2000) studied the relationship between language use and group membership, and found that language inspires deep group loyalties. "It can serve as a symbol of unification on several levels" (Sterling, 2000). In the eyes of Gatti, this is exactly where the danger lies: in the power of a dominant and tyrannical narrative. His long-term theatrical act is to create resistance by breaking up language that is used to ensure obedience and, as he experienced personally, fascist theories of determinism.

A central concern for Gatti is how an individual's adherence to a group's moral code is achieved through language, as language can induce the individual to make moral choices in agreement with his or her membership in the group, or to step away and make choices apart from it. So the use of language becomes a tool with which the individual can move across boundaries and interpret the world around him or herself. "A few months into the process, I knew that understanding everything didn't mean you understand everything. It means you owned the words to say it. It was yours" (A participant cited by M. Melhaa, May 5, 2016).

Conclusion

The philosopher Charles Taylor looked at language, identity, and social justice, and asserted that the language of identity, the words with which we define ourselves or the way in which they define us, reminds us of how much we are in dialogue (Taylor, cited in Mulhall & Swift, 1992, 1996). This dialogue constitutes a narrative with which we not only construct our immediate self but also develop a long-term journey of identity in relation to − and sometimes in opposition to − the narrative of the larger society. As Gatti sees it, it is the dominant narrative that forces individuals to exist not on their own terms but in the language of others. Gatti puts language on its head, breaking words, syllables, and narrative into nonlinear space and time. The goal is to give language to both the individuals represented in the play (the heroes of the French Resistance) and the performers, who live with words and narrative in a completely different form on stage than they do in daily life.

In concluding this exploration, the question arises as to whether the collaborative and rigorous process of Gatti's theatrical world actually changed the lives of the individuals who participated. One performer declared after struggling through learning his lines that he was "richer by three hundred words." In applying Paulo Freire's theory of critical consciousness, the collaborative and word-based approach of Gatti's theater can and did create change. But can art really lead to the kind of change represented by social justice, even revolution?

Erenrich defines social change as a shift or an alteration in the status quo that then leads to systemic change (Erenrich, 2013). This examination of Gatti's work in the context of social justice does not pretend to demonstrate that grassroots leadership or community-based change takes place through his productions. Rather, I would argue that there is a precondition that creates leaders in communities who can engender change by taking up social justice causes. This first step involves changing the status quo mind-set of the individual in part by bringing about a recognition that language is integral to that change. It is Freire's and Gatti's examination and critique of language that allows critical consciousness to change an individual's, and therefore a community's, understanding of the political and dominant narrative surrounding them. It is the initial seed from which grassroots movements can grow.

In the case of Armand Gatti and the complexity of thought that went into *La Traversée des langages* and *L'Inconnu N°5*, a different and perhaps more authentic question is posed: Is change only recognized because outside structures and personal fortunes reflect a change, or is the empowerment of the individual achieved by a shift in language and thought, as theater can so adeptly bring to light? Do we say that a person's destiny has not changed because the confines of that life are still the same, or can we see agency of thought and choice as the authentic expression of an evolved consciousness? As Gatti himself said, "The revolution is both the interior and exterior light of our narrative" (Gatti as quoted in Leterrier, 2012). Freire pondered the great changes that would come when individuals came into their own, as when given power over their own vocabulary, agency, and ownership of their own language and thoughts. He believed that this would happen through a pedagogy that would bring on critical consciousness. In Gatti's world, critical consciousness and agency over language are also what makes human resistance possible.

Acknowledgments

The author would like to acknowledge and thank the following people for their help in researching this chapter: The organization La Parole Errante, Jean-Jacques Hocquard, Mohamed Melhaa, Lee Magill, Evelyne Le Polotec, and Armand Gatti.

References

Banu, G. (2012). Les leaders effectifs et les communautés artistiques. In M. C. Autant-Mathieu (Ed.), *Créer ensemble: Points du vu sur les communautés artistique fin XIX-XX siècle* (pp. 69–73). Montpelier: L'Entretemps Editions.

Biehl-Missal, B. (2010). Hero takes a fall: A lesson from theater for leadership. *The Leadership Quarterly, 21*(1), 64–74.

Bouillaguet, P., & Lenin, J. P. (1982). Armand Gatti on time, place and the theatrical event (N. Oakes, Trans.). *Modern Drama, 25*(1), 69–81.

Dewey, J. (2007). *Democracy and education*. Middlesex: Echo library.

Duflo, C., & Quenet, N. (2006). A grey hope: Thin territorial identity among French suburban youth in Garges and Sarcelles. Retrieved from http://www. humanityinaction.org/knowledgebase/202-a-grey-hope-thin-territorial-identity-a mong-french-suburban-youth-in-garges-and-sarcelles

Erenrich, S. J. (2013). Funding leadership-development training for cultural activists: A reflective essay. *The Foundation Review, 5*(2), Article 8. doi:10.9707/ 1944-5660.1158

Fisher, D. J. (1977). The origins of the French popular theater. *Journal of Contemporary History, 12*(3), 461–497.

Frankenstein, M. (1983). Critical mathematics education: An application of Paulo Freire's epistemology. *The Journal of Education, 165*(4), 315–339.

Freire, P. (1970). Cultural action and conscientization. *Harvard Educational Review, 40*(3), 452–477. doi:10.17763/haer.40.3.h76250x720j43175

Freire, P. (1998). *Pedagogy of freedom, ethics, democracy, and civic courage*. Lanham, MD: Rowman & Littlefield.

Freire, P. (2005). *Pedagogy of the oppressed*. 30th Year Anniversary. (M. B. Ramos, Trans.). New York, NY: Continuum International Publishing.

Freire, P., & Macedo, D. P. (1995). A dialogue: Culture, language and race. *Harvard Educational Review. 65*(3), 377–402.

Friexe, G. (2013). Des communautés d'expériences. In M. C. Autant-Mathieu (Ed.), *Créer ensemble: Points du vu sur les communautés artistique fin du XIX-XX siècle* (pp. 423–428). Montpelier: L'Entretemps Editions.

Gagnon, S., Vough, H. C., & Nickerson, R. (2012). Learning to lead unscripted: Developing affiliative leadership through improvisational theater. *Human Resource Development Review, 11*(3), 299–325

Gatti, A. (1987). *Journal illustré d'une écriture*. In M. Séonnet & S. Gatti (Eds.), *Material description* (vol. 1, p. 255). Paris: Artefact.

Gatti, A. (2012). *Rosier blanc du cimetière d'Arras*. La Traversée des langages (pp. 649–731). Paris: Editions Verdier.

Ilies, R., Frederick, T., Morgeson, P., & Nahrgang, J. D. (2005). Authentic leadership and eudaemonic well-being: Understanding leader–follower outcomes. *The Leadership Quarterly, 16*, 373–394.

Kaak, P. A. (2011). Power filled lessons for leadership educators from Paulo Freire. *Journal of Leadership Education, 10*(1), 132–144.

Knapp, B. L. (1969). Armand Gatti: Multiplicity of vision in action theater. *Modern Drama, 12*(1), 57–63. doi:10.1353/mdr.1969.0033

Knowles, D. (1989). Introduction: Armand Gatti, the wild duck flying against the wind. *Armand Gatti in the theater: Wild duck against the wind* (pp. 1–17). London: The Athlone Press.

Knowles, D. (1992). Armand Gatti's theater of social experiment. *New Theater Quarterly, 8*(30), 76–85.

Knowles, D. (1993). The restorative function of language in Armand Gatti's experimental theater for the 'exclus' of society. *Theater Research International, 18*(1), 36–52.

Kravetz, M. (n.d.). *Biographie d'Armand Gatti, La Parole Errante*. Retrieved from http://www.armand-gatti.org/index.php?cat=biographie

Ladkin, D., Taylor, S. (2010) Enacting the 'true self': Towards a theory of embodied authentic leadership. *The Leadership Quarterly, 21*(1), 64–74.

Leterrier, E. (2012, March). Gatti monumental. *Le Matricule des Anges, 131*, 13.

Mulhall, S., & Swift, A. (1992, 1996). *Liberals and communitarians* (2nd ed.). Malden, MA: Blackwell Publishing.

Shamir, B., Dayan-Horesh, H., & Adler, D. (2005). Leading by biography: Towards a life-story approach to the study of leadership. *Leadership, 1*(1), 13–29.

Sterling, P. (2000). Identity in language: An exploration into the social implications of linguistic variation. Unpublished paper presented at Texas A&M University. Retrieved from http://www.tamu.edu/chr/agora/winter2000/sterling.pdf

Watkins, M. (2012). Revolutionary leadership: From Paulo Freire to the occupy movement. *Journal for Social Action in Counseling and Psychology, 4*(2), 1–22.

Zaubitzer, S. (Photographer). (1996). *L'Inconnu N°5 du fossé des fusillés du pentagone d'Arras. [photograph]*. Sarcelles, France.

SECTION II
Grassroots Leadership and Cultural Activists Part 2: Visual Art and Film

5

Boniface Mwangi: Photo-Journalist/ Social Activist

Nita Hungu and Marta D. Bennett

"**P**eople back home call me a heckler, a trouble-maker …, the voice of the people. But that wasn't always me," began Boniface Mwangi in his talk on "The Day I Stood up Alone" (TEDGlobal, 2014). His childhood nickname, "Softy" highlighted his soft-spoken nature, but today as an award-winning photojournalist and social activist, Boniface Mwangi, is a force for change.

Born on July 10, 1983 in Taveta, Kenya, near the Kenyan-Tanzanian border, Boniface Mwangi was sent to live with his grandparents in Nyeri, Central Kenya, at the age of six, so that his mother could run a small business back and forth across the border. One of his early challenges was finding himself immersed in the Kikuyu-speaking community near Mt. Kenya, yet his fluency was in the national language, Kiswahili. Two years later he rejoined his mother, who by then was in the capital city, Nairobi, living in various low-income areas. In and out of school, Mwangi eventually dropped out completely by age 15 to help his mother sell used books in town. Those early years were marked by the poverty of his various communities and the deep Christian faith of his mother, who would often disappear every few weeks into the city's Karura Forest to pray. However, all the prayers did not seem to change their financial status or the corruption of the nation's leaders (Mwangi, 2014). This observation provoked in Mwangi the determination to not just pray, but also to act, to speak out and confront poverty, injustice, and the corruption of national leaders.

He was in Bible school in 2003, preparing to become a pastor, when one of his lecturers lent him a book by the late Mohamed Amin, a Kenyan born photojournalist who is most notably known for documenting the Ethiopian famine of 1983–1985 (Corfield, 2015). "That book opened a new world for me," said Mwangi. "Here was another high school dropout who went on to conquer the world using his camera" (Perry, 2012). "It was because of his work that the world gave so much help to that country [Ethiopia] – and I saw for myself the positive power of photography" (Corfield, 2015).

Borrowing money from a friend to buy his first "point-and-shoot" camera, Mwangi taught himself to shoot photos and soon began winning awards. He joined the staff of *The Standard*, Kenya's second largest newspaper, and it was while on assignment as staff photographer that he was tasked with documenting the postelection violence of 2007–2008. He took countless photos of the violence and brutality incited by politics and tribalism that would be forever etched in the nation's mind, and photos that reminded him that he was living in a society where the poor were at a greater risk of death at the hands of law enforcers than of criminals. Though he won countless awards for his photo documentation, including the CNN Mohamed Amin Journalist of the Year award in both 2008 and 2010, he came out of the crisis severely traumatized, suffering from posttraumatic stress and depression. He quit his job at *The Standard*, dismayed that after all the destruction, the politicians and much of the country just picked up and moved on as if nothing had happened (Mwangi, 2014).

Picha Mtaani

In 2009, "Picha Mtaani" (a Swahili phrase for "photos on the street") was launched. Mwangi's enlarged photographs of the postelection violence were displayed in open-air venues, providing a context for dialogue, and aiming to help victims, perpetrators, and communities to reflect, discuss, and resolve to work for healing, reconciliation, and peace. The traveling photographic display served as a catalyst for remembering, telling personal stories, and making resolutions for social change. Individuals viewed pictures that were otherwise not published in the media, displayed on the premise that antiwar imagery plays a critical role in deterring further violence (Adhengo, 2010). Prior to Kenya's next elections in 2013, Picha Mtaani was again exhibited in Mombasa, along with discussions and a documentary entitled "Heal the Nation" to challenge the nation to work diligently for peace even as the citizens were heading for the polls.

Rising Up and Speaking Out

Mwangi's anger at the corruption among the political elite launched new forms of social activism. Planning with a group of friends to confront the politicians and to heckle the President during a national address, he arrived at the stadium where the former President Mwai Kibaki was speaking on June 1, 2009. Mwangi's friends did not have the courage to join him in the protest leaving him to protest alone. He stood up, and began shouting down the President (Eng, 2015). Beaten, arrested, and jailed, he was finally released on bail, with a court case that followed for a full year. Much later in his video *Patriot*, he responded to the challenge that he was an irritant. His reply was "If there were more irritants in the country, Kenya would be a better country," (Mwangi, 2014). He further complained that 18 Kenyans can sit in a speeding public vehicle with a drunk driver, and not say a word. "No one speaks up!" he lamented (Mwangi, 2014).

Pawa254

Dissatisfied with the inadequate impact made by the Picha Mtaani campaign, he sold his car, his studio, and other personal assets in 2011 to establish a collaborative space for a network of artists and activists known as Pawa254. Pawa is a youth slang word for power, while 254 is the international dialing code for Kenya, thus even the name "Pawa254" serves as a symbol of national strength and unity. As an organization, Pawa254 seeks to bring power back to the Kenyan masses.

The Pawa254 office site is an open space, near International Leadership University (ILU) where I, Marta Bennett, teach, and where I, Nita Hungu, am a recent Master's degree graduate. Mwangi himself enrolled in the Bachelor of Science in Leadership and Management program at ILU in 2013 as a first year student, but then got caught up in his activities, so as of this writing, has yet to finish. He does continue to meet regularly with one of our leadership department faculty members, however, and thus remains connected.

Pawa254 is a meeting point where creatives from all socioeconomic backgrounds involved in various art forms come together to brain-storm, create art, protest, share ideologies and beliefs, and engage with like-minded people for the purpose of social change. Photographers, musicians, hip-hop artists, video artists and filmmakers, poets, cartoonists, graphic designers, and the like, converge to strategize how to influence Kenya's future for the better (PAWA254 – Africa Rising!, n.d.). In keeping with the Swahili proverb "Kidole kimoja hakivunji chawa" ("one finger cannot kill lice") Mwangi notes that in unity, there is strength.

Like-minded organizations are also invited into the Pawa254 space. One such organization is Art for Abolition, which engages with sexually abused children from informal settlements. Likewise, Pawa254 has worked with Action for Transparency, an organization that calls for the accountability of government funds in the health and education sector. Action for Transparency engages with individuals from Kariobangi, one of Nairobi's informal settlements, enlisting the help of the constituents of Kariobangi in the monitoring and evaluation of projects and funds allocated to them.

By starting Pawa254, Mwangi did not go underground. Together with graffiti artists from Pawa254, in early 2013 Mwangi turned to public protest in the form of huge murals depicting Kenyan leaders as vultures, preying on their constituents. The graffiti movement called MaVulture ("Many Vultures") created the wall murals in the Central Business District of Nairobi during the Kenyan 2012/2013 general elections, which were used as a tool to educate the "wananchi" (local citizens), while speaking against economic and social injustice caused by ineffective leadership. Imagery included vultures displaying vices such as corruption, nepotism, and tribalism, conveying a powerful message that structural violence would not be tolerated any longer. According to Cathychristine Nanzala Keya and Johannes Michael Nebe (Keya & Nebe, 2012, p. 87), graffiti in Kenya "became the new element of conducting civic education as the General Election approached." Alongside the graffiti, posters depicting politicians in suits and ties, but with the heads of vultures, proclaimed: "Vote for me: I am greedy," "I am your favorite killer," "I only care for my bank account," "Vote for Me: Murderer," and "Vote for Rapist" [sic] (Mwangi, 2014).

Graffiti in Kenya has long been viewed as vandalism, and the country's by-laws prohibit this kind of art form. Graffiti was first employed on Kenyan public transport vehicles (matatus), later resulting in a ban enacted by the then late transport minister Mr. John Michuki (Gathenji, n.d.). Mwangi's graffiti was met with mixed reactions. The political elite was shocked and angry at the bold images. On the other hand, it was not uncommon to see groups of citizens milling around the art, pointing and discussing. According to Boniface Mwangi, the outcome was positive, in spite of abrasive comments on his Facebook page, airing incensed reactions as well.

These graffiti works were "an influential force in peace-building and nation-building … through education, and raising awareness, increasing knowledge, and moulding [*sic*] attitudes of the public regarding the acceptance of differences, as well as the shared histories, common goals and aspirations of the Kenyan people as a nation" (Mokua, 2013, p. 242). Banko Slavo as cited by Ombati Mokua (2013, p. 245) argued that graffiti is a form of civil protest that is more permanent than other forms of protests such as public demonstrations. Further, Mokua noted that graffiti in Kenya had its roots in "poverty, marginalization, minority status and grand corruption" (p. 248) all of which are forms of structural violence.

Nonviolent Protests

Mwangi has often denied that he is a public threat, noting that he is just a citizen. Recently he commented, "I am an activist because I am an active citizen, and I think everyone should be an active citizen" (Jesaro, 2015). During an interview on the nation-wide television program #TheTrend, aired on NTV Live (NTV, 2013), he spoke of several such protests, including "Occupy Parliament 2013" and later in the year, "Occupy Parliament Reloaded, 2013." As he describes them, the protests were an "uprising against the collective greed of Kenyan MPs" (Ministers of Parliament). Marching through the streets wearing T-shirts proclaiming "Occupy Parliament 2013," the protesters wrote the names of MPs on large live pigs using blood. The blood-smeared pigs were a demonstration against parliamentarians' lobby for their own salary increase. Kenyans derogatorily refer to Members of Parliament as "M-Pigs" instead of MP's, made in reference to the selfishness and greed of a number of the parliament members. Mwangi capitalized on this term and used living art to create a vivid picture of how the Members of Parliament were bleeding the economy. The protesters were beaten and arrested, but not deterred. Mwangi called for a reconvening of the protests, to march again for "Occupy Parliament Reloaded, 2013," crying out to his fellow citizens, "Come with your tools, your mkokoteni (wooden carts), your drums if you are musicians ..." (NTV, 2013) appealing to all Kenyans to rise up and to make their voices heard.

The year prior, "Love Protest 2012" was staged, to "tell parliament with a piece of art that their time is up" (Mwangi, 2014). The protesters carried to parliament 49 coffins, one for each year of impunity since independence, each with a scandal written on it. When the first act of parliament in 2013 was to raise their own salaries, Mwangi led "State Burial 2013" with 210 caskets, one for each member of parliament, but since there was no place to bury the coffins, they were burnt on site instead (Mwangi, 2014).

Revolutionary Leader or Heckler?

It is no wonder that his approach to activism has been very controversial. After he and his crowd delivered the 49 wooden coffins to the doorsteps of the Kenyan parliament, Mwangi received death threats, and was accused of being on the payroll of Western foreign governments and interest groups, something he consistently condemns and strongly denies (Meffe, 2015). Many have accused him of taking freedom of speech too far.

In 2014, Boniface Mwangi temporarily stepped down from social activism due to the allegations that he was involved in a plot to overthrow the government (Mwangi, 2014). On a video aired live by a Kenyan television station, Mwangi stated "I'm no longer willing to die for my country, I will live for it because my kids need a father," resulting in fierce reactions on social media (Kiboi, 2014). In addition to these allegations, Mwangi had apparently also received death threats from government officials and despite reporting the incidents to the police, no action was taken (Mwangi, 2014). Nevertheless, Mwangi eventually declared that he would continue to be a conduit of social change.

Numerous posts on social media in reaction to his work point to the fact that while many view him as a hero, a good number of Kenyans feel that his protests are not producing the desired outcomes. For example, blogger and socio-political activist Robert Alai wrote harsh comments on social media, criticizing Mwangi's statement that he would resign from activism. He accused Mwangi of not being an authentic change agent due to his decision to quit. Alai made reference to the numerous Kenyan activists who died while fighting for socio-political freedom in previous regimes (Kimani, 2014). Mwangi's actions are therefore both criticized and praised in equal measure.

Ongoing Activism

The use of social media by Kenyans has grown in leaps and bounds: 700,000 + monthly active users on twitter and 4.3 million users on Facebook. These statistics are projected to soar even more in coming years (Blogger's Association of Kenya, 2015). Boniface Mwangi's Twitter account (@BonifaceMwangi) is growing daily, reporting 404,447 followers as of June 25, 2016 (https://twitter.com/bonifacemwangi), and another 162,015 followers have liked his Facebook artist page by June 25, 2016 (https://web.facebook.com/BonifaceMwangiBM/?_rdr). Through these platforms, he has been able to rally his followers against injustice, no matter whether perpetrated by public officials or private citizens. One such example is of a video he posted on his Facebook page and Twitter, which showed a husband physically abusing his six month pregnant wife in full view of neighbors. The video was shared widely on different social media platforms by his followers. This resulted in a prominent local newspaper highlighting the story, causing widespread debate about the ills of domestic violence. His online presence and number of followers has allowed him to magnify stories like these, bringing justice to the oppressed.

In January 2015, a developer attempted to grab the school playground of Lang'ata Road Primary School, a school in Nairobi that caters to children from the neighboring Kibera informal settlement. Using the twitter hashtag #OccupyPlayGround, Boniface Mwangi organized a peaceful protest that was disrupted by riot police dispensing tear gas at the participants, including innocent school children. The president of Kenya strongly condemned state agencies for not resolving the matter quickly, thereby leading to unnecessary injuries. In the end, title deeds were awarded to public schools so as to deter further land grabbing (Burrows, 2016).

Preparing the Baton of Succession

I, Nita Hungu, first visited Boniface Mwangi's workplace while doing my Master's thesis research on leadership development through music (Hungu, 2014). A vocal artist myself, I went to interview one who worked out of Pawa243, to collect his perspective on my topic. Later I met with James Kamau, Mwangi's former personal assistant, interviewing him to learn more about Mwangi and Pawa254 from someone who worked closely with Mwangi, as well as to get perspectives on the movement from an insider. J. Kamau (personal communication, February 8, 2016) noted the challenge of sustainability, observing that "the danger of revolutionary ideas is that they die with the leader."

To counteract this threat, Boniface Mwangi has created a group called "#TeamCourage" that envisions individuals from all backgrounds to step up and make a difference. He uses this group as a means to transmit his own values for change so that in the event of his absence, his ideologies will be carried on into the next generation. Kamau further posited that "the greatest weapon of tyranny is the idea that an individual is powerless" (J. Kamau, personal communication, February 8, 2016). Mwangi is therefore modeling to those around him that they have the power to effect change. In the scheme of life, actions, no matter how small and mundane, can be the impetus for a revolution in different sectors of society.

As part of this agenda, on November 30, 2015 under the logo of #TeamCourage, Mwangi sent a press release to media houses, inviting them to cover a peaceful march from the city center's Uhuru Park to State House the following day. He reminded them that as free citizens, article #37 of the Constitution gives them the right to picket and protest, and the demonstration was advertised on Twitter as #KnockOutCorruption. A petition had been prepared to send to President Uhuru Kenyatta in early November 2015, demanding the President to declare corruption a national disaster. By the end of November, over 8,000 had signed the petition. In his State of the Nation address, the President did declare "corruption a national security threat" and called for religious leaders to also proclaim it a sin against God. When Pope Francis visited Kenya later that month, President Kenyatta appealed to the Pope to pray for him, that he would succeed in his war against corruption (TeamCourage, 2015).

According to J. Kamau (personal communication, February 8, 2016), Mwangi is perceived as a mentor. On many occasions, he has worked with emerging musicians and artists, resulting in a political message for social change in their work. Mwangi believes that any artist is a potential leader, and his commitment is to train and mentor artists from the grassroots level. According to Mwangi, art in all its forms should be used to challenge the status quo in order to bring about lasting change; artists should take pride in being counter-cultural. In addition, Pawa254 houses the "Empawaring Artists Grant Programme," geared at engaging and empowering creative emerging youth, whether in poetry, film, fashion, animation, music, graphic design, or other media.

During his work experience at Pawa254, J. Kamau (personal communication, February 8, 2016) stated that he was trained on how to organize a social campaign, from packaging the message, to networking with the right individuals to funding and leading a social movement. This hands-on training has allowed him to be more aware of what goes into projects geared toward social change. Kamau, who is a lawyer, reported that because of his interaction with Boniface Mwangi, he considers himself an agent for social change. Indeed, following Kamau on his Facebook page one can attest to this. His bold posts are mostly geared at challenging the political elite to change.

Modeling the Way

As a leader and mentor of others, Mwangi is keenly aware that what he says and does impacts the development of leaders around him, including his own young children. According to J. Kamau (personal communication, February 8, 2016), "every battle is a value battle; where there is a lack of value and the need to instill that value." Mwangi has attempted to propagate certain societal values through his personal life and work. These include integrity, value for life and property, and perseverance.

Those who have worked with Boniface Mwangi attest to the fact that he highly values and demonstrates personal integrity. In the long run, this consistency and values-based leadership has influenced the organization as a whole and has been a critical factor in the sustained growth of Pawa254 and all the projects he runs. For J. Kamau (personal communication, February 8, 2016), working with Mwangi has challenged him to make value-based decisions. Kamau stated that "Everything you do has an effect; because of this, I cannot give a bribe" (J. Kamau, personal communication, February 8, 2016). Mwangi has also made public announcements concerning his audited wealth due to allegations of corruption (Jesaro, 2015). He challenges individuals in positions of power to also be transparent about the amounts and sources of their wealth.

During his protests, Mwangi condemns vandalism and injury to individuals. According to J. Kamau (personal communication, February 8, 2016) Mwangi's philosophy is to confront the issues while preserving life. A picture taken during the Lang'ata Primary School protest shows Mwangi tending to an injured policeman. Despite an escalation during this protest, he was able to separate issues so as to fight the real enemy – corruption.

Many pictures from the Picha Mtaani were not published due to their disturbing nature. Mwangi made a tough choice to be sensitive, considering the harrowing experiences of the victims and their families. Balancing the journalistic ethic of protecting the dignity of the subject, versus the story that needs to be told to stop injustice, is a judgment call often faced by every photojournalist. In many instances, Mwangi has been sent pictures that are highly sensitive; many times he has declined posting them on social media.

Despite the government's reactions to his work, he has continued to be a catalyst for change in the nation. Mwangi is currently working on his first solo photography book titled *"Boom Twaff"* a name he derived from the steady beats of the hip-hop music genre. Along with his constituents at Pawa254, he continues to be at the forefront of innovation in Kenya, using the arts to fight injustice and corrupt leaders.

Recognition and Awards

Despite the fact that Mwangi is considered by many officials to be a destabilizer, there are instances in which he has won the support of the government. One such instance was December 2015 when Pawa254 organized an art festival dubbed "Art in the Streets." The event saw an entire street in the Central Business District of Nairobi being closed off to showcase music, art, and film. The collaboration between Pawa254 and the City Council of Nairobi made possible the successful event.

Mwangi's Picha Mtaani postelection violence traveling exhibit has been used in 12 African countries as a tool for reconciliation, and has been seen by over two million people in Kenya (Mwangi, 2008). He has been recognized as a TED Fellow (2010), and has received the Mohamed Amin Photographic Award category in the CNN MultiChoice African Journalist Awards (2008, 2010), Social Media Awards: Occupy Parliament (2013), Global Post Person of the Year (2012), NYU Magnum Foundation Human Rights Fellow (2011), Foreign Correspondents Association E.A Photo (2011), Temple University USA: Society of Emerging African Leaders Award (2013), and the Acumen Fellow (2011), to name a few (Hashtagsquare, n.d.).

In 2009, the United States Secretary of State, Hillary Clinton, wrote a letter commending Mwangi for his work, stating, "Your photography is absolutely stunning and tells an important and powerful story for the world to hear" (Mwangi, 2009). In 2012, Boniface Mwangi was presented with the Prince Claus Award for his contribution to culture. At this event, the Kenyan Chief Justice Willy Mutunga applauded his friend Mwangi for his outstanding campaigns, declaring that Mwangi's activism "… gave me hope that this country has alternative leadership among young people … and that is very comforting" (Prince Claus Fund for Culture and Development, 2012). He added, "I am convinced that the implementation of the Constitution which is very crucial for this country, if we are going to put this country in a social democratic trajectory, will be spearheaded by artists" (Prince Claus Fund for Culture and Development, 2012a, 2012b).

Summary

In an open letter to the nation regarding Kenyan President Uhuru Kenyatta, Mwangi used an African parable to introduce his mission to air public grievances about the President's leadership. He wrote:

Well, being the African I am, I will first use a parable. And not being one to skirt around issues, I will go ahead and confront a real issue that needs addressing.

There once lived a powerful King, ruler of a vast West African Kingdom. This king was known to appoint a commoner as his "truth teller." This truth teller lived among the king's subjects and would periodically be summoned by the King to tell him what the people were saying about the king and his rule. If the commoner lied, the king would put him to death. It was in his life's interest that the commoner told the king the truth.

The king in my story is our President, Uhuru Kenyatta. Unfortunately, the president lacks a "truth teller," a commoner in his presidency to tell him the truth. I would like, as a commoner, to tell the truth to the King, and to tell him what is being said in his subjects' chambers.

(Mwangi, September 21, 2015; Rasqoh, 2015)

Mwangi likened himself to a "truth-teller" whose purpose was to keep the "king" accountable to his people. This was a controversial move; in African cultures, to criticize any elder, let alone one of high rank, is unacceptable, and all the more so if done publically. In a previous era in Kenya, a person who criticized the President would likely, at minimum, merely "disappear." According to Sewanyana (n.d.), parables and proverbs serve as a deterrent and an "opportunity for people to talk about kinds of behaviour which society prohibited them from indulging in" (p. 51). These parables therefore serve as a form of euphemism in which messages of grievances were relayed to the recipient indirectly. Though he is relatively young, has never completed university, nor achieved merit through traditional channels, Mwangi still spoke out boldly, employing the cultural tactic of indirect communication through a parable, to justify his action.

Adamant in his stance against injustice and persistent in his opposition to corruption, Mwangi models courageous values-driven leadership. "My call to Kenyans is become an active citizen. Speak out when things go wrong and remember this, you can never achieve anything without courage," he challenged in an interview with *The Standard* newspaper (Jesaro, 2015). His wife Hellen Njeri added, "He is an activist as a reaction to injustice and the belief just that there is better for this country" (Jesaro, 2015). He says that when he sees his children, he has hope (Mwangi, 2014), Mwangi holds forth a vision of a Kenya where truth and justice prevail for all, a country where his own children can grow up in peace and can thrive. He himself states, "I am a photo-activist, using photography for activism, but mostly, I am a patriot" (Mwangi, 2014).

"The struggle for a better Kenya continues" declares Mwangi (2014). Convinced that the arts provide a force of communication that goes beyond mere words, he and his network employ images, stories, symbols, and music to deliver messages that penetrate the emotions as well as the opinion. As a process of leadership development, over 200,000 youth have been engaged in trainings and outreach programs through Pawa254 (Mwangi, 2014). Thus, through art, collaboration, and mentoring, Boniface Mwangi is raising up a movement of creative leaders from the grass roots, who are determined to promote justice and responsible leadership for Kenya – and beyond.

Acknowledgments

We, the two authors, are deeply grateful for the privilege of delving into the life and work of Boniface Mwangi. With great respect and appreciation, we have been challenged by his courage, convictions, creativity, and persistence. Since he has become a notable public figure in Kenya, much material was available online through videos, blogs, and articles, posted both by himself and by numerous others. We specifically thank him for his quick and open response to us to use any excerpts from his articles, postings, or interviews, including his parable of the truth-teller. In the same spirit, we gratefully acknowledge the invaluable input of James Kamau, whose insight into the life and work of Boniface Mwangi shaped the research significantly.

References

Adhengo, B. (2010). *Peace art: The forbidden expression*. Raleigh, NC: Lulu Books Ltd.

Blogger's Association of Kenya. (2015). *The State of Blogging and Social Media in Kenya, 2015*. Nairobi: Blogger's Association of Kenya. Retrieved from http://www.monitor.co.ke/wp-content/uploads/2015/06/The-State-of-Blogging-and-Social-Media-in-Kenya-2015-report.pdf

Burrows, O. (2016, January 18). #OccupyPlayground, one year later and the issue of titles. Retrieved from https://www.capitalfm.co.ke/news/2016/01/occupyplayground-one-year-later-and-the-issues-of-titles/

Corfield, D. (2015). Boniface Mwangi: Activism, photography and making a difference. *Canon*, May. Retrieved from http://cpn.canon-europe.com/content/interviews/boniface_mwangi_on_photo_activism.do

Eng, J. (2015, February 27). Why I chose to stand up, alone: TED Fellow Boniface Mwangi on risking his life for justice in Kenya [Blog post]. Retrieved from http://blog.ted.com/?cat=blog_posts&s=Boniface+Mwangi

Gathenji, H. K. (n.d.). Writing on the wall. *Destination Magazine*. Retrieved from http://www.eadestination.com/pop-culture/77-writing-on-the-wall

Hashtagsquare (n.d.). *Boniface Mwangi biography*. Retrieved from www.hashtagsquare.co.ke/?s=boniface+mwangi.

Hungu, N. (2014). *Enhancing leadership development through music: Perspectives of professionals in Nairobi*. Unpublished Master's thesis, International Leadership University, Nairobi, Kenya.

Jesaro, M. (2015). I am worth 3 million shillings – Activist Boniface Mwangi and wife publicly declare their wealth. *Standard Digital*, December 10. Retrieved from http://www.sde.co.ke/article/2000185007/i-am-worth-3-million-shillings-activist-boniface-mwangi-and-wife-publicly-declare-their-wealth

Keya, C. N., & Nebe, J. M. (2012). Graffiti – An art form used in political revolt in Kenya. In J. M. Nebe (Ed.), *Peacebuilding and conflict management* (pp. 85–92). Trier: University of Trier.

Kiboi, A. (2014, February 17). Activism and retirement (Giving up? Quitting?) [Blog post]. Retrieved from https://admblind.wordpress.com/category/boniface-mwangi/

Kimani, S. (2014). Robert Alai 'bashes' Boniface Mwangi for 'quitting activism'. *Standard Digital*, February 18. Retrieved from http://www.sde.co.ke/article/2000113939/robert-alai-bashes-boniface-mwangi-for-quitting-activism

Meffe, D. (2015). Boniface Mwangi: Africa's rising firebrand? *New African*, March 18. Retrieved from http://newafricanmagazine.com/boniface-mwangi-kenyas-rising-firebrand/

Mokua, O. (2013). Graffiti: A powerful innovative weapon broadening the horizons of social transformation in Kenya. In Papers presented at the international conference on children and youth affected by armed conflict: Where to go from here? (pp. 239–253). Centre for Children in Vulnerable Situations, Kampala.

Mwangi, B. (2008, December 9). Career achievements. Retrieved from http://www.bonifacemwangi.co.ke/career-achievements/

Mwangi, B. (2009, January 28). Boniface Mwangi. Retrieved from http://www.bonifacemwangi.co.ke/biography/

Mwangi, B. (2014, December 1). Patriot [Video file]. Retrieved from https://www.youtube.com/watch?v=3OUdX0efyt0

Mwangi, B. (2014). WHY I quit ACTIVISM, and why I am BACK. *Kenya Today*, December 3. Retrieved from http://www.kenya-today.com/opinion/boniface-mwangi-quit-activism/

Mwangi, B. (2015). Uhuru is an alcoholic and needs help. *Matukio*, September 21. Retrieved from http://matukio.co.ke/2015/09/uhuru-is-an-alcoholic-and-needs-help-boniface-mwangi/

NTV. (2013, May 3). #theTrend: Boniface Mwangi's Fiery Activism [Video file]. Retrieved from https://www.youtube.com/watch?v=iXb8-k2ppJ8

PAWA254 – Art Rising!. (n.d.). About us. Retrieved from http://pawa254.org/

Perry, A. (2012, December 3). Africa rising. Retrieved from http://www.laveudafrica.com/africa-rising/

Prince Claus Fund for Culture and Development. (2012a, January 29). http://www.prinsclausfonds.nl/en/news/presentation-of-2012-prince-claus-award-to-boniface-mwangi.html

Rasqoh. (2015, September 21). Boniface Mwangi's Daring Letter on President Uhuru Kenyatta's Alcoholism. Retrieved from http://rasqoh.com/boniface-mwangis-full-article-on-president-uhuru-kenyattas-alcoholism/

Sewanyana, L. (n.d.). The use of traditional communications in conflict management: The case of Uganda, pp. 40–69. Retrieved from http://pdfproc.lib.msu.edu/?file=/DMC/African%20Journals/pdfs/africa%20media%20review/vol11no3/jamr011003004.pdf

TeamCourage. (2015, November 30). PRESS RELEASE for the #Knock OutCorruption March to State House taking place TOMORROW from 10am at Uhuru Park: Freedom Corner [Facebook Status Update]. Retrieved from https://www.facebook.com/TeamCourageKE/photos

TEDGlobal. (2014). Boniface Mwangi: The day I stood up alone. Retrieved from https://www.ted.com/talks/boniface_mwangi_boniface_mwangi_the_day_i_stood_up_alone?language=en

6

Benevolent Subversion: Graffiti, Street Art, and the Emergence of the Anonymous Leader

James Jarc and Tricia Garwood

Introduction

In his 2000 book, *The Tipping Point*, Malcolm Gladwell examined the correlations of New York City crime rates and seemingly minor criminal activity such as fare-beating and graffiti in the subway systems. By adopting a zero-tolerance policy against these infractions, Gladwell suggests, the authorities in New York helped "tip" the crime rates in the city toward lower rates across the board (Gladwell, 2000). Gladwell's main point, rooted in the broken windows theory of Wilson and Kelling (1982), is that a reduction in minor crimes (such as graffiti) creates the social perception of safer, crime-free communities and deters would-be criminals from perpetrating delinquent behaviors. While the efficacy and ethics of such policing is under debate/scrutiny, the assumed connection between delinquency and street art implies the strong semiotic power of graffiti and illustrates an important aspect of this chapter. Graffiti, it seems, is more than just spray paint on a wall.

First, graffiti is a powerful communicative tool, capable of inspiring many types of social action. City officials, property managers, and custodians lament the practice of *tagging* or *bombing* as delinquent, criminal behavior. On the other hand, some community members applaud the artists' social commentary as relevant and necessary for cultural progress. Further, wealthy culturati are willing to shell out vast sums of money to own works by noted street artists. Graffiti's mischievous, counter-cultural roots and widely ranging continuum of art versus vandalism make it an art form with a highly specific cultural appeal. Graffiti artists, like their art, exist in *liminality* (Palmer, 2001), occupying dual roles in grassroots social movements. At once, they are both mirrors of their social context as well as influential drivers of change. We assert that graffiti artists play a critical mediating role in society, similar to the Jungian archetype of *trickster* (Jung, 1966). as found in cultural mythology around the world.

Like the trickster, street artists are boundary crossers. They are clever and wise yet often find themselves – like Loki in his fish net (Hyde, 1998) – caught in their own traps (and sometimes in police cruisers). The archetypal artist as trickster infuses society with a much-needed subversive viewpoint. Without this kind of what we call *cultural vaccination*, communities face stagnation, stasis, and a decline into cultural entropy (Barrett, 2006). By injecting a small dose of disorder into the system, graffiti artists and other subversive leaders encourage the community to recognize a threat to its well-being and hopefully coalesce around it to find a solution. It becomes the responsibility of the trickster graffiti artist, then, to lead courageously (and often anonymously) by way of the representations he or she portrays on walls, subway cars, bridges, and tunnels around the city.

Marcis, Clark, and Care (2003) defined benevolent subversive leadership as the practice of undermining ineffectual or failing legitimate power systems in order to achieve organizational or community purpose. In these cases, stakeholders work through unofficial, informal channels to sustain the health of their communities. We believe that benevolent subversive leadership can be practiced not only in organizational settings, but in broader communities and social movements as well. This chapter uses the infamous artist, Banksy, as a point of departure for our discussion of benevolent subversive leadership. We identify ways in which Banksy subverts traditional power structures while working to create productive dialogue around issues of justice, greed, consumerism, animal welfare, and a host of other contemporary issues.

In 2010, Banksy was featured as one of *Time Magazine*'s 100 most influential people of the year, an impressive achievement for an artist who began his career bombing (painting graffiti) walls in

Bristol, England, just two decades earlier. The portrait featured in *Time* pictured the artist incognito with a paper bag over his head (Fairey, 2010). Since then Banksy has bombed cities around the world and, while remaining anonymous and ever subversive, has evolved into an artist whose work can sell for hundreds of thousands of dollars. He has not held a face-to-face interview since 2003 though his organization, Pest Control, continues to both authenticate his work and help maintain control of the artist's narrative (Ellsworth-Jones, 2013). Banksy's anonymity represents a portion of his subversive power. He exerts leadership not through charisma, coercion, or direct influence but rather through the imagery he uses and its careful placement. This is one of the cornerstones of subversive leadership: it is never about the leader himself or herself, it is about the power that the leader's message — in Banksy's case, the iconoclastic street art — has on members of the community in which the leader works.

Defining Graffiti and Street Art Movements

The terms graffiti and street art are often used interchangeably, though it is important to note that there is a clear distinction between the two. More often than not, "graffiti" refers to territorial markings or overt vandalism, typically containing crude language and/or imagery (Yip, 2010). In contrast, "street art" is often considered to be more of a fine art, practiced outside of the confines of traditional studios, galleries, or museums. Street art includes traditional spray paint as well as stenciling, stickering, yarn bombing, projections, installations, or a multi-modal approach seen in much of Banksy's work. The terms "neo-graffiti," "post-graffiti," "urban art," and "guerilla art" have also emerged as synonyms of street art, excluding vandalism and territorial tagging (Yip, 2010). As we are not attempting to analyze the art form itself, we will use many of these terms interchangeably throughout this chapter to signify any visual representation of an idea, displayed in an area not typically designed for the display of artwork. Shacter (2014) deploys the term "independent public art/artist" as a convenient umbrella term for the above-listed art forms; we will also utilize this terminology as well as the abbreviation IPA.

The legal distinction between art and graffiti is permission (Yip, 2010). Ferro (2014) draws the distinction this way: "With

the exception of 'legal walls', where street artists are allowed
to tag, spray painting someone else's property is still a crime"
(para. 8). Most cities are responsible for developing and enforcing their own graffiti-related codes, though municipalities
operate within frameworks laid out by states (Sherwin-Williams
Co. v. City of Los Angeles, 1993). Some local codes attempt to
prevent graffiti from happening by legislating the sale of spray
paints, large markers, or other materials that are often used by
taggers. Some hardware stores may limit quantities of supplies
that can be sold to any one individual. Stores in Portland,
Oregon are required by law to record the buyer's name, address,
phone, and driver's license information along with the brand, lot,
and quantity of the items sold (Graffiti Materials and Sales,
Portland City Codes, Chapter 14B.85, 2007). The City of
Chicago has entirely banned the sale of spray paint within the
city limits since 1980 ("Justice Stevens Allows Chicago to Ban
Spray Paint", 1995). The efficacy of graffiti prevention laws such
as these continues to be hotly debated.

Although the legal distinction holds, should the moral
distinction hold as well? Is it always morally wrong to break
such laws? Or is subversive activity such as independent public
art − or less permanent versions such as projections or yarn
bombing − a way of leading change by communicating dissenting views, expressing concerns, or asking questions others are
reluctant to ask? Isn't the point of street art to make a public
statement against "the system"?

But, Is It Art?

Given the ambiguity of such an art form, there is a great deal of
controversy surrounding street art and the artists that create it.
Sociologist Gordon Douglas (Ferro, 2014) says that despite its
negative reputation, street art can prove to benefit a city economically. Rather than being a signal of disorder, Douglas suggests
that the presence of graffiti can actually increase the appeal of a
neighborhood. In contrast to the "broken windows" theory
introduced earlier, Gregory Snyder (2009) compared rates of
graffiti and violent crime in various neighborhoods in New York
City, and found that there were a number of areas (such as
SoHo) where higher concentrations of graffiti actually correlated
with fairly low rates of violent crime. Economist Elizabeth
Currid-Halkett, an associate professor at the University of

Southern California noted, "When you see graffiti, it's really a sign of many more interesting creative things going on" (Ferro, 2014). Consider street artist Nate Swain. The formerly mysterious "Boston Lego Builder" continually repaired a gaping hole in an old warehouse (being used by a group of local artists) with Legos to make both an artistic and a political statement, drawing attention to the need for additional police stations and more reasonable rental rates. Swain has created public art in a number of spots around Boston. The general response of passersby and building residents was gleeful, some literally thrilled that "guerilla art" had returned (Smith, 2016). In contrast, former Queens Museum of Art Executive Director Tom Finkelpearl believes that while public art may help start dialogue, graffiti is vandalism and should not be considered art ("What is Street Art?", 2010). The prevalence of anti-graffiti laws suggests that many city planners, legislators, and urban homeowners agree with Finkelpearl. Yet street art sells, and this causes some commercially successful street artists to be cast as "sellouts" among their peers and to lose some of the *street cred* that helped them initially develop agency within their communities.

In 2008, Banksy's painting, *Ruined Landscape*, sold for $385,000 at a Sotheby's auction causing Heather MacDonald (2011) to complain that street artists like Banksy and Shepard Fairey (designer of the famous Barack Obama "HOPE" poster) are hypocrites since their initially controversial and subversive street art now commands such a high price on the art market. Graffiti was formally acknowledged by the art community in 2011 when *The Museum of Contemporary Art, Los Angeles* featured the street art and graffiti of 50 artists. Not everyone was ready to embrace street art and a number of critics were dismayed by what they termed the *Banksy effect* (Ellsworth-Jones, 2013). Banksy's work continues to ruffle feathers amongst widely diverse critics from fellow street artists to city commissioners and gallery owners. The work of Banksy, Fairey, and other successful street artists is often vandalized, and their reputations become tangled up as part of the very system they worked to subvert. Hadengust (2014) points to the *tall poppy syndrome* and common jealousy toward artists like Banksy. Those who stand out from the crowd are often the ones with the targets on their backs. Taggers are out working their territories, risking high fines and jail time to create subversive artwork, while Banksy boldly sets up a booth in Central Park, sells his pieces for $100, and gets front page treatment from the local media. Of course other IPAs would be jealous! In a 2007 *New Yorker* interview, Linda Collins asked Banksy about his motivation. Perhaps taking a swing at some of his detractors, the artist answered, "I originally set out to try and save the world, but now I'm not sure I like it enough" (Collins, 2007, para. 69).

In our subversive leadership definition, as long as an artist continued to challenge society's values we would not discount their work because of commercial success. In fact, the commercial success of street art serves as a much-needed catalyst, propelling the artist's work further into the communities they seek to critique and influence. The question is, regardless of income, can an artist who anonymously gives away his work and subversively inspires others to do the same be considered a sellout? The answer is subject to the opinion of the critic or proponent, but we feel as long as the art inspires others to question and doubt – and to make those questions and doubts public – then "sellout" is not a proper or fair label.

Subversive Leadership

As our discussion reveals, subversive leadership is complicated and often dichotomous. The message can be well intended, but its delivery is messy and often illegal. The morals may be high, but the tactics are cast as lowbrow. Subversion will always make people uncomfortable, but as long as no one gets hurt, and some progress toward improvement is achieved, we see it as benevolent. Paint on a wall, in our opinions, is the epitome of nonviolence, yet the messages can still feel threatening to community members who may not understand the work. Banksy's use of rats presents the artist's commentary on the power of social change. Stenciled on walls and literally running through a gallery opening, these vermin represent power in numbers. Banksy (2002) explained in his book, *Existencilism*, "Like most people, I have a fantasy that all the little powerless losers will gang up together" (p. 19). This is the very paradox of the liminal, non-positional, subversive leader. In order to exert influence, the leader must find a balance between significant visibility and expert/referent power (Johnson, 2005, p. 10), and continuing to be seen as a member of the community he serves (Haslam, Reicher, & Platow, 2011).

The challenge – and perhaps inherent paradox of leadership – lies in working within existing power structures while strategically effecting change toward justice, equality, improved processes, or whatever the community needs most. Society says it values leaders who are honest, virtuous, fair, and agreeable. Leadership, in the most popular and traditional sense, values the status quo. But there is a somewhat countercultural element of leadership as well when leaders are called to effect some form of change within a group or society; when they feel constrained and unable to move in the direction to which their ethical compasses point. Civilization is fueled through change, revolution and ideas being expressed in a more subversive way. This can't be easy. Linsky (2009) suggests that a key to subversive leadership is persistence: "Leadership requires the courage and skill to stay in the game for as long as it takes to achieve your purpose and to sustain the disapproval of those who like the game the way it is currently played, because it suits their purposes, whether or not it is in the interests of the organization or community as a whole" (Linsky, 2009, para. 11).

Through the course of his career, Banksy has produced work that comments on everything from corporate greed to animal captivity. In situations when society is perceived as unjust, subversive leaders like Banksy raise their voices – via their paint cans, their stencils, and their brushes – and express their discontent in ways that polite society may call gross, explicit, lewd, or offensive. The subversive leader challenges the very nature of the system in order to shine a light on the plight of those for whom the system does not work. Banksy's international reputation as a cultural commentator (and subversive leader) was likely cemented in 2005 when he painted a series of escapist paintings along the West Bank's concrete dividing wall. A girl with a handful of balloons floats hopefully aloft while a boy props a ladder against the wall; both are powerful visual messages with global impact. *Barely Legal* opened in Los Angeles in 2006 and the show again used sensationalism to draw attention to facts people might prefer to ignore. A live elephant painted red with gold fleur-de-lis represented the "elephant in the room," a message of poverty and greed that apparently Banksy felt society was unwilling to confront. *Barely Legal* drew roughly 30,000 people, waiting in lines five blocks long to see the work (Collins, 2007). In the days after the show, Banksy not only bombed several buildings, he also installed one of his most daring works of art. The artist dressed a blowup doll to look like a Guantánamo Bay prisoner – complete with a hood and an orange jumpsuit – and somehow managed to bypass Disneyland's strict security to leave the "prisoner" along the path of the Big Thunder Mountain Railroad attraction. It remained there for a full 90 minutes (Collins, 2007).

Raymond Smilor (1997) asserted that effective leadership "upsets the status quo, disrupts accepted ways of doing things, and alters traditional patterns of behavior" (p. 341). The success of disruptive leaders comes from four abiding elements: talent, opportunity, capital, and know-how (Smilor, 1997). Banksy has used these elements, with much the same motivation. Douglas and Fremantle (2006) suggested that "artists are increasingly interested in creating the conditions in which the challenges, desires, and tensions of changing social, environmental, and cultural circumstances become exposed or revealed" (p. 1). Artists emerge as subversive leaders through the influence of the quality of the art they produce and through contributing his or her creativity to the public discourse (Douglas & Fremantle, 2006). In both business and the arts, a common source of power is the expertise of the leader and their ability to position themselves opportunistically in optimal social/political/organizational position to affect change. Banksy's work has been successful in large part because his choice of location is so strategically and inextricably linked with the content of the work being displayed.

Whether in the arts, politics, science, technology, or academia, individuals who propose the next great idea is often ridiculed (or even arrested) before the promise of their subversive idea can come to fruition. Subversion will always be an uncomfortable yet critical element of creativity and innovation. It is through benevolent subversion that potential is revealed. Through this view, we see the catalytic role of the graffiti/street artist as the trickster who rejects ridicule and becomes the purveyor of a cultural vaccination that helps prepare society for the change will propel us forward.

Cultural Vaccination

GRAFFITI ARTISTS AS TRICKSTER

In nearly every culture and body of mythology, the character of the trickster plays an important role. Examples include Hermes and Prometheus in ancient Greek mythology, raven and tortoise in Native American tales, and Bart Simpson or Woody Woodpecker in popular culture. These characters are often represented in stories as physically or sexually ambiguous and are often capable of changing forms. The trickster can be rude, gross, perverted, under-handed, and generally not the type of character you would invite to a stuffy dinner party. Tricksters are master negotiators, cunning orators, and stealthy criminals, yet, for all their scheming, strive for a level of acceptance from their communities. The trickster, according to Barbara Babcock-Abrahams (1975), exists in constant transition, somewhere between juvenile delinquent and culture hero, much like the independent public artist in today's urban mythology. In contemporary mythology, shape-shifting his way between criminal and culture hero, Banksy is iconic.

As a teenager, Banksy began bombing in the Barton Hill district in Bristol, England (Ellsworth-Jones, 2013). Early on, he began using his classic stencil style after a near escape from the police. During an early escape, Banksy shared that he was hiding under a truck with oil dripping all over him. When he looked up, he noticed the stencil plate on the fuel tank. In that eureka moment, Banksy realized that he could make his mark far more efficiently by using stencils. His stencils create an esthetic that is clean and instantly readable. The style enables him to reduce complicated ideas to simplest visual elements (Collins, 2007). Simplicity is a communication tactic ideally suited to cultural boundary crossers like Banksy; little is lost in translation. Banksy's first London exhibit was in 2001 where he and some street artist friends displayed their work on the side of a pub to about 500 onlookers. In 2003, his *Turf War* exhibit brought him fully into the public eye. It famously featured a cow with Andy Warhol painted on its side and Queen Elizabeth II looking a great deal like a chimpanzee. It is this type of scene that is caricatured in Banksy's film, *Exit through the Gift Shop* (Baring, Cushing, Gay-Rees, & Banksy, 2010). Banksy subsequently placed secret artwork in many major museums including the Louvre, Tate London, and the Metropolitan Museum of Art. This evolution, and the cultural crossover it represents, demonstrates that the IPA is a liminal figure, constantly translating his ideas, mixing forms and norms, and bridging a critical social gap.

In almost all examples, the trickster is defiant of authority, yet endearing (Babcock-Abrahams, 1975, p. 160). The persistent dual personalities of the trickster and the street artist "are expressive of the social contexts in which they occur and depend upon social experience for perception" (p. 160). The trickster exists to help us figure out what we think is normal or what we consider acceptable behavior. We shun the trickster for his dirty jokes or vulgar paintings on the wall yet in the end, thank him for his help in clarifying our values and helping us recognize injustice. It is precisely this liminal, transitional existence that allows the trickster to venture unharmed into the unknown and return with gifts for his people. He is at once unappreciated and practically necessary for the prevention of cultural entropy. Without the trickster and the independent public artist, we may never think to question how we define terms like good, evil, normal, weird, decent, or fair.

Banksy the trickster-leader helps society move forward by challenging norms, reflecting social values, and bearing the brunt of society's collective harsh judgments. Rather than being admired for his charm, or virtue, Banksy embodies many attributes of the *postheroic* leader (Crevani, Lindgren, & Packendorff, 2007), a leadership style that is focused on decentralizing power. Tricksters are effective as leaders because "they express the generative situation of ambivalence and contradictions that the very basis of culture engenders. Seeming undifferentiation and ambivalence are characteristic of mediating figures ..." (Babcock-Abrahams, 1975, p. 164). In contrast with the heroic, "great man" leadership styles of Carlyle (1841) and Max Weber (1947), postheroic leaders want to create a situation in which everyone can contribute to growth and change, regardless of who gets credit.

Independent public artists such as Banksy, through their anonymity, shield themselves from the harshest of personal critiques and use this veil to sustain their creative, selfless leadership energies. The idea of the anonymous leader fits well within both postheroic and benevolent subversive leadership theory, and can perhaps be held up as the ideal of non-positional, other-focused leadership. We suggest that even though we collectively "know" Banksy, his leadership comes primarily through the quality of work, and its contributions to the public sphere (Douglas & Fremantle, 2006). Banksy takes great strides to ensure his art belongs to the people through its placement in common space, through its discussion of common concerns, and by literally putting his work into the hands of adoring fans. His approach ensures there is no one in the middle interpreting, misrepresenting, or watering down his message.

Conclusion

The independent public artist occupies a unique and important role in contemporary culture. He or she is perceived as both a criminal and a culture hero, walking a fine line between credibility and distrust. Graffiti and street art are gifts brought to communities by picaresque, benevolent leaders who, through ambivalence or altruism (perhaps both), shoulder the burden of holding a mirror to society. We have discussed the role of the independent public artist as one of liminality, much like the character of trickster in many mythological traditions. Graffiti artists, like tricksters, conceal their identities to avoid emotionally draining criticisms and the ever-watchful eye of law enforcement. In doing so, we believe that IPAs are exercising a critical leadership tactic that allows them to sustain their creative energies.

This chapter has attempted to align benevolent subversive leadership with the emerging schools of postheroic leadership thought. Decentralized, non-positional leadership puts the power in the hands of the collective, allowing each individual to lead as needed. In the case of the IPA, we believe that the public expression of countercultural messages serves as a foundation upon which community members may build discourse. Street art as dialogue, however deviant, can inspire collective action, challenge status quo, and lead to real change. The independent public artist, however anonymous, serves as an enabling leader, connecting cultures and generating accessible environments in which we can work toward improving the world around us.

References

Babcock-Abrahams, B. (1975). A tolerated margin of mess: The trickster and his tales reconsidered. *Journal of the Folklore Institute*, 11(3), 147–186.

Banksy. (2002). *Existencilism*. Bristol, UK: Weapons of Mass Distraction.

Baring, Z. (Executive Producer), Cushing, H. (Executive Producer), Gay-Rees, J. (Executive Producer), & Banksy (Director). (2010). *Exit through the gift shop* [Motion picture]. Paranoid Pictures.

Barrett, R. (2006). *Building a values-driven organization: A whole system approach to cultural transformation*. Burlington, MA: Elsevier.

Carlyle, T. (1841). *On heroes, hero-worship, & the heroic in history*. London: James Fraser.

Collins, L. (2007). Banksy was here: The invisible man of Graffiti art. *The New Yorker*, May 14. Retrieved from http://www.newyorker.com/magazine/2007/05/14/banksy-was-here

Crevani, L., Lindgren, M., & Packendorff, J. (2007) Shared leadership: A postheroic perspective on leadership as a collective construction. *International Journal of Leadership Studies*, 3(1) 40–67.

Douglas, A., & Fremantle, C., (2006). When is the artist a creative leader?: A provisional framework. In *Proceedings of the creative rural economy conference*, September 10–13, 2006. Ramsbottom: Littoral.

Ellsworth-Jones, W. (2013). *Banksy: The man behind the wall*. New York, NY: St. Martin's Press.

Fairey, S. (2010). Banksy. *Time Magazine*, April 29. Retrieved from: http://content.time.com/time/specials/packages/article/0,28804,1984685_1984940_1984945,00.html

Ferro, S. (2014). Can graffiti be good for cities? *FastCo.Design*, January 7. Retrieved from http://www.fastcodesign.com/3022524/can-graffiti-be-good-for-cities

Gladwell, M. (2000). *The tipping point: How little things can make a big difference*. Boston, MA: Little, Brown and Company.

Graffiti Materials and Sales, Portland City Codes, Chapter 14B.85, 2007.

Hadengust, A. (2014). Graffiti artists turn on Banksy: The rise of art hate. *The Daily Beast*, August 6. Retrieved from http://www.thedailybeast.com/articles/2014/08/06/Graffiti-artists-turn-on-banksy-the-rise-of-art-hate.html

Haslam, S. A., Reicher, S. D., & Platow, M. J. (2011). *The new psychology of leadership. Identity, influence, and power*. New York, NY: Psychology Press.

Hyde, L. (1998). *Trickster makes this world: Mischief, myth and art*. New York: Farrar, Straus and Giroux.

Johnson, C. E. (2005). *Meeting the ethical challenges of leadership: Casting light or shadow*. (5th ed.). Thousand Oaks, CA: Sage.

Jung, C. (1966). Two essays on analytical psychology. *Collected Works of C. G. Jung Vol. 7*. Princeton, NJ: Princeton University Press.

Justice Stevens Allows Chicago to Ban Spray Paint. (1995). *New York Times*, March 4. Retrieved from: http://www.nytimes.com/1995/03/04/us/Justice-stevens-allows-chicago-to-ban-spray-paint.html

Linsky, M. (2009, June 14). Leadership as a subversive activity. Linsky on Leadership [weblog]. Retrieved from http://cambridgeleadership.blogspot.com/2009/06/leadership-as-subversive-activity.html/

MacDonald, H. (2011). Radical Graffiti Chic: Sponsored by L.A.'s aristocracy, The museum of contemporary art's new show celebrates vandalism. *City Journal*. Retrieved from http://www.city-journal.org/html/radical-graffiti-chic-13369.html

Marcis, A. C., Clarl, S. L., & Care, R. (2003). Subversive leadership. *Update*. Mystic, CT: A.C. Marcis Consultants. Retrieved from http://www.themacrisgroup.com/docs/Update_Oldsite/Vol_1_Issue_0303.pdf

Palmer, R. E. (2001). *The liminality of hermes and the meaning of hermeneutics* [lecture]. Retrieved from https://www.mac.edu/faculty/richardpalmer/liminality.html

Schacter, R. (2014). *Ornament and order: Graffiti, street art and the parergon*. Farnham: Ashgate Publishing Ltd.

Sherwin-Williams Co. v. City of Los Angeles, 4 Cal. 4th 893 (1993).

Smilor, R. (1997). Entrepreneurship: Reflections on a subversive activity. *Journal of Business Venturing*, 12(5), 341–346.

Smith, T. (2016). Unraveled: The mystery of the secret street artist in Boston. *Morning Edition, National Public Radio*, April 5. Retrieved from http://www.npr.org/2016/04/05/471471307/unraveled-the-mystery-of-the-secret-street-artist-in-boston

Snyder, G. (2009). *Graffiti lives: Beyond the tag in New York's urban underground*. New York, NY: New York University Press.

Weber, M. (1947). *Theory of social and economic organization* (A. R. Anderson and T. Parsons, Trans.). New York, NY: The Free Press.

Wilson, J. Q., & Kelling, G. L. (1982, March). Broken windows: The police and neighborhood safety. *The Atlantic*. Retrieved from http://www.manhattaninstitute.org/pdf/_atlantic_monthly-broken_windows.pdf

Yip, E. W. (2010, January 21). What is street art? Vandalism, Graffiti or public art Part I [web page]. Retrieved from http://artradarjournal.com/2010/01/21/what-is-street-art-vandalism-graffiti-or-public-art-part-i/.

7

Innovating Social Change through Grassroots Leadership Practices in the Arts

Anu M. Mitra

A rtists who believe that their work is interventionist in scope and who view themselves as activists have often led communities and societies to transformation and liberation. Through their art-making practices, they have harnessed the leadership values inherent in their communities of choice to create social change. In an important case study, we examine how artists have emboldened community in order to enact participatory action from the ground up. In terms of methodology, we use the protocols of participatory action research (PAR). With its insistence on relevance, urgent mandate to act, and reliance on the leadership values of the community, PAR provokes open-ended solutions that lead to tangible developments in society.

Case Study

JR, the French photographer, has used street photography to reframe social change issues. He believes that people are the actual architecture of the city and that the texture of person and place form the essence of belonging. He wants to create conditions for the center to know the margins — and his photographs deal with serious conflict through the emotional strategy of humor and connection. Conceptualizing, producing, and pasting large-scale portraits of everyday people with the active help of his audience in conflict-ridden places throughout the world, he brings into conversation the oppressor with the oppressed. In Palestine and Israel; in Sierra Leone, Tunisia, Cambodia, and India; and in rich and poor Kenya or Brazil, his portraits inspire connection and reflection. In his work, JR combines grassroots leadership and arts-based social change. Using visual arts as a way to communicate solidarity and unification, JR forces people to reframe the parameters of social interrogation and explore alternative ways in which to make change happen. In all instances, he democratizes the work of change so that it becomes a lateral, participatory, and nonhierarchical transformation model where each member of society serves as change-agent. In this way, he empowers community while provoking radical transformation — all through the deliberate use of art as a tool for active change. "I just want to raise questions, generate dialogue. Not provide answers, because, in any case, I don't have them. My work is to show that the limits are not where we think they are," JR notes (Khatchadourian, 2011, p. 59).

Who Is JR?

JR wears a hat and dark glasses at all times to shroud his identity. By intent, both his persona and narrative remain mysterious but what is clear is the effect that his work continues to have upon marginalized people living in volatile countries worldwide. What is shared by JR about his personal history is bare-bones: he was born in 1983 in Paris to a Tunisian mother and a father who was of Eastern European and Spanish heritage. He shared a home with his two sisters and their parents. JR (these are his real initials but his actual name is unknown) remembers that his parents gave up their bedroom for the three children and instead slept in the living room for years. The extent of this sacrifice created an impression on JR, who commented much later, "Wow, my parents were sleeping in the *living room*! You think *your* surroundings are normal" (Khatchadourian, 2011, p. 60). It was the gap between his personal reality and the world's perception of normalcy that awakened in JR's consciousness the drive to uncover other pockets of dysfunction. From age 12, JR worked in a weekend street market, assisting elderly salespeople. This experience made him comfortable with generations that were far removed from his own while he learned the values of dependability, reliability, and enterprise. His high school years were marked by multiple arrests for juvenile infractions. The final encounter came at 16, when, for reasons undisclosed, JR was expelled from school. As his friends became more entangled with the law, JR decided to find an alternate path. He moved to Paris to live with a cousin and took to the streets as a graffiti artist. It was through his graffiti and the tags that he attached to those of his friends that JR "learned that graffiti is as much a conceptual act as it is a display of color and line" (JR's website, *Portraits of a Generation*). He was already thinking of effect as much as he was of form and content. Fast forward into his future as the youngest recipient of the TED Prize in 2010, and we find another admission: that graffiti taught JR that the results were not as important as the action itself (JR's website). Through his singular act of rebellion, of claiming public spaces with his graffiti art, JR staked his presence while declaring that social change was a two way enterprise: his voice could be heard only if others were open to listening.

While graffiti may have provided an avenue, it all changed in 2000 when, at 17, JR found an old Samsung ECX1 point-and-shoot camera on the Paris metro. "We don't really see ourselves until someone outside ... usually not from here — reflects us back to ourselves," JR noted (JR's website). With this insight becoming embedded in his practice, JR's art + activism came into being. At once, he was an artivist (an artist/activist that reawakens people's social consciousness and viewing habits) and a photograffeur (Kennedy, 2010, p. 2), (neither a photographer nor a graffiti artist exclusively, but both at once); both a conceptual and practical artist, creating art that changed the way in which people viewed each other. The street became a forum for global diplomacy and a space for citizen intervention and social change (Alonzo, 2013, p. 1). The separation between artist and subject was nullified and each became an aspect of the other. Art-making became possible in a forum that was fluid, discursive, free of ego, and therefore capable of surprising innovation and social change.

> What matters is not so much the photo itself than the impact of the action of taking a photo, the effect produced on those who look. JR (JR's website)

From the early stages of his art-making, JR engaged in participatory art projects where an entire community was recruited to use art as a way of forming mutual bonds of understanding and cooperation. In his projects, JR follows the protocols of **PAR**. This methodology became popularized with Paolo Freire's work in the 1950s and 1960s, specifically, his belief in conscientization that emerged from his work with illiteracy in Northeastern Brazil. Freire noted that even in socially oppressive conditions, human beings had the right, desire, and ability to know their reality. "Authentic education," Freire noted, "is not carried on by 'A' for 'B' or by 'A' about 'B', but rather by 'A' with 'B' mediated by the world — a world which imposes and challenges both parties, giving rise to views or opinions about it" (Paolo Freire quoted in Ada and Beutel, 1993, p. 42). Conscientization led to the naming of this world, "to say the right word is to change the world" (Ada and Beutel, 1993, p. 4) and to the authentic articulation of a tangible problem that was real and pressing. Instead of addressing hypothetical and academic situations, Freire's methodology focused on fundamental, systemic, deep-rooted problems that could only be addressed by the collaborative knowledge-base and spirit of the entire community. Freire viewed PAR as emancipatory — aimed at "helping an oppressed group identify and act on social policies" — and in doing this, he brought attention to "generative themes," or issues "that the community agreed had highest priority" and seemed to occur with seeming regularity (Kemmis, 1982, pp. 9–11).

Widely used in business, education, social, government, and other sectors, the defining qualities of PAR are

- A specific, problematic situation emerges from the lived experiences of the community and the research question is articulated, defined, analyzed, and solved by practitioners and community members both collaboratively and cooperatively.
- An egalitarian system of problem solving is put in place, leading to the establishment of a leadership model that is democratic and less hierarchy driven.
- The locus of control is shifted from practitioner to the subject of the research itself — the inquiry is "done *by* or *with* but never *to* or *on*" the community in question (Kemmis, 1982, pp. 9–11). The researcher and community work as co-facilitators and co-educators to produce critical knowledge that could conceivably lead to social transformation.

- Dialog is a central concept of PAR as it is through relationship building, trust, empathy, and mutual respect that knowledge is generated, gathered, and established. The research question and solutions emerge from this space of good will.
- The format of this social space is openly structured, discursive, fluid, and evolving on its own terms. It is public and participatory and a place of perpetual innovation all at the same time (English, 2010, pp. 1–26).
- Reflection or active contemplation of the outcomes leads to the production of further, nuanced solutions that are meaningful. Thus, a solution to a particular problem is not fixed in time. After its resolution, new questions are seen to arise that need the dedicated attention of the community.[1]

In JR's work, the protocols of PAR are put to full use. A community issue is identified; solutions are jointly studied and enacted; art pieces are produced that become the conjoint work of community and artist; and ongoing reflection on outcomes becomes the focal point that leads the social conversation to another, more relevant place. In the *Portraits of a Generation* series, for example, the working class and itinerant population of Les Bosquets is drawn into direct interrelationship with the educated, upper crust of Parisian society through the placement of provocative portraiture. Systemic lapses in society's reach to all citizens becomes the focus of JR's inquiry and the theme continues in the ongoing discussions between the two sections of Parisian society. JR's photographs of "men playing bad boys" (*JR*, 2015. p. 52) challenged the political name-calling in which Parisian leaders were engaged. "Political leaders from all sides — who had failed to make things better — were on air everyday, juggling buzzwords: prevention, repression, integration, immigration, youth, assimilation, education, citizenship, respect, language, generation, soccer. They discussed the symptoms of this sudden fever without looking at the causes behind it" (p. 52). JR noted that when political leadership failed, it remained to the citizenry to discuss and reflect upon social inequities. These active discussions forced the "bobo" of Paris (bourgeois bohemian) (p. 52) to seek an understanding of the larger social phenomena

---

[1]*Note*: This section relies in great part on the consolidated reading of the following texts: Brown and Tandon, (1983); Dickson and Green, (2001); Fals Borda (2002); Kelly et al. (2004); and Tisdale (2003).

that would determine whether Les Bosquets was "France's future or a threat to national identity" (p. 52).

In the *Face2Face* series, JR's placement of Arab, Christian, and Jewish faces provoked conversation, discussion, and reflection. "Passersby were invited to guess who was the Israeli and who was the Palestinian – often they could not tell them apart. By participating, everyone was showing support to a two-state solution in which Israel and Palestine could live peacefully within safe and internationally recognized borders," JR noted (p. 74). In JR's triptych, Sheik Aziz is cast face to face with Brother Jack and Reb Eliyahu and the oversized poster is pasted on the Separation Wall on the Israeli side as well as the Palestinian side. JR noted: "The project showed that what we call 'possible' can change; this artistic action, which experts had thought impossible, proved that limits can move" (p. 74).

In *Women Are Heroes*, the elements of PAR are shown to continue in the ongoing reflective practices that are engineered by the women in the community. Rosiete Marinho of the Morro da Providencia favela in Rio de Janeiro, Brazil, reflects: "This (the favela) is my home. I love this place with all my heart, and that love is what drives me to do things to make it better here ... I'm the mother of two children and I have two granddaughters. My house is called the 'Widow's house' because my mother, aunt, my daughter and I are all widows. But life goes on. Women are the role models here ... What I'd really like is for the kids here to have the same kind of childhood I had, for them to have the respect I had for the elderly and the wisdom I had not to get into drugs. It's so easy to get into drugs nowadays that kids think it's normal. They have no chance of seeing life from the other side, from the side of society that has rejected them but where they might find a place for themselves tomorrow ... that dignity is what we need for the children today" (p. 102). The overarching themes of educating the future generation, of protecting youth from drugs and violence, of having all segments of society gain access to meaningful jobs and lives – becomes the focus of communal discussions.

What is emphasized in JR's many projects is the potential that is inherent in all community members. Subjects are not viewed as victim or aggressor; rather, the similarities among people divided by ideology is shown to be striking enough to begin a conversation on how we may come together as a socially viable force. "My artistic projects always revolve around people's personal stories and the place where they live. My artistic practice is infiltrating," JR comments (JR's website).

Portraits of a Generation (2004–2006), JR's first social action project, began surreptitiously by showcasing the youth of Les Bosquets (a working-class suburb of Paris) in the more exclusive parts of the city. In November 2005, Paris went up in flames when two African youths were electrocuted in a power station while hiding from the police. In JR's portrait gallery, the youth maintain their menacing gaze with their aggressive body language – stereotypes that are perpetuated by the media. The photo of Ladj Ly and others, taken with a 28 mm fish eye lens, is displayed in very large format on the walls of the bourgeois neighborhoods of Paris, evoking the dramatic portraits of the Renaissance artists Van Dyke and Rembrandt. JR's subject uses a camera, instead of a gun, thereby highlighting the tongue-in-cheek aspect of an otherwise volatile situation. JR continues to ask the community to raise provocative questions to which there appear to be limited answers: "Who are (these ruffians)? Model students or gangsters? ... What do they dream of? What are their nightmares? Are we to inspire them or punish them? ... Above all, are we to shut our doors or open our arms?" (JR's website). This series, subsequently used to wrap City Hall in Paris in the tradition of Christo, captures a complex social phenomenon that can neither be dismissed nor addressed with "clever headlines" (JR's website). In this case as in subsequent ones, JR raises the question with his community of choice, frames the issue as a coparticipant of the project, provides perspective and scale, and then leaves the resolution open for discussion and dialog. JR's *Portrait of a Generation* series is a pervasive form of change making from the ground up where broad spectrums of society are involved to reflect on systemic inequities. "To change the way you see things is already to change things themselves," he notes (JR's website).

In 2005, JR traveled to the Middle East to understand the essential sources of conflict between the Israelis and the Palestinians. While doing his research in the two communities and harnessing the wisdom of ordinary people, JR noted: "After a week, we had the exact same conclusion − these people look the same, they speak almost the same language, like twin brothers raised in different families ... A farmer, a taxi driver, a teacher, has his twin brother in front of him. And he is endlessly fighting with him ... We must put them face to face. They will realize" (JR's website).

In the *Face 2 Face* series (2007), portraits of Palestinians and Israelis who have similar jobs are pitted side to side and face to face. Very large photographs of cooks and tailors and teachers and taxi drivers − all making funny faces and showing their lighter side − are juxtaposed on the West Bank and the segregation wall in the Palestinian side of Bethlehem. In JR's work, ideology is shown to demonstrate division but humanism is used to display unification; through the prism of humanness, controversial subjects and volatile divides are bridged. Commenting on the *Face 2 Face* project, a rabbi writes: "The Torah's message is that every human being is created in the image of God. That is why it is important to respect the person in front of you" (JR's website). JR adds, "Everywhere I try to break down clichés. It's about breaking down barriers. With humor, there is life" (JR's website).

In the *Women Are Heroes* (2008–2010) series, JR's mission is to highlight the dignity and independent mindset of women everywhere, especially as they endure crimes of indiscriminate proportion. In his site-specific research, JR listened to the stories of women in the favelas of Rio de Janeiro and chose to capture their faces as they relived their unique narratives. These were pasted not only in the streets and walls of their villages and favelas but also in London, Paris, New York, and other major cities of the world, as a testament of the power, strength, and dignity of women everywhere.

In Rio, JR traveled to the Favela Morro da Providencia, where he heard that three young men had been arrested by the police for minor infractions. The favela was deemed so violent that neither police nor ambulance would venture inside. JR created trust with drug traffickers and the favela dwellers, alike, and found an entrance into the community. He discovered that in an act of apathy, the police had handed over the young boys to the enemy gang, who had hacked them into pieces and shipped them in body bags to their families. The grandmother of one victim,

Benedita, was used as the poster photo on the main stairway of the favela, looking reflectively on the goings-on of a community. Images of women's eyes were pasted on the houses in which they lived, facing the city center of Rio. JR left the interpretation, analysis, and ongoing conversation to be carried on *by* the community and in the interest *of* the community. In Rio as in Kibera, Kenya, social engagement among warring factions thus became a catalyst for a much larger social conversation. Portraits in public spaces were used as a means of protest, propaganda, and a provocation for social action. The street became a gallery for urban intervention while also serving as spaces of beauty, vulnerability, and the enactment of social justice. "He's putting a human face on some of the most critical issues while redefining how we view, make and display art," noted Amy Novogratz, TED Prize director, at the presentation of JR's TED Award in 2010 (http://www.ted.com/talks/jr_one_year_of_turning_the_world_inside_out.html).

How

JR works with a 28 mm lens which captures every wrinkle of a person's face. To get an image of the subject, the photographer must be 10 inches away, as JR notes, he can literally "smell the breath" of his subject (JR's website). An ambience of trust and open communication must be developed in order to achieve his goals. In the *Inside/Out* project, for example, JR's subjects take photographs of themselves, which are printed by JR on large-scale paper. With a squeegee, a bucket, and glue (that JR teaches folks how to make), subjects then launch a guerrilla campaign of pasting the photos in highly visible public spaces. There is no credit given to JR, no sponsorship, no logos or branding; this is simply JR serving as a catalyst to change the world.

Inside Out (since 2011) began with JR being the youngest person to receive the TED Award in 2010. As part of this experiment, JR invited people worldwide to collaborate in a large-scale participatory project in which everyone used b&w photographic portraits to discover, reveal, and share their stories. The digitally uploaded images, which come with a statement, are made into posters by JR and then sent back to the project's cocreators for exhibition in their own communities. The photos are free and making glue is inexpensive. Through this project, JR demonstrates "that messages of personal identity … can be transformed into pieces of artistic work" (JR's website).

In Tunisia, in March 2011, six photographers scoured the country to identify 100 Tunisians who represented the broad swath of Tunisian diversity – young and old, rich and poor, intellectual and farmer. Their faces were pasted where pictures of the former dictator, Zine-el-Abidine Ben Ali, long stood. Both confusing and intriguing to Tunisians, JR provided enough room for dissent as communal discussions ensued. Foreseeing heated discussions, he chose to leave Tunisia so that the conversation could continue without him. "For the first large street exhibition of the Arab world, the posting promised to be surprising and the confrontation with art not always simple," he noted, "nobody suspects the forces that are hidden behind art" (JR's website). "'Looking out from the inside – rather than outside in' – What a fascinating concept. From a humanistic lens, this quote impacted me because it allowed me to understand how we can, as Kaan Turnali states, open our nerve endings, so to speak, and increase our awareness in 'a state of design mindfulness' … We cannot accomplish this from the office behind a desk, or behind closed doors. We must be right in the trenches, working, observing, and suffering side by side … within their authentic circles and under realistic conditions. Only then can we have a chance to live the experience rather than experiencing it in a distant light," JR said in his TED talk. (http://www.ted.com/talks/jr_one_year_of_turning_the_world_inside_out.html)

In JR's terms, art can, indeed, amplify the capacity for self-knowledge, empathy, imagination, and social creativity, and leverage the forces of transformational change from the inside out. "With a bullet, you hit one man; with a photo, you can hit a hundred of them" (Thompson, 2015, p. 32).

In Conclusion

JR's work offers multivocal perspectives on social/cultural/political issues and runs counter to the one-dimensional view of the world that is disseminated through mainstream media. Through his work, JR challenges the media to look at immigration, crime, poverty, and other issues with alternative perspectives. JR's art is confrontational, unsettling common beliefs about social limitations through dialogue. He asks people to think about their representation, while revealing the politics of looking and showing. His activist frame of looking serves to provoke questions but not necessarily provide answers. JR also perpetuates an ongoing relationship with his larger audience through updates on social media; currently his Instagram account has close to a million followers who seek updates on his recurring projects.

I felt pulled to JR's work because of the raw emotional energy that he invests in his artistic practices in order to lift an entire community with intentionality. At the opening of his exhibition in Cincinnati in September 2013, JR described in great detail the large scale, photographic eyes that he had printed on vinyl that Kenyans were then using as roof protectors and sealants from rain. This unique functionality of art moved me deeply, as I grew up in India and saw first-hand how poverty affects human spirit but not entrepreneurship and potential. The slum-dwellers of Kibera were proud of their piece of JR and displayed it on their roof-tops for all to witness! As well, the animated, humanized, and fully aware portraits that were being photographed by JR seemed to go free of the scars of inequity and injustice. This limitless optimism in the human condition gave me hope that seemed to go beyond the confines of reason!

Acknowledgments

Unqualified thanks go out to:

> My endearing and enthusiastic editors, Dr. Susan Erenrich and Dr. Jon Wergin who deserve much of the credit for this chapter being written. Without their active engagement with my work, I may have floundered.

> JR, who served as a strong beacon of light in an otherwise challenging world. His work gave me hope and a sense of unending possibilities. I was especially touched with the reality of most JR portraits focusing on the strength of those being photographed; their limitations were hidden by the force of their character.

> JR's office in Paris, and especially Marc Azoulay, for helping me with logistics.

> At the Contemporary Art Center in Cincinnati, Pedro H. Alonzo (guest curator), Steven Matijcio, and Jaime L. M. Thompson who provided exposure and insight into JR's work − for which I am most grateful.

> The Union Institute & University, my workplace for almost three decades, and especially Dr. Arlene Sacks − whose constant encouragement compelled me to take measured risks in my work.

> To Shekhar, Priyanka, Arnav, and Shaheel − who provide me with the architecture of belonging. Without your constant presence in my life, none of this makes sense.

References

Alonzo, P. H. (September 21, 2013−February 2, 2014). The Contemporary Art Center, Cincinnati. Exhibition Notes on JR.

Brown, L. D., & Tandon, R. (1983). Ideology and political inquiry: Action research and participatory research. *The Journal of Applied Behavioral Science*, *19*(3), 277−294.

Dickson, G., & Green, K. (2001). The external researcher in participatory action research. *Educational Action Research*, *9*(2), 243−260.

English, D. (2010). *How to see a work of art in total darkness*. Cambridge, MA: MIT Press.

Fals Borda, O. (2002). Participatory (action) research in social theory: Origins and challenges. In: P. Reason & H. Bradbury (Eds.), *Handbook of action research: Participative inquiry and practice* (pp. 27–37). Thousand Oaks, CA: Sage.

JR. (2015). *JR: Can art change the world?* London: Phaidon.

Kelly, J. G., Azelton, S., Lardon, C., Mock, L. O., Tandon, D., & Thomas, M. (2004). On community leadership: Stories about collaboration in action research. *American Journal of Community Psychology, 33*, 205–216.

Kemmis, S., & McTaggart, R. et al. (1982) *The action research planner*. 2nd ed. Waurn Ponds Vic, Australia: Deakin University.

Kennedy, R. (2010). Award to artist who gives slums a human face. The New York Times, October 19, Section C-1, p. 2.

Khatchadourian, R. (2011). In the picture. The New Yorker, November, pp. 50–56.

Tisdale, K. (2003). Being vulnerable: Being ethical with/in research. In K. deMarrais & S. Lapan (Eds.), *Foundations for research: Methods of inquiry in education and social sciences* (pp. 13–30). Mahwah, NJ: Lawrence Erlbaum.

Thompson, N. (2015). If a smile is a weapon: The art of JR. In *JR: Can art change the world?* (pp. 30–41). London: Phaidon.

List of Resources

Ada, A. F., & Beutel, C. (1993). *Participatory research as a dialogue for social action*. San Francisco, CA: Chrysalis.

Bartunek, J., & Louis, M. R. (1996). *Insider/outsider team research*. Thousand Oaks, CA: Sage.

Bray, J. et al. (2000). *Collaborative inquiry in practice: Action, reflection, and making meaning*. Thousand Oaks, CA: Sage.

Freire, P. (1982). *The pedagogy of the oppressed*. New York, NY: Herder & Herder.

Jason, L. et al. (Eds.). (2003). *Participatory community research: Theories and methods in action*. Washington, DC: American Psychological Association.

JR's website: http://www.jr-art.net/jr

Local News: http://www.citybeat.com/cincinnati/article-28632-street_artist_jr_visits_the_cac_for_his_first_us_show.html.   http://wvxu.org/post/street-artist-jr-contemporary-arts-center

Press articles from JR's website: http://www.jr-art.net/sites/default/files/downloads/JR-REVUE-DE-PRESSE.pdf

From L'Express: http://www.lexpress.fr/culture/photographie/jr-s-affiche-a-paris_474525.html

From Beaux Arts: http://lezartsurbains.blogspot.com/2010/12/jr-dans-beaux-arts-magazine-janvier.html

From GQ: http://www.gqmagazine.fr/pop-culture/cinema/articles/jr-une-experience-auditive/6705

TED Talks: http://www.youtube.com/watch?v=0PAy1zBtTbw. http://www.ted.com/talks/jr_one_year_of_turning_the_world_inside_out.html

Blog posts: http://m2jc2010.wordpress.com/enquetes-fevrier-2011/le-graffiti-a-la-lumiere-des-galeries/au-dela-du-graffiti-rencontre-avec-jr-colleur-daffiches-engage/. http://saracornett.blogspot.com/2011/09/jr-photo-graffeur.html

TV news: http://www.youtube.com/watch?v=J86Ri8v28y0

From the World Policy Institute Website: http://www.worldpolicy.org/blog/2010/10/21/street-artist-jrs-empowering-art

From Le Figaro: http://www.lefigaro.fr/culture/2012/01/10/03004-20120110ARTFIG00740-jr-fait-salle-comble-au-centre-pompidou.php. http://www.lefigaro.fr/lefigaromagazine/2011/01/15/01006-20110115ARTFIG00680-jr-art-la-loi.php

From Le Figaro Madame: http://madame.lefigaro.fr/art-de-vivre/laureat-ted-prize-2011-171211-203971

From the *New York Times*: http://www.nytimes.com/2011/02/27/magazine/27Photograffeur-t.html?pagewanted=all&_r=0

From Environmental Graffiti: http://www.environmentalgraffiti.com/beaten-track/news-women-are-heroes-teds-winner-prize-2011-jr-screens

8

Peter Young: The Filmmaker as *Agent Provocateur*

Margot Edwards and Ralph Bathurst

> That's the beauty of making a film: What makes it powerful is that you condense three years [of filming] into 85 minutes and you put one dynamic and energy next to another. That is how you end up with a very powerful piece of work. As a director that is where I find the greatest challenge and reward … to convey a story that is truthful, dynamic and exciting for the audience so that everyone goes away and feels satisfied and that they have been represented well.
>
> Peter Young (Interview, 2016)

Introduction

Our opening quote is taken from our interview with artist and filmmaker Peter Young. His film is a documentary, *The Art of Recovery* (Young, 2015), set in the aftermath of a deadly earthquake that occurred in Christchurch, New Zealand, in February 2011, and illustrates the struggle between grassroots citizens and government organizations as they battle to determine how the city should be rebuilt. Telling a story of residents taking control of their devastated city through artistic interventions, Young's documentary exemplifies the impact of grassroots leadership utilizing the arts to fight for social change.

127

Having watched Young's documentary, we were compelled to explore the motivations behind his artworks and we arranged an interview with him. Our chapter focuses firstly on Young's career and his leading role in bringing his documentaries to completion. The second part of our chapter defines Young as a grassroots leader, describing his role in leading and his focus on social issues in settings that range from local to global communities. The final section analyses the key themes in *The Art of Recovery*. In this documentary Young shines his spotlight on the artists who, in collaboration with the grassroots organization, Gap Filler, fight for their rights to redesign the post-quake city. Young has given us permission to quote directly from the transcript of his documentary and we highlight the key themes including the value of collaboration, building connections, the acceptance of transition, and the importance of experimentation in the process of working for social change.

Peter Young — An Interview with the Artist

Our *agent provocateur*, Peter Young is a self-confessed photographer and story teller. Movies are his preferred format and he uses this process to capture ordinary people doing everyday things to tell extraordinary and compelling stories. Young favors projects that highlight injustices — he is motivated by social change and his films provide a forum for participants' voices and provide avenues for reflective thinking on leadership roles and democratic processes.

His stories are not comforting. His intention is not primarily to entertain, but rather to provoke and stir, to illustrate injustice and provide a platform for reflective thinking about important issues that could otherwise remain buried and forgotten.

Peter Young learned his craft by being apprenticed to other movie makers. He was their cameraman and he followed *their* instructions. He confessed that there is certain security about having other people take the responsibility for creating movies, but there came a time in his life when he wanted to tell the stories that energized *him*; that he knew were of importance to the characters in his movies, as well as those of us watching the finished product.

Probably this shift from turning up to shoot, to creating an important narrative came with an invitation to make a movie in one of the most inhospitable places on the planet: The Ross Sea, a deep water bay in the Southern Antarctic Ocean, and quite possibly the one place on Earth where there are still no effects of human habitation. Young had spent time, some years earlier, laboring as a dishwasher in the Antarctic and developed a love for the place, in spite of its being inhospitable. He had finished studying directing at TVNZ's Natural History Unit in Dunedin, New Zealand, and in 2011 when he received the invitation to return and make a film about Antarctic wildlife, he considered that it was an opportunity too good to pass up. He felt he was ready at this time of his life and career journey to take on the challenge of making a feature film.

The *Last Ocean* was released in 2012 and won numerous awards on the international film festival circuit in 2013. More than just a wildlife movie, *Last Ocean* tells a compelling story of humanity's insatiable appetite for fish. The official web site reports:

> Californian ecologist David Ainley has been traveling to the Ross Sea to study this unique ecosystem for more than thirty years. He has written scientific papers describing it as a "living laboratory." Largely untouched by humans, it is one of the last places where the delicate balance of nature prevails. But an international fishing fleet has recently found its way to the Ross Sea. It is targeting Antarctic toothfish, sold as Chilean Sea Bass in upmarket restaurants around the world.
>
> (Young, 2013)

And this is the core of the documentary's story: it is another account of human greed where financially endowed corporations seek to enhance their return for a limited number of shareholders at the expense, ultimately, of the rest of humanity. With the pillaging of the Ross Sea comes the end of its delicate ecosystem and any hint of sustainable fishing. The Antarctic is surrounded by a pristine ocean; it is the "last" ocean not to be exploited by resource-hungry fishing conglomerates. Young felt strongly motivated to join with other people who were fighting to bring attention to this story and his actions on this film were the first time he had become part of a grassroots action team that fought large conglomerates.

Last Ocean is a movie of global significance and Peter Young took considerable risks by investing his time and energy into the development of the story without any definite idea about how the project would unfold, where he would receive funding, or how the final product would come to fruition and be reviewed. Its success on the international stage was reward for his efforts, and vindication of his provocative story.

During this period of working on *Last Ocean*, another community project was gestating in Young's consciousness. He was a long-time resident of Christchurch and in 2010 and 2011 that city experienced devastation through a series of earthquakes.

Peter Young started collecting images of the recovery process. He had a hunch that there was a story to tell but he was not clear about the orientation of the narrative. Initially, he was unable to secure financial support but was driven by the need to tell the story, demonstrating a grassroots response to a compelling need. Through perseverance, he eventually received funding from several agencies and was able to complete the work, releasing *The Art of Recovery* in 2015. The documentary is about the people of the city who took control of the wasteland and through their art gave traumatized residents places to connect, play, and express themselves. Our chapter now moves to analyze Young's artful projects on behalf of grassroots leadership and social change.

Young's Grassroots Leadership

If we analyze Young's artful actions, in producing *The Last Ocean* and *The Art of Recovery* documentaries, against Freire's (1970/1994) seminal conceptualization of grassroots philosophy, the fit is clear. Grassroots leadership involves groups of people taking collective actions, joined together by a common cause and a strong desire for change.

Paulo Freire (1970/1994) lays the foundations of grassroots philosophy, the complexities behind cooperative action, as he argued that humans, facing certain obstacles in their personal and social lives, make decisions about how to tackle those "limit situations" (p. 31) and, if they decide they can overcome the barriers, they can then devote themselves to social change using action and reflection. The key aspect to Freire's philosophy is the divide between the people in power – the dominant, and those who are at the bottom of the power hierarchy – the oppressed – who are denied or curbed from overcoming limit situations. The limit situations (also described as barriers or goals) are typically related to big issues such as "collective consumption, cultural identity, and political self-management" (Castells, 2005, p. 328); they are the drivers for grassroots action. Freire (1996) believed that "the persons who have understood [the limit situations] seek to act: they are challenged and feel themselves challenged, to solve these problems of the society in which they live, in the best possible manner, and in an atmosphere of hope and confidence" (p. 205).

Thus, grassroots leadership is founded on the identification of the barriers, the *cause* itself, and the perception of a hopeful outcome in the belief that changes are possible. In addition, Addy (2002) highlighted the importance of dialogic reflection in the strategic change process associated with grassroots projects:

> We, as humans, have the means to critically objectify the world and our experiences within it. By engaging in processes of reflection and analysis, we can gain understanding and transform that understanding into strategies for change. Therefore, this dialogue process is revolutionary in its inherent call to action.
>
> (Addy, 2002, p. 196)

An exploration of Freirean grassroots social movements provides evidence that the leadership practices that emerge are commonly centered on issues of justice and depend heavily on dialogic processes that enable community groups, and those who align with their collective dreams, to unite around a common desire to take action. Extending beyond this collective agenda, there is also the recognition that individual strategies are worth pursuing, including raising awareness so that others may become involved, enabling them to accept greater responsibilities, and enhance wider understandings.

The promotion of issues is a key dimension of grassroots movements. Castells (2005) highlights the importance of alternative forms of media that engage in purposive, horizontal communication. One such form of communication is the documentary movie, a recognized art form originally described as "the creative treatment of actuality" by Grierson (1933, p. 8) and this practice is now seen to be part of a systematic, staged, and collaborative process (Kerrigan & McIntyre, 2010) involving discussion, information sharing, and reasoning. We therefore argue that Young is an artist who uses his skills to promote sensitive issues and bucks the media trend to present stories from "the elite perspective" (Addy, 2002, p. 196), representing instead the voices of the disenfranchised and marginalized. He focuses uniquely on the oppressed and in doing so, challenges his audiences to think more deeply about issues of ethics and justice. We argue that Young uses his art form to identify limit situations, question the dominant status quo beliefs, and provide opportunities for greater dialogue about the chosen issues in the public realm. If we analyze Young's actions through a Freirean lens, in *Last Ocean*, we could name the limit situation, as sustainability. Of more significance, though, is the limit situation in *The Art of Recovery*: the right to join the democratic process.

Young also weaves an element of hope into his stories; as viewers we leave the theater believing our habits can change, that a better outcome is a real possibility, and we are spurred to change our actions. This hopeful element aligns strongly with grassroots philosophy (Ekins, 1992). In this way, Young's documentary enables ideas to spread to other applicable environments (Mars, 2009) and aligns with recognized activist strategies (Ricketts, 2012). Thus, he provides an example of artistic activism, a concept that has previously been linked to grassroots leadership, and although we have not interviewed audience members, others have found evidence that post-film discussions can provide "theoretically meaningful independent determination of political attitude change" (Lenart & McGraw, 1989, p. 710). Other evidence of the impact of artistic works on community members attitudes are found in documentary (Whiteman, 2004), photography (Gawthrop, 1993), and installation art. For example, Bathurst and Edwards (2012) explored the role of artist Tyree Guyton in social change in Detroit's Heidelberg St neighborhood. Guyton's colorful installations helped his oppressed community recognize the problems they faced and served to communicate their desperate socioeconomic issues to a wider audience. Evidence of the impact of Guyton's art is provided by one teacher who reported that her students were able to "establish connections between the project and local politics" (Kinloch, 2009, p. 169) as a direct result of their encounter with the installations. Bathurst and Edwards (2012) claim that the artists, as leaders, ask, "where are we going and what are our needs?" (p. 69), questions that resonate with Freire's (1970/1994) belief that the dialogic process needs some form of provocation and "the response to that challenge is the action of dialogical Subjects upon reality in order to transform it" (p. 149).

Young's documentaries influence his subjects as they reflect on their stories and what and how to tell them, and his audiences as they view his reconstructed scenes and later as they reflect on the issues at hand. When we analyze Young's artistic endeavors in light of Ladkin's (2010) definition of leadership "as a moment of social relations" that involves "collective mobilisation towards an explicit or implicitly determined purpose" (p. 28), it is clear that the elements of purpose and context take precedent over the follower—leader dichotomy. Purpose and context are key elements in grassroots leadership, as individuals and groups make a commitment to overcoming the "limit situation" by engaging in "limit acts" (Freire, 1996, p. 80). Freire argues that the acts are best signified by their desire to mobilize and "burst through the barrier in question" (p. 206). This group action is reflective of Grint's (1997, p. 17) argument that collective mobilization is the key component of leadership, and not only does Young provide documentaries that stoke barrier-breaking dreams, the subject material of his latest documentary, *The Art of Recovery*, provides an array of examples about how the arts can be used in collective action for social change. Our argument at this time, before the film is widely released, rests with evidence on the roles of documentary in "bolstering the feeling of status of their members and communicating their activities to their supporters" (Tarrow, 1994, p. 127) and with the recognition that films can also influence policy-making processes (Whiteman, 2004).

This chapter now backgrounds the context of the earthquake events and describes the problematic issue of the city's subsequent redesign before exploring Young's Gap Filler movement and his documentary.

The Christchurch Earthquakes

The city of Christchurch, originally built on swampland by Europeans in the early 19th century, was designed to reflect some of the cultural values the immigrants left behind in mother England (Johnson, Lochhead, Shapcott, & Shaw-Brown, 1986). Named "Christchurch" after its English origins, its major buildings were constructed of stone reminiscent of English architecture and yet, during the quake that occurred at 12:51 pm on February 22, 2011, those rigid walls crumbled (Lochhead, 2011) and 185 people lost their lives. Over 80% of the buildings within the Four Avenues which define the central city area have had to be demolished because of their instability. With the closure of the central city and the buildings that housed the commercial sector, businesses quickly re-established themselves in suburbs on more stable ground. Overnight, the city became a wasteland, and as buildings were demolished, vast sections were left covered with gravel. A once vibrant city was turned into a car park. Many of the houses and entire suburbs in the suburban areas beyond the city center were deemed uninhabitable by local and central government authorities.

The devastation of Christchurch cannot be underestimated. The stories of loss, grief, near death experiences, and triumph over adversity have been well canvassed in written accounts and movie documentaries. What has been less understood is the process by which the city has begun to recover its identity and rebuild its infrastructures and, most critically, the barriers that became the focus for many of the inhabitants, and the struggles citizens experienced during the rebuilding became Young's focus.

When we interviewed Young he told us how, as he moved through the city collecting images, he began to conceive the problem – the disconnect between the official Canterbury Earthquake Recovery Authority (CERA) and the populace – and our chapter now moves to examine this issue.

The Art of Recovery – Addressing the Limit Situation

Young's documentary focuses on the democratic right of the citizens of Christchurch to have a place at the decision-making table about how to best rebuild their city.

Young's documentary thus is founded on what could be described as a "limit situation" (Freire, 1996, p. 80), the power struggle over who would take charge of the city rebuild. On the dominant side, the task of making something habitable out of the rubble was firmly claimed by the Government-created decision-making organization CERA with the stated purpose, "To lead and partner with communities to return greater Christchurch to a prosperous and thriving place to work, live and play, as quickly as possible" (CERA, 2016). On the one hand, the government minister in charge of the recovery, the Honourable Gerry Brownlee comments: "The thing I am most pleased about is the level of excitement amongst investors" (Young, 2015). The Minister's primary focus was on bringing investment capital into the city, and to create separate zones for different activities – arts, commerce, and recreation, for instance. The city would be reconstructed around these high profile precincts, "Legacy Projects" as they came to be known (Barnaby, Boidi, & Boles, 2012; Borrowdale, 2016).

On the other side, are the stories Young captures with his camera. As he wandered the devastated city, looking to document material for his project, he discovered groups of people engaged in action projects that opposed established authority. One such group was the grassroots movement Gap Filler — a community of change agents that included graffiti artists, sculptors, and musicians, who participated together to make social changes in the city. Recognizing that their stories were not widely known, Young took on the challenge of engaging with them, making the documentary, and promoting their cause to a wider population.

Young's story focuses on a grassroots leadership and highlights the power of art to provide a mechanism for social change. In his interview, he stated:

> The real story, on the ground, is that the people want the gaps to stay. The gaps are needed so that people have the freedom to decide what to *do* and how to fearlessly enact their vision for their community, and yet, because of their opposition to the grand plans for redevelopment, their voice is ignored.

> (Young, interview, 2016)

The divide between official organizations and the Gap Filler's objectives is profound in Young's documentary. The contrasts are starkly portrayed. Quotes from his documentary include an array of statements in opposition to the CERA philosophy, for example:

> Dr Ryan Reynolds: "Suddenly you feel quite helpless you are facing a total city rebuild more or less and it's up to the government, some architects, some planners and some property developers what the whole city becomes … but I live here and I have no way of inputting into that and a ton of people felt that way."

> (Young, 2015)

> An unidentified woman: "watch out everyone we are going to rebuild your city and we'll let you know when it's ready for you to come and use."

> (Young, 2015)

> Coralie Winn explains, "They're so project-focused. It's all on the outcome. Not the process. Not on the communities. It's like Frankenstein. Make it and Bzzzzt — [but] will it come to life?"

> (Young, 2015)

Young also illustrates the concern of urban architects and designers by highlighting the controversies at play. In his film, architect Reed Kroloff cautions the "legacy project" approach:

> When you have large scale infrastructure improvements, like the whole "Justice" precinct … those can be deadening because they take the energy of the small scale and they replace it with the economy of the large scale. And not properly managed, it can sap a lot of the excitement.
>
> (Young, 2015)

The disconnection between Gap Filler and the "Establishment" is the limiting situation that spurs the Gap Fillers to action. The central government's responsiveness to the locale appears to be lacking, and in our interpretations of the reports and Young's documentary, we think that the divide between the officials and locals reveals how leadership plays out. We argue that Young, through his filmmaking, illustrates the role of artists who generously create positive social change in their city though their purposeful actions. The next section of this chapter describes the grassroots movement, Gap Filler, and their philosophy.

Gap Filler

When Young first ventured back to the post-quake city, he was struck by the range of artistic projects he encountered. He discovered that these social change projects sprouting up on vacant sites were designed and implemented by members of the creative urban regeneration initiative called Gap Filler. The creative activists' key purpose, as explained by Coralie Winn, director and co-founder of the Gap Filler project, is "to bring life, energy, positivity and creativity to vacant sites in Christchurch and to connect everyday people with their city here and now" (Gap Filler, 2016). To achieve their aims the group focuses on motivating and providing guidance to a large number of like-minded community volunteers enacting their leadership values by "fearless implementation – by *doing*" (Gap Filler, 2016), as they collaboratively design, develop, and build their creative projects.

The Gap Filler project exemplifies grassroots leadership because it takes a bottom-up approach, empowering "the average citizen to be able to transform the space of their city and their surroundings at least in some small way" says Ryan in a video description of the project on their web site (Gap Filler, 2016).

Community engagement is at the very core of the group's values and a key driver is the belief that "through developing and investing in gap sites, communities will recognize the value of social/cultural activities and communal endeavor in building social capital and resilience, stimulating economic development and creating connectedness" (Gap Filler, 2016).

This approach mirrors the "leading learnership" model proposed by Laudeman (2012, p. 37) where the group members and volunteers are in effect involved in the development and mobilization of human capabilities as they engage in large-scale dialogues about ideal outcomes. The first step is learning, and this begins with listening to each other, and then working together to produce something new out of those conversations. Laudeman claims that such "community visioning" (2012, p. 53), flips the power structure toward ordinary people and lets the followers set the direction.

Young obtained permission to cast members of the Gap Filler project into his documentary. His scenes capture moments of social leadership with community members stretching themselves to hone their skills, pushing their capabilities as they strategically devise new ways of being together. The process of leading is spread, not by conventional methods, but rather like paint: when a full can is accidently spilt, the ideas spread fluidly, indiscriminately, oozing around obstacles with ease and then becoming tightly cohesive. Thus, the "doing" is shared in an open and deliberate manner; as one project is successful, it is handed off to other people to run and this leaves the team free to generate new projects. In this way, grassroots leaders draw on "existing networks and social movements" but expand these in order to meet the pressing demands of the moment (Mars, 2009, p. 340).

The final section of our chapter provides our analysis of Young's documentary, *The Art of Recovery*, describing four key grassroots leadership themes that emerge from his documentary: collaboration, connection, acceptance of transition, and the importance of experimentation in social change.

The Art of Recovery – Key Action Themes

THE VALUE OF COLLABORATION

The dominant theme in Young's documentary is the collaborative nature of grassroots leadership as community members work together to create artistic interventions (Mars, 2009). His scenes illustrate the process of "gap filling" — how the group activities encourage collaboration and create space for new possibilities of interacting with city spaces. Young shows us how previously disparate groups garner resources from among community volunteers and use that energy for fundraising needed to keep the project viable (Gap Filler, 2016).

For example, Young's documentary highlights the building of the Pallet Pavilion: an entire performance venue built out of discarded blue wooden pallets, etched with the names of over 300 helpers who aided in the construction of the project. The pavilion was always intended to be temporary; crowd-sourced money meant that it was on site for a year longer than originally intended, and the achievement has been nominated for an International Award for Public Art (Gap Filler, 2016). Before it was dismantled, a range of events were held, including music, comedy, and theater productions, and the success of those events was attributed to the people's vested interest (Gap Filler, 2016).

The documentary provides evidence for collective power, as one Gap Filler, Ryan Reynolds, explains: "the process of creating something has an incredibly profound impact on how it is used and its success ... they want to see it succeed because they were involved" (Young, 2015).

BUILDING CONNECTIONS

The Gap Filler proponents argue that collaboration opens up greater possibilities for change and that new ways of interacting in the city spaces are enhanced by connection to previously disparate groups (Gap Filler, 2016). Young's film provides a powerful example of how the Gap Fillers bridged the connection between street artists, who prior to the project, felt alienated from other community groups, including more traditional artists. Young captured the bonding between mainstream and marginalized artists, and the growing realization that they "were on the same side" (Young, interview, 2016).

The creative projects built by these innovative thinkers drew Young to cast them as key characters early in the filmmaking process. He focused on the speed of the artists' reactions: "I just really believed in them and I really liked them for the courage that they had. They just went and did stuff" (Young, interview, 2016). Graffiti artist Wongi Wilson "went out there and just painted walls" (Young, interview, 2016). Prior to the earthquake,

Wilson was on the fringes of society, hounded by the police for "tagging"; but as he forged his craft on the vast expanses of vacant, post-quake walls, he was wall-by-wall remaking the city (Young, interview, 2016). Young's film deliberately casts these fringe dwellers as heroes of the post-quake and in doing so they project "civic courage," a key component of democratic change (Giroux, 2011, p. 8).

ACCEPTANCE OF TRANSITION

Young also draws our attention to the transitory nature of our existence. Young explains: "what the transitional project offered us is that life is transitional: it's like family, friends – they come and they go" (Young, interview, 2016). Early in the film we are introduced to Dr Ryan Reynolds and he surprises us with his statement on how he felt after losing his house:

> I found my insurance paper work, a couple of changes of clothes, couple of tins of food from the pantry, not much, and had my backpack on and was out front of the house and I actually felt on a bit of a high – it's like you don't get much freer than that in a way.

> > (Young, 2015)

Reynold's "high" alerts the audience to alternate possibilities – that a person's spirit can be uplifted and new optimism may emerge, despite losing all worldly possessions.

Young's story of transition is further reinforced with his footage of the collaborative installation titled *186 Empty Chairs* – each representing a lost life. The chairs, painted in white and laid out in rows, were set up in the open air, and subject to the extremes of weather. Artist Peter Majendie was not concerned about the deterioration of the chairs, because he believed that the temporary nature of human life needed acknowledgment. He states, "you can create beautiful things that are temporary. There is a bit of engagement that connects with us – that we are not here forever" (Young, 2015).

Similarly, the coverage of the dismantled pallet pavilion cracks our complacency and challenges our notions of comfort and control. As viewers of the documentary and on reflection of our own temporality, we could not sit in our own living rooms surrounded by our treasured possessions and not be moved by the impermanent nature of the artists' creations.

Young forces us to see that the bureaucrats did not recognize the value in transition – and never took it seriously. "Transitions were just like little things that were happening while the main job was getting done. And actually, the reality is, that the main job was happening on the ground and not up the ivory tower" (Young, interview, 2016).

Transitions were also important for the city's rejuvenation. For example, *The Art of Recovery* places a special significance on small actions in the process of rejuvenation. As the documentary opens we follow Liv Worsop as she bikes around the city, under cover of dark, planting succulents in the rubble to beautify the ruins. She says, "a weed is only a plant that's in the wrong place" (Young, 2015). Although this action might seem to be insignificant, it contributes to the belief that "it is in the countless small moments such as these that leadership is enacted" (Taylor, 2012, p. 165). The role of artists in creating such small moments are featured throughout Young's documentary; for example, he films Café owner Sam telling us that the artists and musicians are like weeds as they are the first to take on early re-colonizing opportunities (Young, 2015). The tenacity of the artists who bravely acted, painting murals, designing garden and performing, helped bring change to the central city and further served to inspire the Gap Fillers to be equally courageous and experiment widely with social projects.

THE IMPORTANCE OF EXPERIMENTS

The Art of Recovery also provides ample evidence of how grassroots leaders effectively deal with adversity. It comes as a relief to see that no solution is flawless and yet the work continues, and when something doesn't work, the Gap Fillers may improvise, or try something new, but they never stop. Even at the documentary's conclusion Coralie Winn, one of the co-founders, laughs at her own stupidity as she reflects on the group's processes and the scene places a spotlight on bravery and stubbornness as key qualities in grassroots leadership.

The experimental nature of the projects is celebrated throughout the film. Young captured the dynamic energy of the dance-o-matt. With the dance halls destroyed, Young focused on strangers grooving together to their choice of music on a public dance arena; the concept was conceived in doubt but Young found that he "loved the idea of people dancing amongst the ruins" (Young, interview, 2016). The dance-o-matt novelty drew crowds and allowed community connections to flourish in ways that were unanticipated.

Young's leading influence is evident in his artful approach as he focused on two serious young rappers as they observed the dance-o-matt, as they suddenly and unexpectedly broke into a smile. The ability to read what's happening and create it within a shot is a particularly beautiful moment in the film and one Young said was lauded at the movie's Christchurch premier (Young, interview, 2016). That scene allowed those from outlying suburbs, who had adopted a more satellite approach by attending to their own pressing local needs, to be energized by the vibrancy they witnessed in the city's center. In turn, the film primes the audience to become involved in future projects and, it could be argued, to move the leadership energy elsewhere (Mars, 2009).

It is possible that viewers will follow the examples of Young's characters as they explored the change options opened up as a result of the earthquake. They might, like Bailey Perryman, design and build a city farm. Young captures Perryman, explaining his actions: "The earthquake really shook me up big time. I realized how ill equipped I was to deal with a disaster like that. My instinct was to plant seeds, sow seeds" (Young, 2015). Wasteland became productive land as he grew crops for local consumption, transforming "victims" into active agents, leading literally from the ground up.

When we watch Young's documentary, the message is clear: everybody has a role to play in leading social change and yet these acts of revivifying the cultural fabric of the City cannot be sheeted back to the work of one individual, and this may account for the successes of the Gap Filler projects. No single person had a vision that galvanized people into action. For, as Keith Grint (1997) argues, in situations that require innovative and courageous decision making, leaders are hamstrung by the organizations within which they work. The need for stability and certainty overrides the desire for bold and creative solutions, because "when the penalty for failure far exceeds the reward for success, the system induces a high level of anxiety that inhibits decision-making and risk-taking" (Grint, 1997, p. 12).

Young's hopeful story promotes a way of overcoming the inhibitions Grint (1997) discusses, and the stifling behaviors frequently associated with top-down leadership (Uhl-Bien, Marion, & McKelvey, 2007). He showcases the struggle of the citizens of Christchurch to "regain their humanity" (Freire, 1996, p. 26), to create innovative and elegant solutions for the issues they face, and provide a solid platform for reflection on the processes involved in grassroots action, about what works, where the energy should be focused and how change might be extended.

Conclusion

Peter Young is an artist who provokes his audience to consider how we can engage in social change. In our interview with Young, his activities as a grassroots leader were evident. He is motivated by visions of a better future, and he engages bravely with projects that address limit situations. His influence is exemplified in his latest project, *The Art of Recovery*, which provides us with powerful clues about how grassroots leadership can help mend the broken city.

Young's artwork allows us to reflect more fully on the place of arts in our society and provides evidence that transitions can be positive and the benefits should not, like that spilt paint, be mopped up, tidied away, and covered over with something bright and shiny. Peter Young and his story of the Gap Filler project have provided us with a powerful reflection on leading change, of human capabilities and limitless possibilities that occur from collective action.

In particular, Young contrasts the divide between official city leader's visions and the Gap Fillers while simultaneously showing us how relationships were forged between disparate groups, the mainstream and marginalized, as a result of artistic activities taking place on the ground. By envisioning what needs to be done, generating the resources, enabling others to act, to engage in the *doing*, and having the courage to try innovative approaches, the grassroots leaders in Young's film exemplify the energetic mobilization espoused by Grint (1997). The future of Christchurch's identity and cultural focuses will be as a result of grassroots leaders taking action in spite of, and instead of, officially sanctioned processes. Grassroots leaders will create *their* city as they collaborate, connect, play with transitional projects, and enjoy artistic experimentation and foster new ways of working and living together.

References

Addy, D. E. (2002). Community dialogue: A tool for social engagement and class awareness. In J. J. Slater, S. M. Fain, & C. S. A. Rossatto (Eds.), *The Freirean legacy: Educating for social justice* (pp. 184–197). New York, NY: Paeter Lang.

Barnaby, B., Boidi, E., & Boles, I. (Eds.). (2012). *Christchurch: The transitional city part iv*. Wellington, NZ: Freerange Press.

Bathurst, R. J., & Edwards, M. F. (2012). Aesthetic leadership: Walking towards economic recovery. In P. Shrivastava & M. Statler (Eds.), *Learning from global financial crisis: Building the future creatively, reliably, and sustainably* (pp. 55−75). Stanford, CA: Stanford University Press.

Borrowdale, L. (2016). Strength to strength. *Kia Ora*, February, pp. 41−46.

Castells, M. (2005). Grassrooting the space of flows. In L. Amoore (Ed.), *The global resistance reader* (pp. 363−370). London: Routledge.

CERA. (2016). Canterbury earthquake recovery authority. Retrieved from http://cera.govt.nz/. Accessed on March 31, 2016.

Ekins, P. (1992). *A new world order: Grassroots movements for global change*. London: Routledge.

Freire, P. (1970/1994). *Pedagogy of hope: Reliving pedagogy of the oppressed* (R. R. Barr, Trans.). New York, NY: Continuum.

Freire, P. (1996). Pedagogy of the oppressed *(M. B. Ramos, Trans.)*. London: Penguin Books.

Gap Filler. (2016). Retrieved from http://www.gapfiller.org.nz/. Accessed on March 2, 2016.

Gawthrop, L. (1993). Images of the common good. *Public Administration Review*, *53*, 508−515.

Giroux, H. A. (2011). *On critical pedagogy*. New York, NY: Continuum.

Grierson, J. (1933). The documentary producer. *Cinema Quarterly*, *2*(1), 7−9.

Grint, K. (1997). *Leadership: Classical, contemporary and critical approaches* (pp. 1−17). Oxford: Oxford University Press.

Johnson, R. D., Lochhead, I., Shapcott, P. M., & Shaw-Brown, D. (1986). *The architectural heritage of Christchurch: Government buildings* (Vol. 5). Christchurch: Christchurch City Council Town Planning Division.

Kerrigan, S., & McIntyre, P. (2010). The 'creative treatment of actuality': Rationalizing and reconceptualizing the notion of creativity for documentary practice. *Journal of Media Practice*, *11*(2), 111−130. doi:10.1386/jmpr.11.2.111_1

Kinloch, V. (2009). Suspicious spatial distinctions: Literacy research with students across schools and community contexts. *Written Communication*, *26*(2), 154−182.

Ladkin, D. (2010). *Rethinking leadership: A new look at old leadership questions*. Cheltenham: Edward Elgar.

Laudeman, G. (2012). Leading learnership: The transformation of leadership via convergence with learning. In J. D. Barbour, G. J. Burgess, L. L. Falkman, & R. M. McManus (Eds.), *Leading in complex worlds* (pp. 37−62). San Francisco, CA: Jossey-Bass.

Lenart, S., & McGraw, K. (1989). America watches "Amerika": Television docudrama and political attitudes. *Journal of Politics*, *51*, 697−712.

Lochhead, I. (2011). Christchurch architecture and the earthquakes of 4 September 2010 and 22 February 2011. *Fabrications*, *20*(1), 120−127. doi:10.1080/10331867.2011.10539674

Mars, M. M. (2009). Student entrepreneurs as agents of organizational change and social transformation: A grassroots leadership perspective. *Journal of Change Management*, 9(3), 339–357. doi:10.1080/14697010903125597

Ricketts, A. (2012). *The activists' handbook: A step-by-step guide to participatory democracy*. London: Zed Books.

Tarrow, S. (1994). *Power in movement: Social movements, collective action and politics*. Cambridge: Cambridge University Press.

Taylor, S. S. (2012). *Leadership craft, leadership art*. New York, NY: Palgrave Macmillan.

Uhl-Bien, M., Marion, R., & McKelvey, B. (2007). Complexity leadership theory: Shifting leadership from the industrial age to the knowledge era. *Leadership Quarterly*, 18(4), 298–318.

Whiteman, D. (2004). Out of the theaters and into the streets: A coalition model of the political impact of documentary film and video. *Political Communication*, 21(1), 51–69.

Young, P. (Writer). (2013). *The last ocean*. Christchurch: Fisheye Films.

Young, P. (Writer & Director). (2015). *The art of recovery*. Christchurch: Fisheye Films.

SECTION III
Grassroots Leadership, Participatory Democracy, and the Role of the Arts in Social Movements in the United States

9

They Were All Leaders: The IWW and Songs for Revolution

Greg Artzner and Terry Leonino

In the early part of the 20th century one labor union established as its goal to organize all the wage-earning workers in the world regardless of skill, nationality, ethnic background, race or gender. Rather than just organizing "craft" unions of workers with specific trade skills, they sought to bring all workers, all laborers who toiled for wages into "one big union." It was known as the Industrial Workers of the World, and its members were called the "Wobblies." The IWW was known as, and remains today, the "singing" union, using music and song effectively to build a strong organization, fighting to abolish the wage system, bring about a better world and secure justice for the working class.

Greg Artzner

In the summer of 2015 in our capacity as singers, musicians, and activists, we participated in a centenary commemoration concert tour in various towns and cities in the northeastern United States. We joined with fellow IWW members, singers, and songwriters, Charlie King and George Mann, along with other Wobblies and union activists in the local areas, in celebrating the life and work of famous IWW martyr Joe Hill, who was murdered by the state of Utah on November 19, 1915. The commemorative concert tours, called "The Joe Hill 100 Road Show," were produced by the IWW all around the country in regional sections, and ours was the portion that took place in venues from Ithaca, NY, to Barre, VT, from Philadelphia to Boston, from New York City, to Baltimore and Washington, DC.

We have come to find out over the years that around the country a surprisingly large number of people don't really know who Joe Hill was. Like abolitionist John Brown, who was immortalized in a well-known folksong, Joe Hill is a figure whose story has largely been consigned to legend and myth. The famous song from the 1930s written by Alfred Hayes and Earl Robinson, "I Dreamed I Saw Joe Hill," sung by Paul Robeson, Joan Baez and many others, is quite often all that people know about him, if that much. Some people are actually surprised to find out that Joe Hill was, in fact, a real person.

Traveling around the country, singing the songs of Joe Hill, along with other IWW songs portraying the struggles and triumphs of working people, we were repeatedly inspired not only by our Fellow Workers on stage, but also by our audiences, most of whom *did* know Joe Hill's story and his songs and sang along with us heartily. The experience motivated us to explore even more deeply the history of our union, and its use of music and the arts. It is a deep and colorful story, and one of the best examples of the successful utilization of song in organizing and fostering solidarity in mass struggle.

With each stop along our tour, after every show, as we traveled to the next, we reflected on our own history, coming from union families and singing these songs in our youth and throughout our four decades as professional musicians. Growing up in the working class in northeastern Ohio, both of us were tied to unions from childhood, with my grandfather, Terry's father, and our siblings all belonging to industrial unions where they worked. When we teamed up in 1973 and began to play music professionally the next year, the first thing we did was to join our musicians union. We had learned at an early age the power of music to promote solidarity, to inspire, to educate, and, as the IWW said many years before, to "fan the flames of discontent" (IWW Songs, 1917, front cover). When we moved to Washington, DC, in 1974, one of the first people we met was Joe Glazer, the late singer and songwriter known as "Labor's Troubadour." Joe had been singing for unions since the early 1950s and was famous across the country for joining workers on picket lines and in union halls, often singing the old IWW songs, including the songs of Joe Hill. We joined with Joe and sang back-up for him in the studio and at numerous union functions over the years until his death in 2006. We recorded an LP of songs of working people entitled *Working My Life Away* on Joe's Collector Records label in 1982. With this background, for us to share the honor of playing the songs of Joe Hill on the 2015 tour was another valued link in the chain of our activist musical lives, and instigated a deeper examination of the preceding links, going back beyond the 100 years since Joe Hill's death.

Joe Hill, the IWW and the Power of Singing Together

So just who was Joe Hill and why were we commemorating him in our concert tours in 2015? Joe Hill was born Joel Emmanuel Hägglund in 1879 in Gävle, Sweden. He was the third child in a family of nine. There was music in the Hägglund home and Joel played the organ, accordion, violin, piano, and also later learned the guitar (Smith, 1969, p. 44). In about 1902, after his father died, Joel and his brother immigrated to the United States. He changed his name to Joe Hillstrom, and ultimately shortened it to "Hill." Joe became an itinerant worker, traveling and working various jobs from New York to Cleveland, and various other places, ultimately arriving on the west coast, where he joined the IWW in 1910 while working the docks in San Pedro, California (Rosemont, 2002, pp. 45, 46). He became well known among his "Fellow Workers" as an organizer and as a cartoonist for IWW publications, but more importantly as a writer of parodies for the union's songbook. His best-known and most widely sung songs were parodies of popular tunes and hymns of the time, *Casey Jones, the Union Scab*, *There Is Power in a Union*, and *The Preacher and the Slave*, otherwise known as *Pie in the Sky*, a well-known phrase he coined which forms part of the last line of the refrain in the song. Joe's songs became the best-loved ones among Wobblies all across the country and his name was known far and wide. Hill was working and living in a Swedish immigrant community in Salt Lake City, Utah, in January of 1914 when an armed robbery occurred there. Two masked men gunned down John Morrison, a former policeman, along with his son in the grocery store they owned and operated. That same night Joe Hill had an argument with a friend over a woman for whose affections they both were vying. Joe's friend pulled a gun and fired, and Joe suffered a gunshot wound in the abdomen, similar to one suffered by one of the armed robbers in the grocery store. After Hill sought medical attention, the doctor who tended to the wound notified the police, thinking Joe might be one of the robbers. Hill was arrested and charged with robbery and murder. The prosecution was swift and unrelenting, painting the famous Wobbly bard as a rabble-rousing miscreant, a subversive member of the IWW. There was little doubt that Joe's active membership and high profile as a songwriter in the IWW was a major factor in the prosecution of the case (Kornbluh, 1964, p. 128). The police described the shooting of Morrison as a "revenge killing," yet Joe Hill had never met him and had no connection to him at all (Adler, 2011, p. 53). Hill refused to name his friend as his assailant, and also refused to name the woman over whom they were arguing. He naively assumed the court was required to prove him guilty, and that it was not his own duty to prove his innocence. But the standard of proof for the jury was low, and on circumstantial evidence and flawed testimony, he was convicted of murder and sentenced to death. Given a choice between hanging and a firing squad, the famous Wobbly songwriter chose the latter (Kornbluh, 1964, pp. 127–131). While in prison awaiting execution, Joe continued to write, including a brilliant parody to the popular song *It's a Long Way to Tipperary* entitled *It's a Long Way Down to the Soupline*. Despite having no access to a musical instrument, he also composed words and music to three of his greatest songs, *The Rebel Girl, Don't Take My Papa Away from Me*, and *Workers of the World, Awaken!* (Adler, 2011, pp. 271–279, 327). Despite a worldwide campaign asserting his innocence, which even involved the Swedish Foreign Minister to the United States, and President Woodrow Wilson's plea for a stay of execution and a thorough reconsideration of the sentence, the authorities of the state of Utah executed Joe Hill on November 19th of the following year (Kornbluh, 1964, p. 130). At his own request, his body was transported to Chicago, cremated, and the ashes divided among 600 small envelopes which were distributed to IWW members through their membership branches in various places around the United States and around the world (Adler, 2011, p. 340). His life may have ended, but as the song intones, he truly became the man who "never died."

The Industrial Workers of the World was founded in 1905 in the city of Chicago, Illinois. From its inception it was revolutionary in nature, aiming to ultimately organize all wage-earning members of the working class worldwide into one big syndicalist union, with an ultimate goal to abolish the entire wage system. Furthermore, their aim was to enlist the industrial workers that had been considered "unorganizable." They sought to bring into the big union the unskilled workers who were unwelcome in Samuel Gompers' skilled crafts amalgamation, the American Federation of Labor (Rosemont, 2002, p. 7). Due to the structure of the AF of L, being a federation of individual "craft" unions for workers only in their specific trades, Wobblies commonly referred to it as the "American Separation of Labor" (Bird, Georgakas, Shaffer, 1985, p. 4). As Vincent St. John described the "One Big Union" in his famous pamphlet, *The IWW: Its History, Structure and Methods*:

> ... In a word, its basic principle makes the IWW a fighting organization. It commits the union to an unceasing struggle against the private ownership and control of industry .... There is but one bargain the IWW will make with the employing class – complete surrender of all control of industry to the organized workers. [1912, revised edition 1919]

> (Rosemont, 2002, pp. 10, 11)

At its founding, the IWW brought together workers, union leaders, and organizers from around the country, including Bill Haywood of the Western Federation of Miners, Eugene Victor Debs of the American Railway Union, Mary Harris "Mother" Jones of the Knights of Labor and the UMW, and Lucy Parsons, labor organizer and widow of famed Haymarket Square martyr Albert Parsons (Kornbluh, 1964, p. 1).

From the beginning, the IWW was the ultimate grassroots organization. Big Bill Haywood, when he addressed the founding convention, said, "We are going down into the gutter to get at the mass of workers and bring them up to a decent plane of living" (Rosemont, 2002, p. 11). And so they did. The union organized ordinary laborers regardless of skill, race, gender, or ethnic background in industries all across the United States and around the world. When any Fellow Worker was asked who was their leader, their standard reply was, "We are *all* leaders!" (Rosemont, 2002, p. 8). The end goal was to bring about a "new world from the ashes of the old" in the words of Wobbly poet and songwriter Ralph Chaplin (IWW Songs, 1917, p. 25). Their means were direct action and the general strike, but those were not the only means (Kornbluh, 1964, p. 35).

The IWW utilized various means of artistic expression broadly and effectively. Their press was, and remains to this day, a vivid example of the creative brilliance of workers at the grass-roots. James Stodder, who penned an essay on Wobbly poet and organizer Covington Hall, wrote:

> ... In the Wobbly press we find poems and polemics by innumerable unknown proletarian authors; freewheeling, humorous, and often savage debate on every aspect of revolutionary values in the broadest sense ... individual styles ranging from hard-boiled prole-talk and lyrical utopianism to surprisingly modernist forms of "insanity" suggesting expressionism or surrealism ...
>
> (Rosemont, 2002, p. 32)

The union utilized visual art, including the art of satirical cartoons, broadly and to great effect, both in their publications and in posters, banners, and other forms of visual propaganda.

Wobbly Songs

And then, there were the songs. The Wobblies used song effectively to help organize and more importantly to foster solidarity and raise morale. Singing was part of every action, whether it was a union rally, meeting, strike, picket line, or just sitting around a campfire with Fellow Workers in a hobo jungle (Rosemont, 2002, pp. 479, 480).

The man considered by many Wobblies to be most responsible for the effective use of song among IWWs was J. H. Walsh. It was Walsh who suggested and advocated for publication of the famous pocket-size songbook chock full of lyrics, mostly parodies, officially titled *IWW Songs*, but better known as "The Little Red Songbook." Members of the rank and file who were poets, songwriters, and lyricists contributed parodies and songs to the book, which has been revised and reprinted many times over the years. One of its most famous contributors, Richard Brazier, explained the first steps in its development:

> The IWW understood the power of song long before J.H. Walsh came to Spokane and IWW had been printing and selling a little brochure that contained several songs and sold for five cents a copy .... The little card brochure was the foundation of the songbook. We had the idea of the song book before J.H. Walsh ever came to Spokane but could never get enough support to put it over

[nationally]. Where J.H. Walsh came in was his strong support of the idea [throughout the union] and the strength he built up by his continual presentation of the idea ... before the membership .... In that sense J.H. Walsh might be called the father of "the Little Red Song Book."

(Rosemont, 2002, p. 55)

The book was an extremely effective means of making the songs available to members of the union and others, being 4 inches by 5½ inches in size, so it easily fit into any Fellow Worker's hip pocket. The lyrics of the songs were set to the melodies of either currently popular songs or well-known folk songs from days of yore. Well-known hymns became vehicles for the songs, too. In 1910, in one of the numerous "free speech" fights, Wobbly "soapboxers," Fellow Workers who delivered IWW recruiting speeches while standing on one or two upturned wooden boxes to whatever crowd had assembled, found themselves in competition with a Salvation Army band. The Salvation Army is a fundamentalist Christian organization that provided assistance to poor, unemployed people in exchange for the unfortunate souls attending sermons and listening to proselytizing speeches. They would dress in quasi-military uniforms and sing well-known hymns loudly, often accompanied by an equally loud small brass band, complete with bass drum. The IWW sarcastically referred to them as the "starvation army." The Salvation Army band and singers would strategically position themselves nearby and drown out the soapboxers. Joe Hill and the other IWW parody writers jumped into action writing new words to the hymns that were most popular with the band. When the band began to play, each Fellow Worker could reach into his or her pocket, take out their copy of the "The Little Red Songbook," and all could sing the new lyrics together loudly.

Famed folksinger, songwriter, raconteur, and long-time member of the IWW, the late Bruce "Utah" Phillips tells the story:

One of the songs for the Spokane Free Speech Fight was composed by Joe Hill ["The Preacher and the Slave"] and was introduced to the streets by Haywire McClintock, a well-known singer very active in the IWW in those parts. Haywire would hide in a doorway with T-Bone Slim. They had a tube and a garbage can lid for percussion and a guitar. A mass of workers would be gathered around the Starvation Amy donut dollies. A man would walk by carrying an umbrella and a briefcase and dressed in a tight suit with a string tie and a bowler hat. He looked just like banker, but functioned like a carney shill. He'd yell, "I've been robbed! I've been robbed! Help, I've been robbed!" Everyone would rush over to him. "What's the matter?" they'd ask. When enough had crowded around, he'd shout, "I've been robbed by the capitalist system!" And then the boys would jump out from the doorway and start singing Joe Hill's song ...

(Bird et al., 1985, p. 28)

Most of the songs in the "*The Little Red Songbook*" were, and are, simple and direct. In order to fulfill their purpose and be successful, they had to be. In the early twentieth century, many union members were recent immigrants from various countries with limited English, both in speaking and understanding. Moreover, the songs were direct expressions of the class struggle in which they were engaged: criticism of the employer class, praise for the union and its tactics, enjoining the workers to organize and engage in direct action. The songs were meant to be straightforward and to be sung in the course of whatever action was being undertaken, whether strike, meeting, march, or rally. Utah Phillips wrote: "Our protest music of today tends to be a little more abstract. It's harder to understand. There's a lot of difference between, 'How many miles must a white dove sail before it can rest in the sand?'[sic] and 'Dump the bosses off your back'" (Bird et al., 1985, p. 25).

Wobbly songs are not maudlin, sentimentally emotional or nostalgic; they are not designed to elicit tears or romantic wistfulness. They are not filled with abstract symbolism or metaphor. They are songs for and by workers, and they have their own work to do. The emotions they are designed to provoke might be indignation and resentment or strength of determination and perhaps to do it through humor. As an ad for the songbook in an IWW pamphlet described them:

... Songs that strip capitalism bare; show the shams of civilization; mock at the masters' morals; scorn the smug respectability of the satisfied class; and drown in one glad burst of passion the profit patriotism of the Plunderbund.

(Rosemont, 2002, p. 477)

Fellow Worker Phillips also commented on how, in fulfilling their mission, the songs were universal in their simplicity and directness:

> … to help people define their problems and to suggest what the solutions might be. A lot of working folks came from other countries and couldn't speak very much English and didn't have a chance to go to school here. If the songs were going to communicate, they had to be simple.
>
> (Bird et al., 1985, p. 25)

The songs were, and remain today, an integral part of the IWW experience. They were sung by everyone, and in nearly every worker's struggle, the free-speech fights and strikes. Many Fellow Workers have commented upon the songs being used to inspire and unify the crowds, such as in the Lawrence, Massachusetts strike of 1912. Mary Heaton Vorse wrote about it in her autobiography *Footnote to Folly*.

> They were always marching and singing. The gray, tired crowds ebbing and flowing perpetually into the mills had waked and opened their mouths to sing, the different nationalities all speaking one language when they sang together …. It was as though a spur of flame had gone through this audience, something stirring and powerful, a feeling which has made the liberation of people possible; something beautiful and strong had swept through the people and welded them together, singing …. The workers sang everywhere: at the picket line, at the soup kitchens, at the relief stations, at the strike meetings. Always there was singing.
>
> (Rosemont, 2002, p. 480)

A young journalist named Louis Adamic, covering an IWW dockworkers strike in San Pedro, California, in 1923, commented on the singing as police rounded up the strikers, and marched into trains that took them off to several different jails:

> While the strike was thus being broken, the Wobblies — rough, strong men; native-born and foreigners — sang their songs. They sang in the prison stockade in San Pedro, on the way to the trains, in the trains, and finally

in jail. "God!" another young newspaperman remarked to me. "One feels like singing with them. They got guts!"

(Rosemont, 2002, p. 481)

Franklin Rosemont, in his book *Joe Hill: The IWW & the Making of a Revolutionary Workingclass Counterculture*, described the function of the songs:

> Singing these songs ... was an *education*: morally, intel-
> lectually, and politically, Singing these songs provoked
> thought, stimulated the imagination, stirred the spirit of
> revolt. Singing these songs was often the first big step in
> the learning process by which deceived and disheartened
> wage-slaves, who had long cowered in ignorance, fear,
> and silence, became clear-thinking, brave and outspoken
> fighters for working class freedom. In short, singing these
> songs was instrumental in making Wobblies.

(Rosemont, 2002, p. 481)

IWW songs also had specific purposes to suit specific needs. While some songs were well-suited for rousing a crowd, and stirring up a rally or meeting, such as "There Is Power in a Union," "The Preacher and the Slave," or "Workers of the World, Awaken," others were meant to tell a story or make Fellow Workers chuckle in contemptuous assent such as "Mister Block" or "The Popular Wobbly." Still others became anthems that remain powerful ritual songs still sung ceremonially by unionists throughout the world such as "Hold the Fort," and "Solidarity Forever." Some songs were meant to be sung together in direct action, on picket lines and marches, while others were sung around campfires among "bindlestiffs," hoboes traveling by freight train to whatever job they might find (Rosemont, 2002, pp. 479, 480).

Enemies and Critics

Over the years, the songs of the IWW have been subjected to criticism ranging from dismissive contempt to outright moralistic condemnation, including disparaging comments from scholars and writers one might have considered to be friendly to the IWW and its goals. Some of these critical remarks might be considered as badges of honor, while others betray a class bias and surprising lack of understanding of the working class and the purpose of the songs. In David Noebel's 1966 book *Rhythm, Riots and Revolution*, published by Christian Crusade in Tulsa, Oklahoma, the author gives two full pages to the "vicious" songs of Joe Hill, condemning him as forebear to the sinister protest songwriters of the 1960s, themselves direct descendants of the communist "conspirators" of the thirties, forties and fifties (Rosemont, 2002, p. 478). Novelist Wallace Stegner, who penned a novel based on the life of Joe Hill, glibly dismissed the Wobbly bard's songs as "crude" (Rosemont, 2002, p. 479). Even playwright Barrie Stavis, who wrote a play about Joe Hill entitled *The Man Who Never Died*, and also compiled Joe Hill's songs into a collection published by Oak Archives in 1960, wrote with condescending disdain about Hill's classic anti-war song *Don't Take My Papa Away from Me*, "It is a poor song, a sentimental song, representative of the poorer taste of the popular song of that day" (Stavis & Harmon, 1960, p. 44).

The Singing Legacy

Despite the troubles the union endured, the IWW did not die and did not fade away. The story of the Wobblies is inspirational and has a lot to teach activists and organizers in any movement today regarding the use of music and other art forms to advance any struggle for progress.

The Joe Hill 100 Road Show brought us poignantly and powerfully face to face with the musical legacy of the Wobbly bard and his union. Everywhere we sang, our audiences sang along enthusiastically, obviously long familiar with the songs, many joining in without benefit of printed lyrics in their hands. In our conversations with audience members during intermissions and after the shows, we found that many were not only long-time union supporters and union members, they were also long-time social activists involved in other progressive causes including the Civil Rights Movement, environmental and peace action groups. Some of our concertgoers remarked on how long they had known and sung these songs, and how they carried the messages and the underlying philosophy expressed in them into other aspects of their lives. They made the connections between the fight for justice for workers in the early twentieth century and the work they themselves were committed to do in the latter years, well into our new century. We were particularly moved to see and to meet many younger people attending the concerts, men and women in their twenties, who clearly made those connections too. Joe Hill and the Wobblies apparently had a broad appeal, rebels, heroes, and heroines inspiring and touching the hearts of concerned and dedicated young activists a hundred years later.

To be sure, in the century since the founding of the IWW there have been other social movements that have utilized song in similar ways to those of the Wobblies. The labor movement learned well from the IWW, even as it organized in different directions and with different social philosophies, with the various industrial unions whose membership of unskilled workers some- times included Wobblies, or former Wobblies, joining the Congress of Industrial Organizations (CIO) and then merging with the American Federation of Labor (AF of L). Many of the songs sung by IWW workers in the early twentieth century are still sung by AFL-CIO union workers in their meetings and ral- lies, and on their picket lines. New singers and songwriters have become "links on the chain," following in the footsteps of Joe Hill and the Wobbly writers. The list is long and illustrious, including writers and singers such as Aunt Molly Jackson, Jim Garland, Florence Reece, and Sarah Ogan Gunning, Woody Guthrie, Pete Seeger and the Almanac Singers, Joe Glazer, Utah Phillips, and contemporary writers Elaine Purkey, Anne Feeney, Charlie King, Si Kahn, Joe Jencks, George Mann, and many more.

The Civil Rights Movement of the 1950s and 1960s used music and mass singing to greater effect than perhaps any other socio-political movement in history. Their use of the parody reached back over a hundred years into the traditional songs sung in fields and churches by their antecedents in the struggle to abolish slavery. Like the IWW, Civil Rights leaders and organi- zers understood the power of singing together, and wrote new words to one hundred year-old-songs to apply to the ongoing struggle to achieve true freedom and equality in human society. The songs they sang in mass meetings and on marches and in demonstrations remain some of the most powerful songs in our history, and rank among the greatest cultural testaments to the indomitable spirit of human beings fighting for justice.

So the question remains: what does the example of the IWW, as well as other social movements that have used song effectively, have to teach us about grassroots leadership and the arts for social change here in the twenty-first century? With new technol- ogy and new musical forms, aren't the old ways and old songs just an antiquated device that is no longer relevant? Our answer is a resounding, "no." Time and again we have heard our dear friend the late, great songwriter, song leader and union supporter Pete Seeger say that if this world was going to be here in a hundred years, and that if we as a human family were going to survive that century, one of the reasons would be that we learned to sing together, to raise awareness, and to unify us to fight against our common enemies which have always been hatred, fear, prejudice, violence, and injustice. We agree. In marches, the use of chants and percussion is and has been an effective means of unified expression of purpose. In rallies and demonstrations, the use of songs written for the purpose of group singing with easily sung chorus refrains is a powerful and active way for everyone's voice to be heard – together. The parody remains an excellent way of getting large groups of people to sing together quickly. And there are many excellent songwriters today following in the footsteps of Joe Hill whose music speaks to the ongoing struggles. It is important that activists in the current socio-political movements understand the power of song to inspire, unify, teach, and embolden people to action. Artists who provide this kind of musical motivation are much needed "Fellow Workers," and when that work is utilized thoughtfully, strategically, and appropriately as an equal component to other means of expression, it can make a profound and lasting contribution.

So today, as we reflect on the various means available to us to advance our work in direct action for progressive social change, we can still take a lesson from the Wobblies in the use of song and the other creative arts. Franklin Rosemont said it well:

> And today? Does anyone really believe that we can find effective solutions to the pressing problems of *our* time – not only the persistent and agonizing problem of wage-slavery, but also the problems of "whiteness," misogyny, homophobia, homelessness, and ecocide – with anything *less* than the freest and most revolutionary imagination and creativity? The reason why Joe Hill and the old-time Wobblies are still so popular among young radicals and have so profound an influence on so many contemporary social movements – from Justice for Janitors to micropower radio, from anti-globalization to animal rights, from Earth First! to feminism, from gay liberation to Critical Mass, and all the various new abolitionisms: from the group around the journal *Race Traitor* to the

movement to abolish prisons — is because The Wobblies' dreams of a better world, and the means they imagined and improvised to realize those dreams, have never ceased to touch the hearts and minds of those who value freedom above all, and who now dare to dream revolutionary dreams of their own.

(Rosemont, 2002, pp. 588, 589)

References

Adler, W. M. (2011). *The man who never died: The life, times and legacy of Joe Hill, American Labor Icon*. New York, NY: Bloomsbury.

Bird, S., Georgakas, D., & Shaffer, D. (1985). *Solidarity forever: An oral history of the IWW*. Chicago, IL: Lake View.

IWW Songs. (1917). *To fan the flames of discontent*. Chicago, IL: IWW Publishing Bureau.

Kornbluh, J. (ed.). (1964). *Rebel voices: An IWW anthology*. Ann Arbor, MI: University of Michigan.

Rosemont, F. (2002). *Joe Hill: The IWW & The making of a revolutionary workingclass counterculture*. Chicago, IL: Charles H. Kerr.

Smith, G. M. (1969). *Joe Hill*. Salt Lake City, UT: University of Utah Press.

Stavis, B., & Harmon, F. (eds.). (1960). *Songs of Joe Hill*. New York, NY: Oak Archives.

10 Women's Music: The Mothership

Holly Near

Music Changing Lives, Lives Changing The Music

I was standing in the wings, waiting with my collaborators to walk on stage. It was 1974. We were on a seven-city tour in California produced by women for women. What we were about to do had never been done before. Three "out" lesbians and one straight woman, who avoided the safety of calling herself a heterosexual in an act of solidarity, listened nightly to over 1,500 women shouting and stamping as the lights dimmed in the house. I remember thinking, "Oh my! It's like we are the Beatles!" I had sung on Broadway in the musical "Hair" and I had shared the Philharmonic stage with Jane Fonda, Nina Simone, and the cast of the "Free The Army" touring troupe. But I had never experienced such an electrifying audience as the one waiting for us to walk on. Something life- and world-changing was about to take place that would have consequences far beyond my imagination. We walked out on to the stage – Meg Christian, Margie Adam, Cris Williamson, and me. The crowd was cheering and waving. They were saying hello to us and to themselves. As the audience quieted and four voices in tender harmony began to sing, we were immediately drowned out by cheers, as if the audience could not contain itself. It was hard to continue as we too were overwhelmed by the beauty of the moment. But we did – singing "Hello Hooray."[1]

---

[1]Words and Music by ROLF KEMPF © 1968 (Renewed) WB MUSIC CORP. All Rights Reserved; Used by Permission of ALFRED MUSIC.

Hello hurray let the show begin

I've been ready

Hello hurray – let the lights go dim

I've been ready …

I've been waiting so long to sing my song

I've been waiting so long for this day to come

I've been thinking so long I was the only one

To this day women tell me they were in the audience of one of those concerts. We did two concerts in each city – one for women only and one for the general public. My father and mother drove to the one closest to their home. They attended the open concert together and then Dad waited in the car so Mom could go to the women only. (I love the men who understood this need for women to gather alone, but it made some men, and women, really agitated.)

The energy in the concert halls was palpable and for over a decade women who might not have attended a workshop, visited a women's center, or gone to a rally made their way to a concert featuring feminist and lesbian feminist artists. And for those who were longtime organizers, the music was an uplifting and unifying force where so often there was tension and exhaustion. Music has always been a major influence in grassroots organizing and although there are those who think of social change music as "entertainment," this music is, in my experience, an agent for change. Women's Music proved this to be true again and again. So how did that happen, and why?

In the 1970s and 1980s, as a result of blossoming lesbian feminism that was personal, political, theoretical, and cultural, a new music found its way out into the open. Women began writing songs in the privacy of their homes, sharing their stories quietly with one another. It was as though there was a collective jaw drop; "They are writing about that?" One woman might translate a particular song into Spanish, another into American Sign Language. Roughly made cassette tapes were slipped from one pocket to another. Soon the living rooms got too crowded and the artists were performing their work in church basements, hotel multi-purpose rooms, folk music venues, and eventually on major stages around the country, including Carnegie Hall. It was called "Women's Music" but in truth that was a code word for music inspired by feminism and lesbian feminism. One group of women who were thinking about starting a feminist laundromat as a way of organizing women decided, instead, to start a record company.

This was not the first time in recent history that people turned to music as the messenger. Coal miners striking in West Virginia sang *Which Side Are You On* written by labor organizer Florence Reece and made famous by Pete Seeger and the Weavers. African American jazz singer Nina Simone exploded onto the stage with her song *Mississippi Goddam*, which articulated the horrific conditions of Jim Crow, the state and local laws enforcing racial segregation in the southern United States. Rock artist Country Joe McDonald sang to thousands of soldiers with his cutting *I-Feel-Like-I'm-Fixin-To-Die-Rag*. And even pop singer Lesley Gore's hit, *You Don't Own Me*, fed a flame in the hearts of so-called "proper" white teenage girls. Radio DJs went out on a limb to play music inspired by grassroots organizing that challenged the system.

So when feminists spoke up and lesbians came out, they were met at the front door by songs. The songs were written by both lesbians and straight women who had walked away from the music business in order to find the music of their hearts. The music reflected the changes they were determined to make in the world – a world in which Pandora's Box was open and there would be no more secrets. Lesbians and feminists put it all on the table. I doubt talk show host Oprah Winfrey could have had such a revealing television show had it not been for feminists who first bravely began to talk about the secrets and complexities of women's lives. Feminism challenged violence against women, worked for the Equal Rights Amendment, pointed out inequality in pay, struggled to make space for women in the fields of science, sports, and medicine, and to end the lack of representation in government. Women learned to be outspoken about birth control, sexual liberation, having children outside the tradition of marriage, and the right to an abortion. Perhaps the most "dangerous" act was openly promoting the idea of women loving women and becoming so independent they no longer needed a man in order to live happy lives. This independence was often "felt" as man-hating when, in fact, it was more about loving women than hating men. And most importantly, it was a grassroots movement that inspired the music for social change, and that music in turn inspired grassroots movements on a community, national, and international level.

The lyrics spoke to the experience of women through the eyes of artists who believed feminist women held a unique perspective on economics, race, war, community, children, violence, politics, history, and art. They did not see or hear themselves in the dominant culture nor were they much included in the music business. If they were to have careers, if they were to have the space to present feminist and lesbian feminist songs, if they were to have an impact on the culture, they would have to create the space; it would not be given to them.

What Is Women's Music?

In the early 1970s, lesbian feminist singer/songwriter Meg Christian asked me if I had ever written a song about a woman, just a woman. I said of course. But when I combed through the lyrics of my newly penned feminist songs, each lyric had a male character that the heroine was loving or leaving. Or the song was about a patriarchal institution she was protesting. I was shocked. I sat down to write a song about a woman but it wasn't so easy. I realized I wasn't quite sure what women thought about independent of men or patriarchy. I came to understand that it is very hard to know one's self if one is steeped in dominant culture; that it would require some separating to make room for independent thought. I also realized that with every new song I wrote, even if it included male characters and institutions, I had to make a vigilant effort to put the song in a woman-identified context. That vigilance was the most important lesson I ever learned. It is from this place that I wrote "Hay Una Mujer Desaparecida" about women missing in the Chile of Augusto Pinochet; "The Rock Will Wear Away" about a woman's fierce journey for independence; "Fight Back" written to inspire resistance to rape.

I did not stop writing songs about class, race, gender, genocide, war, peace, environment, children, love, and passion. I had learned to do that from the international peace and justice movements. Rather, I began to write about those conditions through a feminist's eye. And I learned to do that through this movement of radical feminists and lesbians who dared to ask how they would think if they thought for themselves. This self-awareness opened another door along the way and that was understanding that other cultures might write a song or run a meeting or arrive at a consensus differently from a white-dominated conclusion. Understanding myself as a woman informed my whole political perspective and made me a better activist and ally. Songwriting offered me an opportunity to be a poetic practitioner.

Yes, but How Do We Reach an Audience?

Like so many who went before us, we were making it up as we went along. It became clear that if this music was to be heard, viable structures had to be developed. Out of necessity, we created record labels, distribution networks, music sections in feminist bookstores, as well as in major record stores. We encouraged philanthropists to fund the recording projects. We knew of only one woman recording engineer in the whole country, Joan Lowe, who lived in the northwest. She was generous with her knowledge and patient with beginners. We learned from her and then we trained other women recording engineers. Later we met Leslie Ann Jones, another trained engineer, and our production skills took another leap forward. We needed to tour so we trained concert producers and wrote a step-by-step guide to concert production. The songs as well as the structure became a lifeline and a university. Women dared to take on tasks they had never imagined doing, teaching themselves and each other. Almost without exception the concerts were connected to local community organizing.

Hundreds of women volunteered in one way or another. For example, over 100 women became record distributors in their regions. They would load the records (they were records in those days!) into their cars and drive to music outlets all over their state or region. Imagine walking into a retail store with a new album in hand called "Lesbian Concentrate." This was a recording put out by Olivia Records, a lesbian collective working out of Los Angeles. Their new collection of lesbian songs flew in the face of Anita Bryant, a brutal anti-gay spokeswoman for an orange juice company. I think fondly of those women who dared to represent a kind of music that had not ever been recorded. They were presenting this record to store owners who may have never said the word "lesbian" out loud, much less displayed the record in the store window.

Were we succeeding in reaching out? Finding an audience? Way beyond my wildest dreams. Reading my "fan mail" revealed to me that we were not only correct in our efforts to put Women's Music at the heart of community organizing, but we had unleashed a deep and troubled discontent that had been waiting to escape the souls of women. The music helped women to survive. Their letters to the artists revealed that most of them worked in a "man's world" where they were unwelcome, paid less, promoted less, scrutinized more. They drove to work with cassettes of Women's Music in their cars that emboldened and inspired them to face their day. On the drive home the music healed and loved them so hard that by the time they got home they felt they could stand long enough to get in the front door. Sometimes their letters told of their sick children with no health care, bosses who intimidated them, husbands who beat them, and parents who were dependent on them. But they held on to the music.

Reaching an audience was a logistical challenge for sure; how to build structures that would alert women to the music. But what we were really doing was building a cultural movement that would organize communities with song the way the labor movement used to hand out leaflets.

Most mysterious to me is when I reflect on the artists who walked away from commercial music careers to dedicate their lives and their talents to Women's Music. Classical instrumentalists and composers, rock drummers and guitarists, jazz pianists and percussionists, Celtic fiddle players and Appalachian banjo players, R&B soul singers and gospel choir directors, indigenous drummers and new age cellists, garage bands and Broadway singers. They were all called to join this new feminist orchestra for change.

Perhaps for some the choice was not so hard. What we were leaving was not all that attractive. My mistrust of the music business started early. I was a preteen, maybe 10, when my singing teacher (who had been Johnny Mathis's early singing teacher) took me to Los Angeles to audition. I don't remember the company or the man behind the desk but when all was said and done he wanted me to sing "Does Your Chewing Gum Lose Its Flavor on the Bedpost Overnight" and dress like Shirley Temple. I was already singing "Wasn't That A Time," learned from a Weavers recording, and I was singing "Joe Hill" learned from a Paul Robeson record. And I was familiar with material sung by Judy Garland, Judy Holliday, Ella Fitzgerald, Edith Piaf, Mary Martin, Peggy Lee, Eartha Kitt, and Joanie James. So it is understandable that when I got home, although tempted by the bright lights, I felt no interest in spending any more time in that world. There had to be something better. By the time I was 21 years old, I had started my own independent record label.

Festivals — A Place to Gather

Music festivals became an important part of the dissemination of information as well as a place to network and expand our education as artists and organizers. In Illinois, Kristen Lems started a Midwest festival when she was excluded from a folk festival that had no women performers in headliner positions. She got pissed and said, "Well, I will start my own damn festival and invite only women!" She thought it would be a one-time thing to make a point, yet the National Women's Music Festival recently celebrated the 40th anniversary of its inception in 1974. The festival was a place for artists to meet other women artists, distributors to find and train other distributors, and for activists to lead workshops investigating every possible issue from a feminist perspective.

In the next state over, Michigan, a more lesbian-identified festival was created; it was a gathering place in the woods for women to camp, play music, dance, fall in love, and discuss lesbian feminist theory. Women came from all over the United States and from many parts of the world. It took a massive amount of organizing to help the local citizens feel safe with such a gathering, but soon they saw lots of happy women arriving each year with their camping gear and instruments and nothing disastrous happened. In fact, the festival organizers bought food from local farmers and called on local businesses for supplies. At the height of the festival 8,000 women attended. It was good business and soon, the front lawns en route to the festival had signs that read "Welcome Back Mich Fest Women!" Participants had a magical week full of music, thunderstorms, and starry nights. We also fought about everything from issues of drugs and alcohol to whether there should be more bands and less folk music. But year after year, we returned to a powerful family reunion of lesbian feminists that provided an experience not found anywhere else in the world.

Daring to Grow

There were some who were willing to keep this a small private party. I understand. It was a great party. On the other hand, there were many of us interested in expanding the vision so it would be in keeping with our global politics. The excitement for Women's Music was growing fast. Now jazz, classical, blues, and rock artists were finding their way to the festivals. At the same time, my career was rapidly growing and I was in need of help. For every invitation I received to do a concert, I got at least five invitations I had to turn down. At the National Women's Music Festival, I ran in to my friend Amy Horowitz.

I first met Amy in the early 1970s when she produced a concert for me in Ashland, Oregon. She wasn't a concert producer, but she had been International President of B'nai B'rith so she knew how to organize. After her journey into International Affairs, Amy moved "back to the land" and started one of the first women's health collectives. She not only produced my concert, she learned how to distribute Women's Music in Southern Oregon. I asked Amy if she wanted to move to LA to help me and she said yes. We brainstormed together about how to handle the invitations. These were not simple booking requests, they were requests for me to come help build community, to educate, to heal, to celebrate. The concert was to be a beacon as well as a fundraiser. In many cases, artists coming in from the outside could say the things the women who lived in that community could not. All the way back to the time of Shakespeare, the troubadours have carried the news and it was true now. Feminists wanted to hear songs about the issues facing them in daily life. After much discussion, Amy concluded that she wanted to start a multi-racial cross-cultural organization dedicated to putting outspoken feminist artists on the road.

Around the same time, in 1975, a recording by Bernice Johnson Reagon found its way into my house. Bernice Reagon had been one of founding members of The Freedom Singers, a group formed in 1962 in Albany, Georgia, to educate communities about civil rights issues through song. She was also field secretary for the Student Nonviolent Coordinating Committee, one of the most important civil rights organizations of the 1960s. I had heard of the Freedom Singers and how they sang everywhere from schools to concert halls to churches and living rooms. I felt I had a lot to learn from her. Stunned by the power and beauty of her songs, I wrote to her.

On a trip to visit her parents in Washington, DC, Amy sought out Bernice and told her of our work together in LA. Bernice told Amy about a group she had formed that presented "black woman sound"; it was called Sweet Honey In The Rock and Bernice wanted us to produce a California tour for them. Amy called me. "I'm saying yes. Can I say yes?" Within months, Amy and I welcomed Sweet Honey In The Rock to California for their first tour. When they arrived in LA, I cooked them a turkey dinner at my house. A coalition formed, which attempted to share power across race; this would forever change my work as an artist and an organizer.

Amy moved to DC to work with Bernice Reagon and to get her organization, Roadwork, on its feet. Roadwork booked over 20 artists — tours for Sweet Honey In The Rock, Wallflower Order Dance Collective (a feminist dance company), and a powerful collaboration of women of color called the Varied Voices of Black Women. She also booked me, still assisting me in my ever-growing desire to take feminist perspective to the left, and global peace and justice movements to feminists on the wings of song. Even though I was often the only feminist artist at a leftist event and the only leftist artist at a lesbian event, I was learning to be a link in the chain connecting movements where they so obviously needed to be connected. If one is to work in the peace and justice movement, it cannot be successful without the full participation of women. Similarly, the lesbian feminist community would benefit from having a global perspective. And in both cases, confronting homophobia and racism was essential. The friendship and collaboration that was established between Bernice Johnson Reagon, Amy Horowitz, and me became the anchor I badly needed. It made growth possible.

Changing the Face of Women's Music

On the west coast, women of color began to question the perpetuation of white folk in the context of Women's Music. The work of R&B singer and producer Linda Tillery, rock and roll pioneer June Millington, jazz pianist extraordinaire Mary Watkins, and poet/professor June Jordan redefined the form and feel of lesbian music. They deepened the definition of Women's Music and created an essential dialogue without which feminist song would have died a white death. By this I mean that if we were part of developing global feminism, Women's Music by nature had to reflect the racial and cultural diversity of women. Women's Music could not reflect one story.

As a result of my sister Timothy Near's work with the National Theater of the Deaf, I saw my songs "signed." I initiated having my concerts signed by an American Sign Language interpreter. We found that deaf women had little access to feminist and lesbian thought and the concerts opened that door for them. Disability rights activists, many of whom were scholars attending the University of California at Berkeley, confronted me and educated me so I became more aware of accessibility issues at the venues at which I sang. Older women asked me to meet with them so they might point out the lyrics in a few songs they felt were ageist. I revised the lyrics. The close relationship I developed with grassroots activists informed my music so I was able to be an ambassador as well as a musician.

I was also coming to terms with the fact that lesbians were not all alike. We were not all feminists and political. Some were separatists, some worked in complex global movements. There were lesbians who wanted to be like upper-class men and enjoy the benefits of heterosexual acceptance. There were struggles around class and race, culture and ticket price, children and language.

We had become an identifiable group of musicians, production people, distributors, record labels, managers, booking agents, and audience. Through the door of music we began to understand feminism. At various times we were angry and resentful and we hurt each other. We were unnecessarily mean – the kind of meanness that comes from insecurity. But we learned; we gained wisdom; and softened into stronger women. The lessons learned continued to be reflected in the songs we wrote.

Our songs had helped to demystify lesbianism and feminism. The live concerts were a huge part of this. People brought their parents, met their sweethearts, and came out at these concerts. They redefined their whole lives, decided to change jobs, got the courage to ask for a raise, and felt for a moment what it would be like if they didn't have to be on guard all the time. Ranging from bold love songs to tender lullabies to rallying cries for change to electric condemnations of oppression, Women's Music gave voice and visibility to feminism. Seldom acknowledged by the mainstream or even by traditional folk circles, we built an invisible bridge that opened doors and changed the public discourse so that the next generation of opinionated women moved right into the mainstream and made themselves heard and at home.

And my music got better as did my critical thinking. The lyrics became less rhetorical, the poetry blossomed, the quality of the music elevated, the sound of the recordings improved, the concert production got more professional. And I became a better activist. The higher the standard of the presentation, the more professional we became, the more we legitimized the ideas and the movement. When I was featured in *People* magazine, when I performed at Carnegie Hall, it wasn't just a personal artistic achievement; it opened up more space into which people could walk without having to first make a commitment to an idea. I worked very hard to make sure no one had to show their political credentials at the door even though some in my audience might not have agreed with that principle.

Decades later, I sat on a stage in Columbus, Ohio, with Dr. Bernice Johnson Reagon, Pete Seeger, and Harry Belafonte. We had been invited by Dr. Amy Horowitz to speak and sing on the subject of music and the effect it has had on public policy. History shone its light on us as the audience rose to its feet, not only to thank us but to acknowledge in themselves that they had built the movements for which we had sung all those years. There we were in an academic environment discussing the social change movements that had directed our lives as artists, and sharing the music we had made to serve the movements. And because of our personal growth there was no subject we could not discuss or write songs about. We held a repertoire that included songs of civil rights, labor, environment, disability rights, gender and sexual identities, feminism, and more. Women's Music had found its place in a world of cultural exchange. When the four of us walked on stage I felt it was indisputable proof that social change artists are grassroots leaders. We are cultural workers and our work is profoundly influenced by the grassroots movements that rise up out of extraordinary necessity.

To young people coming up, I hope you know that if you are not included you can build it. If you don't like the way it is being done, step outside of it and build something you like. Is it easy? No. Will it break your heart? Yes. Is it worth it? I look forward to seeing how you answer that question in a few decades. Jazz had to build it. R&B had to build it. Folk had to build it. People of color had to build it. Lesbian feminists had to build it. Here's to the music that changed our lives and to the grassroots movements that changed our music.

Acknowledgment

Lifelong thanks to Kathy Goldman and Amy Horowitz for their historic clarity and to Alison de Grassi and Susie Erenrich for their spot-on editorial skills.

11

Acting Up and Fighting Back: How New York's Artistic Community Responded to AIDS

David Edelman

I t was a small article buried inside the *New York Times* on July 3, 1981. The headline read, "Rare cancer seen in 41 homosexuals" (Altman, 1981). Few took notice. Only a handful of researchers at the U.S. Centers for Disease Control and Prevention and a few doctors treating these perplexing cases of the rare Kaposi's sarcoma cancer in New York and California were even aware that something was happening. All of these first 41 patients were terrified, no one could tell them what was wrong, and all of them would be dead within two years.

Fear and panic can spread like a wildfire and so it was with AIDS in New York City in 1981. I know. I was there as both a witness and participant as the AIDS crisis unfolded. I arrived in August of 1981, a 25-year-old gay actor ready to make my mark in the theater. Shortly after, I read the first reports of this new disease and felt a shiver. By the end of the year, and over the course of the decade, that shiver would turn into the same anger and grief experienced by most of my generation. I became a volunteer at Gay Men's Health Crisis, handing out condoms and bleach kits on the streets of Greenwich Village and in the gay bathhouses. I was an early member of the Gay and Lesbian

Anti-Defamation League that, thanks to a threatened lawsuit by the ADL, would become the Gay and Lesbian Alliance Against Defamation. I served on its oh so gaily named Swift and Terrible Retribution Committee. I marched and rallied and protested. I did this to expiate the fear and to help my community in its time of abandonment.

And I wasn't alone. The history of America's early response to AIDS was largely written by the collective anger of a large community of gay artists who were both victims of the disease and leaders of the movement to fight back. They found their "ordinary" artistic careers recast in an unexpected and unasked for direction and changed the world's response to AIDS. It's a story of compassion and heartbreak, of raising fists and raising funds, and waking the public health establishment and the legislators who provided the funding. That history is far wider and deeper than can be written in this brief chapter; it begs its own book. But we can catch a glimpse in the stories of a few.

The Beginning: 1981

If you were young and gay in New York City in 1981 you were likely to be living life with an abandon unlike anything seen in prior generations. The Stonewall riots were just over a decade in the past. Gay identity politics was confronting endemic homophobia and oppression head on and gay sexuality was busting the closet wide open, nowhere as unabashedly as in New York City. A gay man could take his morning run with Front Runners, a gay running club, spend lunch hour at a gay bookstore, meet up with friends after work at a gay pub and then attend a gay professional networking meeting, head out for some gay two-stepping, or attend a gay theater performance. And on the weekend, he could dance the night away and expect to hook up with, if not Mr. Right, then certainly Mr. Right Now. It was as if the tightly coiled libidos of an entire generation of gay men were finally sprung and the effect was exhilarating.

New York City was also America's cultural mecca and home to a large and vibrant LGBT artistic community. Unlike Los Angeles' film and television industries, out gay actors and dancers could actually make a go of it in New York while gay authors and visual artists found that the ethos of the City nourished their work. Publishing of gay-themed books took off in the 1970s and soared by the end of the 1980s. The Stonewall Book Awards, begun in 1971, and Lambda Literary Awards, launched in 1989, bookended this extraordinarily productive period in gay literature. Visual artists like Andy Warhol, Robert Mapplethorpe, and Keith Haring were perhaps the most iconic of a flourishing community of gay visual artists who made New York City home. Gay designers with household names like Perry Ellis, Roy Halston, and Calvin Klein created American fashion from New York in the 1980s.

It truly was the best of times to be gay and living and working in New York. And it was soon to become the worst. From July of 1981, when this mysterious cancer was first reported, to the end of the decade, life in New York City's gay community was both a heart pounding and a heart breaking experience. Gay men, finally free to live life as they desired, were about to confront the plague. It would leave none untouched and would devastate an entire generation.

As AIDS began to take its toll, what started as a response to cope with this new disease turned into a social movement unlike anything that had come before. Its impact was broad and deep, from increased public awareness of the LGBT community to grassroots fundraising on an unprecedented level; from the symbolism of a red ribbon to the speed with which new drugs were approved and introduced into the market; from gay pride to gay power. And artists took a leading role.

Larry Kramer and GMHC

On August 11, 1981, soon after the initial reports of the new gay cancer had appeared, a group of eight gay men met in a New York City apartment to discuss their growing fear and alarm. They didn't need the *New York Times* to tell them something was wrong. Most of them had shared a summerhouse on Fire Island and they had already buried two of their lovers. Two more housemates were ill and another was dying. These eight were among the first to recognize the impending devastation of AIDS. The apartment belonged to Larry Kramer, the Academy Award nominated screenwriter of *Women in Love* and most recently the author of the highly provocative satiric novel about gay life, *Faggots*. Larry had called them together to hear from Dr. Alvin Friedman-Kein, the only researcher at New York University who was investigating this new illness. At the end of the evening they passed the hat and raised over $6,000 for Friedman-Kein's research. This gathering launched the nation's first and largest community organization devoted to the disease, Gay Men's Health Crisis (Shilts, 1987).

GMHC was formed with a mission to care for those stricken with AIDS, provide education to the gay community, and advocate on AIDS issues. The group of eight formed the nucleus of the board, including Kramer and writer Edmund White, author of a score of novels that would earn him a Guggenheim Fellowship and a National Book Critics Award. But it was Larry Kramer who quickly became the discomforting conscience of the AIDS movement.

Three years before, Kramer had written in his novel, *Faggots*:

Why do faggots have to f**k so f*****g much? It's as if we don't have anything else to do. All we do is live in our ghetto and dance and drug and f**k — there's a whole world out there, as much ours as theirs. I'm tired of being a New York City-Fire Island faggot, I'm tired of using my body as a faceless thing to lure another faceless thing, I want to love a person!

(Kramer, 1978)

Many in the gay community did not like Larry Kramer. He was accused of being a kill-joy and a traitor to gay liberation. Nor was he the image of a temperate, buttoned-down, and professional gay that many in the leadership of the community wanted to project to the world. He was loud and demanding and often obnoxious; to his friends at GMHC he could sometimes be an embarrassment, even if they knew he was right. When the board finally forced a meeting with New York Mayor Ed Koch in early 1983 to discuss the city's response to AIDS, Kramer was secretly disinvited for fear that he would insult the mayor to his face. In anger, Kramer threatened resignation but it backfired and the board accepted. Betrayed by his friends and cast out from the organization he had founded, Kramer would henceforth become an independent and unequivocal voice within and for the gay community.

In March 1983 he published a manifesto in The New York Native that rocked the gay world. Kramer titled it *1,112 and Counting* and he used it as a cudgel to drive home his message: "If this article doesn't scare the shit out of you, we're in real trouble. If this article doesn't rouse you to anger, fury, rage, and action, gay men may have no future on this earth …."

And then, like Emile Zola's *J'Accuse*, came the indictments:

I am sick of our elected officials who in no way represent us …

I am sick of closeted gay doctors who won't come out to help us fight to rectify any of what I'm writing about ...

I am sick of gay men who won't support gay charities. Go give your bucks to straight charities, fellows, while we die ...

I am sick of closeted gays. It's 1983 already, guys, when are you going to come out? By 1984 you could be dead ...

I am sick of everyone in this community who tells me to stop creating a panic. How many of us have to die before you get scared off your ass and into action? ... Get your stupid heads out of the sand, you turkeys!

I am sick of guys who moan that giving up careless sex until this blows over is worse than death... Come with me, guys, while I visit a few of our friends in Intensive Care at NYU ... They'd give up sex forever if you could promise them life ...

I am sick of "men" who say, "We've got to keep quiet or they will do such and such."...

Okay, you "men" – be my guests: You can march off now to the gas chambers; just get right in line ...

And I am very sick and saddened by every gay man who does not get behind this issue totally and with commitment – to fight for his life.

(Kramer, 1983)

It was a jaw-dropping indictment of the establishment, the gay community, and men who continued to have unsafe sex. Many in the LGBT community would see in Kramer's article the dividing line in their lives – before AIDS and after AIDS. For many, however, Kramer was still an incendiary and panic-monger, attempting to undermine the gay sexual revolution at its high point. Exhausted by two years of building GMHC, tilting at windmills, and the death of so many friends, Kramer left for Europe to find some peace. But he would soon be back and he would rechannel his anger through his art.

Michael Callen

Michael Callen was a 27-year-old aspiring singer-songwriter in New York when he was first diagnosed in 1982. Callen was unwilling to be victimized by the disease and felt a driving need to do something about the dearth of practical AIDS information available to gay men. At the time, it was still not known that a virus caused AIDS or that it was transmitted through blood and semen. Less than a year after his diagnosis, along with his friend Michael Berkowitz, he had written a short book entitled, *How to Have Sex in an Epidemic: One Approach*. It was published by Tower Press in a one and only limited run of 5,000 but that was enough. The book's plainspoken descriptions of gay sex pulled no punches and its common sense strategies for protecting oneself resonated with the gay community as no other AIDS educational material had.

It was the first published guide to "safe sex" and it catapulted Callen from a relatively unknown musician into the national spotlight. In short order he was appearing on local New York and national television shows to talk about safe sex. He testified before Congress, coined the term "Person with AIDS" (PWA) that helped to devictimize those who had contracted the disease, founded the People with AIDS Coalition, served on the New York State AIDS Institute, and spoke before national and international AIDS conferences. He published numerous articles, in both the popular and academic presses, and two more books on living with AIDS. Remarkably, Michael Callen accomplished all of this within a period of eight years, rising from a little known cabaret singer to become a worldwide voice of the AIDS movement. Like Larry Kramer, he too would return to his art at the end of the 1980s, channeling the fight against AIDS through his music (Callen, 1996).

Not every powerful artistic voice within the gay community of the 1980s was a solo act, however. The New York City Gay Men's Chorus began in 1979 and quickly emerged as a source of both pride and joy within the gay community. The Chorus' success was so astounding that by December 1982 it was performing a Christmas concert in Carnegie Hall. By April 1982 it had performed at its first AIDS fundraiser, a benefit performance at the Paradise Garage for the newly formed Gay Men's Health Crisis, and by November it had performed at its first memorial service for a member who had died (Vivyan, 2004). This interweaving of celebration, raising money, and memorializing the dead became a hallmark of the Chorus for the next 25 years. It represented a unique expression of the gay community in the time of AIDS; the joy of living in the midst of despair and the drawing together of gay people to care for their own.

Rock, Liz, and AmFAR

But still, the world took little notice of the devastation that AIDS was wreaking on the gay community. And then the bombshell hit. Rock Hudson became mysteriously ill and died in October 1985. The handsome American move icon had contracted AIDS and the world was shocked; this was no longer a disease of "those people" but of someone they knew (or thought they knew) and admired. And then Hudson's friend Elizabeth Taylor decided to make AIDS her personal mission and things started to change. Along with Dr. Mathilde Krim, a wealthy medical researcher who had been working on AIDS since 1981, she founded the American Foundation for AIDS Research, launched with a major gift from Rock Hudson just one month before his death. AmFAR was soon to become the world's largest privately funded organization to support AIDS research and advocacy. And because it was Elizabeth Taylor, the world could no longer stick its head in the sand.

Some in the gay community were resentful of AmFAR, a "straight" celebrity organization that would steal all the thunder and money away from the gay community's own efforts. But others capitalized on it and none more than gay artists. Many saw Elizabeth Taylor's newfound cause not as a threat but as a way to destigmatize the disease and those affected by it, opening doors that had hitherto been closed and loosening pockets.

It was the power of collective action rising at the intersection of grief, anger, and caring with an ever deepening need for social justice and the very human desire to not only survive, but to live. These complex forces, combined with the public voice of Elizabeth Taylor, formed a nexus of action that was replicated over and over within the gay artistic community of New York in the second half of the 1980s.

Working the Audience

By the middle of the decade, Broadway performers were soliciting cash from the stage at the end of their performances using a heartrending appeal: our fellow performers are sick and dying. Hurrying to the lobby after the curtain, contribution buckets in hand, actors and dancers began collecting pocket money from their audiences. In 1987, what started informally was officially organized under Actors' Equity Association, the performing arts

union, as Equity Fights AIDS. By the end of the decade, Equity
Fights AIDS was supplementing its direct audience appeals with
special events like Gypsy of the Year and the Easter Bonnet
Competition. In 1988, Broadway producers got on board with
their own AIDS fundraising arm, Broadway Cares. The entire
Broadway community realized that the audience − theater lovers
and those who loved theater people − was a natural ally, primed
to support an emotional appeal from the stage to aid their fellow
performers. By 1992, when the two groups merged to form
Broadway Cares/Equity Fights AIDS, the efforts of performers
and producers had raised nearly $4 million (Broadway Cares/
Equity Fights AIDS, 2016).

The Design Industries Foundation Fighting AIDS was
launched in 1984, just before Rock Hudson's death, by textile
designers Patricia Green and Larry Pond. Then, in 1986, designer
Perry Ellis died and the fashion industry was dealt a blow. In
short order other noted designers succumbed, including Willi
Smith, Angel Estrada, Antony Moorcroft, and at the end of the
decade, Halston. DIFFA emerged from this devastation as a
powerful grassroots fundraising organization in the fight against
AIDS and in 1988 produced a major gala at New York's 26th
Street Armory, hosted by Metropolitan Home magazine. It was
an art world A-list fundraiser: Peter Allen, Bette Midler, and
Robin Williams provided the entertainment, David Hockney
designed the sets, chefs such as Alice Waters from Chez Panisse
provided the food. Shearson Lehman Hutton donated the steaks
and the lobsters, Tiffany donated the engraved invitations, Tele-
Flora gave all the floral arrangements, Neuchatel provided
the chocolates. Waiters and wine stewards from throughout
Manhattan staffed the event and New York University students
washed the dishes. 1,200 guests paid $350 per ticket to see, be
seen, and send a message that people with AIDS and those in the
trenches were not alone. "It's the event of the season to spotlight
the issue of the decade," Ms. [Marlo] Thomas said. "One would
hope that such exuberance, with so many people putting so much
time into it, would have some effect on policy" (Hochswender,
1988). Wishful thinking. The policy changes did not materialize
until the next decade was well underway.

In 1989, responding to the United Nation's second annual
World AIDS Day, visual artists organized the first Day Without
Art, bringing together museums and galleries throughout the
world to commemorate, raise funds, and organize peaceful protests. At the end of the decade, two members of the Paul Taylor

Dance Company gathered a group of professional dancers at their home in NYC and within a year Dancers Responding to AIDS was born. By 2016, DRA was raising over $12 million per year to support the Actors Fund Home in New Jersey and making grants to hundreds of AIDS organizations in the United States and abroad (Dancers Responding to AIDS, 2016).

But not every event was designed to gather the artistic fold together to raise large sums of money. Some events were small, personal, but no less distinctive of a community caring for its own. The Pyramid Club in New York was a mecca for gay artists and the leading venue for the downtown performance art scene — freaky, fabulous, and an incubator for many avant-garde performers. On a summer night in 1986, 500 artists and performers gathered for a party to honor their colleague Martin Burgoyne, 24 years young and dying. They only raised about $6,000 for his medical expenses, but it was more about a family coming together to love one of their own. Madonna came by and Keith Haring, too, and others with names like Lady Bunny, Jean Caffeine, and John Sex. Steve Rubell, the owner of Studio 54 (who would himself die of AIDS three years later) said in the *New York Times*, "We know many AIDS patients who have been deserted, treated like lepers by their own families." "A year ago," he said, "probably a lot of people would not have come to a party like this." But then and there they came, to party and dance and to hold and kiss their friend, and to tell him how much they loved him. As for the guest of honor, he said simply "great party" (Geist, 1986).

Making Art and Acting Up

Larry Kramer and Michael Callen both returned to their art and realized that they could do as much, if not more, to raise consciousness of AIDS through their creative work than through polemics alone. Larry Kramer's self-imposed exile came to an end in April 1985 when his play *The Normal Heart* opened at Joe Papp's Public Theatre, where it ran for nine months. It was Kramer's highly autobiographical interpretation of the unfolding AIDS crisis and his response to a negligent government, a gay leadership that could not agree on direction, and a gay community that seemed tone deaf to the personal risks associated with the disease. It was another wake up call, but unlike his earlier highly charged article in the New York Native, this was a work of art that had the capacity to move an audience. In his review of the play in the *New York Times*, Frank Rich wrote, "Although Mr. Kramer's theatrical talents are not always as highly developed as his conscience there can be little doubt that 'The Normal Heart' is the most outspoken play around — or that it speaks up about a subject that justifies its author's unflagging, at times even hysterical, sense of urgency" (Rich, 1985). Papp, the hard boiled producer of the play, shared the same visceral reaction that audiences experienced on seeing it for the first time. Vanity Fair writer Michael Shnayerson recalled Papp saying in an interview:

> I found it difficult to watch The Normal Heart when it came to that place toward the end of the play with the two guys, one is withering away and the other is trying to insist that he eat something. And the first guy says, I'm not going to eat anything, I don't want anything, and the other guy says, You'll get a lot sicker if you don't eat anything. I'm sick of you, I'm tired of you, forget it — and he smashes a container of milk on the floor, and it spreads all over, and he throws the bread on the floor. It's a violent scene, and then it's quiet, and he turns away, and then the guy who's stricken with AIDS sort of crawls toward him — Suddenly, across the desk from me, Joe Papp puts his head in his hands and begins to cry.
>
> (Shnayerson, 1987)

Larry Kramer succeeded in galvanizing both the gay and straight communities as no one else had — through his art. His voice still resonates today. While few artifacts of the time have remained in contemporary consciousness, the 2014 HBO movie version of Kramer's play is testament to the lasting power of art within a movement for social justice.

Michael Callen returned to his art in 1988 when he formed The Flirtations, a cabaret quintet that toured the country at the end of the decade and released two albums of music. He and "The Flirts" were among the most successful performers within the gay-music scene of the 1980s, singing songs with wit and humor and pathos and rage. In the last year of his life Michael Callen recorded 40 songs and made a special appearance in the Tom Hanks film *Philadelphia*. He died in December of 1993 at the age of 38. One of the last songs that Callen recorded included the refrain

We've had enough

Won't take no more

We've had enough

Gonna win this war

We've had enough

We've had enough

Of the hate and the lies

This is genocide

We've had enough.

(Callen, 1996)

Larry Kramer's radical behavior was far from over when The Normal Heart finished its run at The Public Theatre in the fall of 1985. Within two years his anger and energy had once again burst over when he helped form the street action group ACT UP (AIDS Coalition to Unleash Power), whose Silence = Death slogan would become an international emblem of AIDS activism. As Charles Kaiser wrote in *The Gay Metropolis*:

> ACT UP's charter described it as a coalition of "diverse individuals united in anger and committed to direct action"; one of its chants identified it as "loud and rude and strong and queer." As the novelist David Leavitt put it, its members were determined to disprove the idea that a community in the grip of AIDS was "weak, ravaged [and] deserving only of charity." Instead, "they presented an image of community powered by anger and willing to go to almost any length in order to defend itself."
>
> It was a fabulous combination of the practical and the theatrical.

(Kaiser, 1997)

Other artists joined Larry Kramer in the initial formation of ACT UP, including filmmaker Vito Russo, author of *The Celluloid Closet*, fashion designer Tim Bailey, actor Ron Goldberg, and an army of thousands who took to the streets. Their modus operandi was disruption, at once colorful and confrontational, and police arrests were not only common but desired. From its founding in 1987 through the early 2000s, the group would be recognized worldwide for its particular brand of civil disobedience with branches in cities around the globe. ACT UP forced the U.S. public health service and the pharmaceutical industry to speed up the funding, testing, and approval of new drug therapies, it helped secure the passage of the Ryan White Comprehensive AIDS Resources Emergency (CARE) Act and of other federal laws and regulations designed to protect the civil rights of persons with AIDS, and it ensured that PWAs were at the table. Without ACT UP and the artists who conceived it, who knows how many more years would have elapsed before AIDS was transformed from a deadly disease into a managed chronic illness?

The End of the Beginning

The forces that shaped the AIDS crisis of the 1980s were complex: an unprepared public health system, a slow to respond medical research establishment, a burgeoning gay rights movement in the midst of an American society permeated by homophobia and unable to discuss sex, Reagan era small government and budget cuts, a mainstream media that stumbled and lurched in its reportage, local politics as usual, and the suffering of the dying, the ill, and the worried well. The response was equally complex. In New York City, ground zero for AIDS in 1981, artists helped give form to the anger that erupted in the gay community. Some, like Michael Callen and Larry Kramer, were compelled to action, albeit in very different ways. Callen was an insider, seeking change by pressuring the system. Kramer was an outsider, banging on the doors and making a ruckus. Both artists created political and social change not only by harnessing their artistic talent for polemical purposes but also through the creation of art that was infused with a political sensibility.

Members of the NYC Gay Men's Chorus responded to AIDS collectively and in unison; gathering up the community's financial resources at charity events, consoling the community at memorial services, and reflecting the community's strength and courage in public performances. Others, like the members of Actors Equity Association, represented an entire arts industry sector in a collective response. Noted leading actors and unknown chorus gypsies alike appealed to nearly every audience of nearly every Broadway show for years to come, raising millions of dollars for AIDS organizations in New York and around the world. They may have competed at Tony Award time, but in the struggle against AIDS these performers spoke the same message and shared the same goal. DIFFA and DRA represented the struggle of their own artistic communities with many gay men among their ranks who would die young. And then there was Elizabeth Taylor, who focused the celebrity spotlight on AIDS. In 1987, when I was president of the New Jersey Lesbian and Gay Coalition and we were starting up the first statewide AIDS education program, I somehow got a hold of Elizabeth Taylor's home phone number and dialed, completely on a lark and totally unprepared. I had no thought other than to leave a message with a housekeeper that would of course go ignored. I was thoroughly gob smacked when that unmistakable voice answered the phone and I'm sure I fell out of my chair when I realized I was talking with Elizabeth Taylor herself. But once I recovered, she was gracious and kind and eager to hear about our work.

Thinking back 30 years to that brief phone chat, I am reminded of Malvolio, reading from his love's pretended letter in Shakespeare's *Twelfth Night*:

In my stars I am above thee; but be not afraid of greatness: some are born great, some achieve greatness, and some have greatness thrust upon 'em.

That seems a fitting description of the grassroots leadership within the artistic community as it responded to AIDS in that first awful decade. We were all just actors, singers, dancers, and painters, some with "names" but most without. We just wanted to pursue our craft and make a career — a life really — in the arts. But then our passion and talent were hijacked by a disease that thrust us into action, collectively and individually. We took our anger, mixed it with our art, and fought for change. And each of us became greater for it. As Larry Kramer wrote in The Normal Heart, "We're all different in many ways and alike in many ways and special in some sort of way."

In 1978, Gloria Gaynor released "I Will Survive" and within a year it reached number one on Billboard's Hot 100. It would soon take on a whole new meaning. So many artists of my generation did not survive and we will never know what greatness they might have achieved.

Acknowledgment

Permission for use of Michael Callen's lyrics by Tops and Bottoms Music (BMI) (1996). Michael Callen, Legacy, Significant Other Records.

References

Altman, L. K. (1981). Rare cancer seen in 41 homosexuals. *The New York Times*, July 3, p. 20.

Broadway Cares/Equity Fights AIDS. (2016). Retrieved from http://www.broadwaycares.org. Accessed on April 16, 2016.

Callen, M. (1996). We've had enough [Recorded by M. Callen]. On Legacy [CD]. New York, NY. Retrieved from http://michaelcallen.com/. Accessed on March 19, 2016.

Dancers Responding to AIDS. (2016). DRA history. Retrieved from www.dradance.org. Accessed on May 26, 2016.

Geist, W. E. (1986, September 6). ABOUT NEW YORK; In the face of a plague, A party. Retrieved from http://www.nytimes.com/1986/09/06/nyregion/about-new-york-in-the-face-of-a-plague-a-party.html. Accessed on May 4, 2016.

Hochswender, W. (1988, October 6). Designers (and friends) hold gala to help AIDS charities. Retrieved from http://www.nytimes.com/1988/10/06/garden/designers-and-friends-hold-gala-to-help-aids-charities.html. Accessed on May 2, 2016.

Kaiser, C. (1997). *The gay metropolis*. New York, NY: Harcourt Brace & Company.

Kramer, L. (1978). *Faggots*. New York, NY: Random House.

Kramer, L. (1983). 1,182 and counting. *The New York Native*, March 14, 59.

Rich, F. (1985). Theatre: 'The Normal Heart' by Larry Kramer. *The New York Times*, April 22, p. 17.

Shilts, R. (1987). *And the band played on*. New York, NY: St. Martin's Press.

Shnayerson, M. (1987, April 1). Retrieved from http://mshnay.com/blog/2015/2/22/one-by-one. Accessed on May 2, 2016.

Vivyan, J. (2004). *New York City Gay Men's Chorus 25th Anniversary Journal*. New York: New York City Gay Men's Chorus.

SECTION IV
Theatre of the Oppressed as a Form of Grassroots Leadership

12 Truth Comes in Many Colors: Theatre of the Oppressed for Conflict Transformation and Trauma Healing in Kenya

Mecca Antonia Burns,
Bonface Njeresa Beti and
Maxwel Eliakim Okuto

How can theatre promote leadership? How does it serve to "encourage autonomous activity, to set a process in motion, to stimulate transformative creativity?" (Boal, 1992, p. 245). How does leadership arising within a group differ from leadership imposed from the outside? And how might Kenya serve as a case study?

Theatre of the Oppressed (TO) is an arsenal of theatre games and techniques designed to motivate people, restore true dialogue, and create space for participants to rehearse action. Everyone has the capacity to act in the "theatre" of their own lives; everyone is at once an actor and a spectator.

Brazilian director and activist Augusto Boal began developing Theatre of the Oppressed in the 1960s, during a military dictatorship. Following educator Paulo Freire, Boal viewed oppression as a power dynamic based on monologue rather than dialogue. Freire believed that the oppressor—oppressed dynamic destroys the humanity of both and the task is to liberate both. However, "only the power that springs from the weakness of the oppressed will be sufficiently strong to free both" (Freire, 1970, p. 44).

Boal's work has mobilized theatre activists worldwide — including the authors of this chapter. We use Theatre of the Oppressed for conflict transformation and trauma healing, as key precursors to social change in East Africa. Conflict can hinder social change — but can also propel it forward. Theatre brings dissenting voices, emotions, and motivations into an "as-if" world. This artistic frame provides freedom from harm: Because violence is represented *within* the aesthetic space, none get hurt — and all get heard.

Trauma researcher Bessel van der Kolk and peacebuilding expert John Paul Lederach describe the potential of theatre from their own perspectives:

> Conflict is central to theatre — inner conflicts, interpersonal conflict, family conflicts, social conflicts, and their consequences. Trauma is about trying to forget, hiding how scared, enraged, or helpless you are. Theatre is about finding ways of telling the truth and conveying deep truths to your audience. This requires ... exploring and examining your own internal experience so that it can emerge in your voice and body on stage.
>
> (Van der Kolk, 2014, p. 335)

> The stage creates a shared space where people can feel the voices moving and touching ... The stage created enough distance, enough security for [people] to tell their stories without fear of rejection, without fear of public shame.
>
> (Lederach & Lederach, 2010, pp. 284, 287)

* * *

Burns: When Augusto Boal died in 2009, his son Julian Boal conducted their planned New York workshop alone. At the water fountain I made a comment to Julian about inheriting his father's mantle. He demurred and I realized with a shock that the mantle had descended upon us all. In this crowd of mourners I felt jubilant about the future, about holding onto the mantle's hem in Africa. As a quintessential transforming leader, Augusto would appreciate this; he would want his work to evolve and transform, as it had through every journey life took him on.

Boal left us this metaphor: Theatre of the Oppressed has grown like a tree, branching out and bearing fruit in its migration from Brazil to France to India and back home. What are the roots of the tree? Images, Sounds, and Words – which draw sustenance from social forces like Politics, Economics, and Philosophy. The trunk of the tree transfigures these elements into art through a sequence of dynamic games and Image Theatre techniques, helping the tree branch out and reproduce, and spreading seeds of solidarity and multiplication.

Boal and his colleagues showed a remarkable capacity over the years to transform failure into artistic triumph. Disaster sprouted new branches out of creative necessity. For example, Forum Theatre grew out of Brazilian and Peruvian audiences' demanding a loosening of the troupe's control. And Rainbow of Desire grew out of an incongruence of Forum Theatre's oppressor/oppressed dichotomy in Europe (L. J. Epstein, personal communication, 2016; Erenrich, 2010).

Many Colors of Boal: Techniques and Roles

"When conflict and oppression seem overwhelming, drama can offer a sliver of hope, a playful way in, a pathway of incremental steps. Theatre bridges the actual with the possible, letting people imagine how tensions and circumstances could be transformed" (Burns, Beti, Okuto, Muwanguzi, & Sanyu, 2015, p. 138). In this chapter, we will focus on three branches of the TO tree: Image Theatre, Forum Theatre, and Rainbow of Desire, as practiced in East Africa.

IMAGE THEATRE

In Image Theatre, participants form a tableau of frozen poses to capture a moment in time, dramatizing an oppressive situation. This image becomes a source of critical reflection, facilitated by various interventions. First the *real image* may be depicted, next an *ideal image* envisioning liberation from oppression. Then a sequence of *transitional images* shows movement from real to ideal. Images may be reshaped from multiple perspectives.

Image Theatre is an invitation to take a stand, to strike a pose, to use physical gesture to reveal truths without uttering a word. Human sculptures — living, breathing, but unmoving and unspeaking — portray the essence of a predicament, emotion, or abstract idea, drawing on rich somatic vocabularies. Generally, several people step into the aesthetic space to form an image together, a moment suspended in time. Those watching provide their own meaning, not knowing the "true" story. They may assign captions to the tableaux. The figures next become animated, rhythmic, moving toward what they desire, speaking aloud in an interior monologue.

Image Theatre highlights the difference between subjective and objective realities, revealing the human tendency to assume one's own interpretation is the only correct one. "Moreover, working with images avoids privileging those who are more verbally adept, or are native speakers of the language being used" (Sullivan, Burns, & Paterson, 2007, p. 221).

Jokers and Spect-actors

Who engineers these theatrical encounters? A facilitator, renamed the *joker*, helps transform audience members into *spect-actors* — activated spectators. The joker is like a wild card, unbound to any suit or faction, but sympathetic to all. "The word implies a playful, exploratory attitude, an invitation to wonder together, 'what if…?'" (Sullivan et al., 2007, p. 223).

Image Theatre Example: "Real to Ideal"

A street theatre piece on election violence in Kibera, Nairobi's biggest slum, stopped short with a real image: figures frozen in place with raised fists holding rocks. The joker invited the audience to resculpt the figures to create a more ideal image. But what would be the transitional images — how could the Kenyan populace move from strife to reconciliation?

FORUM THEATRE

Forum Theatre is an exercise in democracy and human rights in which anyone can speak and anyone can act. A short play dramatizes a situation with a terribly oppressive ending that spectators cannot be satisfied with. It is immediately shown again; however this time the spectators become spect-actors and can at any point yell, "Stop!" They step onstage to replace the protagonist and take the situation in different directions. The people acting as oppressors will maintain their oppression until they are authentically stopped – and just as in life, stopping them isn't easy. Forum Theatre thus becomes a laboratory within which to experiment with different courses of action.

The protagonists should be characters with whom the people in the room identify, so that when intervening they are rehearsing their own action. The point is not to show what we think other people should do – this is not theatre of advice. The point is to discover what *we* can do. Theatre thus becomes rehearsal for real-world action.

"Boal describes the emancipatory qualities of this creative space where realities can converge, be constructed, stretched, reduced, amplified and deconstructed at will" (Sajnani, 2009, p. 476). Forum Theatre has the ability to convey a powerful and memorable message to its audience because it presents real situations for the public to consider and provokes them to explore real strategies together. Through its interactive approach it provides important information, emotional support, and problem-solving skills that may be difficult to obtain elsewhere.

Forum Theatre originated in a military regime, with battle lines clearly drawn between oppressors and oppressed. It transformed in Europe where there was less need for an external police presence; people had internalized their oppressors.

RAINBOW OF DESIRE

Rainbow of Desire is a branch of Theatre of the Oppressed invented by Boal in exile in France. There he saw people who were free from the brutal repression of his native Brazil yet suffered from deep loneliness and despair. Europeans enjoyed prosperity and freedom, but drug abuse and suicide rates were alarming. How could this be? Boal was accustomed to life "in the southern hemisphere, where dictatorships murdered people, but where fewer people pointed weapons at their own heads" (Boal, 2001, p. 324). Boal concluded that in France the cops who were absent on the street had become internalized within people's heads (Boal, 1995).

In Rainbow of Desire, the conscious *will* of the protagonist engages with each *desire*, via gesture, rhythm, and text. Living sculpture, verbal and nonverbal dialogue, and dynamization of images reveal the spectrum of a protagonist's desires, emotions, and attitudes, and an *antagonist's* "rainbow" can also be portrayed. Specific techniques will be described below.

Rainbow of Desire explores the premise that healing the fragmentation of the psyche can help heal the fragmentation of societies. Facing inner adversaries — moving toward them with love, listening to their messages — can build the inner strength, the soul force, to face difficult characters encountered in the outer world. Rainbow of Desire elaborates on Forum Theatre both by humanizing outer opponents and by identifying adversaries that lie within, hidden from awareness. Thus the personal is bridged with the political.

Amani People's Theatre: A Kenyan Perspective

Amani People's Theatre (APT) is an initiative of African artist-peacebuilders based in Nairobi, Kenya. Founded in 1994, APT employs an interactive multiarts approach to conflict. Inspired by indigenous East African theatre and the theories of Freire and Boal, the people's theatre process integrates education, entertainment, and research in exploring context-specific issues and searching for creative nonviolent responses. Weaving together performance art, peace education, reconciliation dialogues, and traditional African rituals, APT trains groups in conflict transformation, interfaith dialogue, trauma healing, street-child rehabilitation, and crime prevention.

Burns: When I first visited Kenya in 2010, my husband, daughter, and I immediately traveled with Amani People's Theatre up the Great Rift Valley to a remote village. There we had a chance to see Forum Theatre applied to democracy building on a grassroots level. The play showed a marital dispute in a poor family over whether to vote for the upcoming Constitutional referendum. We saw firsthand how APT engaged people with political processes through Forum Theatre.

APT uses participatory theatre in all its interventions with communities, whether conflicts are rooted in historical injustices, poverty, ownership and access to land, or political violence and ethnic identity.

AUTHORS' OWN STORIES

Beti: I went to primary school in rural Kenya in the village of Isulu before moving to Nairobi where I was street-based in the Kangemi slums of Nairobi. I joined Shangilia street theatre by

1997–1998 and it became the turn-around for my life. It was a home and theatre center to many former street children, whose lives were transformed by the power of the stage. Shangilia fused the dance and movement with drama, as vehicles for social transformation and behavior change among the children in Kangemi slums. I learnt these skills and started training the youth there and later in Kawangware, where we started an outreach.

At Shangilia, advocacy songs provided opportunities for youth to showcase their talent, for churches, schools, villages, and corporate events to win support for the plight of street children. Dance and acrobatics were applied as self-reflective tools for street life and for engaging in dialogue. Church groups heard stories of children's experiences in the streets and were invited to performances to see how the children themselves represented their experiences. By 2002, Shangilia had a national impact on children's rights advocacy in Kenya, performing at the UNICEF anniversary of the Convention on the Rights of the Child, in New York and Cologne.

In 2003, I became trained by Amani People's Theatre in Theatre of the Oppressed to work with communities in conflict. This work has taken me to Somalia, South Sudan, Canada, and Ethiopia to apply theatre in peacebuilding, human rights, and social justice. Theatre brings to the fore issues of conflict in a playful but transformative way, through storytelling and self-reflection. Theatre affords both antagonist and protagonist the opportunity to share their fears and hopes, and thereby the chance to transform such standing fears. Lederach (2005) argues that the arts and moral imagination help peacemakers understand the complexity, paradoxes, and indigenous knowledge needed to bring the field of conflict analysis and resolution to the next level.

Okuto: I grew up in different parts of Kenya because my father worked for the government. We lived in Nairobi, Garissa, Nakuru, Nyeri, Isiolo, Mombasa, Kisii, Kakamega, and rural Oyugis. Wherever we lived, singing and drumming played a key role in my culture. Every evening as a young child, I could hear music playing and drums from the neighborhood. My parents used lullabies to soothe children, to express their love and joy, and to interact. Drums and shakers engaged people in vigorous and creative dances in homes, village, schools, and churches.

Through Music, Dance, and Drama (called MDD in Africa), the community gathered together and this brought about harmonious living, especially during ceremonies like childbirth, circumcisions, weddings, and burials. MDD created a sense of belonging where everyone was treated equally. In times of war or conflict, music relieved negative emotions that could lead to violence. It had the potential to express a sense of belonging to one's group — and antagonistic attitudes toward other groups.

My first experience with Paulo Freire was a university workshop that involved dialogue and problem posing. I became more involved with Popular Education and Theatre of the Oppressed in 2005 when I began working with Amani People's Theatre. Forum theatre was a methodology which I found educative, creative, and entertaining. Forum performance has been particularly valuable in presenting scenarios that the entire community can relate to. Young Forum performers and facilitators work with leaders to develop a conflict scenario reflecting real problems, then ask the community how they might prevent the conflict from escalating. Audience members are then invited to step in and enact their suggestions.

Burns: My troupe, Presence Center for Applied Theatre Arts, had spent years wrestling theatrically with Virginia's racial history before I traveled to East Africa. At my first meeting with the acclaimed Amani People's Theatre, the leaders mentioned their interest in drama therapy and Rainbow of Desire for trauma healing in Kenya. In 2010 and 2011, my husband Brad Stoller and I trained teachers, actors, social workers, and APT interns in Theatre of the Oppressed.

In subsequent years, APT began sending me to far-flung areas of Kenya. I thought I would be working alongside them, but I became used to going solo. I felt singularly safe and comforted in packed vans brimming with African music, hurtling all day toward a destination where I knew no one. I traveled on wings of trust: I trusted APT to keep me safe even from afar; I felt trusted by them to deliver a workshop fitting of their reputation, and I trusted whoever hosted me because we shared common ground through participatory theatre.

In a postcolonial era, participatory processes move beyond the dichotomy of black and white into full color. Through this pluralization, Forum Theatre helps diverse groups recognize their common humanity and unify to contend with their common oppressors. But Forum Theatre may perpetuate enemy images — which Rainbow of Desire serves to mitigate. The dramatization of personal narratives offers a chance to shift perspectives beyond simplistic notions of who is good and who is bad.

In Senegal I saw several West African troupes perform Forum plays in which jokers asked audiences to decide which

characters should go to heaven and which to hell. Later I won-
dered if this practice might stem from African traditions of public
shaming of wrongdoers, and requiring them to repent and swear
oaths. In Boal's aesthetic space, the citizenry themselves can par-
ticipate in a fictionalized, open-air, judicial decision.

 I was initially surprised to be asked to lead Rainbow of Desire
workshops in a land so rife with outer oppression. In our Senegal
Lightning Forum, *a crowd of antagonists tries to drive out a preg-*
nant protagonist, throwing her bag after her. Again and again, new
spect-actors pick up the bag to portray the girl, dramatically sup-
porting her refusal to accept undeserved exile. My next impulse —
to explore the "rainbow of the antagonist" — was preempted by a
call to prayers. [video link]

 In Uganda, we used TO to explore cultural barriers to repro-
ductive health services as we laid the groundwork for a clinic.
Rather than vilifying men for demanding large families, partici-
pants took turns embodying a father's inner landscape, perceiv-
ing his fear of dying alone, the loneliness of a small family, the
desire to increase one's clan.

 We created a Forum scene in Western Kenya in which a
young woman is sexually harassed on her way to school. Years
later in her office, she finds herself face to face with her former
harasser, whom she is now interviewing for a job. Does she exact
her revenge? Or will she show forgiveness? Raising the questions
is even more important than receiving the answers.

WEAVING A RAINBOW

How is social change in Kenya hindered and sabotaged by politically maneuvered tribal conflict and land grabbing? What role
does trauma play? And how can Theatre of the Oppressed be a
source of healing and transformation?

 Weaving a Rainbow was an APT project that helped integrate
ex-militia members on Mt. Elgon back into the community after
land issues led to violence in 2006–2008. The objective was
peace and healing through participatory theatre, which offered an
interactive forum for creative and redemptive dialogue. Both victims and perpetrators shared painful memories, using theatre techniques to move toward reconciliation in the region.

 Burns: On a mountaintop linking Kenya and Uganda, former
militia members have gathered in search of acceptance back into
the community. Amani People's Theatre is conducting a year-
long project here and has asked me to offer a warm-up today.
I quickly choose two themes: sharing leadership and playing with

conflict. Stepping into a conventional leader stance, I direct the group to move through the room as I call out "start" and "stop." This is simple; the chain of command is clear. Next we rotate the leadership role. Now leaders take turns, but still stand outside giving directions.

Then a crucial shift: the group must start and stop together — in silence. Leadership now emerges from within the group along with social engagement, awareness of proximity, breath sounds, and footsteps. Finally we turn to iconic games from the arsenal of Theatre of the Oppressed — West Side Story and Columbian Hypnosis — to further experience responsive leadership. [video link]

Case Study: Participatory Theatre on Election Violence in Kenya

BACKGROUND

From December 2007 to February 2008, Kenya was on the brink of collapse from disputed general elections, with "1,500 killed, 3,000 … women raped, and 300,000 people left internally displaced…. The magnitude of the trauma and structural violence … took both Kenyans and the international community … by surprise" (Roberts, 2009, p. 2). Many actors in these clashes were both victims and perpetrators; thus the conflicts are difficult to resolve through criminal justice approaches that seek only to assign blame and punish perpetrators. Forum Theatre can interface with restorative justice practices to allow everyone's grievances to be addressed.

The 2013 election saw a country working together to suppress conflict, but in 2016 a strong sense of fear remains because of hate rhetoric by politicians, rumors of voter manipulation, and rigging of upcoming elections. Nairobi's largest slum, Kibera, has remained a hot spot involving diverse ethnic groups with competing political interests. Mainstream politics stays dominated by ethnic patriarchy and political clientelism, keeping women and youth of all tribes on the margins.

ENEMY IMAGES

In Kenya, Kikuyu remains the largest ethnic group, dominating the political scene since independence, more recently in concert with the Kalenjin. Bitter rivalry has ultimately pitted the

Kikuyu–Kalenjin axis against the Luos, who have spent decades opposing what they see as Kikuyu hegemony over the Kenyan state. The smaller tribes remain excluded from political power altogether, further fueling ethnic tensions during elections. The Luos, political arch-rivals of Kikuyu power since independence, lost senior politicians to assassination during the first two presidencies (Kenyatta and Moi regimes). These assassinations reinforced the Luos' self-image of victimization, cemented mental images of Kikuyu as enemies and aggressors, and strengthened their stereotypes of Kikuyus as thieves obsessed with money.

Kikuyus have spearheaded campaigns to delegitimize the Luos as "hungry for power," with attendant dehumanizing narratives. The belief is spread that Luo may not understand how to rule a nation – after all, it's the Kikuyu who fought for independence from colonialists. Other stereotypical prejudices include cultural practices, with circumcision being seen as an important credential for state leadership. Since Luo do not practice this rite, how could they manage matters of the Kenyan state?

> [W]hen they are engaged in a serious conflict, people will normally project their own negative traits onto the other side, ignoring their own shortcomings or misdeeds, while emphasizing the same in the other. Enemy images also involve "scapegoating." It is common for each side to decide that it is the other side (the "enemy") that is the source of all their problems. If only the enemy could be vanquished or eliminated, then those problems would go away ... You do not have to be a world leader to break down enemy images among the people with whom you come into contact.
>
> (Burgess, 2003, p. 1)

One of Martin Luther King's (1958) principles is that "nonviolence seeks to defeat injustice itself, not people. It recognizes that evildoers are also victims" (p. 102). The field of political psychology and unofficial diplomacy has developed this idea further. "[E]xaggerated enemy images can be viewed as a shadow – a counterpart to an individual that is impenetrably linked to him or her" (Volkan, 1985, p. 21).

BOAL'S INTROSPECTIVE TECHNIQUES

Screen Image

The Screen Image technique of Rainbow of Desire reveals the projections that interfere with authentic dialogue between individuals, groups, and even nations. These stereotypes or mis-perceptions block us from actually seeing the other. Reclaiming projections means taking the plank out of one's own eye, to see more clearly how to be the change wished for in the world. Theatre can forge a dialogue process with specific enemy images, to avoid displacing them onto others.

As an American friend wryly commented recently, "If we build a fence to keep immigrants out, maybe we can keep out all the unwanted parts of ourselves that we have projected onto them" (P. Leavitt, personal communication, May 2016). What is projection? It happens when another person serves as a mirror, reflecting back tendencies one is blind to in oneself.

In Screen Image, two people enact a scene of conflict, then each selects an additional participant to embody her projection. Each sculpts this human "clay" into a screen image or *body mask*, which she places in front of the opposite actor. The figure might be shown turning away in disdain, or standing on a pedestal, or poised to attack. Often metaphorical, this is her *true image* – her subjective experience of the other person.

Now when the two people in conflict stand facing each other and attempt to interact, they cannot see each other, because the screen images are in the way. Soon the images become autono-mous and playfully intensify the conflict – still distorted by their body masks. When the original actors return and "shadow" them, the distortions slowly melt away and repair has a chance to begin, as a newly humanized *other* comes into focus.

Example: A Ugandan brother and his older sister enact a simple domestic scene in which she feels patronized by his instructions on using a charcoal burner. She creates an image of him scoffing at her. He in turn sculpts an image of her turning away, ignoring his concern for her. Ultimately they recognize each other's compassion and competence. Masha Maitha, cofounder of APT, wandering by, observed that this technique could be used with stereotypes and rivalries between the East African countries.

The Rainbow of Desire Technique
"To the phrase 'as clear as daylight' we counter: 'No, as dark as daylight, which lies – as clear as the rainbow, which tells us the truth' (Boal, 1995, p. 150).

When light hits a raindrop, it refracts and disperses, revealing all the true colors that the white light concealed. In the Rainbow of Desire technique, a group functions as a prism, as each member reflects a different hue of the protagonist's personality.

Each human being has an inner diversity of emotions, attitudes, and desires — and a kind of inner governance is necessary to help these coexist. *When I experience internal conflict, can't make a decision, or keep making wrong decisions, perhaps I have marginalized facets of myself and overlooked their wisdom. I've driven bits of my humanness into exile: my fears, hurts, competitive impulses, need for love and belonging. Suddenly one emotion, attitude, or desire becomes a monochrome — a rainbow with only one color — as when fear or vengeance sweeps over me and I know nothing else.*

This technique begins with a brief scene of a protagonist's dilemma. Then participants sculpt each other to represent the full spectrum of the protagonist's unseen desires — ideally, the antagonist's inner conflict as well — which are animated through physical and verbal monologues and dialogue.

Van der Kolk (2014) describes "the mind as a kind of society. In trauma the self-system breaks down, and parts of the self become polarized and go to war with one another ... The internal leader must wisely distribute the available resources and supply a vision for the whole that takes all the parts into account" (pp. 280–281). Self-governance means everyone has the capacity to empower themselves rather than project authority and power upon someone else.

Internal Oppression and the Cops in the Head

"*Boal realized that internal antagonists could be just as threatening to human life as external cops*" (Blair, 2011, p. 33).

Cop in the Head is a brilliant game brimming with insight and laughter. Someone enacts a situation in which something she desires eludes her. Nothing external is stopping her; she simply cannot engage her will. The joker asks her to silently sculpt the "cops" that were present in her memory or imagination during the improvisation. These are actual people from her life: a relative, teacher, employer from whom she has received a limiting message.

"*Do you remember when ...?*" she asks each one, then elaborates: "*... and that is why ....*" She arranges her cops in a constellation around herself, and the cops use both their physical formation and the verbal information she has given them. Muttering admonitions, the cops inexorably creep forward, even though she pushes them back. This becomes a game in which the protagonist tries to change the outcome while the cops try to keep it the same.

What might be the cops in the head of a white woman traveling to Africa? *"You'll do more harm than good." "Outsiders shouldn't meddle." "You're neglecting your own community in Virginia." "You're just like your British ancestors, feeling entitled to go gallivanting off to any continent you choose."* These inner "authorities" are intrusive – but potentially instructive. They don't have to take over. They just want to be heard!

Three Wishes

Though at first glance it might seem like a superficially happy ending to a sad story, Three Wishes is a potent way to imagine a "way out of no way." People with whom the authors have worked – suicidally depressed patients, elders living with buried racial trauma in Virginia, street youth in Kenya – often could not imagine things being different. Sometimes despair offers solace when it's become too painful to hope.

Granting someone three wishes seems childlike, whimsical, and noninvasive: What harm is there in wishing? Harmless indeed, yet so powerful to formulate an intention and then immediately see it enacted. For example, a story is shared of a little girl who wanders away from camp one night and gets lost. Then upon her triumphant return the next morning she discovers that no one even noticed she was missing. Watching this scene, our hearts break a little. So we offer a glimpse into what could be: her heart's desire, the heroine's homecoming.

In war-torn societies, one's first wish might be to exact vengeance. The second wish might be to see the perpetrator beg for mercy. After seeing these wishes gratified in fantasy, could wish number three be an enactment of forgiveness? What would it look like, feel like – what would happen next, what might it lead to?

PEACE MARSHALS: A FORUM THEATRE TOOLKIT AS A WAY FORWARD

For over two decades Amani People's Theatre has worked with vulnerable youth populations to fashion peace in their communities, mobilizing and training county youth volunteers to be Peace Marshals. Young people demonstrate extraordinary zeal in addressing socio-political and ethnic identity-based issues. Yet when disillusioned by lack of economic options and limited opportunities to engage in decision-making processes, they are easily enlisted as foot soldiers and rioters. Anticipating the 2017 national election, the authors have been preparing a Forum Theatre toolkit to place youth — the major drivers and victims of election-related violence — at the forefront of change.

Local experts who know and live the subject matter and cultural context can become trained by APT as Peace Marshals, through an approach grounded in nonviolence and transformative leadership. They learn to analyze scenarios using Image Theatre exercises and create Forum Theatre performances to engage with the larger community.

Peace Marshals can provide early warning and on-the-spot guidance to influence behavior patterns before, during, and after the elections. Training prepares them to intervene in crises and settle group disputes to stave off violence. Participatory theatre methods are used afterwards for debriefing: sharing experiences with each other, troubleshooting, and sustaining morale.

Thus we seek to combine the potential energy of the youth and the power of participatory theatre with the committed vision of APT's artist-peacemakers, in order to forge constructive relationships between youth and elders for a lifetime of civic engagement and mutual peacebuilding.

Conclusion

Van der Kolk links trauma and conflict, describing how theatre helps trauma survivors find their shared humanity. Kenya's history shows how people associate emotional expression with "losing control and ending up on the losing side again ... In contrast, theatre is about embodying emotions, giving voice to them, becoming rhythmically engaged, taking on and embodying different roles" (Van der Kolk, 2014, p. 335).

When a group listens and then enacts someone's true story — walking the walk, running the same risks — there is a unique experience of being understood and cared for. It is a thought experiment conducted with the whole body, a soul-storming session. Art changes the world through its both soft and disruptive power.

The world of "What if?" lies waiting within every moment: an opportunity to experiment before taking risks in the outer world. Dramatic reality serves as a bridge between imagination and action. Two individuals — or groups — may stand at an impasse. Yet an audience watching from outside recognizes both the love *and* the lack of understanding between them. From this aesthetic distance, spect-actors may see a way to step into the scene and pose a spectrum of solutions. Thus, theatre gives the public a chance to take the initiative − to stand at the threshold of a transformative moment and devise a script for real-world change.

> The Theatre of the Oppressed is located precisely on the frontier between fiction and reality − and this border must be crossed.
>
> (Boal, 1995, p. 245)

Acknowledgment

The authors wish to thank Amy Taylor for editorial assistance.

References

Blair, B. (2011). Theatre of the Oppressed, trauma, and the seventh shift. In E. Friedland & T. Emert (Eds.), *Come closer: Critical perspectives on Theatre of the Oppressed*. New York, NY: Lang Publishing.

Boal, A. (1992). *Games for actors and non-actors*. London: Routledge.

Boal, A. (1995). *The rainbow of desire: The Boal method of theatre and therapy*. London: Routledge.

Boal, A. (2001). *Hamlet and the Baker's Son*. New York, NY: Routledge.

Burgess, H. (2003). Enemy images. In G. Burgess & H. Burgess (Eds.), *Beyond intractability*. Retrieved from http://www.beyondintractability.org/essay/enemy-image

Burns, M., Beti, B., Okuto, M., Muwanguzi, D., & Sanyu, L. (2015). The domain of the possible: Forum Theatre for conflict transformation in East Africa. *African Conflict and Peacebuilding Review*, 5(1), 136−151.

Erenrich, S. (2010). *Rhythms of rebellion: Artists creating dangerously for social change*. Doctoral dissertation. Retrieved from https://etd.ohiolink.edu/

Freire, P. (1970). *Pedagogy of the oppressed*. New York, NY: Continuum.

King, M. L. (1958). *Stride toward freedom: The Montgomery story*. San Francisco, CA: Harper & Row.

Lederach, J. P. (2005). *The moral imagination: The art and soul of building peace*. New York, NY: Oxford University Press.

Lederach, J. P., & Lederach, A. J. (2010). *When blood and bones cry out: Journeys through the soundscapes of healing and reconciliation*. New York, NY: Oxford University Press.

Roberts, M. J. (2009). Conflict analysis of the 2007 post-election violence in Kenya. *New Dominion Philanthrometrics Journal, 1,* 2. Retrieved from http://www.ndpmetrics.com/papers/Kenya_Conflict_2007.pdf

Sajnani, N. (2009). Theatre of the Oppressed: Drama therapy as cultural dialogue. In D. R. Johnson & R. Emunah (Eds.), *Current approaches in drama therapy* (2nd ed.). Springfield, IL: Charles Thomas.

Sullivan, J., Burns, M., & Paterson, D. (2007). Theatre of the Oppressed. In A. Blatner (Ed.), *Interactive and improvisational drama: Varieties of applied theatre and performance*. Lincoln, NE: iUniverse.

Van der Kolk, B. (2014). *The body keeps the score: Brain, mind and body in the healing of trauma*. New York, NY: Viking.

Volkan, V. (1985). *Enemy images: A resource manual on reducing enmity*. Washington, DC: Psychologists for Social Responsibility.

13 Theater Research Methodology of a Split Society: Ukrainian Reality

Natalia Kostenko and Kateryna Tiahlo

One little tree is better than a heap of stones.
Augusto Boal

Social Theater at the Time of "Emergency"

More than 2 years have passed since the followers of Augusto Boal in Ukraine created a new generation of the social theater called *The Theater for Dialogue*, originating from *The Theater of the Oppressed* (TO). The latter is known for giving a person the creative power to turn art from a consumer's act to a creative one. This is a social theater, and it strives not only to expose the contradictions that exist in the society, but also to invite the audience to consider and resolve them. In doing so, in the opinion of theorists of the *TO*, it is neither a psychological/social project nor exceptionally artistic act. Instead, it transcends each of those elements, enhancing their influence on participants and spectators and creating a special atmosphere that generates a desire to change social order and people's lives.

TO prompts people to ponder why there is so much injustice in the world, and what can be done to change it. As its founder and theorist Augusto Boal, a Brazilian stage-manager, dramatist, and politician, said, this theater "is the beginning of a necessary social transformation and not a moment of equilibrium and repose" (Boal, 2006, p. 6).

This social theater is a branched art method with a great number of special techniques, which may be used both within and beyond the stage – in teaching, public discussions, psychological consultations, conflictology, journalism, literature activities – and that is only the tip of the iceberg. The *tree* of the TO symbolizes the growth of the method from philosophy, through games and images, to direct action and relieving social stress (Fig. 1) (Boal, 2006, p. 3).

So, what is the TO in the Ukrainian context, a society where extraordinary events have become routine? Where, in conditions of uncertainty, depression is not an individual state, but a long-term state of the society? Social contradictions have become considerably more aggravated in Ukraine since Euromaidan – a broad movement protesting the authorities' refusal to support the European Union for European values, which resulted in the

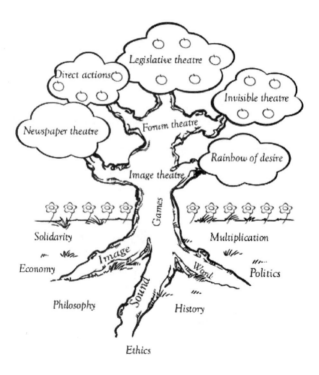

Fig. 1.   Tree of the Theater of the Oppressed.

Revolution of Dignity and an overthrow of the previous regime in Winter 2014. Maidan is the Independence Square in the center of Kyiv where protesters and sympathizers gathered. It has become a symbol of civil disobedience and resistance to authority and has given its name to the whole protest movement. Then followed annexation of the Crimea and continuing armed conflict in the East of the country, in Donbas, with the opponents of a sovereign democratic Ukraine. As a result of these events the Ukrainian society was suddenly put in a state of *"emergency,"* which is more often discussed in connection with today's financial-economic, political, cultural crises (Žižek, 2010; Adey, Anderson, & Graham, 2015; Kostenko, 2015). System turbulence, political instability, economic downturn, and an atmosphere of "temporality" are features of the present-day Ukraine. These circumstances do not allow ordinary citizens to trust any guarantees (institutional or personal) about the duration of this "temporality"; the culture of *"emergency"* has become part of everyday life. Still, people hope for positive changes in the society, to have new opportunities to experience fortitude and solidarity.

Innovatory Theater Prospect

Culture and art phenomena inspire current forms of civil protests, manifesting democratic ideals and values. They attract attention to cultural diversity, reduce psychological tension, and excite esthetic pleasure. The cultural effects of Maidan in the capital and other cities stimulated creativity and increased cultural and symbolic capital. The national anthem of Ukraine became the most popular melody of 2014, which spontaneously led to gatherings of people of various ages and social status; fences along public gardens and arterial roads were of yellow-and-blue colors of the Ukrainian flag. Art statements like a medieval catapult made by protesters, or the chime of St. Michael cathedral at night to call Kyivites to gather in the city center, are only two examples of art creativity connected to the Maidan. Another vivid example is a piano on Grushevsky Street. Both unknown performers and stars, such as singer Ruslana, played in the smoke of burning tires. There was also an unforgettable concert in the square by Sviatoslav Vakarchuk and his team in the evening cold with the phone-lights of thousands of people. Gadget cameras shot details not only with the aim to inform ad locum the whole world in media but to create later an authentic documentary. All of this was captured by Judith Butler's words about the people's protests of the last decade: "revolution happened because everyone refused to go home, cleaving to the pavement, acting in concert" (Butler, 2011).

This was the time when TO appeared in Ukraine. TO is the well-known world theater practice used to discuss social contradictions by modeling how "to live together," without the intended oppression of others, when "everyone is a leader for himself." However TO is new to the Ukrainian society. Though such theatrical-performative methods were in the framework of educational programs and psychological trainings, they have remained somewhat localized. Nevertheless the wave of public enthusiasm caused active development of alternative formats of arts, including theatrical art, where direct participation of citizens is most appreciated. Theater, and to a lesser extent cinema and fiction, are always first to react to social changes.

One of possible forms of TO in social communities is **forum-theater**. Actors, producers, and dramatists in the performance are not professional actors but people which have found themselves in complex and oppressing life conditions. During the preparatory seminar or workshop a group of participants analyzes the set problems with the help of facilitator – the "joker" – through games, exercises, discussions, and separate scenes. This activity as well as the groupwork before the performance permits participants to understand their problems better, to confide a personal story to others and to find support in the group.

The philosophy of this socio-artistic activity may be conventionally divided into three structural elements: discussion, creation of image, and transformation.

The first step is discussion; its aim is to elicit the problem, to define its acuteness and urgency, to narrate individual stories. The TO resembles here a "documentary theater." All the images are not given but created during the discussion of individual narratives; they are built of the standard social experiences. Then the most interesting things occur: live and bright images, models of situations are formed on the basis of personal emotional feelings. That is the second step when the participants can create miniatures, standing sculptures, as well as the esthetic context – surrounding sounds, movements, and other elements that symbolize senses and content. At this point the first stage of the theater is over, and then comes a time of dialogue. The spectators, as the coauthors of theatrical interaction, may intervene in the plot and change it according to their own sight. That may be repeated many times until all present people demonstrate their understanding of the situation and the possibilities of change.

In TO there is no strict division into actors and spectators, but collective interaction when the actors and conventional audience switch the roles. TO can take place not only in the enclosed space, but also in the open social environment, as in the case of the "invisible theater," when several actors perform in the social environment – for example, on the street or in transport – starting the play as in everyday life, enlisting other participants who do not know that they are in a "play." Such a secret experiment with reality can elicit rich material for the subsequent creative work – and future direct action.

But before speaking about the prospects of the *Theater for Dialogue* in Ukraine developed on the principles of the TO, it is worth recalling everything from the very beginning.

How Did It All Begin

In Winter 2014 well-known jokers of the TO from Belgium, Germany, Italy, and other countries came to Ukraine by invitation of Ukrainian activists. They had great experience with societies in crisis and thus demonstrated their solidarity with the Ukrainian people's protest. The action was called *Joker Tsunami in Ukraine* (Theater for Dialog, 2015), and this title corresponded well to reality. Three-day seminars of theatrical orientation with the use of the methods developed by Boal (1993) were held simultaneously in Kyiv, Lviv, Chernihiv, Chernivtsi, and Donetsk.

The first public performance of the *Theater for Dialogue* took place in Kyiv on February 16, 2014 in the Ukrainian Home near the Maidan and gathered a great audience (Tiahlo, 2015) (Fig. 2). The spectacle touched the theme of Euromaidan, embracing both activist supporters and opponents, those who had not approved it and stood for the former system. They presented miniatures, created by the methods of forum-theater, favoring further expression of opposite positions. They aggravated contradictions between peaceful and more radical protesters, between neutral observers and activists, between elder persons and impulsive youth – between those social groups which wanted, in one way or another, to change this reality. It seems that after the dialogues in the Ukrainian Home the participants experienced all possible emotions but indifference. At the same time performances took place in other Ukrainian cities

Fig. 2. *Theater of the Oppressed* Company. Kyiv, February 16, 2014. Inscription on the building pediment: "Combining true values."

and towns, sparking keen interest and heated discussions in the society.

But within several days there were mass shootings of protesters by government specialized forces, and Institutska Street turned into the avenue of dead heroes, and Maidan from a space of liberty to one of mourning. More than 100 protest participants died in those days; people have called them the *Heavenly Hundred*. The participants of the Kyiv theatrical group received information about first victims on Maidan by phone, when they were working over controlling their own desires and strivings by the methods of *The Rainbow of Desires*. Reckless guys left for Maidan, to defend those who remained and were helpless before this tragedy. The response of the theater of direct action was prompt.

It was difficult to overestimate the role of socially active art and art resistance to violence after those tragic events, captured by the peaceful and not indifferent "*Theater of the Oppressed* is a rehearsal for reality" (Declaration of Principles, 2015). In other words, people had to train to oppose the force without bloodshed, to discuss conflicts, to come to common decisions, and, at last, to search for the projection of the joint and personal future. But under existing conditions a call for dialogue seemed impossible. The world had broken into "ours" and "foreign," becoming black-and-white and an attitude of "struggle to the end." That is why cultural trainings of people with different opinions as to what is happening and especially dialogues among them became rather strained. The everyday and public communication was semantically loaded with incompatible values and with serious problems.

Nevertheless, TO in Ukraine at the time of Maidan has shown its potential in both social and esthetic plays, demonstrating how the formation of civil consciousness can emerge through the self-reveal of a person as an actor or spectator.

Value Dilemmas of Forum Spectacle about Maidan

What are these irreconcilable values that excited the imagination in performances about Maidan, values expressed in the slogans of protesters – the "true" values, as shown in Fig. 2 – and those of the opposition, inspiring conflicts in discussions of participants and spectators? The "live" material generated by the TO – narratives, the language of gestures, images, symbols, scenography of performances, and discussions – answers this question. Thus, we offer the reader to move with us into that value-based space that was created by TO in the period of Maidan, where conflicts were made tangible by participants and spectators.

Performance plots were not focused on the activity of politicians. They were about the life of ordinary citizens, mainly young people who had found themselves in the state of "emergency," involved in the events of the Revolution of Dignity. The video recordings of all 11 performances of the cycle *Joker Tsunami* in different cities show how specific life situations – family, business, recreation, relations with people – were correlated with social reflection and civil reaction, with the actions both "here and now" and in the near and distant future.

PRIORITIES

The "meaning field" of the performances conveyed an "either/ or" or "pro/con" mentality. Some of the values announced by the characters as "most important" had no alternative and counter arguments, as they were shared to some degree by all, such as a need for change *and* for maintaining some semblance of stability and order. Such values as *benevolence, independence,* and *social justice* prevailed among Maidan participants, while the values of *traditionalism, conformism,* and *achievements* prevailed among residents of Ukraine as a whole (Naumova, 2015).

These value complexes can also create a situational tension and an expression of essential conflicts. Those who value change believe in social justice, patriotism, moral values, freedom, personal choice, and the possibility of a better future. But in the actors' performance they also actively oppose the values of stability, which have led to "chaos," society dissidence, and separation of people:

"I've come to Maidan to build new Ukraine!"

"Better go and work! We need stability!"

(Kyiv, "The Birthday")

"Glory to the heroes! Ukraine is above all!"

"This movement in Maidan is pure nationalism, I don't support it."

(Kyiv, "Three Scenes about Maidan")

Humanism, love for people, when sanctifying peace protests, mutual aid, compassion, faith, and the world harmony as a whole, may be called in question in the theater narrative, if it restrains the readiness to engage in decisive actions and social activity.

Priest: "These are the same people, a prayer is stronger than an attack."

A fellow in Balaclava: "No, we needn't any prayer, it's time to act."

(Kyiv, "What Next")

Patriotism is a self-evident imperative of Maidan activists and sympathizers, confirmed symbolically by Ukrainian songs sounding from the stage. It also may be displayed with more personal intimacy, as it is with a young girl who, in spite of her girlfriend's proposals to leave Ukraine for more prosperous countries, does not understand how she can leave her parents, friends, and the land where she lives. Her conclusion sounds like an oath to herself.

"I'll make my fate myself; that will be my fate in my country."

(Lviv, "The Fair of Fates")

But if patriotic values do oppose anything, it is the public declarations about patriotism, more often ascribed to authorities and politicians. Politicians are rather presented with irony as persons who are not able to settle a conflict due to their own interests.

> "Patriotic" revelation of a politician: "I was born on this land, and as a true politician, I will grow rich on it."
>
> (Kyiv, "Three Scenes about Maidan")

As a result the image of today's Ukraine presented to spectators in a pantomime differs considerably from an ideal image. If ideal society looks in actors' performance as harmonic, balanced and constructive, the asymmetry, embarrassment, and somberness come across as symbols of the current society. Still, participants in the performance think that while Ukraine is torn apart today by opinions and actions, it manages to maintain balance.

VALUE "CROSS OF REALITY"

Maintaining balance requires dialogic thinking. The Rosenstock-Huessy metaphor (Rosenstock-Huessy, 1970) symbolizes dual tensions: *inside-outside* and *forward-backward*. Applied to the Maidan phenomenon, axes forming "a conflict cross" or "stress cross" may be interpreted as *paternalism – personal responsibility* and *love – envy* (Fig. 3).

Paternalism as a complex of motivations ascribes control of human behavior to "outside" forces, be they the state, traditional and nontraditional communities, family circle, friends, strangers, or even a concurrence of circumstances. For example, in a spectacle shown in Donetsk the situation of employment of a nonqualified pretender recommended by an influential person passes

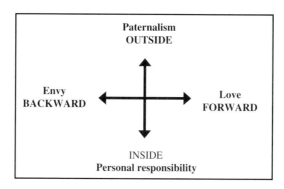

Fig. 3.   Stress Space in to Spectacles (Ukraine, February 2014).

without notice, and no corruption is implied. Assuming personal responsibility is too difficult for ordinary people, because since the Soviet period, when the behavior of citizens was almost completely regulated by the state, paternalist inclinations have taken root in a considerable number of Ukrainians, especially elderly ones. Among socially and professionally active people of youth and middle age, another mood is demonstrated. They appreciate their rights for the personal choice and human dignity, specifically manifested by Euromaidan.

To take responsibility for oneself and for others a person needs, besides understanding and feelings, an existential or volitional spurt, which is not always possible and can be made only with mutual support and persuasion by those who are ready for such action.

"I'd be a civil activist

And defend human rights

If one else except ministers

Asked me help all people in strike

I would come from words to deeds

Would forget all "ifs" in head

If someone made fog to run,

Showed us road in the dark"

(Kyiv, "What Next").

"Let's take part in the Maidan."

"And do you understand where is truth and where is lie?"

(Chernigiv, "Ukrainian Girl")

"I want to fight for my rights first in my life, but I thought before that I am alone and can do nothing."

(Kyiv, "What Next")

The constructive solidarity is accompanied with *love*, but its antipode – *envy* – is capable of forming negative solidarities, up to armed violence, with powerful energy. In the temporal continuum, lettered in Fig. 3, that is the *backward* movement, because Ukraine did not suffer from military conflicts from the time of the Second World War, and the fact of military opposition in the Crimea and Donbas was comprehended by people as something perverted and impossible. Nevertheless, envy, which does not exclude violence, is expressed on a stage too weakly compared to love. Envy is not articulated in a special way and avoids verbalization. But, using theatrical resources it is sometimes expressed with gestures, body language, reaching a scuffle, with intonations and facial expression of actors. Judging from spectators' reaction, purely theatrical techniques work here rather effectively (Fig. 4).

The "stress cross" just symbolizes the atmosphere created on the stage, outlining the rushing-about of confused identity. But it pales in comparison with the attempts to overcome the plot conflict and to take the path of dialogue (Fig. 5).

Fig. 4.   *Envy.* Miniature *What Next.* Kyiv, February 16, 2014.

Fig. 5.   *Consolidation.* After a Spectacle. Donetsk, February 16, 2014.

DONETSK PRECEDENT: BEYOND THE STAGE

Local conflicts in theater performances look rather dramatic, but they are usually settled by compromises or mutual leaving of the conflict sphere. For example, characters with opposite opinions toward Maidan might take part in some entertaining arrangement that allows them to stay away from politics, to forget the conflict for a while — life of full value goes on. Actually, the same decisions were rather infrequent in that period of time: friends stopped contacts because of uncompromising positions, families, and ties of relationship broke apart due to political disagreements. The dilemma *game — reality* appeared more than once in discussions after the spectacle, for example in the form of a proposition to move the stage to Grushevsky Street in Kyiv (the hottest site of protests) to correct scenic interpretation.

When the theater event itself comes into collision with real life, the problem of dialogue becomes rather complicated. In Donetsk, in the time of spectacle performance there appeared in the street a group of people on behalf of a youth political organization allied with the former authorities. They were aggressive and insisted on talking with representatives of TO. The theater troupe and spectators refused to get into contact with them for the reasons of security and threats to spoil a theater show. The phrase "we have to enter into dialogue with those who are ready for it" sounded rather persuasive. But TO participants had dual impressions with respect to such decisions: "*It was perceived ambiguously. We have come to make a theater of dialogue, but refuse to enter into dialogue, when it is proposed. It is clear that one of the parties manipulates the dialogue attempts. ... We are still asking ourselves: if it were otherwise, could it change just a little what is going now in Donetsk?*" (Joker Tsunami in Ukraine, 2015).

When the theater goes beyond the stage, and intrudes into the reality of conflict, the importance of understanding the context of what is going on, displaying social and cultural sensitivity, and making wise, sometimes bold decisions becomes obvious. And the role of the future leader, who is formed in such conditions, assuming the responsibility and inspiring the group, certainly becomes evident.

Two Years Later

Not all of the participants of first performances in February 2014 take an active part in the theater projects now. In a continuous state of "emergency" many people have given up the idea of the-atrical dialogues with society; they have chosen more efficient, as it seems to them, more "real" methods of participation in social life, or have been occupied with personal problems.

However, judging from interviews with some first actors 2 years later (February–March 2016) and analysis of blogs of those infatuated with this work even now, their first experience of TO on the eve of the armed power offensive against the pro-testing Maidan has not passed without a trace. Most of them joined the theatrical process understanding and feeling its civil spirit and social benefit, and remember being bewitched by that special symbolic reality which only a theater can produce. Some of them confessed that they performed for the first time in their lives and, having had an opportunity to try themselves in several roles, received "a golden experience" of combining their own civil position with pleasure from theatrical action. The opinions were divided as to the question of how would they play their parts today. Some of them would refuse to play their old heroes (Maidan antagonists) whose opinions were opposite to their own. Others were ready to play their parts as they did it before, since their characters believed in success of the common cause and distrusted authorities, which charac-terizes the current situation as well. Everybody valued the potential of theatrical interactive methods which, by highlight-ing the problems disturbing different classes of the society, stim-ulate reflection. The participants of first performances remember that in the Ukrainian Home they were staggered by the force that the methods of TO gave people, creating a dia-logue with "other party," exciting self-reflection of the sur-rounding reality that seemed impossible before. They are sure today that they have to analyze their life to understand what oppresses them and others like them, and how they can try to change it.

One of the authors of this chapter also took part in those per-formances in Maidan. And it seems to her that if it were not for those theatrical experiments with the sense, desire, and expres-sion of all the dispiriting moments on the stage, the consequences of that Winter could have been different for her. Each of coa-ches-jokers gave her and her friends, besides knowledge and skills, something that they needed then – confidence, faith, the understanding of significance of actions or passivity. Properly speaking, their task was also to teach people to present their own images, to copy experience so that it could be demonstrated to other people.

According to actors of forum-theater, it is important for them to feel the authenticity of their participation in the community of congenial souls, in collective action on improving mutual life in the society — more so if this collective action is performed in such expressive theatrical format that helps free personal potencies, to reinterpret current events. "*I have comprehended a new definition of activism,* — said Ukrainian joker Oksana Potapova after first performances, — *I have understood that I can do something important for me with other people, and that is also activism. That is not always people with transparency on the street …*" (Joker Tsunami in Ukraine, 2015). Today, she works with TO in the towns of Donbas and East of Ukraine, where people's convictions are often opposing and result in direct conflicts. And because forum-theater is one of those methods which helps conflicting parties come into contact, "*possibly, it will inspire the town residents to make the life around themselves such as they want*" (Potapova, 2015). Leadership is what is engendered, not unfounded promises of changes in society.

Instead of Conclusion

Today *Theater for Dialogue*, which has employed the ideas and tools of the TO, is a rather branched system of interpersonal and interorganizational interactions directed to educational, social, psychological, and creative activity. Its geography is persistently extended, embracing cities and towns of Ukraine. It broadens the circle of its participants, forms local theater troupes, gathers new audiences. Time dictates its conditions, suggests new plots that are different from those in the very beginning.

Flows of displaced persons from the Crimea and Donbas, where war is going on, aggravation of social contradictions and personal tragedies caused by these events, have added new topics to theatrical dialogues. These are the problems of constrained emigrants, family conflicts, inner and outer borders arising between people, and helplessness of a person facing social challenges. *Theater for Dialogue* deals with these and accompanying problems, presenting performances created by already experienced Ukrainian jokers. Theater-educational workshops for representatives of the social sector, trade unions and volunteers, initiative groups anxious about the state of their towns and settlements, and organizations that defend the rights of women and LGBT-communities also have become popular (Theater for Dialog, 2015).

The tour *Maidan Today*, adapted for the stage, was recently organized in the Museum of Maidan. Its main purpose was to reinterpret the experience of Euromaidan of 2013–2014. The Museum guests could meet the images of rebellions, volunteers, members of specialized forces, policemen, sit at decorative barricades and decide which of these images they support today. People are not in a hurry to leave those museum barricades; they are pondering over what has happened with them and the country in recent years.

In the course of time there appeared a very important task for the *Theater for Dialogue* – to issue the book by Augusto Boal *Games for Actors and Non-Actors* (Boal, 2002) in the Ukrainian language and to present it in various cities and towns of Ukraine. The book is intended for a broad audience – from students of artistic higher educational institutions to civil activists.

No doubt the theatrical interactive methods offered by the TO have demonstrated with the example of Ukraine their efficiency as teaching techniques of understanding problems of other people, training of the *culture of dialogue*, reflexive *entering in social life*, and producing new collectivities ready for social changes. Such abilities and practices are deficient in everyday life and civil communication. That is why the *Theater for Dialogue*, being the successor to the TO, has inherited its creative potencies and is the important part of the civil society that is being intensively formed today in Ukraine.

Acknowledgment

The authors are grateful to Susan Erenrich, who worked with Augusto Boal, for valuable advice and recommendations during the chapter preparation, as well as to Jon Wergin for final chapter editing. And, certainly, we very thank all Ukrainian activists of forum-theater, who took part in our study by a different way.

References

Adey, P., Anderson, B., & Graham, S. (2015). Introduction: Governing emergencies: Beyond exceptionality. *Theory, Culture & Society, 32*(2), 3–17.

Boal, A. (1993). *Theatre of the oppressed.* New York, NY: Theatre Communications Group.

Boal, A. (2002). *Games for actors and non-actors.* A. Jackson (Trans., 2nd Ed.). London: Routledge Taylor & Francis Group.

Boal, A. (2006). *The aesthetics of the oppressed.* A. Jackson (Trans.). London: Routledge Taylor & Francis Group.

Butler, J. (2011). *Bodies in alliance and the politics of the street.* Lecture held in Venice, September 7, 2011, in the framework of the series The State of Things, organized by the Office for Contemporary Art Norway (OCA). Retrieved from http://www.eipcp.net/transversal/1011/butler/en

Declaration of Principles. (2015). International Theatre of the Oppressed Organization, n.p., 2004. Retrieved from www.theatreoftheoppressed.org/en/index.php?nodeID=23

Joker Tsunami in Ukraine.(2015). *Theatre for Dialog,* November. Retrieved from https://mail.google.com/mail/u/0/#inbox/15331bf77aabbdf4?projector=1

Kostenko, N. (2015). Belonging to a certain culture in the state of 'emergency'. *Ukrainian society: Monitoring of Social Changes,* 2(16), 390–405 (in Ukrainian).

Naumova, M. (2015). Values of EuroMaydan: The projection of possible society. In N. Kostenko (Ed.) *Changeabilities of culture: The sociological projections.* Kyiv: Institute of Sociology, National Academy of Sciences of Ukraine, 314–341 (in Ukrainian).

Potapova, O. (2015, November 24). A forum-theater in Konstantinovka: To glance on a home town newly. Retrieved from http://tdd.org.ua/ru/forum-teatr-v-konstantinovke-glyanut-na-rodnoy-gorod-po-novomu

Rosenstock-Huessy, E. (1970). *Speech and reality.* Introduction by Clinton C. Gardner. Norwich, Vermont: Argo Books, Inc.

Theater for Dialog (2015). (In Ukrainian). Retrieved from http://tdd.org.ua/

Tiahlo, K. (2015). "Theatre of the Oppressed": From sociology of analyses to the sociology of direct action. *SVOYE – Ukrainian Sociological Journal,* 1(11), 22–29 (in Ukrainian).

Žižek, S. (2010). A permanent economic emergency. *New Left Review,* 64(July–August), 85–95.

14 From Needs-Based to Asset-Based Community Development: The ABCD Method as an Effective Strategy for Engaging with Grassroots Leaders in South Africa

Kennedy C. Chinyowa,
Mziwoxolo Sirayi and Selloane Mokuku

Introduction

It has become increasingly evident that "developing" grassroots communities is a much more complex issue than previously imagined. Despite their best intentions, national governments, non-governmental organizations and international aid agencies have come to realize that people cannot be developed but they develop themselves (Nyerere, 1978). It is not enough to try and change people's attitudes and behavior by creating awareness, bringing new knowledge, and influencing their values and beliefs toward development interventions. What development workers, activists, researchers, and policy makers thought to be of benefit to grass-roots communities has often been rejected by the would-be bene-ficiaries. Byam (1999) argues that those most likely to work to change their circumstances are the people most affected by them.

What do grassroots communities really want from develop-ment initiatives? How can development workers approach their work? There have been calls to search for effective strategies for communicating development but what still remains is an under-standing of the most sustainable approach to such development. In African contexts, theater for development (TFD) has emerged as a more people-centered and participatory approach to grass-roots intervention. TFD can be viewed as an embodied process for communicating the needs and aspirations of target communi-ties. Mlama (1991) has described a typical TFD workshop as an animating process for building up the people's capacity to create their own performances, and through that, to analyze their situa-tion in order to start a more sustained process of community organization. Both facilitators (or animators) and their partici-pants grapple with the problems affecting the community in order to arrive at a critical awareness, and if possible, plan a course of action to solve those problems. The workshop therefore acts as a basis for improving the community's well-being.

The Laedza Batanani Workshop in Botswana has been regarded as the pioneering experiment that paved the way for other prominent African Theater for Development (TFD) projects such as Kamiriithu in Kenya, Murewa in Zimbabwe, Kumba in Cameroon, and Marotholi Travelling Theatre in Lesotho. Laedza Batanani (1974–1976) aimed at awakening the creative potential of villagers in the Bokalaka region of Botswana. The major task was to "overcome problems of low community participation and indifference to government development efforts in the area" (Kidd & Byram, 1982, p. 23). As the Setswana term for the proj-ect implies, *laedza batanani* sought to raise the community's con-sciousness by enabling villagers to participate in their own development and replace apathy with collective action.

However, in spite of its best intentions, Kidd and Byram (1982) report that nothing happened at the end of the Laedza

Batanani experiment. Why? They attribute the failure to the dual nature of TFD projects, their intention to create critical awareness among participants on the one hand, and to disseminate dominant ideologies that tend to domesticate participants on the other. Laedza Batanani ended up having community leaders, government officials, and development workers imposing their ideas on the local villagers by dealing with issues and concerns of the dominant class rather than giving voice to the marginalized. For this reason, Kidd and Byram (1982) have lamented how Laedza Batanani laid the foundation for most TFD projects that have tended to reduce community participation to an instrumental exercise, critical awareness to false consciousness, problem posing to symptomatic problem-solving, and collective action to external imposition. The situation then, which still prevails now, is that most TFD projects in Africa are once-off events with limited or no follow-up in terms of building capacity and organizing the community for action (Chinyowa, 2005).

This chapter seeks to demonstrate how best to negotiate with community or grassroots leaders without overshadowing the primary beneficiaries of TFD projects. Drawing illustrations from a baseline survey workshop held with community leaders in the Eastern Cape Province, the chapter shows how the Asset-Based Community Development (ABCD) method could be perhaps the most effective strategy for initiating sustainable community driven TFD projects. The ABCD strategy rests on the premise that local communities can drive their own development by identifying and mobilizing their own existing, and often unrecognized assets.

From Top-Down to Bottom-Up Approach

The shift from an exogenous, "top-down" or "outside-in" approach toward an endogenous, "bottom-up" or "inside out" approach in contemporary development discourse has necessitated the search for more people-centered intervention paradigms. The "endogenisation" of development discourse recognizes that processes of conscientisation (or raising people's awareness), empowerment and transformation are internal to the mechanisms of social structures and cannot be entirely dependent on external interventions.

In the case of TFD, two major intervention approaches have been identified. The first approach is based on an "outside-in" or "top-down" interventionist model that has been widely criticized for imposing development initiatives that are "foreign" to target communities (Epskamp, 1989). In this exogenous approach, the decisions made from outside the community have been found to be largely ineffective in changing established attitudes, beliefs, and practices. The target community feels as if the externally driven development initiative is being imposed upon them. Thus as a development strategy, the "top-down" model tends to underestimate the target community's ability to shape their own destiny. On the contrary, the community lacks the necessary commitment since they often remain passive, uninterested, and unmotivated. As a result, the exogenous approach has been widely discredited as a form of manipulative propaganda that lacks reciprocity, dialogue, and feedback (Prenki, 2009).

Perhaps the main shortcoming of the top-down development model lies in its needs-based approach. As Keeble (2002) explains, needs-based approaches start with outsiders evaluating what is deficient in a community and how to fix the problems. Instead of working with the community to bring about change, external agents tend to set the agenda in order to "bail out" what they regard as "distressed communities" (Keeble, 2002). Thus, outsiders take up the responsibility of making judgements on the needs of communities which they may not be fully aware of. Even though the needs-based approach remains popular, it is apparent that communities are made to feel as if they are lacking, dependent, and problematic. Such an externally driven focus can be detrimental to development because it leads to deficient-oriented interventions where the community in question continues to rely upon outsiders.

TFD practitioners are now advocating for an "inside-out" or "bottom-up" approach that allows more room for active grass-roots participation in development communication. This endogenous model focuses on internal social structures rather than external agents. In so far as it constitutes an internal process of dialogue, action, reflection, and change, the endogenous model has come to be characterized by a strong tendency to make use of the local community's own resources, and therefore commands a considerable degree of credibility, participation, and sustainability. The shift from viewing the community in terms of its needs to viewing it in terms of its resources places the asset-based approach at an advantage.

The Asset-Based Community Development (ABCD) Approach

Although most contemporary TFD interventions are still dominated by the "top-down" or "outside-in" approach, the gradual shift from a needs-based to an asset-based paradigm could, to a considerable extent, be credited to the ABCD method. According to Keeble (2002), ABCD begins with what is present in the community and builds on the assets and capacities of individuals, associations, and institutions. Rather than focus on what is lacking or deficient in the community, Kretzmann and McKnight (1993) have proposed a drastically different approach that involves the total investment of the grassroots in their own development. For instance, while the popular Kamiriithu workshop in Kenya involved both facilitators and the community finding ways and means of using TFD as a means of influencing social change, Ngugi wa Mirii admits that such theatre can also be a means of mystifying as issues of concern would not have emanated from the people as the community's problems. It does not follow that once you have engaged with the community, then you have solved their problems (Byam, 1999, p. 187). In the case of this community there was a deficit mentality in terms of what could be achieved, thus Ngugi's argument seems to concur with Kompaore's (2004) popular theatre experiences in Burkina Faso who points out that the mere fact of involving the community, or even coming from the community, does not necessarily guarantee the effectiveness of an intervention.

How can the grassroots communities shift from a needs-based to an asset-based paradigm? Jourdain (2005) argues that the process begins with the individual who needs to view his/her community as a place of opportunity and not a place of problems. Jourdain (2005) poses four questions that communities need to ask themselves about what they observe in their locality as follows:

i. What opportunities are available?
ii. How can we turn these opportunities into advantages?
iii. What do we want to have in our community?
iv. What is working in our community?

These questions are meant to prompt community members to identify and develop their own asset mapping strategy before they can turn to external agents. Kretzmann and McKnight

(1993) have argued that asset mapping enables communities to see the wealth of resources in their locality and sets them on the path to utilizing their assets in order to create change for themselves. External assistance can then be sought when communities are actively engaged in developing their own resources.

However, the ABCD method has been criticized for failing to address the role of external agents, discouraging interdependency among community members, dealing with unequal relations of power and fostering community leadership in different contexts. Since ABCD focuses on the building of social capital, this can only happen when all members are recognized and valued according to their disparate abilities, and when the grassroots work together for the common good. Thus adopting a one size fits all strategy does not seem to work in favor of the ABCD method. But, in spite of these shortcomings, ABCD still has an edge over the needs-based approach to community development. When it comes to grassroots leaders in particular, the deficiency model tends to discourage them from taking the initiative to tap on local resources by highlighting the negative aspects of the community.

Mpingana Senior Secondary School Case Study

The trip to the Eastern Cape for a TFD project was undertaken from July 26–28, 2014. The target of the community engagement project was Mpingana Senior Secondary School located in the Eastern Cape Province of South Africa. This trip was a follow-up to previous trips that Tshwane University of Technology (TUT) had carried out in 2013, with a joint partnership that included the local community, the Faculty of Arts and the Faculty of Humanities. This partnership has since been broadened and includes an independent production company called ShakeXperience which makes use of the creative arts to facilitate teaching and learning in educational contexts. The TUT team consisted of Mzo Sirayi, Dean of the Faculty of Arts and Kennedy Chinyowa from the Department of Drama and Film Studies. ShakeXperience was represented by Selloane Mokuku, a program developer and researcher in the company's Arts in Education unit.

On arrival at Mpingana Senior Secondary School, the team was introduced to the school teachers and community leaders who were members of the School Governing Body (SGB). The SGB is regarded by the Department of Basic Education (DBE) as an important structure that contributes to the administration of the school by making decisions that affect its operations. After preliminary introductions, Sirayi acknowledged the presence of community leaders whom he described as "village professors." He proceeded to point out that the "village professors" serve as an invaluable resource that will inform TUT's engagement with the community. Having been born and bred in the Mpingana area, Sirayi remarked that he was not impressed by people from the community who go to study but do not return to add value to the community.

In Sirayi's view, TUT's collaboration with ShakeXperience and engagement with Mpingana Senior Secondary School and the local community was aimed at exploring capacity building strategies for the development of the school. The teachers and community leaders were therefore encouraged to take advantage of the opportunity to improve the school's persistently low matriculation pass rate. Sirayi went on to challenge the gate-keepers saying, "We cannot afford to settle for better, when there's best." The idea was to share the "dream" of making a difference in the community by improving the school's "matric" pass rate which stood at only 6% in 2012. In his response, the school principal acknowledged that the school was under-performing but was quick to add that, "That does not mean we cannot perform. The school must perform with the little it has, we need to have a bigger vision and move forward." At the time of this visit, the school had set itself a target of 50% "matric" pass rate for 2014. The principal indicated that they were ready to listen, work together and do what was needed in order to improve.

In South Africa, education is governed by the DBE as well as the Department of Higher Education and Training (DHET). The former is responsible for primary and secondary schools, and these are further divided into bands, namely, General Education and Training (GET), which includes learners in grade 0 to grade 9 as well as Further Education and Training (FET), which includes grades 10–12. Non higher education vocational training facilities are also included in FET. Within the FET phase, the final year of school (grade 12) is referred to as Matric or Matriculation. Learners who complete matric receive a Senior Certificate, and are said to have matriculated. Depending on the quality of their pass points (Admission Point Score/APS) such learners may be admitted to universities or technical colleges to further their career paths.

Community leaders such as the SGB and teachers make up the gatekeepers of the community who often want to attract resources from outside the community by playing up the severity of its problems (Kretzmann & McKnight, 1993). Such leaders believe that their success lies in the amount of resources they will have brought from outside the community rather than on how self-reliant the community can be. As a result, the community itself begins to believe in its own deficiency. People begin to see themselves as incapable of taking charge of their lives. They are regarded as people who "do not know," and therefore treated as people who "beg to know." In most situations, they are viewed as "empty vessels" (Freire, 1967) who need to be filled with out-side knowledge in order to articulate and solve their problems. Alison Mathie and Gord Cunningham argue that such community members "no longer act like citizens, instead they begin to act like clients or consumers of services with no incentive to be producers" (2002, p. 4). In their book aptly entitled, *Building Communities from the Inside Out*, Kretzmann and McKnight argue that the process of recognizing the people's capacity to solve their own problems begins with the construction of a new lens through which communities can begin "to assemble their strengths into new combinations, new structures of opportunity, new resources of income and control, and new possibilities for production" (1993, p. 6). In the case of the Mpingana School community, it was necessary to begin by changing the mind-sets of the grassroots leaders themselves, to make them "lead by step-ping back" through realizing their own and the community's capacity to shift from being "clients" to "citizens."

Facilitating the Baseline Survey Workshop

The school principal's use of words such as "the school must per-form with the little it has" set an interesting entry toward intro-ducing a different approach to the school's situation. The perspective was to use an ABCD approach. Accordingly, the presence of the SGB and teachers in the workshop was recog-nized as an invaluable opportunity to establish a shared vision toward improving the school. Although the school's "problems" were not ignored, the team introduced action laden games and exercises followed by reflections to come up with a baseline survey whose purpose was

i. to establish the situation in the community in order to plan the parameters of the community engagement project;
ii. to negotiate with the gatekeepers in order to obtain their permission and buy-in before working with the school community;
iii. to establish baseline indicators against which the project's outcomes will be "measured";
iv. to collect data that will assist in designing, planning, implementing, monitoring, and evaluating the project;
v. to establish the priorities of the school community which will inform subsequent interventions;
vi. to map out the envisaged activities that will be carried out during the project.

The baseline survey workshop was led by co-facilitators from TUT and ShakeXperience. The workshop process began with playful games and exercises aimed at building trust, creating team spirit, and instilling a sense of focus. According to Eriksson (2009), play acts as a distancing device for making the familiar strange by allowing participants to "step back" and look more critically at events, happenings, and situations. Even though the distancing might create the impression that the events are rather detached from the real, its power lies in the capacity to arrest attention while creating space for involvement, absorption, empathy, and detachment. Eriksson (2009) further argues that "distancing effects" in play such as enjoyment and freedom help to mediate the seemingly disparate worlds of fiction and reality. As Soyini Madison (2012, p. 2) has argued, by applying performance-based strategies, we enter a poetics of understanding and an embodied system of knowledge concerning how activism can be constituted through imagination, fantasy, and creativity. The playfulness deployed through warm-up games and exercises therefore acts as the means for subverting and reconstituting reality.

For instance, during the baseline survey workshop, the teachers and community leaders were made to participate in warm-up games and exercises. The first warm-up game involved participants finding partners and counting up to three in turns. As the counting continued, the numbers were replaced with gestures and other bodily movements. Participants were then made to reflect on the significance of the counting game. Through this game, participants were able to appreciate each other's learning capacities, to realize areas that they are strong at and those that they were not. As one SGB member pointed out, "When this exercise was introduced, it looked so easy, but when you actually do it, it is a different story."

The reflective session opened an opportunity for more discussion and enabled participants to realize how parents and teachers needed to work together in order to make a difference to the school. Thus through warm-up games, the mood of "playfulness" (Sutton-Smith, 1997, p. 148) was able to arouse feelings of laughter, mirth, and relaxation while simultaneously subverting familiar norms, values, and beliefs. The intense absorption evoked by the "playful" experience had the power to move participants to other states of being. In the process of being distanced from familiarity, participants were transported into an alternative world that offered them a sense of being liberated from the limitations and constraints of their lived reality. Play created space for them to experiment and generate new symbolic worlds that could eventually be transferred to reality. As the Brazilian theatre practitioner, Boal (1995) once argued, when participants create images of their reality, they can eventually translate such images into their real lives. In other words, "the image of reality" can be translated into "the reality of the image."

It was perhaps the "give and gain" exercise that brought the teachers and community leaders closer to the ABCD approach. The primary purpose of this exercise was to enable participants to express their workshop expectations and to commit themselves to the workshop process. Each participant voiced what he/she expected to contribute and what he/she would get from developing the school. Table 1 shows a summary of participants' contributions during the give and gain exercise.

The give and gain exercise was based on the premise that each participant had something to contribute to the betterment of the school community. Therefore, it was important for each member to take responsibility for making the process a success. The exercise acknowledged the existence of potential assets within the community at any particular point in time. As a team, participants begin to realize how they can tap into each other's potential ability to solve their problems rather than wait for outside experts. Thus the give and gain exercise negated the tendency by communities to define themselves in terms of their

Table 1. Outcome of the Give and Gain Exercise.

Give	Gain
Participate in an engaging way	How to make change concrete
Learn by doing the activity	How teachers can make teaching to be fun
Giving information and learners give back	How to make teaching right
Allowing extra time to learners	How to make learners excel
Thoroughly engaging with learners	To gain creative skills in teaching and learning
Learners to be at the center of learning	To get information on leadership
By giving off our best	How to inspire ourselves including learners
Having a positive or right attitude	How to be dedicated to our work
Giving the learners love	What's the best way of getting quality results
Not beating up and punishing learners	What methods can we employ to make learners successful
Through dedication to our work, and being prepared to learn	How can things be made to change
Going an extra mile with learners	What difference can we make to learners

problems, needs, and deficiencies. It discouraged the participants from internalizing such negativity. As Elliot (1999, p. 12) concludes, like plants that grow toward their source of energy, communities should also move toward what gives them a progressive and sustainable livelihood.

The Asset Mapping Strategy

It has already been argued that the needs-based approach has a negative effect on how grassroots communities think about themselves and tend to create poverty stricken mind-sets. In contrast, the ABCD approach recognizes what the communities have, so that these resources become the springboard for building capacity within the communities. To this end, facilitators engaged participants in an asset mapping exercise in order to "build an inventory of their assets and ... to see value in resources that they would otherwise have ignored, unrealized or dismissed" (Mathie and Cunningham, 2002, p. 5). Such unrealized assets include the following:

   i. Human assets — skills, knowledge, labor, and health
  ii. Social assets — social networks and relationships of trust, confidence, and reciprocity
 iii. Natural assets — land, water, soil, animals, and climate
 iv. Financial assets — cash crops, livestock, and savings
  v. Physical assets — roads, bridges, clinics, schools, transport, houses, and sanitation.

To apply the ABCD approach, participants were grouped into pairs and asked to identify those assets that were already available to the school community. At first, it was difficult for participants to identify any assets since the school was located in a rural area where people are often perceived to have "nothing really." This negative perception was familiar to the facilitators but through persistent probing and questioning, participants were able to come up with the list of assets given in Table 2.

From feedback given after the focus group discussions, it was evident that participants had begun to realize the potential assets at their disposal. These assets could be mobilized to develop not only the school but also the wider community. Mathie and Cunningham (2002) assert that the key to ABCD lies in the power of local communities to drive their own development while leveraging additional support from outside experts. The recognition of their strengths, talents, and assets helps to inspire positive action for change than an exclusive focus on needs and

Table 2.   Outcome of Asset Mapping Exercise.

Human	Social	Natural	Financial	Physical
Teachers	Culture	Land	Government	Buildings
Parents (SGB)	Traditions	Water	Donors	Electricity
Learners	Councilors	Trees	Sponsors	Gas
Community	Church	Vegetation	Alumni	Desks and chairs
Council offices	Police	Manure	Computers	Roads
TUT facilitators		Climate	Laptops	Television
ShakeXperience facilitators			Internet	CD/DVD player
				Textbooks

problems. Thus the asset mapping exercise enabled the teachers and SGB to

    i. identify their unrealized capacities;
    ii. map out the diversity of available assets;
    iii. realize the relationships between local and external assets;
    iv. mobilize their resources for potential action;
    v. have more clarity on the school's vision and mission;
    vi. be aware of the opportunities for building on their assets.

Indeed, it was heartening to discover the enthusiasm that was present among the school's gatekeepers toward the end of the asset mapping session, especially when they began to reflect on what they could do to develop their school and community. When facilitators asked the participants to give a summary of what they had learnt during the course of the baseline survey workshop, their responses included the following:

    i. "Games can create a sense of focus and concentration."
    ii. "People can learn through play."
    iii. "The primacy of communication through dialogue should be observed."
    iv. "Leadership needs to be properly managed as observed in the group counting exercise."
    v. "We need to make the best out of our assets."
    vi. "The importance of dialogue and team spirit between teachers and learners."

It is evident that the ABCD method can transform mind-sets that had become locked in negative constructions of the self toward an appreciative construction of reality (Elliot, 1999). Community leaders who had "failed" to recognize any assets in their community were able to realize the potential strengths and capacities available to them.

Conclusion

The prevailing community engagement partnership between TUT's Faculty of Arts, Faculty of Humanities, ShakeXperience, and the Mpingana School community constitutes a formidable team geared toward advancing the school's vision, namely, *To develop a creative and original learner through effective teaching and learning.* The baseline survey workshop demonstrated how the ABCD strategy can enable TFD facilitators and practitioners to make a difference to the grassroots leadership. Instead of pursuing the usual needs-based problem-solving paradigm, ABCD provides a remarkable departure toward an asset-based problem-posing paradigm. The community was able to explore what it could do for itself by identifying and mobilizing its own strengths, capacities, and capabilities. The ABCD approach can therefore be regarded as one of the most effective strategies for sustainable community driven development. It seeks to discourage grassroots communities from focusing on needs, problems, and deficiencies that can only be solved by outsiders. In a way, ABCD practitioners are being called upon to capitalize on the strengths and opportunities that can release the potential of target communities to exercise their own sense of agency, ownership, and responsibility.

The school principal's willingness and readiness "to listen, work together and do what was needed in order to improve," was indicative of a shared vision and an indelible ingredient that will make the community intervention work in the best interests of all stakeholders. It will be necessary to come up with a practical action plan that has clear targets for a more comprehensive turnaround strategy that will encompass the school management, parents, teachers, and learners who are the primary stakeholders. The core of the intervention process will be to come up with more sustainable strategies for community empowerment, transformation, and development. And in the process come up with less intimidating strategies that can enable communities to find their strength. In the gate of community leaders in Mpingana, the arts seem to have played a significant role in creating such an environment.

References

Boal, A. (1995). *The rainbow of desire: The Boal method of theatre and therapy.* London: Routledge.

Byam, D. (1999). *Community in motion: Theatre for development in Africa.* Westport, CT: Bergin and Harvey.

Chinyowa, K. C. (2005). *Manifestations of play as aesthetic in African Theatre for development.* Unpublished PhD thesis. Centre for Applied Theatre Research, Griffith University (Mt Gravatt Campus), Brisbane.

Elliot, C. (1999). *Locating the energy for change: An introduction to appreciative enquiry.* Winnipeg: International Institute for Sustainable Development.

Epskamp, K. (1989). *Theatre in search of social change: The relative significance of different theatrical approaches*. The Hague: Centre for the Study of Education in Developing Countries (CESO).

Eriksson, S. (2009). *Distancing at close range: Investigating the significance of distancing in drama education*. Bergen: Vasa Press.

Freire, P. (1967). *Pedagogy of the oppressed*. London: Penguin Books.

Jourdain, K. (2005). Asset based community building. *Approaching Change*, 6(1), 8–17.

Keeble, S. (2002). Asset Based Community Development: A literature review. Department of Sociology Project, Humboldt State University, California, USA.

Kidd, R., & Byram, M. (1982). Demystifying pseudo-Freirian non-formal education: A case description and analysis of Laedza Batanani. *Community Development Journal*, 17(2), 91–105.

Kompaore, P. (2004). Artistic expression and communication for development. Paper presented at the 'Performing Africa' International Conference held at the Leeds University Centre for African Studies (LUCAS), Leeds, May 14–16.

Kretzmann, J., & McKnight, J. (1993). *Building communities from the inside out: A path toward finding and mobilizing a community's assets*. Evanston, IL: Institute for Policy Research.

Madison, M. (2012). *Acts of activism: Human rights as radical performance*. Cambridge: Cambridge University Press.

Mathie, A., & Cunningham, G. (2002). From clients to citizens: Asset Based Community Development as a strategy for community driven development. Occasional Paper Series No. 4, St Francis Xavier University, Antigonish, Nova Scotia.

Mlama, P. M. (1991). *Culture and development: The popular theatre approach in Africa*. Uppsala: The Scandinavian Institute of African Studies.

Nyerere, J. (1978). *Freedom and socialism*. Oxford: Oxford University Press.

Prenki, T. (2009). *The applied theatre reader*. London: Routledge.

Sutton-Smith, B. (1997). *The ambiguity of play*. Cambridge, MA: Harvard University Press.

SECTION V
People Power, Community Building, and the Arts for Social Change

15 Finding a Line from Fight Club to the Kennedy Center: How We Learned to Cross Invisible Bridges

Garth A. Ross

For 10 days in September of 2015, there was a skate park in front of the Kennedy Center. Where did it come from? Why did that even make sense? And why does it matter?

Finding a Line is our name for this multidisciplinary skateboard culture initiative that we describe as an ongoing, community-sourced public art project. The project caught attention and piqued curiosity, but just as often confounded. Skeptics and admirers alike have asked me all three of the above questions. I hope this story provides some answers and, like any good performance, leaves you wanting more.

I entered this story in a place called Fight Club. My role is that I have the pleasure of serving as the Vice President for Community Engagement at the John F. Kennedy Center for the Performing Arts in Washington, DC. The Kennedy Center is America's national cultural center in the nation's capital. It's more known for ballet, opera, and lifetime achievement awards than for skateboarding, punk rock and urban youth culture. Why then, would someone who leads community engagement at an arts center like this be working with skateboarders? And what would that person be doing in a place called Fight Club?

Fight Club, Ben Ashworth, and *Finding a Line*

Fight Club DC was a privately owned creative space in Washington, DC, for skateboarding, live music, visual art, construction, and documentation. It emerged on the scene in 2004 in an unoccupied and deteriorating building near the Washington Convention Center, which had opened one year earlier, initiating the eventual gentrification of the Shaw neighborhood. Fight Club arose when the Vans skate park in suburban Virginia just outside of DC closed its doors, leaving DC area skaters without an indoor alternative in bad weather. Ramps scavenged from the shuttered Vans park were the seeds of the space, but what would come to be known as Fight Club grew from an outsider ethos of collectivity and bricolage – improvisational creation from a diverse range of available things. In a scene dominated by white teenage boys, the community at Fight Club was more diverse in ethnicity, age, and gender. A donation at the unmarked door admitted those in the know to these weekly skating sessions that also included art exhibitions, film screenings, live bands, and DJs. As word of these wildly creative and energetic BYOB happenings spread and their popularity grew, it was generally understood that Fight Club DC would ultimately be a moment in time, a utopian scene destined to be displaced by development pressures, police, or both.

People called it Fight Club in reference to the film of the same name and its famous quote: "The first rule of Fight Club is: you do not talk about Fight Club. The second rule of Fight Club is you DO NOT talk about Fight Club!" (Uhls, 1999). So I didn't learn about this "underground" spot until 2009 when I was invited by a visual artist and skateboarder friend of mine. The moment I passed through the rusted metal door I was struck by an awareness that I'd become part of a whole that was greater than the sum of its parts. The point wasn't whether the skater in the bowl, or the band on the stage, or the art on the walls was the best ever. The power of the experience was in the balance of the technical and aesthetic with the core purpose of creative expression and engagement, amplified by intense positive energy. Everyone there was fully present and involved. It was there that I met skateboarder, artist, educator, and community activist Ben Ashworth, a driving force at the center of the scene.

When the Vans skate park closed, an important community asset was lost. Leadership was needed to transform a problem that was beyond the community's control into a solution that they did control. Ben and his collective of artists and skaters responded by transforming a dilapidated building on a dark alley into a vibrant venue in which multiple creative communities could converge and thrive. The situation called for transformational leadership, and Ben was happy to provide it. It's just what he does, like a calling. By the time the era of Fight Club DC came to a close in 2010 (allowing me to write about it without violating the first and second rules of Fight Club), Ben had already completed another project working with volunteers to transform community blight into a community asset by dredging tires out of DC's historically neglected Anacostia River (which separates the rest of the District from the historically neglected neighborhood of the same name) and using them to build an outdoor skate bowl dubbed "Green Skate Lab" (GSL) at Langdon Recreation Center in Northeast DC.

Then in 2012, with support from the DC Commission on the Arts and Humanities' public art installation commissioning program "5 × 5," Ben brought together residents of the Navy Yard and Capitol Hill neighborhoods with skaters, artists, and musicians to transform a dicey freeway underpass into a safe and accessible community space for arts and recreation that would come to be known as "Bridge Spot." Ben called this project *Finding a Line*, describing it as "a project which takes the improvisational act at the core of skateboarding – *Finding a Line* through physical space – and applies it to the process of transforming community space."

At the heart of each of these projects, from Fight Club to GSL to *Finding a Line* is Ben's commitment to the transformative power of dialogue through action. "*Finding a Line* is ultimately about presence," says Ben. "It reinforces the value of work in shared territory. It's a collective body that's forced to be present, thinking with our hands and our feet. It's a free zone, not a defined zone. Finding a Line opens up so many questions about how we can be together in this place."

When we first met at Fight Club, Ben and I struck up a conversation that continues today and is unlikely to end. From our earliest discussions, we agreed that the Kennedy Center would be a perfect platform on which to showcase this multidisciplinary collection of creative communities that come together around the expressive act of skateboarding. At the same time, we both acknowledged the unlikeliness of such a radical mash-up. For us, the appropriateness was so apparent that it felt like an imperative. A uniquely American phenomenon, skateboarding emerged from

1960s southern California surf culture and proceeded to spread across the country and around the globe, thriving outside the rules of sports and society anywhere green space was displaced by pavement. With audacity and imagination skaters turned wastelands into wonderlands using only a small board with four wheels. *Finding a Line* needed to be at the Kennedy Center. But how would we make the case for something that represented such a departure from current organizational practice? How would we make the bridge between the skate community and the national center for the performing arts as visible to others as it was to us?

An Invisible Bridge, Jason Moran, and Bandwagon and Live Skateboarding

In order to answer those questions to the best of my ability, I beg your indulgence as I refer to a pivotal moment in a big screen Hollywood action-adventure classic. In *Indiana Jones and the Last Crusade*, the climax of the plot plays out in the temple where the Holy Grail is hidden, and where Indy's mortally wounded father is being held for ransom. Indy must rely on an ancient text to make his way safely through the booby-trapped temple and retrieve the life-giving Grail in order to save his father. His final obstacle on the way to the Grail is a bottomless crevasse. Indy is so certain of the authenticity and veracity of the text that, after a dramatic pause to summon his faith, he takes a step away from the cliff edge into what looks like thin air, to find that his foot lands on an invisible bridge which he then walks safely across. When he reaches the far side of the crevasse, he crouches down and scoops up a handful of dirt, then turns and tosses it back over the surface of the bridge, making it plainly visible to all.

As much as I'd like to portray myself as Indiana Jones, in our story it was Jason Moran, jazz pianist and the Kennedy Center's Artistic Director for Jazz, who was the first to cross the invisible bridge between the performing arts establishment and skate culture, and then toss dirt back across it for us to follow.

In 2013, in addition to his visionary artistic leadership role at the Kennedy Center, Jason was also serving as artist-in-residence at SF Jazz in San Francisco, CA. At SF Jazz, he developed "Bandwagon and live skateboarding," an event in which he and his band "The Bandwagon" improvised a single 90-minute jazz jam session while Bay area skateboarders improvised their own skating session on a half-pipe installed in the theater right in front of the stage. The interdisciplinary dialogue and creative exchange between the skaters and musicians was inspiring for the performers and thrilling for the audience. With this project, Jason drew on his personal history growing up skateboarding and playing jazz in Houston, TX. As a teen torn between what seemed like the two different worlds of skateboarding and jazz, he was inspired by "Video Days," a film in which the path-breaking skater Mark Gonzales joyously reinterprets the concrete jungle of early 1990s New York City as a playground for his completely original skating to the music of the great jazz saxophonist John Coltrane. Over 20 years later, Jason would access that inspiration as a way to expand shrinking jazz audiences by demonstrating the parallels between the two seemingly disparate forms of expression.

Not only are both based in improvisation, but they also both develop and thrive in "sessions." Jason understood that sessions are typically for insiders of a creative community, while performances are designed for presentation to outsiders. He mindfully aimed to strengthen the connection between artists and audiences by inviting audiences into the authentic experience of a session. He believed this would help audiences understand and enjoy the exploratory trial and error creative process as the artists themselves do. He saw this raw format and this juxtaposition of forms as a way to reframe falling and failing in the pursuit of a new musical phrase or skateboard trick as exciting, courageous, and beautiful.

Having crossed the invisible bridge, Jason tossed dirt back across it by inviting me out to SF Jazz to experience it for myself. In San Francisco, I witnessed the leadership of an artist transforming the challenge of audience-building into the joy of community-building. After the success of the SF Jazz sessions, Jason asked if I thought we could do something similar at the Kennedy Center. With sold out shows and strengthened community relationships as evidence, and with Jason *and* Ben as partners, I was finally certain that we could.

The Bridge Connecting *Finding a Line* and the Vision of Kennedy Center President Deborah Rutter

The fact that now Jason, Ben, and I could all see the bridge still didn't mean that the Kennedy Center's new President Deborah Rutter could see it. The track records of Ben, Jason, and me would together have to serve as the ancient text on which Indy relied. Would our experience provide sufficient evidence? Would our conviction justify the step into what looked like thin air that this project would require of Deborah and the rest of the organization?

Before answering these new questions I need to continue answering the questions posed at the outset, and proceed from the initial question of "Where did it come from?" to "Why did a skate park in front of the Kennedy Center make sense?"

Addressing the question of why a skate park should be built at a cultural center is perhaps the most challenging, and at the same time the most important. Any attempt to answer must necessarily begin with the Kennedy Center's mission and leadership. As an expression of our mission, the following words precede our strategic plan: "Imagine a future where art and artists are embraced as central in society and represent our common humanity ... Where we are inspired, moved to reflect on who we are, and changed for the better by the artistic expression we experience ... where artists and audiences interact for greater understanding ... where boundaries of art forms are reduced to allow all of the arts to thrive ..." (Rutter, n.d., p. 2).

And who better to imagine such a future than bold, daring, and creative artists? Artists imagine the future into existence. They draw upon the aggregated accomplishments of history while understanding that the past is not a proof for the future. In a speech to the Irish parliament in 1963, President John F. Kennedy, after whom the Kennedy Center is named, eloquently testified to his understanding of the transformational power of artists. Kennedy, America's first Irish-American President, lauded the artistic heritage of the Irish people when he paraphrased a quotation from George Bernard Shaw, saying "The problems of the world cannot possibly be solved by skeptics or cynics whose horizons are limited by the obvious realities. We need men who can dream of things that never were and ask, 'why not?'" (Kennedy, 1963).

So back to the questions of: (1) "Why was there a skate park at the Kennedy Center?" and of (2) "Was Deborah willing to put her faith in Jason, Ben and me?" the answers were clear. Kennedy himself answers the first question with a "Why not?" that resounds across the years. And Deborah answers the second in her introduction to the Kennedy Center's strategic plan, where she asserts that "The Kennedy Center is dedicated to being artist-centric in our programming and to welcoming our audiences on a journey of exploration, discovery, joy and delight." And she invokes President Kennedy's own inspiring vision as she explains further, writing:

> We are now on the verge of a new frontier for the arts. As participation in the arts evolves, relationships between artists and audiences have intensified. With audiences increasingly interested in becoming their own curators for arts engagement, artists are even more responsive to societal influences and trends, while providing a reflection and commentary on the world around us. The important role of artists as spokespeople for our society has increased as they, and audiences, develop as Citizen Artists. Further, the traditional performing arts are evolving rapidly. Old and new art forms are colliding; Hip Hop and DJ music fold into symphonies and operas, modern dance and ballet express current musical and theatrical ideas. The power of the performing arts to speak to us individually and collectively has never been more valued or important.
>
> (Rutter, n.d., p. 1)

It turned out that Deborah didn't need convincing. She is able to imagine the bridges she can't yet see. And she's relying on artists to make them visible to us all so we can then work together to build them into bridges to our collective future that she challenges us to imagine.

The Bridge Connecting *Finding a Line* and the Vision of Eisenhower, Kennedy, and Bernstein

Having explored reasons why a skate park at the Kennedy Center was deemed appropriate in a contemporary context, it's important to also examine the history Kennedy Center in order to understand how *Finding a Line* fits in a historical context.

The legislation to create the institution was passed in 1958 during the Eisenhower administration (Becker, 1990, p. 1). President Eisenhower believed we needed a cultural institution that would play three critical roles. (1) It would be a world-class venue. With multiple theaters able to host the world's great companies from the Royal Shakespeare Company to the Mariinsky

Ballet, as well as to present the best of American performing arts, such a venue would erase the perception that Washington, DC, was an unsophisticated cultural backwater. (2) It would be a capacious and symbolic space for all citizens to utilize as a social commons where they could gather to exchange ideas and perspectives on matters of shared civic and cultural importance. And (3) it would be a center for mass communications, able to utilize radio and television to extend culture's power to positively influence domestic and international perceptions of the American people as a nation optimistically, dynamically, and creatively emerging from World War II and stepping onto the world stage to play a leading role promoting democracy, peace, and social welfare (Becker, pp. 16, 26, 32).

When President Eisenhower left office in January of 1961, President Kennedy and First Lady Jacqueline Kennedy took on the project with the energy and optimism, style and conviction with which they would inspire the nation and define an era (Becker, p. 46). The First Lady led fundraising efforts, while President Kennedy spoke eloquently to the public about the value of culture in our national life. "The life of the arts," he famously said, "far from being a distraction in the life of the nation, is close to the center of a nation's purpose" (Kennedy, 1962). Two months after his assassination in November 1963, Congress designated the National Cultural Center as a "living memorial" to President Kennedy.

The John F. Kennedy Center for the Performing Arts finally opened to the public in September of 1971 with a world premiere performance of *Mass*, a requiem for President Kennedy commissioned from Leonard Bernstein. Bernstein shared Kennedy's and Eisenhower's original vision for the National Cultural Center. He believed in the importance of a national theater, and was a passionate advocate for the power of culture to bring us together, and for the potential of mass communication to amplify and extend that positive force (Becker, p. 170).

The Bridge Connecting *Finding a Line* and the Spirit of the Times

The initially intended purposes of the National Cultural Center connect directly to the intended purposes of *Finding a Line: Skateboarding, Music and Media*. They also help to answer the question of why this project made sense at this particular moment in history. With the 50th anniversary of the Kennedy Center in 2021 beginning to emerge on the horizon, we built a skate park in front of the Kennedy Center because we needed a laboratory where artists, audiences, and communities could begin to explore this new frontier in the arts on their own terms, a place where today's citizen artists could work hand-in-hand with the Kennedy Center to find ways to connect the mission and purpose of the center to our contemporary cultural context. This is a tremendous challenge for any enduring institution. Participation *is* evolving. Relationships between artists and audiences *are* intensifying. Audiences *are* increasingly interested in becoming their own curators. Artists *are* more responsive to trends in contemporary society. And the traditional performing arts *are* evolving at a feverish pace as old and new forms collide. What will that look like? How will it work? We all wanted to find out.

So, 44 years after the original vision for a national cultural center was realized, we collaborated with artists and the community to construct a new venue for a new era. Like the Kennedy Center itself, it would be purpose-built. But rather than being designed for theater, ballet, or opera, it would be designed for skateboarding, music, and media.

Just as President Eisenhower had intended, this new venue would play three critical roles. (1) It would include multiple "theaters" – a street course and a skate bowl, complete with bleacher seating for spectators – designed and constructed to world-class standards for hosting the very best skaters, musicians, and artists from around the city, the nation and the world. (2) It would be a capacious and symbolic space. With the 100-foot marble façade bearing the president's name as a backdrop, it occupied the entire arrival plaza of the Kennedy Center, serving as a social commons that welcomed all to gather to exchange ideas and perspectives in all-day sessions of skateboarding, music-making, art-making, and socializing. And, (3) it would become an active hub for mass communication, with amateur and professional photographers and filmmakers producing a steady stream of creative documentation, utilizing social media to extend the power of the live experience over digital channels, and connecting with people across the country and around the globe.

Building with Community, and Relationships as Returns on Investment

Where the idea for a skate park at the Kennedy Center came from, and *why* that idea resonated with the mission, leadership, and history of the Center, as well as the spirit of the times, leads to *how* the park was constructed.

The Kennedy Center didn't buy the skate park itself from a sporting goods supplier or build it in our scene shop. Both the park and the programming that animated it were products of the imagination and initiative of the skate community.

The next time Jason was in DC, I arranged for him to meet Ben. They toured skate spots across the city from Freedom Plaza, known to skaters worldwide, to Ben's community projects at Bridge Spot and Green Skate Lab. Jason tapped out rhythms on a chain link fence in syncopated counterpoint to the sounds of birds chirping, basketballs bouncing, and the clack and whir of Ben's skateboard wheels. In one day spent sharing histories, ideas, and a roadside lunch from Mr. P's Ribs and Fish, they'd begun finding the line that would connect them. Jason and Ben enthusiastically agreed to join forces as cocurators of the Kennedy Center festival, *Finding a Line: Skateboarding, Music and Media*, combining their separate West Coast and East Coast endeavors into a shared national passion project.

As the Kennedy Center's Artistic Director for Jazz, Jason was the direct connection to the institution, while Ben was the direct connection to the skate community. Ben's relationships were a tremendous asset to the project – the cornerstone of all we would build. In community engagement, relationships are the primary asset class just as dollars are in traditional business dealings. They're the currency we trade on to do this work in a way that results in mutual benefit for all involved. And when the time comes to consider our returns on investments (ROI) in community engagement projects, the mission bottom line must be measured in relationships – the enduring bridges between people and the organization. The financial bottom line is measured in dollars. This is the "double bottom line" we strive for. To succeed in this work, we have to learn to regard *mission* return on investment (MROI) as the primary goal, and financial return on investment (FROI) as secondary.

With that accounting in mind, it was clear that Ben brought a tremendous amount to the table, making a huge investment in our collaboration and setting us up for success.

Nevertheless, Ben's relationships were just the starting point of the process. A skate park needed to be designed and built. Programming needed to be curated and produced. In order to develop the initial ideas from Jason, Ben, and my Kennedy Center team into meaningful outcomes for the community we aimed to serve, more members of the community needed to be at the table in positions of leadership, involved in decision-making at every level. We engaged the local knowledge and networks that were needed by convening an extended series of community meetings we call "creative ecosystems." These working group sessions included skaters, artists, activists, educators, and young people. Over the course of several months, the sessions took different forms from chairs-in-a-circle conversations, to ramp building sessions, to skating sessions, to a food and clothing drive we called "Skate It Forward." In time, trusting relationships grew through dialogue, transparency, intentionality, and responsiveness.

Stepping Up with Community, and Losing My Resolve

Meanwhile, colleagues within the Kennedy Center who weren't directly involved in these relationships with the eclectic ecosystem weren't able to recognize the relationships as returns on our institutional investment. Our press and marketing teams for example, were acutely aware that a festival was coming up that they were responsible for pitching to the press and advertising to the public. They needed information that they'd expected to have in hand already. They didn't need relationships. They needed a skate park, a press release, and a brochure.

As July turned to August, the September start date of the festival loomed. One creative ecosystem participant, Mike High, put a fine point on my personal predicament, saying, "You really put your head on the chopping block. There was a tremendous amount of institutional and personal vulnerability and risk involved. But someone has to do this to move forward. Saying to the community, 'Hey guys, what do you think? What do you want to do?' It was a gracious and giving thing to do. We were so proud that there was a bowl in front of the Kennedy Center.

Being at the Center gives prestige to the sport. We (skaters) appreciate it, and we'll step up."

As gracious as it seemed, asking, "What do you want to do?" was really the only way forward. This is because the Kennedy Center, with all of its experience in set design and construction for opera, ballet, and theater, had no such experience with skateboarding. There would be no top-down gift of a skate park from the magnanimous Kennedy Center to the grateful skate community, but rather a bottom-up cooperative effort between us. The primary feature of the skate park would be a 40 foot by 20 foot, by 4 foot high kidney bean-shaped bowl. Ben referred to it as the "seed" from which the rest of the project would grow. The bowl was ultimately the result of conversation and collaboration with a team of builders who'd each designed numerous skateable structures, from backyard ramps to public skate parks. Some were licensed contractors and some weren't. And although none of them built skate ramps as a living, all of them built skate ramps as a lifestyle. They were citizen artists, and amateurs in the purest sense of the word. They did it for the love of it.

Ben, who teaches in the art department at George Mason University in Fairfax, Virginia, stepped up and offered to host the building sessions at the university's beautiful and well-equipped sculpture studio. The Kennedy Center stepped up and provided the funds for the raw materials as well as for the hours of physical labor the team dedicated to the effort. As the bowl began to take shape in the capable hands of the building crew, we turned our attention to other essential aspects of *Finding a Line*, like music, visual art, and digital media.

While the Kennedy Center has long experience curating a classical or jazz season, even with Jason Moran's input we're short on experience choosing music to skate by. And since the goal was to invite musicians that reflected skate culture's history and current tastes, and that people would be psyched to skate to, our approach was simple. Building on our new relationships, we asked, "Hey guys, what do you think?" We were immediately introduced to people in the ecosystem who were fans in the scene, played in bands, booked clubs, and deejayed on local radio. Each day of the festival was ultimately hosted by a different skate shop or skate crew who, among other vital functions, proposed the bands and DJs for their day. We quickly had more bands and DJs to choose from than we had available set times in the 10-day festival.

Developing the visual art program followed a similar path of dialogue and discovery. Skateboard culture has long been an interdisciplinary lifestyle that revolves around the creative act of enjoying skateboarding as a form of self-expression. From photography and filmmaking, to painting, graphic design and fashion, visual arts characterized by a Do-It-Yourself, multimedia, antiestablishment aesthetic have always been integral to the whole of skate culture. This piece of the puzzle also took us out of our typical areas of expertise and again required us to rely on our community collaborators for direction and connections. Sure enough, someone knew a DC muralist who'd painted at a number of local skate spots including Bridge Spot. Someone else introduced us to an LA-based photographer who specializes in skateboarding and fashion, shooting catalogues for skate companies and covers for skate magazines. The LA photographer, in turn, introduced us to the founder of a major skateboard company, who is also a skater, musician, visual artist, and collector. Then Converse, our lead corporate sponsor, even commissioned a prominent artist in the skate scene to paint a mural on the inside of the bowl, resulting in a spectacularly visceral fusion of art and skate. Before we knew it, we'd cocurated a major skate art exhibition.

As August sped by with so much of our collective vision becoming a reality, a huge piece of the puzzle was still missing — digital media. Filmmaking and photography are perhaps the most ubiquitous visual expressions of skateboard culture today. From full-length documentaries to web series, and from promo reels for skate brands to teens posting clips on social media platforms, skate culture has flooded the media landscape. And yet, we didn't have a solid plan for authentically featuring this aspect of the culture in *Finding a Line*. With just weeks until the festival would begin, our promotional materials were set to go to print, including two 30-foot-tall banners for the front of the building, and all were boldly emblazoned with the title, *Finding a Line: Skateboarding, Music, and Media*. But with no substantial media-making strategy in place, no more ideas, and no more time, I lost my resolve. I actually contacted the printer to find out if we could remove the word "Media" from the title of the project. But it was too late. All the materials had gone to print.

Stepping Out on the Invisible Bridge with Faith and Freire

Later that same evening, we were to have our final creative ecosystem meeting out at the GMU sculpture studio. I dreaded facing our collaborators with this situation. As it happened, my new boss had gamely accepted my invitation to attend his first creative ecosystem meeting on this particular day, compounding my stress. And to make matters even worse, we'd arranged for a Kennedy Center film crew to document this one session, which I now fully expected to be a disaster.

When I arrived, I quickly found Ben and pulled him aside, nervously confiding that I didn't know what to do. We were stuck advertising a festival that we couldn't deliver in full. And I didn't know how to solve the problem. As I shared my fears, I could see over Ben's shoulder the cameras being set up near the circle of chairs where our collaborators were beginning to gather as my boss surveyed the scene.

What was going on? I thought I was supposed to be the leader of this group effort; in charge and in control. But instead, my ignorance and failed leadership were about to be laid bare for Ben, for my boss, for my staff, and for the whole creative ecosystem community of collaborators to witness. The entire journey up to that point flashed before my eyes. I saw Jason's leadership utilizing skate culture for audience development at SF Jazz. I saw Ben's leadership utilizing skate culture for community development from Fight Club to *Finding a Line*. And I saw other creative ecosystem members making practically every critical decision from the design of the park to the amateur and professional musicians, visual artists, and skateboarders we'd invited, and ultimately booked, to participate.

WHERE DID THE KENNEDY CENTER EVEN FIT IN TO THIS EQUATION? WHERE DID I FIT IN?

Just opening up to those questions had a power — like extending a hand to offer or receive help. That *was* the role of the Kennedy Center. In fact, my curiosity motivated by love for the arts and community had always shaped my specific role — to ask questions. And with every question, I'd been met with well-intentioned, well-considered answers. These questions initiated the latticework of bridging that made the project possible, and that made the project strong. The questions transformed this incredibly risky project into one that was practically fool-proof, able to be fouled up only by a fool too foolish to ask questions when he was in desperate need of answers, or too foolish to act on the answers he received.

The Brazilian educational philosopher Paulo Freire described this as the "problem-posing method" which invites the teacher and the student, or in this case the institution and the skate community, into "coinvestigative" dialogue with each other. This type of dialogue is built upon what Freire regarded as the "true word" which was comprised of two dimensions, "reflection and action," and which constituted a praxis – a unity of theory and practice. In complete agreement with a transformational educator of our own time, Ben Ashworth, Freire asserted that reflection without action was an empty word that lacked the ability to transform; for there could be no transformation without action (Freire, 1972, pp. 80, 87, 88). As mentioned earlier, Ben refers to this same dialogical phenomenon as "dialogue through action" and it's the basis of his own praxis. And then there's Jason Moran, an endlessly curious musician, for whom dialogue through reflection and action at the keyboard is the foundation of the jazz improvisation for which he's been honored with a MacArthur "genius award."

If I truly believed this Freirean, Ashworthian, and Moranian pedagogical practice, then transforming our digital media-making problem into a solution that would fit the final puzzle-piece into our festival could be as simple as posing the problem. These wonderfully generous people who'd all driven out to Fairfax, Virginia, at 7:30 on a Thursday night to share some gazpacho and engage in the collective task of *Finding a Line* from Fight Club to the Kennedy Center would answer the question of how we would feature filmmaking and photography.

This flash of clarity revealed that I had held the ancient text in my hand all along. My questions were all I needed to safely overcome this final treacherous trial. With my resolve restored, I pulled a chair up to the circle. Cameras were rolling as a boom mic swayed over my head to capture every word. Standing on this cliff edge of vulnerability, I was now so certain of the truth of that ancient text – the power in asking a question – that, after a dramatic pause to summon my faith, I took a step forward into what looked like thin air, and posed the problem.

Where the Bridge Has Taken Us So Far

On May 7, 2016, the 10-day festival and the throngs of super-diverse audience, reams of positive press, and unprecedented levels of social media engagement were 8 months behind us. By this time, the skate bowl had been relocated to Gallaudet University in NE Washington, the world's oldest institution of higher learning for the deaf and hard of hearing. The ramp was being utilized as a learning laboratory in which deaf, skateboarding undergrads would study robotics and data visualization. Meanwhile, collaborative engagement with the skate community continued, and on this date I stood at the corner of Rhode Island Avenue and 11th Street, NW in Washington, DC, at the Shaw Skate Park. The Kennedy Center was co-hosting, along with the DC Department of Parks and Recreation, another day of *Finding a Line*. But this time, it was situated in the skate community's own space, not at the Kennedy Center.

Reflections on Why the Journey Matters

I spent much of the day talking with folks at the park who'd shared the journey from Fight Club to the Kennedy Center. And to each of them, I asked the same question: "What does the *Finding a Line* project mean for you?" What follows is just a small sample of responses:

> For me, *Finding a Line* means finding my own line in life. It means getting out into the city, discovering other people and discovering myself.
>
> (Tatiana Kolina, skater, clothing designer, entrepreneur)

> *Finding a Line* is the embodiment of music and skating. I don't know a skater who skates without music. Having your music in your ears and skating is being in the zone. With live music, you don't have your earbuds in. You can be in the zone with other people. It's super inclusive and diverse, and we're all doing what we love together. Coming up, it was hard to get people together to skate, especially if you weren't on a team. Now, this is a new generation of skating that is becoming a community – all rooting for each other. *Finding a Line* is about creating an event; creating the conditions for us to come together. There's so many more people in the park today. We never have over a hundred people out in the park together all day.
>
> (Javier Starks, skater, MC, educator)

Finding a Line is like a mixing bowl of otherwise different ingredients — people who wouldn't have been in the same place without confrontation coming together to confront the stigma of skating. The Kennedy Center as a backdrop was priceless. And Jason Moran was the perfect partner. It's the same stigma that jazz had.

It gave legitimacy to a form and a community that was fringe. You could appreciate the form as truly high level art. How you treated my son as an artist was life changing. It made him feel legitimate. I've performed at the Kennedy Center. Now he has too. *Finding a Line* was high level art.

> (Kevin Green, bass-baritone, father of 12-year-old pro skater Cordell Green)

Being in skate for thirty years, I appreciate an institution willing to embrace sport, culture, and the family of it. I love the multi-generational aspect. In my neighborhood, my crew was four kids — black, Latino, white, and Asian — and a skate mom. My friend's mom would drive us to the parks and all the spots we wanted to skate. Back then, we were all marginalized. But the simple act of skating bonded us. There are so many lines to find — at the Kennedy Center and in the community. It's what skate is all about.

> (Ray Llanos, skater, photographer)

I wish every weekend could be like this. *Finding a Line* at the Kennedy Center was one of the best weeks we've ever had as a family. I can't wait till it happens again at the Kennedy Center. It's such a diverse and positive scene.

> (Mike Harbin, father of 8-year-old skater Quinn Harbin)

Finding a Line is about rethinking the purpose of public institutions as centers for individuals to come together across gender and class; bringing people together under a positive current of creative interest that can create ties and build new initiatives; finding the line that connects, but that wasn't initially apparent. Lines can divide or connect. *Finding a Line* makes lines that connect. Kennedy Center is taking the inventiveness and energy of skate and using it to inspire cross-disciplinary collaboration.

With all of the changes and gentrification taking place in D.C., *Finding a Line* strengthens the foundation of the city by finding ways for all to be welcome and present. *Finding a Line* is a sustainable way to do this; not a top heavy way, but a bottom up way to grow together from a community level. It's good for D.C. We don't want diversity pushed out as the city builds. We want the city to grow from diversity being the foundation. *Finding a Line* doesn't have a frame that keeps anything out. Skating is that way.

> (Max Kazmezadeh, skater, professor of art and robotics at Gallaudet University)

Finding a Line is about being open to it, and letting it evolve on its own. It's a living project that's continuously producing. It begins before and continues after – in the community activity and in social media.

> (Sue High, artist)

It validates what people already do for the love. They'd do it anyway. But it changes the public perception for major institutions to say that this is a valuable form of expression. Someone said they feel like they're at a wedding.

> (Ben Ashworth, skater, artist, educator, activist)

A Vision of Where This Journey Can Take Us – Grassroots Leadership, and the Arts for Social Change

Finding a Line is the product of balanced and reciprocal relationships. And as such, the project produces benefits for all involved. The statements above convey some of the reasons why the project matters to individual community participants. Equally important are the institutional and collective benefits – the reasons why a project like *Finding a Line* matters to the Kennedy Center, and why it matters to the community at large.

From a mission perspective, many not-for-profit cultural organizations focus on their intrinsic motivation to strengthen relationships between their organization, artists, and audiences. And yet from a business perspective, extrinsic financial motivations influence many of these same organizations to focus on cultivating transactional relationships with their constituents in order to drive earned revenue through selling the cultural products they produce. Unfortunately, an unintended consequence of this structural orientation towards sales is the cultivation of relatively weak ties with constituents that result from these primarily transactional relationships (Hyde, 2007, p. 96). If an organization evaluates its effectiveness relative to the "double bottom line" of dollars *and* relationships, then even strong ticket sales (FROI) can result in weak service to an organization's mission (MROI).

As a compliment to the more transactional and traditional among the Kennedy Center programs, *Finding a Line* has been an exercise in intentional codesign of a program that engages artists, community members, and the organization in working together toward shared goals, with an interdependence that cultivates reciprocal relationships (Hyde, p. 96). The strong ties established through working in this way result in the MROI we measure in relationships.

The great promise of promoting this type of cultural coproduction is that the benefits of increasing the number and strength of relationships within a community accrue to that entire ecosystem, not just to the organization.

Today, perhaps more than ever, we need to use all the tools at our disposal to strengthen the communities we live in. Locally, nationally, and internationally, individuals and communities suffer negative consequences of weak ties and strong divisions. And since many of the problems our communities face are cultural, *why do we invest so little in cultural tools for responding to cultural problems?*

We can no longer afford to ignore this obvious value proposition for society. Just as we turn to financial tools for responding to financial problems, and military tools for responding to military problems, we must turn to cultural tools for responding to cultural problems. The intrinsic motivations that drive participation in the arts support personal actualization, social engagement, and civic activation. These prosocial effects make grassroots cultural coproduction a uniquely effective tool for strengthening communities by cultivating individual and collective flourishing.

And if we currently lack sufficient cultural tools, then investment in the design and implementation of such tools is not a luxury, it's an imperative. We can no longer afford to regard the arts as a "nice to have" that we indulge in when times are good. We must awake to the realization that the arts are a "must have" that we need most when times are hard.

Artists can be transformational leaders with the vision to reframe shared problems as shared opportunities. With *Finding a Line*, we put into practice what Jason Moran learned in San Francisco from reframing the problem of shrinking jazz audiences as an opportunity to revitalize jazz audiences, and the musical experience itself, through the union of skateboarding and jazz. Artists have the ingenuity to design creative projects that bring together disparate groups and individuals to realize these visions. *Artistic leaders see invisible bridges, use questions to make them visible and strong, and then lead us across.* In order to answer the question of how might we transform the Kennedy Center plaza into a creative community space for music, art, and skateboarding, *Finding a Line* drew upon what Ben Ashworth had learned through activating his powerful visions of engaging the ethos and participants of the skateboarding community to answer similar questions of how they might transform a warehouse, a highway underpass, or tires polluting a river into dynamic community spaces anchored by the creative act of skateboarding. With an energetic reciprocity at the core of their practice, artists make relationships while making art. *Artists and artistic leaders can be creative problem-posers who use the arts as a tool to galvanize communities into collective problem-solvers.* Through the experience of cocreating *Finding a Line*, I came to understand the institutional and community benefits of the "problem-posing method" described by Freire and practiced by Ben. But in order to reap the returns from artistic leadership, institutions must invest in artists' visions. As active partners with shared goals, institutions need to take on some of the risks in the calculated hope for returns, as with any investment − financial or mission. In the case of *Finding a Line*, the Kennedy Center assumed financial and legal risks (not entirely dissimilar from risks inherent in undertaking original theatrical or operatic productions), compounded by the unfamiliar risks of embracing the unknown and turning to community partners for decision-making guidance in navigating institutionally underexplored territories of culture.

With the support of our institutional investment and tolerance for risk, Ben Ashworth, Jason Moran, the skate community, the Kennedy Center Community Engagement team and I succeeded in *Finding a Line* from Fight Club to the Kennedy Center. The returns on the Kennedy Center's investment have been art, attention, and curiosity, for sure. But more importantly, the mission of *Finding a Line* is accomplished in what these new relationships and experiences are teaching us about the power of creative grassroots leadership to utilize the arts as a tool for social change. The cultural coproduction achieved through the application of a Freirean process cultivated reciprocal relationships that resulted in strong ties between the institution and the community – a significant mission return on the Kennedy Center's investment. The project transformed an institution formerly off-limits to the skateboarding community into a platform for that community to authentically reveal itself and its relevance through shared cultural action in cultural common space. The unity achieved across this chasm of difference has tremendous value for the Kennedy Center, the skateboarding community, and for society at large. Let's put the artists and the tools to work. There's much to be done.

Acknowledgments

Writing this chapter would not have been possible without the endless love and support of my wife, Christy, the editorial enthusiasm of my daughter, Eva, and the inspiration of my skateboarding son, Si. For the experiences on which this story is based, I owe a tremendous debt of gratitude to Ben Ashworth and Jason Moran, as well as to my indefatigable team at the Kennedy Center: Diana Ezerins, Matt Kattenburg, Margaret Bushko, Bobby Hunter, Margot Pien, AJ Jelonek, Owen Burke, and Baye Harrell. Thanks to Michael Kaiser for his many years of service to the Kennedy Center and support of this work, and to Deborah Rutter for her continuing support and powerful vision for the future of the Kennedy Center. I would also like to thank James Early for encouraging me to write, and Susie Erenrich for inviting me to contribute to this journal.

References

Becker, R. E. (1990). *Miracle on the Potomac: The Kennedy Center from the beginning.* Silver Spring, MD: Bartleby Press.

Freire, P. (1972). *Pedagogy of the oppressed.* (Reprint: 1992, published through Continnuum in New York).

Hyde, L. (2007). *The gift: Creativity and the artist in the modern world.* New York, NY: Vintage Books.

Kennedy, J. F. (1962). Look magazine, 'The Arts in America' (552), December 18, 1962, *Public Papers of the Presidents.*

Kennedy, J. F. (1963). Retrieved from http://izquotes.com/quote/243211. Speech delivered to the Dail (Parliament of Ireland), June 28, 1963.

Rutter, D. (n.d.). *Strategic Plan 2016–2021.* Unpublished manuscript. John F. Kennedy Center for the Performing Arts, Washington, DC.

Uhls, J. (Screenwriter), & Fincher, D. (Director). (1999). *Fight club* [Motion picture]. 20th Century Fox.

16 Crafting Community and Change through Books and Pads: The Tikondwe Teachers Project in Domasi, Malawi

Kevin Bottomley, Justin Snyder,
Alinane Misomali, Denise Archuleta,
David H. Davenport, Marsha Dwyer,
Destenie Nock, Lucy Kapenuka,
Chifundo Ziyaya, Ann Potts and
Liz Barber

Since 2004, U.S.-based college students and faculty, partnering with Rotary clubs in North Carolina, have collaborated with teacher leaders in three rural schools in Domasi, Malawi, on participatory action research projects (PAR) designed to save the lives of children and youth through education. In Malawi, one adult in five, and one child in ten, test positive for HIV/AIDS. The only correlate of remaining disease-free is staying in school, but multiple oppressions involving poverty, language, literacy, gender, and a lack of teacher empowerment operate to severely limit access. While many initiatives have addressed needs determined by teachers as critical, this chapter focuses on how the arts operate as tools for *tikondwe* — freedom — in the Domasi context. Malawian teachers now author culturally congruent texts in the languages their pupils speak, so they can learn to read and write. U.S.-based graphic design students then craft illustrations and layout for these teacher-authored books, and raise funds for printing classroom sets. In response to the needs of older girls, another project gathers them in the afternoons to sew their own sustainable feminine pads so they do not miss a week of school each month. Our aim in this work has been to knit together those whose expertise can be brought to bear on problem-solving with diverse others, and in that action, expand the moral circle and facilitate leadership development through side-by-side engagement. Our chapter explores the potential for Brazilian educator, Paulo Freire's (1970), conscientization — or *tikondwe* — of heads, hearts, and hands within this trans-global community.

Crafting Power and Tikondwe in the Domasi Context

Freedom is important to Malawians, who won independence in 1964, and strive for increasingly democratic forms of government in each presidential election. They know well that freedom rests upon a literate electorate. However, Malawi was only 10 years into a public school initiative when university faculty members Ann Potts and Liz Barber first traveled there as part of a Fulbright team in 2004. Their objective was to spend the summer working in schools with teachers as part of a one-time knowledge exchange, but what they encountered convinced them to seek continued involvement. A shortage of schools and teachers prevails, and many schools are under the trees. With as many as 125 + learners crowded into early standard classrooms, as few as 60-some remained in classes by Standard 8. One outcome of British influence is that in Malawi, the term "standard" means the same as U.S. "grade level": Standard 8 means eighth grade.

The teachers there explained the primary school attrition rate, and low pass rates on the Standard 8 exams that structure access to secondary school, as the result of multiple factors. Poverty alleviation is the major goal of education in Malawi, but many families can spare only the children deemed the brightest to attend school, as others are needed to help with farming and household management. The hopes and dreams of whole families, sometimes whole villages, rest on the shoulders of those who get to attend school. Schools lack writing and instructional materials. Many learners sit on the floor, trying to memorize lessons, often unable to understand the language of instruction. Hunger constitutes a profound barrier.

Language politics also form a significant barrier. Against a background of 17 indigenous languages, only English and ChiChewa are the languages of schooling. In Standards 1–4, instruction takes place in ChiChewa, with English taught as a second language. From Standard 5 onward all instructions, texts and tests are in English. Learners who come to school with Yao, Lomwe, or another indigenous language, and lack ChiChewa, do not understand the language of instruction, have no bridge language to English, fail to learn to read, and eventually drop out. Gender further restricts access to education. In 2004, the majority of learners who persisted in school to Standard 8 were male. Compared to waning traditions of female oppression, the deepest need is a simple and practical one: older girls lack feminine pads. Limited teacher training and a lack of further opportunities to build teaching skill once teachers are in-service, compound other problems.

However difficult the educational endeavor, children in classrooms were joyous, and teachers shouldered their loads with energy and hope. In Sub-Saharan Africa, people do not ask God – or American friends – to solve their problems. They ask only that *we be with them.* Potts and Barber were new to African Ubuntu, a worldview in which the one exists only through the others, but as their 2004 trip drew to an end, they knew could not abandon the Domasi teachers with whom they had worked side-by-side – striving, striving – that summer. It felt like being in love, and knowing you would never see your beloved again. On the plane during their flight home, they leaned across the aisle and hatched a plan for teams of U.S. university students and faculty to spend a month in-country every summer, merging their strengths and skills with the wisdom and tenacity of Domasi teachers, to create needed resources.

U.S.-based university faculty and students needed opportunities to experience building community within the Ubuntu worldview, learn cross-cultural competency, become global citizens, and develop skill in non-colonizing ways to make knowledge with diverse others. The Tikondwe Teachers Project embodies a mutual commitment across American friends and Domasi teachers to *be there for each other* across time and global distance. Participatory action research (PAR) grounds our work: action research projects originate, are defined, analyzed and solved in and by the community. Projects involve the active participation of the community at all levels of the process, and build capacity and awareness of the resources that can be leveraged for development. Skills brought to the endeavor include insider and outsider knowledge: participants become researchers, and researchers become facilitators and committed members of the new community that forms around each PAR project (Lincoln, Lynham, & Guba, 2011). Through PAR methods, Freire's conscientization occurs for both insiders and outsiders: community participation allows for a thorough analysis of the social reality, with the goal of transformation and improvement of the lives of all involved.

Initiatives to date address hunger, health, literacy, HIV-AIDS education, among other needs identified by Domasi teachers. Crafted from the inside out (Toms & Burgess, 2014), projects arise from needs within the school community, and across a year of trans-global negotiation they bring together assets from both sides of the world. In the side-by-side of *being with* each other as teachers and learners in collective striving, freedom is realized and power gets generated – on both sides of the globe – often in ways we could never have foreseen.

Making Stories and Drawing Across the Continents

Doctoral student Justin Snyder traveled to Malawi in 2012 to start a school garden. When he got there, though, the currency had been devalued, people were starving, teachers were afraid the crops would be stolen, there were no funds to pay for a guard, and the project was shelved. Snyder set about helping with other projects, particularly the mother tongue literacy (LMT) seminar held in the afternoons for teachers from Domasi Demonstration Primary (Standards 1–8) and two nearby schools. In 2009, teachers designed the LMT seminar to build knowledge about how to teach reading across multiple languages. Rotary clubs in the Carolina Piedmont supported the venture, and yearly seminars were launched in 2010.

One afternoon in the seminar Snyder noticed Alinane Misomali, a blind teacher who taught 95 sighted Standard

6 learners, unable to move forward on a multilingual big book he wanted to craft. Snyder offered assistance, and the two became an every-class pairing. Misomali had achieved more than most sighted individuals, yet held some unfulfilled dreams:

> While I am blessed to be working as a teacher and able to support my family I feel I am not given the same opportunities as my fellow teachers. I want the same opportunities, to be asked to mark the national exams, and given opportunities to further my education. I know I can do these things, but because I cannot see I am over-looked when these opportunities arise. I want to be viewed just as a teacher, not as a blind teacher.

Snyder and Misomali completed and collaboratively performed his big book, *Vain Hope*, for his Standard 6 class. The two friends said their goodbyes, and their story could have ended there.

VAIN HOPE

To document their collective striving, Snyder photographed the pages of Misomali's book. Back in North Carolina he approached Alamance Community College (ACC) graphics design instructor, Denise Archuleta, to see if she had a student who might craft the story into a small multilingual reader. Brittney Gaither took on the task as a service learning project, Snyder's horticulture students raised funds for printing, and the 2013 team delivered 100+ copies of *Vain Hope* to Misomali's students. The distribution of the books opened floodgates of story-making and a new reality of self-as-author that was contagious. That year teachers authored 18 new multilingual titles, some in as many as four languages, and the LMT book project was ensconced within the design curriculum at ACC. Domasi teachers send "About the Author" drafts and photos for inclusion in their books. A celebration for teacher authors, complete with cake, takes place on the final day of each year's seminar. Then teacher texts jump across the internet multiple times before each book is finalized. American colleagues edit the English text, while a Malawian secondary teacher, Tadala Kapenuka, edits all other languages. ACC design students provide lush illustrations on every page to support literacy acquisition, and learners reap the rich cumulative benefits.

LITERACY IN THEIR HANDS

In 2014, Snyder and graphic design instructor David Davenport
traveled with the team to distribute the first production of multiple titles of LMT readers. According to UNESCO (2008), the
greatest need in mother tongue literacy are texts written in the
children's languages. The Domasi readers included traditional
tales like *Vain Hope*, fiction, accounts about health practices
and HIV/AIDS instruction, ABC books, and lessons for daily
living. Snyder described the first day of giving out books at the
Demonstration School:

> Extreme highs and floods of emotions as we handed out
> the books to the standard 3, 5, 6, 7 learners. The stu-
> dents celebrated that they now had a book of their own.
> All this from one teacher sitting me down to tell a story.

District supervisor, Alippo Ussi, looked out in astonishment
at the scene unfolding as learners left school that day. In classrooms, the textbooks that exist must be shared across many learners; in some classrooms, only the teacher has a book. Few
Malawian children have a book that they can take home, read
again and again, and share with family members. However, that
day the road had sprung up with multiple groups of learners, all
clustered around the ones who were joyously holding and reading a book to their friends. When she arrived home, Ussi's grand-
daughter shared her copy of *The Miraculous Lion*. Snyder
recounted:

> … we watched over 400 learners walking away carrying
> books proudly. They wandered through the school read-
> ing their books without a care of their surroundings. A
> group of girls huddled around one as she read hers to all
> her friends. Boys sat to the side of the soccer field, leaned
> up against the goalpost, reading. Even those playing had
> the book held tightly against their chest.

The head teacher, returning from town, commented, "I see
you handed out books today. All the learners look very happy.
They all have their books and look very proud."

Davenport described distributing over 2,000 books to learners at three schools:

> One true joy was handing out the books to the children
> in the primary classrooms. First they would stand
> and greet us in unison, 'Welcome, how are you today?'

all 95 to 125 of them with beautiful smiling faces as they sat in rows on concrete or hard dirt floors. Each child eagerly grasped a book — they clearly enjoyed having a book in their own hands. The teachers were proud to share their books, and read with enthusiasm, sometimes singing and dancing as they performed the stories. Curious schoolchildren outside peeked in the windows with their noses pressed to the glass — some climbed up and sat in the windows to hear the stories.

At one point Snyder encountered a young boy from Standard 4 in a classroom doorway. The child could not communicate much in English but was clutching his copy of an LMT book about farming:

> I asked if we could read it together. I read the English and then he read the ChiChewa. It was a special moment to be sharing the book this way with this child, in the hallway of the school, in an unprompted and unscripted event. I could not understand his language and he understood very little of mine, however at that time because of the book written by his teacher in both languages, we were together in our understanding of the story. We both left this chance encounter with a smile.

This book ends with the farmer getting a car and a blackberry, and no longer talking to his old friends, but someone had torn out the last page. The story now had a different ending. Whoever made the edit by removing the page wanted that child to learn a more valuable lesson that fit with traditional Malawian values: rather than material gain, a plentiful crop is its own reward.

Teachers gathered at the LMT seminar with copies of each other's books, and shared how they had come up with their ideas. Many penned stories told in their villages. Misomali explained that his second book, *The Miraculous Lion*, was told as a true event from his grandfather's village. Another teacher wrote her story to help girls make good life decisions. Snyder and Davenport described how authoring took the school by storm during the final days that year:

> First a Standard 7 student started writing her own story and had classmates illustrate it. Then a second, and a third child began to write. Writing is taking place

everywhere, in the classrooms, hallways, the teacher workroom, even in the spaces outside the door. The last few days of school, exams are done and many students are out in the field playing, but a growing faction have parted from their friends to write stories. There are two groups, one of boys and one of girls, huddled in the tea break room, others sitting in an empty classroom writing, and even more outside in storm drains with pencil and paper spread out, working away. The head teacher is hidden away in his office working on three different titles, each suited for a different grade level. At tea break many teachers excuse themselves: 'I have to get back to my classroom because I am working on my stories.'

One afternoon Davenport arrived early to prepare for a storyboarding workshop for teachers in the seminar:

Before I knew it, I was surrounded by five curious young girls, 10–12 years old, each watching what I was doing as I prepared for class. Once they felt at ease, the girls started asking me questions about art, drawing and graphic design. They shared their hopes and dreams of being a teacher, nurse, artist, and visiting the U.S. some-day. Then boys started to show up: 'Mr. Davenport, I want to tell my story. Can you help me draw pictures for my story?' I handed each child a pencil and paper and they immediately started to write and draw. As I watched them leave and walk across the school yard, I thought to myself – those children will walk a long distance home from school and do more chores like feeding the chickens, sweeping and even guiding an ox cart.

As children made stories, they needed ways to polish them:

More and more students are requesting to spend their last days with us instead of out on the playground. We started the day with Mr. Misomali coming to get us and asking if we could work with some of his students. He had an early standard girl who had written a story yes-terday but who did not get to come see us and was in tears that she thought she missed her chance. Then we had a boy that just showed up and said he, too, had a story. They kept coming from everywhere.

That year teachers started afterschool writing clubs for learners at all three schools. ACC design faculty and students pledged to craft anthologies of these learner-authored stories for all club members.

In summer 2014, teachers wrote 23 more books, and the next year, 25. Malawian news media covered the story of the LMT teacher-authored books, and Misomali, who by then had authored four, figured large in the report. That September, after years of rejection based on his blindness, he was accepted into the bachelor of education program at Domasi College, to fulfill his dream of becoming a teacher educator.

DRAWING ACROSS THE CONTINENTS

Back in the United States, Davenport reflected on the meanings of his experiences:

> On the last day of the LMT workshop each teacher got up and proudly read aloud their stories, the books I would take back to my own design students to craft into more readers for children. Having been there, immersed in the teachers' literacy work in classrooms, I more deeply than ever understand the significance of what our ACC design students add. With drawings on each page, the children learn to read and write much faster because art is a universal language that breaks down barriers. Including drawings in the story the children recognize words and learn to read much faster. The teachers pattern reading with pictures and writing, the children read the words aloud again in unison, repeated over and over again, and the lessons are learned forever.

> One ACC student artist expressed a similar understanding:

> Illustrations are tools for learning. The origin of literature is storytelling, and when we begin to write down stories, images are tools that bridge our understanding of the words used to articulate them.

> According to design instructor Denise Archuleta, the book project constitutes a "fantastic real world experience" for students at ACC:

> It not only teaches them about vector illustration, page layout, imposition and publishing; it gives them a project

that connects them with the lives of children on the other side of the world. Other graphic design curriculums teach vector drawing, however with the book project, our students learn how to 'reverse engineer', research the environment and way of life of the people that the stories are about. These are not your typical fairy tales. They address social and economic issues faced by the people of Malawi on a daily basis, and that has an impact on our students when they do the research and illustrate the book. Each student puts their self-portrait on the back of the book along with a brief biography, so that when the books are distributed, the teacher authors can see the student illustrators and learn about them. ACC has put into place 'Writing Across the Curriculum', but our graphic design students are 'Drawing Across the Continents'.

With Destiny Pads, A Girl Can Go Far

The same year that Snyder planned a school garden, engineering student Destenie Nock organized the sewing of Destiny Pads, so-named by Domasi teachers who ululated — called out in a culturally specific expression of joy — over the long-distance telephone when they heard her idea. Nock was moved by accounts from teachers like Jane Pwhetekwere regarding the problems for older girls:

> The learners are shy coming to school when they know they have started their monthly period. They make excuses. They say 'I can't go to school' because they are afraid. For example, the teacher teaching in front of the class, when you choose a girl learner to answer a question they feel shy to stand up, and they check their backside, because maybe there is blood on her dress.

Girls in Malawi do what the great-great-grandmothers of women in more developed contexts did — they fold old towels or bits of cloth and place this in their clothing. However, folded fabric does not stay in place when a female moves about, restricting her mobility substantially. As a result, many girls miss so many days that they cannot keep up with their studies, and eventually give up on school altogether.

NEGOTIATED POSSIBILITIES

Nock investigated the possibilities for a sew-able, washable pad that, made properly, could last up to 5 years. She proposed two versions, both designed to provide comfort and reliability using cost-effective materials that were easily accessible. With an ideal outer layer fashioned from cotton flannel, the most absorbent inner layers are made using cotton terrycloth. If a girl lacked access to these fabrics, old shirts would work as a cotton source. The school had a treadle sewing machine, but teachers decided on hand sewing; the ability to sew and mend their own pad would provide girls with the greatest flexibility.

Teachers, including males, affirmed that Destiny Pads were much-needed at the school. All children learned to sew in Standard One, and by Standard 5 the backstitch needed for pad construction was familiar. Teachers settled on introducing the project with Standard 7 and working down to include Standard 5. Although Standard 8 girls needed the pads, by the time of the team's arrival they had already left to study for end of school exams. Pwhetekwere, head teacher Lucy Kapenuka, and assistant head Chifundo Ziyaya each sewed a pad of their own so they knew fully how to describe the project, and Pwhetekwere agreed to explain the Destiny Pad's purpose, construction, and use.

HANDS ON

Before the girls came to the school's tea break room to make their first pad, team members laid out examples of the pads in different stages, fabric for the inner and outer layers, safety pins, needles, and thread. Nock recalled:

> The girls gathered around our makeshift sewing table and listened as Jane explained the purpose and construction of the Destiny Pad in ChiChewa. Many giggled and smiled, especially when they heard that upon completion of their first pad they would receive their own pair of underwear. Jane ended her discussion by showing how to secure the pad in a pair of underwear, which produced a fresh round of laughter and smiles from the students. While Jane's explanation was rendered in ChiChewa, we understood when she told them that with these pads, girls could leave home, go to school, go to the markets. With these pads girls could go far − Jane demonstrated with walking hands, showing this over and

over — with Destiny Pads a girl could go far. As many times as Jane or other girls explained the purpose of the pads to new groups, this message rang out with every telling.

Afterward Pwhetekwere sent small groups of 10 or so to the tea break room to begin stitching their first pad. As each girl came through the line, eager to pick the fabric they liked and begin sewing, team members modeled how to sew along the seams, and made sure they understood they could come back for help or more thread. The girls sat together, working and helping each other, sometimes singing softly. When the first group returned to the classroom, Pwhetekwere brought 10 more, but kept back one who had just sewn a pad. This time, this girl gave the directions in ChiChewa. This process continued until every girl started a pad.

Girls were not the only ones interested in pad-making. Little children clustered at the windows, staring in wonder at rows of funny dolls with two arms and no faces. Female teachers asked for pad materials, and male teachers requested start-up supplies for their wives. Pwhetekwere wanted to take one of the pads home to show:

> I have a girl working for me as a maid. She is in second-ary school, and I was telling her that we have Destiny Pads at our school, and I want to teach you. She was happy, saying, 'Auntie please try to bring it for me so that I can learn how to do it, so that I can use it.' And when I introduced it to her yesterday, she was happy, I tell you. She was telling me 'Auntie I will do a lot. I will do about ten so that I can use two-two.'

Pwhetekwere earlier modeled how a girl could use two pads at the same time on days of heavy flow. Schoolgirls were clearly not the only ones who needed to be able to go far. Teachers agreed that once all girls had sufficient personal supplies of pads, sewing should continue for the purpose of selling these to local women, the proceeds to fund Destiny Pads and a child feeding program at the school.

Nock attributes project success to several factors: the research she did beforehand which allowed her to locate and pro-vide options from which teachers could choose, planning for sus-tainability, and building on the community assets of teacher wisdom and learner sewing skill. The project continues each year, and horticulture student Marsha Dwyer reflected on her participation in 2014:

> I made my way back to the tea break room, a large room with broken tables and chairs on one side and a small, closet-sized library on the other. Older girls assisted with teaching the younger ones, helped us communicate with the children who had little English. These girls became leaders overnight, empowered by the skills that they gained in single day. With these tools, they now had the ability to stay in school and get an education. I began to understand the depth of my role – this project was important for every female there, teachers included.

Dwyer explained how, in addition to her role with Destiny Pads, she was drawn in to facilitate learner writing groups:

> At the other end of the school, people in our group were assisting teachers with LMT, writing stories that my school, Alamance Community College, in Graham, North Carolina, was going to publish into books. The book project inspired students to write their own stories – at every corner of the school, children were asking for paper and pencils so they, too, could author a story. Groups sat in doorways writing feverishly. In the sewing room, girls waiting their turn to make pads asked if they could write stories, fantastic stories about love, heartache, hunger, and AIDS. By this time, boys piled up around the windows of the room wanting to be a part of what we were doing, so we erected another table for the young men authors. That room with broken tables and chairs took on a life of its own. No one was unhappy in that room, because everyone was on an important mission. The girls were empowered with the ability to create their own destinies – with a little fabric, thread, and their skills, they crafted a way to stay in school and get an education. The art that we created together was hope.

Books and Pads: Threads in a Trans-Global Community

A goal of development is to increase a community's social capital or networks of engagement (Saxton & Benson, 2005).

Communities with high levels of social capital which engender reciprocity and trust are happier, more cohesive, vibrant, and prosperous. Community development methods range from diagnostic models to participatory perspectives.

Diagnostic models are deficit-based. They can be compared to Freire's (1970) banking concept of education, in which the "scope of action allowed ... extends only as far as receiving, filing, and storing the deposits" (p. 72). Many social and non-governmental organizations rely on the deficit-based model in which members of the community are clients and the agency, the program provider (Kretzmann & McKnight, 1993). However, outsiders lack prior knowledge and experience working in the community (Arbuckle & DeHoog, 2004), and this method fails to recognize what the community is already doing and has done on its own behalf.

The gifts model examines the capacities and possibilities posed by a community (Block, 2008). It can be compared to Freire's (1970) problem-posing method of education, which "affirms men and women as beings in the process of becoming − as unfinished, uncompleted beings with a likewise unfinished reality" (p. 84). Focusing on gifts of the head, hands, and heart, this model encourages participatory development in which community members make the change they have identified and decided to work toward (Kretzmann & McKnight, 1993).

Participatory development engages the community, and involves a long-term focus on transformation and self-reliance. Through participatory development outsiders and insiders facilitate and mobilize resources to co-create long-term change (Ewert, 1991). Sustainability can result from a consistently applied philosophy of participatory development. Sustainable community building can include three components: asset mapping, connecting assets, and creating a compelling vision (Kretzmann & McKnight, 1993). According to Hargreaves and Fink (2006), "Sustainable leadership reaches out to communities. It invites direct engagement; two-way, jargon free communication; and meaningful participation" (p. 262).

The Tikondwe Teachers Project cobbles together ways of thinking and working that make sense for a trans-global community. We started by co-authoring across continents, students, and faculty. Co-authoring makes sense as once in-country only the Domasi teachers are the experts. We found a fit within conceptions of PAR. Brydon-Miller, Kral, Maguire, Noffke, and Sabhlok (2011) compare PAR to jazz:

> ... knowledge generation is a collaborative process in which each participant's diverse experiences and skills are critical to the outcome of the work. PAR combines theory and practice in cycles of action and reflection that are aimed toward solving concrete community problems while deepening understandings of the broader ... forces shaping these issues. ... PAR is responsive to changing circumstances, adapting its methods, and drawing on the resources of all participants to address the needs of the community. ... the process provides a space within which community partners can come together and a process by which they can critically examine the issues facing them, generating knowledge and taking action to address these concerns. (p. 387)

Attwood's (2007) definition of PAR resonates particularly well for us. It is based on

> ... the concept that people have the right to determine their own development ... [it] recognizes [the need] for people to participate meaningfully in the process of analyzing their own solutions, over which they have power and control, in order to lead to sustainable development. (p. 2)

McTaggart (1989) argues that PAR should start with small groups; starting small allows for minor changes to be managed and controlled, and for participants to experience the success that leads to greater reforms. As small groups achieve their goals, gradually more and more people are included and affected.

Doctoral students among us discovered Chilisa's (2012) indigenous research strategies that emphasize relational ontology. Reality, through the African philosophy of Ubuntu, is based on relationships. We learn about reality through our relationships with others; the ethical and aesthetic criteria for this work include reciprocity and tracing knowledge production to the knower by name. The work must be fair, have catalytic and tactical authenticity (be able to prompt action), raise awareness, recognize standpoint and positional knowledge (knowledge that is tied to the viewpoints and purposes of different interest groups), recognize communities as the judges of quality, provide voice to participants, and involve critical reflection on self in the roles of knower/redeemer/colonizer/transformative healer (pp. 173–174).

Oakes, Lipton, Anderson, and Stillman (2015) provide yet another evaluative lens in their criteria for educational innovations:

1. Is it educative? Do people learn from it?
2. Is it participatory? Are there opportunities for stakeholders to have a voice, be involved?
3. Is it just? Is it fair to all involved?
4. Is it caring?

Adler (2006) proposes the arts as a way to lead positive change and create innovation in leadership and across society as a whole. Other authors have discussed the use of arts in leadership to increase creative thinking and solve complex problems (Katz-Buonincontro, 2008; Sutherland, 2012). Emergent leadership also seems useful in thinking about the Tikondwe Teachers Project (Northouse, 2016). Individuals in a group perceive and then accept someone as an influential person within the group dynamic. The continued growth and success of the group depends on such leadership.

Teacher leader Robert Stovala provided a 2016-report on the progress of the books and pads projects:

> With the Destiny Pads absenteeism has been reduced in girl learners, and the number of girls has increased at this school. Learners are gaining skills on how to make their own pads, e.g. cutting and sewing. It has brought motivation to learners. The mother tongue literacy class has brought creativity and critical thinking in both learners and teachers. Teachers have increased their vocabulary, and learners are able to learn more, and have developed reading spirit.

In 2004, only three of 65 learners had scored high enough on the Standard 8 exam to apply to secondary school. Eight years later, 40 out of 66 made the needed score. The next year, 67 of 67. Then 75 out of 75, with the difference all in females, followed by 85 of 85, the difference all females.

Now through the combined arts of storytelling, writing, graphic design, and sewing, Domasi teachers craft cutting edge knowledge about how to level the playing field for learners with linguistic diversity, and female students, in their part of the world. All we can say for sure is that in the side-by-side of *being with* each other and worrying together over time as global teachers and learners, freedom is realized and power gets generated, often and most delightfully, in ways we cannot foresee.

Acknowledgments

We owe everything to our Domasi teacher partners who have opened their hearts to us every year since 2004. Their names are legion, but we especially want to thank Gift Kawiza and Hamilton Kamwendo, teacher leaders at Domasi Demonstration Primary who now teach elsewhere, but whose participation has been central and compelling. Through her position as District Supervisor, Alippo Ussi negotiates our access to each other and guides our collaborative struggles with the love of a mother leader. Tadala Kapenuka, son of Lucy Kapenuka, was a Standard 8 student when Potts and Barber first traveled to Malawi; he now teaches secondary school and handles email and on-the-ground communication for our group when we are apart from each other, along with editing all LMT book text written in languages other than English. Jane Pwhetekwere provided skillful and loving leadership to the inception of the Destiny Pads Project, and teacher Tisi Ngalande now does so, fostering further leadership development among the girls who sew them. Robert Stovalla, a young emerging leader, has joined Chifundo Ziyaya as spokesperson for our more recent collaborations at the Demonstration Primary School.

Critical is the energy and ingenuity of the university students who have traveled to Malawi across the years to see a dream through to fruition by joining hands with a teacher whose life they could barely imagine before they arrived there. Their ability to shift gears, acclimate, move across points of view, and grow by breath-taking leaps inspires those of us who have been at this for a while. Also, we want to thank University of North Carolina Wilmington graduate student, Claire Kenney, for her careful editing and keen ear in editing our manuscript.

Finally, we want to remember two Malawian educators and dear friends who have died: Reuthers Malembanje and Absolom Phiri. We offer our chapter in their memory.

References

Adler, N. (2006). The arts & leadership: Now that we can do anything, what will we do? *Academy of Management Learning & Education*, 5(4), 486–499.

Arbuckle, M., & DeHoog, R. (2004). Connecting a university to a distant neighborhood: Three stages of learning and adaptation. *Journal of Community Practice*, 12(3), 53–70.

Attwood, G. (2007). *An action research study of the REFLECT approach in rural Lesotho*. PhD thesis, University of the Witwatersrand.

Block, P. (2008). *Community: The structure of belonging*. San Francisco, CA: Barrett-Koehler Publishers, Inc.

Brydon-Miller, M., Kral, M., Maguire, P., Noffke, S., & Sabhlok, A. (2011). Jazz and the banyan tree: Roots and riffs on participatory action research. In N. K. Denzin & Y. S. Lincoln, (Eds.) *SAGE handbook of qualitative research* (4th ed., pp. 387–400). Thousand Oaks, CA: Sage.

Chilisa, B. (2012). *Indigenous research methodologies*. Thousand Oaks, CA: Sage.

Ewert, D. (1991). NGOS and self-sustaining development: Bridging the theory-practice gap. *Institute for African Development Newsletter*, Cornell University.

Freire, P. (1970). *Pedagogy of the oppressed*. New York, NY: The Continuum International Publishing Group, Inc.

Hargreaves, A., & Fink, D. (2006). *Sustainable leadership*. San Francisco, CA: Jossey-Bass A Wiley Imprint.

Katz-Buonincontro, J. (2008). Using the arts to promote creativity in leaders. *Journal of Research on Leadership Education*, 3(1), 1–27.

Kretzmann, J. P., & McKnight, J. L. (1993). *Building communities from the inside out: A path toward finding and mobilizing a community's assets*. Skokie, IL: ACTA Publications.

Lincoln, Y., Lynham, S., & Guba, E. (2011). Paradigmatic controversies, contradictions, and emerging confluences, revisited. In N. K. Denzin & Y. S. Lincoln (Eds.), *SAGE handbook of qualitative research* (4th ed., pp. 97–128). Thousand Oaks, CA: Sage.

McTaggart, R. (1989). Principles for participatory action research. *Adult Education Quarterly*, 41(3), 168–187.

Northouse, P. (2016). *Leadership: Theory and practice* (7th ed.). Los Angeles, CA: Sage.

Oakes, J., Lipton, M., Anderson, L., & Stillman, J. (2015). *Teaching to change the world*. New York, NY: Routledge.

Saxton, G., & Benson, M. (2005). Social capital in the growth of the nonprofit sector. *Social Science Quarterly*, 86(1), 16–35.

Sutherland, I. (2012). Arts-based methods in leadership development: Affording aesthetic workspaces, reflexivity and memories with momentum. *Management Learning*, 44(1), 25–43.

Toms, F., & Burgess, S. (Eds.). (2014). *Lead the way: Principles and practices in community and civic engagement*. San Diego, CA: Cognella.

UNESCO. (2008). *Improving the quality of mother tongue-based literacy and learning: Case studies from Asia, Africa, and South America*. Bangkok: UNESCO.

17 The Shape of Water … Palestine, Badke and Lets Make Noise for Gaza: Three Journeys of Intercultural Choreographic Practice in Palestine

Nicholas Rowe, Noora Baker and Ata Khatab

Introduction

But art should be above politics!

We have heard this comment from artists, audiences, authors, and academics; expressed in festivals, workshops, conferences, and reviews. It suggests that some universal hierarchy exists, in which "politicized" artistic expression is culturally inferior to "nonpolitical" artistic expression. The phrase is insidious and hopes to silence the voices that dissent and question the power surrounding an intercultural exchange.

As dancers who share Palestinian culture abroad, the authors of this chapter consider the idea that art should transcend politics is nonsensical. Dance is inherently political. Dance embodies the diverse sociopolitical contexts in which it is created, amplifying a community's ideals, norms, and distinctions. This can inevitably present challenges and choices within an intercultural artistic collaboration. Which political ideals, norms, and distinctions need to be maintained when working with others? How might the politics of art be acknowledged and honored, while leaving space for intercultural dialogue? Which ideals may be reconfigured in the hybrid imaginings of collaborating artists?

As dance artists who work in "third spaces" (Bhabha, 1994), navigating the terrain between Palestine and other cultures, we three recognize the complexities and the importance of intercultural artistic projects, and their implications for grassroots leadership. More than just a political amplifier, an intercultural dance forum is a *political laboratory*. It allows participants to physically realize relevant new ideas and envisage diverse potential futures (Zeitner, Rowe, & Jackson, 2015). Through creative dance activities with an *Other*, the diverse pasts, presents, and futures of those participating in the experience can be deconstructed and reimagined. When managed equitably, these forums can inform political and cultural directions across the globe. When inequitable, however, intercultural exchanges can simply extend the oppression of one cultural group over another.

Through this chapter we reflect on the emergence of political-artistic philosophies within Palestine, and consider how these ideas have shaped the ways that the three authors of this chapter (from Palestine and Australia) have approached intercultural arts projects. Within the context of dance in Palestine, El-Funoun Popular Dance Troupe has had a prodigious influence. While the centralized, national governance of culture in Palestine has been impeded for decades, this volunteer-based, nonprofit, nongovernmental arts organization has been at the forefront of grassroots artistic and political leadership (Huleileh, 2014).

This leads us to share our own autonarrative accounts of recent intercultural dance projects, which consider how three core political/artistic values developed within El-Funoun have informed our approaches to intercultural dance processes and products. Our stories do not present perfect models of intercultural dialogues in dance, but offer some insights into the growing discourse on how artists may engage in international political actions. The hostile intensity of the current global climate, along with cultural arguments for political segregation (Huntington, 1992; Lewis, 2002), present challenges for peaceful discourse among Europe, America, and the Middle East. Advancing such understanding has therefore become an increasingly urgent issue for arts activists and grassroots leadership organizations.

Dance, Equitable Interculturalism, and Post-Identity Leadership

The sensations of movement, touch, and sight that are evoked by dance do not carry universal, essential, or inherent meanings. Like all forms of cultural knowledge, these kinaesthetic, haptic, and visual sensations are given meaning as dance. They are socially constructed into concepts that are diverse, complex, and often contradictory. Within an intercultural creative process, these contrasting assumptions and values about dance can be placed under scrutiny, revealing that differences not only exist, but are also rationalized from different sociopolitical standpoints. Each artistic choice can therefore challenge well-entrenched ideas of *how* movement carries meaning. Each artistic choice can also provide an opportunity to embody ideas and imagine the world from another's context. This disassembles the idea that one's own cultural identity is static and homogenous (Anderson, 1991; Bhabha, 1994; Hobsbawm, 1983) and questions whether traditional dance practices can ever actually affirm an authenticity and exclusivity within that identity (Buckland, 2006; Grau, 1992; Karayanni, 2015; Shay, 1999, 2014). Through such deconstruction and reconstruction, dance, as a creative art form, can be a wonderful tool for reimagining shared spaces, between cultures and between individuals.

To remain *equitable* locations of exchange however, *all* participants must enter intercultural collaborations in a state of "becoming" (Rowe, Buck, & Martin, 2015, p. 184). This means that each participant is willing to take constructive steps along "the developmental continuum from *ethnocentricism* to *ethnorelativism*" (Bennett, 1986, p. 179). Such a journey involves a shift from assuming that all values are universal, to recognizing differences, to tolerating differences, to integrating and celebrating differences. Currently across the world, locations for intercultural dialogue are rarely so neutral. As a legacy of the Imperial Era, hegemonic systems of cross-cultural interaction remain predominant, in which more powerful economic and military parties continue to determine the aims, procedures, and outcomes of the interaction (Beresford, 2007; Bharucha, 1993; Said, 1993). Through colonizing processes of cultural interaction, the indigenous dance culture of Palestine has historically been subject to extensive cultural hegemony and appropriation by Zionists, Pan-Arabists, and Palestinian nationalists (Kaschl, 2003; Rowe, 2008, 2011), in which dance movements are decontextualized and transferred across cultural and political boundaries, disempowering local artists and devaluing cultural differences. As we will discuss within this chapter, such exchanges have provoked an intercultural wariness amongst dance artists within Palestine.

Retreating into cultural isolation ultimately supports the cultural appropriation and hegemony of dominant global powers however, allowing the sites and processes of contemporary acculturation to be determined centrally. The participation of Palestinian artists in intercultural creative arts projects is therefore critically important, as such participation can potentially decentralize and diversify the *how* and *where* of intercultural innovation. Their active involvement can transform globalization from being a new tide of cultural imperialism and into a movement in which marginalized people can more equitably realize and share their collective visions with others.

For those visions to be relevant to others, they must contain values that transcend a particular ethnic or cultural identity. An intercultural artistic exchange project therefore provides an opportunity to sort and sift through a cultural history, to identify the deeper meanings and political values that might be shared across borders. For the authors of this chapter, that history within Palestine has been largely shaped by the critical discourses emerging from El-Funoun Popular Dance Troupe.

El-Funoun: A Brief History of Grassroots Leadership and Dance for Social Change in the West Bank

Throughout the first seven decades of the 20th century, the hilltop city of Ramallah, just north of Jerusalem, grew as a cultural hub and site for intercultural arts events. This culminated in the annual Ramallah Nights Festivals of 1962–1966, in which tourists from across the Middle East gathered in Ramallah throughout the Summer to experience cooler mountain air and cultural events staged by local and imported dance and music groups. This cultural landscape was massively transformed by the Israeli military invasion of the West Bank in 1967. The local residents became politically separated from their families and cultures in the wider region, as Israel imposed military restrictions on movement and cultural expression. This ended the Ramallah Nights Festivals, and effectively isolated the local culture from the outside world for the next quarter of a century (Rowe, 2010a). At the same time, a dominant Israeli national discourse sought to deny the existence of Palestinians, while appropriating local cultural heritage and further colonizing land and water resources (Haddad, 1994).

In response, the Palestinian national movement established local folklore festivals and publications. Through the Heritage Society in Al-Bireh (a town adjacent to Ramallah), festivals featuring displays of the folkloric dance dabkeh were held in public gardens throughout the 1970s. These were increasingly subject to censorship by the Israeli military, however, which withheld permits and disrupted such cultural gatherings through military intervention. Dabkeh troupes were denied permission to travel between towns and individuals attempting to promote dabkeh became subject to house arrest, detention, interrogation, imprisonment, and physical abuse (Abu Hadba, 1994). The Israeli military occupation can thus be considered as a major stimulant in the politicization of folk dance. By denying such public performances of cultural identity, the Israeli military increased the significance of dabkeh as an act of political resistance.

In 1979, *Firqat El-Funoun Ash-shabiyeh* (El-Funoun Popular Dance Troupe) was formed and in 1980 won an annual folklore competition at Birzeit University. El-Funoun went on to become the longest established and most popularly renowned dance collective in Palestine. While aligned with more leftist Palestinian political parties, the members of El-Funoun were clear from the outset that the group was not simply a political mouthpiece. As Wassim al-Kurdi, one of the founding members, recalled

> All (Palestinian political) parties wanted to have their own folk groups, magazines, their own festival ... We started to take a distance from political slogans

(of Palestinian factions). We asked are we dabkeh for art,
or just posters for a political party? It was not in our idea
to become a dancing group for any political party.

(Cited in Rowe, 2010a, p. 136)

The socially inclusive political mandate of leftist political
ideals nevertheless pervaded the group's vision, as they began to
challenge the patriarchal gender norms that had been established
by the wider nationalist Palestinian folkloric movement. In large-
scale productions throughout the 1980s, El-Funoun advanced the
role of women on stage as dancing alongside, and in the same
manner as, the male performers. Productions such as *Mish'al* and
Marj Ibn'Amer also drew on historic narratives of rebellion, to
encourage resistance against the Israeli military occupation.
Through dance, El-Funoun explored and advocated for political
independence, cultural pluralism, and social cohesion (Huleileh,
2014; Rowe, 2010a).

In 1987, El-Funoun established the Popular Art Centre, as an
independent cultural center focused on advancing dance and
music in Palestinian society. The Popular Art Centre subsequently instigated the annual *Palestine International Festival*,
engaging local youth volunteers and international performance
troupes, and directed *Art for Everyone* and *Our Kids*, the largest
community arts education projects to have taken place in the
West Bank and Gaza Strip (Rowe, 2015).

While the Israeli military occupation continues to this day,
the 1992 Oslo Peace Accords allowed for greater freedom of
movement between the people of the West Bank and the rest of
the world. This introduced new opportunities for intercultural
exchange and cooperation, although sometimes with problematic
results. The cooperative Israeli-Palestinian Al Khan/Al-Kasabah
production of *Romeo and Juliet*, which toured the world sponsored by the Israeli Ministry of Foreign Affairs, was widely
condemned within Palestinian society as a whitewashing of the
ongoing Israeli oppression of Palestinians. El-Funoun and the
Popular Art Centre had refused any such cultural normalization
with Israeli artists within the context of military occupation.
Their stance preempted, and supported the emergence of, the
global Boycott, Divestment, and Sanctions Movement to prompt
Israel to abide by international law (Rowe, 2002).

Through workshops and performances from visiting artists
and international tours, dancers within El-Funoun engaged in
increasing intercultural activities with artists from across the

world throughout the 1990s and 2000s. During this period, one of the authors of this chapter (Nicholas) was a visiting artist from Australia who had danced with contemporary and classical companies in Europe, and subsequently moved to live in Ramallah for 8 years and work with El-Funoun and the Popular Art Centre. The second author (Noora) grew up in Palestine as an artist within the second generation of El-Funoun in the 1990s, and by 2000 had begun to choreograph for the group, traveling abroad to study and engage in international artistic cooperation projects. In 2003, both cocreated and performed in *Access Denied*, the first large-scale "contemporary" dance work set in the West Bank (Rowe, 2016). The third author (Ata), the son of one of the founders of El-Funoun, began dancing and choreographing for El-Funoun in the late 2000s, by which time intercultural arts projects had become a norm within the cultural landscape of Palestine.

While our artistic and cultural experiences stem from different places and eras, all three of the authors of this chapter credit El-Funoun with establishing a relevant, critically reflexive consciousness for artistic innovation in Palestine.

Through its sensitivity to the dangers of both cultural imperialism and nostalgic parochialism, El-Funoun's creative practice has been fueled by reflective questions that collectivize cultural innovation: who can contribute ideas to a work of art? Who can select ideas that make up a work of art? Whose concerns are addressed by a work of art?

Within this chapter we will focus on responses to these questions that for us remain central pillars of El-Funoun's artistic leadership: (A) the collective generation of ideas, (B) the gaining of collective consensus in composition, and (C) the presentation of art that has broad social relevance. After expanding on these three themes, we reflect on how they have informed subsequent intercultural exchanges that we have been involved in.

COLLECTIVE AND CONSENSUAL GENERATION, COMPOSITION AND RELEVANCE

From its establishment, El-Funoun sought to practice an egalitarian creative process, and their final productions were always credited as *choreographed by El-Funoun* (Rowe, 2010a). This egalitarian practice begins when a new dance is created, through the collective generation of ideas. Within the studio, the group set tasks to improvise dance and music, and integrate these tasks with group discussions on the concepts surrounding the new work. These creative tasks and reflexive discussions allowed everyone involved to contribute movement inventions and theatrical ideas to the final production. Such a collective model of movement generation is not unique, and has been identified in diverse cultural locations (Butterworth, 2004; Martin, 2016). El-Funoun rationalizes this socially improvised creative practice as an extension of their cultural heritage: rooted in the improvisational nature of local traditional social dance forms (Rowe, 2009).

Within the development of these improvised ideas toward performance, El-Funoun has also established a collective *compositional* practice. This involves consultation and consensus-building while the generated ideas begin to take form, through open forum discussions within the group and with other community members during work-in-progress feedback sessions. This collective compositional approach contrasts with more predominant decision-making processes undertaken by a director/choreographer within classical and modernist Western Dance theater contexts (Rowe, 2010b). This desire to reach consensual agreement on the final artistic product can be seen as stemming from the inclusive and antihierarchical socialist values of the groups' leftist politics.

The presentation of socially relevant art has also been central to every work produced by El-Funoun, which in either a narrative or embodied way seeks to make comment on contemporary Palestinian politics, identity, and cultural directions. From the political drama of 1986s *Mish'al* (advocating the right to resist foreign domination) to the wedding festivities in 1997s *Zaghareed* (advocating a woman's right to choose her husband), the works of El-Funoun have consistently carried locally relevant topical and contentious social commentary (Huleileh, 2014; Rowe, 2010a).

Through these artistic processes and imperatives, El-Funoun has illustrated how arts for social change can be entwined with grassroots leadership. While these processes may not be unique to El-Funoun and the Palestinian context, the collectivization of creative practices provide us with a reflexive guideline for intercultural exchanges. By bringing these three artistic/political values to the cultural exchange, we can feel greater confidence that the intercultural dance dialogues we engage in can maintain a broader sociopolitical relevance, and extend beyond a simplistic collapsing of ethnic identity and exchange of dance "moves."

To consider how these three themes have been applied beyond the work of El-Funoun within intercultural exchange projects, we reflect here on three intercultural dance projects that we have recently been involved in. Through our narrative reflections we identify how collectivized creative practices continue to inform the ways that we navigate diverse cultural norms and barriers, to create dances that evocatively speak to Palestine and the world.

NOORA: THE SHAPE OF WATER … PALESTINE

While living in London in 2012 I came together with two other artists, Dafne Louzioti from Greece and Thais Mennsitieri from Brazil. The three of us dreamt of creating a collective where we can throw our ideas into one pot, so we created a performing art collective called CACTUS. Our first project was entitled *The Shape of Water*, a series of residencies in different countries, bringing together artists from diverse backgrounds and disciplines to explore new ways to engage the audience in site-specific performance.

The *Shape of Water* explores the diversity of ideas that each culture has of occupation and territory. It follows the principle that water has no form but takes instead the shape of the space it fills, and that that occupation is inherently unstable and temporary. The project explores how this concept of occupation can be developed artistically through the body (water) in the context of a specific space (the container), "space is transformed by those who occupy it and in turn, the occupants are also transformed after residing in it" (Cactuspac, 2016). Individual stories and cultural and political reports introduced into the process by each of the participants form the core material of performance action.

In May 2014, *The Shape of Water* was reshaped in the village of Bir Nabala, Palestine, as a collaboration between CACTUS, El-Funoun and Al Harah Theater. The work directly addressed the impact of the segregation wall around and through the West Bank, which restricts the movement of Palestinians. While the wall was constructed by the Israeli government under the pretext of Israeli security, it ultimately appropriates Palestinian land and forms a divide around and between Palestinian communities (Usher, 2005). The chosen place that called for this project was a factory that had been abandoned after the segregation wall cut through the main commercial street that had connected the village of Bir Nabala with Jerusalem. This factory was amongst many residential buildings, businesses, and houses abandoned in the area as a result of the wall.

During the residency, seven local artists (including myself), along with Dafne and Thais, inhabited the abandoned factory. We spent 10 intensive days working with dust, broken glass, and holes in the structure of the building; the segregation wall in front of us and an Israeli army jeep watching us like a hawk. During this period we explored the space through theater, dance, and visual arts, discussed the concept of an active audience, and experimented with objects, light, and sound to create different images, actions, and stories.

The idea of having artists from different disciplines – dance, theater, visual arts – devising work together is not a new method, however it is fairly new in Palestine. The artists involved in *The Shape of Water ... Palestine* were for the first time involved with other Palestinian artists outside their discipline. All nine of us had a bumpy start understanding each other, having to rely on language at first. Being the translator from English to Arabic and vice-versa was a bit difficult for me. Spending 8 hours a day in one space, eating, drinking, speaking, and working physically together allowed us to bond, break down, and understand our differences; to become one group, working toward one goal.

In the beginning of the process there was a feeling of ownership of ideas. It was not easy to give one's ideas to be criticized, questioned, and reshaped. As creators we can be very defensive of ourselves and our ideas; it is difficult to open oneself to another and allow others to question and challenge one's thoughts. This ownership turned into sharing slowly and with each of the artists trusting in the process and being curious about what will develop. There were times when the group felt frustrated, going around in circles and feeling agitated with each other. This is when breaks were needed, some food and silence. For the most part, we put our frustration to work, to create and to question. It was food for the mind working with interesting artists. A glue in creating one group came from working in a politicized space that mattered to us all; whether one is Brazilian, Greek, or Palestinian, there is a segregating wall built in the 21st century and no one is stopping it!

In the process, CACTUS members made it clear that we as a group will use what is in the space and what the place gives us. We worked with the architecture of the building and its surrounding as our aesthetics. We worked with shadows, windows, stairwell, roof, metal rods sticking out, broken floors and the echo of our voices, water from the taps running, walls, doors, and doorframes. There was so much material to work and experiment with. We also used what we brought into the place, such as the bottles of water that we drank. One day one of the artists brought with him a flower in a pot. This flower could not be ignored and quickly became part of the piece. It was the hope that everyone left with at the end of the performance.

Inspired by the powerful energy, physical state and history of our abandoned site and the personal experience of each participating artist, we invited and led the audience through a ghost factory – which uses as fuel the presence of the audience – and works through the manipulation of water and dust to keep a pot of flowers alive. Two intimate 20-minute promenade performances took place with an after performance discussion, in afternoons when Palestinian workers climb up the segregation wall "illegally" to cross over to Jerusalem seeking work.

One interesting observation from the audience and the artists was that they were amazed by how they have become blind to the destruction the segregation wall has imposed on Palestinian life and land. Some said that they recall many years passing through this road to Jerusalem and after the wall was built they simply stopped coming near the area. People bring life to places, so through their absence are they helping kill these places?

ATA: BADKEH

My first arts exchange outside Palestine was in 2012, in a collaborative dance project sponsored by the Qattan Foundation, between Les ballets C de la B and KVS Theater from Belgium and 10 Palestinian dancers from different groups and styles: folk dance, capoeira, hip-hop, and circus. The production was entitled *Badke*, a distortion of the Arabic word *dabkeh*, which describes a typical Palestinian folk dance. The production was about searching for identity between Palestine and a global culture, and breaking down movements through dabkeh into other forms. The ideals of collective solidarity and celebration are concepts that extend from the dabkeh in its traditional folk dance form, and in *Badke* these concepts were given new movements from different contemporary dance styles, gestures and movement (AM Qattan Foundation, 2016).

Badke was the first step for me out of the comfort zone, allowing me to question myself about what dabkeh means, and whether it can be a form that allows me to be expressive. During the creation process I was thinking of how to break the patterns of my movement, how to move differently. It was not easy expressing my individuality, in the sense of what I am facing right now, not just representing the past. This process opened the door to questions: if we want to rethink how collective identity can be revived, we first need to explore our individual differences. This will broaden our knowledge and experiences and allow us to work in a collective.

During the process of creating the work there were many discussions. In the beginning I was confused with some topics, such as being naked on stage. What is the difference between the things we *should* not do, and the things we simply *do* not do? I found it interesting exploring how the things that we are "not allowed to do in our society" helped us shape our cultural and artistic collective identity in the production. It helped us find answers to our research and vocabulary to work with in movement. For example, we do not use our lower-torsos in dabkeh. Is this because we should not, or simply do not? So we had to think how we might incorporate ideas and movement with the lower torso.

There was a question raised in the group as to whether we should include some videos related to refugees from the 1967 war. As artists are we supposed to advance our understandings of our collective identity through our work, or should our work always reveal to us where our unique collective identity comes from? This led into a huge discussion, in which questions allowed us to take apart, develop, expand, and start rebuilding ourselves artistically and make space for new ideas to appear.

At the same time, I was aware that many dances that are being performed in Europe represent the society there and reflect the conditions of living there. To me, it is not healthy to accept something just because somebody else is doing it, and to copy other's experiences without looking at mine first. As an artist I need to understand my culture and past and build my own understanding and art, then I will be able to learn from other cultures. I will be lost if I just take the art of another culture without connecting to it to my roots and context of where I live.

In a discussion with the audience from one of the European cities that *Badke* visited, I was faced with the question 'What do you mean by Palestinian identity?'

This kept me questioning what "identity" means, what it represents, and if a collective identity truly exists for those living apart from their homeland in a different culture. Is being a Palestinian connected to a history, or a geography, or a shared contemporary circumstance?

NICHOLAS: LETS MAKE NOISE FOR GAZA

A return visit to Ramallah with my family in 2014 coincided with the bombardment of Gaza through the Israeli military's "Operation Protective Edge." It was the Summer school holidays and so usually a time of daily arts activity, but most cultural events (including dance classes, rehearsals, workshops, and performances) were canceled in empathy for the people of Gaza.

At the same time, social media was abuzz with international declarations of solidarity with Gazans, often in the form of very creative videos. Some younger members of El-Funoun, in the junior Bara'em dance group, were gathered at the Popular Art Centre and wanted to somehow creatively participate in the "intifada" taking place through Facebook and YouTube. This seeded the idea of *Lets Make Noise for Gaza*, a short dance video I created with 18 members of Baraem and El-Funoun over the next week. The video was uploaded and rapidly shared on social media, and subsequently screened at international film festivals.

The basic intent of the work was to make body-percussive dance theater that might reflect the frustration and impotence that comes from watching the televised onslaught of an overpowering military on a civilian population. The group first divided into small teams and developed rhythmic body-percussion phrases. Each team then reconfigured these repetitive rhythmic phrases in different locations around the Popular Art Centre building, creating movements that responded to stairwells, windows, kitchens, and domestic objects. These phrases became scenes that emphasized and contextualized the frustration in very mundane, urban landscapes. The scenes transitioned into each other within the video collage, and built to a crescendo as everyone ran outside for a collectively devised body-percussion dance.

The scenes took 4 days to create and record. I then spent 2 days editing a rough draft, which I shared with the dancers, their parents, and others in the local community. While they enjoyed the spectacle, many felt it remained irreverent and did not comment directly enough on the issue of the bombardment in Gaza.

This was a useful provocation. I had previously spent years in Palestine cocreating dance and theater productions. The intervening years as a dance academic in New Zealand had, however, shifted my artistic sensitivities away from creating work that (to me, at that moment) appeared too literal and dogmatic. I had been less observant of the daily news cycles of carnage being wrought upon Palestinian children by so-called "smart" bombs;

I had paid less attention to the foreign media reports that insinuated the children themselves were somehow responsible. The local community was approaching this artistic production mindful that 551 children in Gaza had been killed and over a thousand permanently injured as a result of the 7-week military attack (United Nations Office for the Coordination of Humanitarian Affairs, 2015). My artistic imperatives had drifted out of alignment with the community that I was working with. I had to acknowledge that intercultural competence is never a completed task, but an ever-unfolding journey of sensitization.

Through further dialogue with the dancers, we added a section at the end in which individual children identified themselves as a Palestinian child, and expressed an enthusiasm for different parts of their own bodies (exclaiming "I love my arms," "I love my knees"), with a final child calmly declaring that she did not want to be a victim of war. Following another round of consultation, it was agreed that subtitles at the start should politically contextualize the artwork.

When I shared this short film with colleagues in Australia and New Zealand, some of the commentary I received was critical of the political didacticism of the work. This reminded me that cultural alienation at home can be an unfortunate result of intercultural artistic collaborations, as intercultural creation inevitably involves forging a new culture that is yet to be acknowledged and shared. How can we, as artists, effectively transport realizations in and out of this border zone of intercultural exchange?

Conclusion: The Homeland of the Body

Intercultural arts exchanges can challenge our cultural ideals, norms, and distinctions. This can lead to a very embodied frustration, as captured by the Palestinian poet Mahmoud Darwish's desperate call,

> Where can I free myself of the homeland in my body?
> (2013, p. 15)

As dancers, we are seeking intercultural arts processes in which we are not forced to abandon the "homelands" within our bodies, but to confidently and competently carry these homes into new, creative landscapes.

Through the production processes of *Badke, the Shape of Water ... Palestine* and *Lets Make Noise for Gaza* we have sought to foreground dialogue, with our artistic colleagues, communities, and audiences. These intercultural projects, while often disturbing, nevertheless allowed space for three themes relevant to the cultural/political ideals of the authors involved: the collaborative generation of ideas, a consensual method of composition, and the production of artwork that has clear social relevance.

This allows us to return to our cultural communities and rationalize our intercultural artistic choices, which in turn extends our ability to engage in artistic leadership. By not seeking to place art above politics, our role as artists has maintained relevance within a highly politicized and contested space.

Acknowledgments

This research has been undertaken as part of the ArtsEqual – project funded by the Academy of Finland's Strategic Research Council from its Equality in Society – programme (project no. 293199).

References

Abu Hadba, A. (1994). How Zionist authorities dealt with Palestinian folklore. In S. Kanaana (Ed.), *Folk heritage in Palestine* (pp. 55–92). Ramallah, Palestine: Al-Shark.

AM Qattan Foundation. (2016). *Badke-a Belgian-Palestinian Dance Production.* Retrieved from http://www.qattanfoundation.org/en/cap-badke-dance-production-en. Accessed on May 1, 2016.

Anderson, B. (1991). *Imagined communities: Reflections on the origins and spread of nationalism.* New York, NY: Verso.

Bennett, M. (1986). A developmental approach to training for intercultural sensitivity. *International Journal of Intercultural Relations*, 10, 179–196.

Beresford, R. (2007). *Lying abroad: A critical study of cultural diplomacy.* Buffalo, NY: Merril Press.

Bhabha, H. (1994). *The location of culture.* London: Routledge.

Bharucha, R. (1993). *Theatre and the world.* London: Routledge.

Buckland, T. (2006). *Dancing from past to present: Nation, culture, identities.* Madison, WI: University of Wisconsin.

Butterworth, J. (2004). Teaching choreography in higher education: A process continuum model. *Research in Dance Education*, 5(1), 45–67.

Cactuspac. (2016). *The shape of water*. Retrieved from http://cactuspac.com/portfolio/the-shape-of-water/. Accessed on March 27, 2016.

Darwish, M. (2013). *Unfortunately, it was paradise: Selected poems*. (M. Akash, C. Forche, & F. Joudah, Trans.). Oakland, CA: University of California Press.

Grau, A. (1992). Intercultural research in the performing arts. *Dance Research*, *10*, 3–27.

Haddad, M. (1994). The relationship of Orientalism to Palestinian folklore. In S. Kanaana (Ed.), *Folk heritage in Palestine* (pp. 93–117). Ramallah, Palestine: Al-Shark.

Hobsbawm, E. (1983). The invention of tradition. In E. Hobsbawm & T. Ranger, (Eds.), *The invention of tradition* (pp. 1–15). Cambridge: Cambridge University Press.

Huleileh, S. (2014). *In the mayhem of dance: The story of El-Funoun popular dance troupe*. Beirut: Dar Al Adab.

Huntington, S. (1992). *The clash of civilizations?* Washington, DC: American Enterprise Institute.

Karayanni, S. S. (2015). Modernism and dance in the Middle East and North Africa. In S. Ross & A. Lindgren (Eds.), *The modernist world* (455–463). New York, NY: Routledge.

Kaschl, E. (2003). *Dance and authenticity in Israel and Palestine: Performing the nation*. Leiden: Brill.

Lewis, B. (2002). *What went wrong? The conflict between Islam and the West in the Middle East*. London: Weidenfeld & Nicolson.

Martin, R. (2016). *Women, dance and revolution: Performance and protest in the Southern Mediterranean*. London: IB Tauris.

Rowe, N. (2002). Cultural boycotts. *Dance Europe*, *52*(May), 50–51.

Rowe, N. (2008). Dance education in the occupied Palestinian territories: Hegemony, counter hegemony and anti-hegemony. *Research in Dance Education*, *9*(1), 3–20.

Rowe, N. (2009). Post-salvagism: Choreography and its discontents in the occupied Palestinian territories. *Dance Research Journal*, *41*(1), 45–68.

Rowe, N. (2010a). *Raising dust: A cultural history of dance in Palestine*. London: IB Tauris.

Rowe, N. (2010b). Movement politics: Dance criticism in the occupied Palestinian territories. *Forum for Modern Language Studies*, *46*(4), 441–459.

Rowe, N. (2011). Dance and political credibility: The appropriation of dabkeh by Zionism, Pan-Arabism and Palestinian Nationalism. *Middle East Journal*, *65*(3), 363–380.

Rowe, N. (2015). Dancing beyond the post-trauma paradigm: Community projects in the occupied Palestinian territories. In S. Burridge & C. Svendler-Nielsen (Eds.), *Dance education around the world* (pp. 55–63). New York, NY: Routledge.

Rowe, N. (2016). Access denied and sumud: Making a dance of asymmetric warfare. In G. Morris & J. Richard Giensdorf (Eds.), *Choreographies of 21st century war* (pp. 25–45). Oxford: Oxford University Press.

Rowe, N., Buck, R., & Martin, R. (2015). The gaze or the groove? Emerging themes from the *New Meanings and Pathways: Community Dance and Dance Education Symposium* in Beijing. *Research in Dance Education*, *16*(2), 184–197.

Said, E. (1993). *Culture and imperialism*. New York, NY: Vintage Books.

Shay, A. (1999). Parallel traditions: State folk dance ensembles and folk dance in 'the field'. *Dance Research Journal*, *31*(1), 29–56.

Shay, A. (2014). *The dangerous lives of public performers*. New York, NY: Palgrave Macmillan.

United Nations Office for the Coordination of Humanitarian Affairs. (2015). Fragmented lives: Humanitarian overview 2014. Retrieved from https://www.ochaopt.org/documents/annual_humanitarian_overview_2014_english_final.pdf. Accessed on June 1, 2016.

Usher, G. (2005). Unmaking Palestine: On Israel, the Palestinians, and the wall. *Journal of Palestine Studies*, *35*(1), 25–43.

Zeitner, D., Rowe, N., & Jackson, B. (2015). Embodiary leadership: Dance, leadership and experiential learning. *Organizational Aesthetics*, *5*(1), 167–187.

18 In Case of Emergency, Break Convention: Popular Education, Cultural Leadership, and Public Museums

Darlene E. Clover

> Museums are such dominant features of the landscape, that they shape our most basic assumptions about the past and about ourselves.
>
> Marstine (2006, p. 1)

anadian poet Marlene Nourbese-Philip once argued that culture was not an insignificant site of struggle, but that its power lay in masking that very fact. There are perhaps no better masters of disguise than public arts and culture institutions. Their is often a facade of authority, reverence, and motionlessness: places where once living artifacts and artworks go to die. Museums seem to cloak themselves in veils of impartiality and neutrality, and seek refuge in a pretext of "detachment from real world politics" (Phillips, 2011, p. 17). They appear to shirk responsibility as pedagogical sites in favor of conserving

299

and preserving, and thereby, evade the torchlights that search for solutions to the disorientating array of contemporary social, cultural, and ecological problems facing the world today. Janes (2009) thus concludes that as social institutions, museums lack the pedagogical and leadership capacities needed to contribute to the dramatic change this troubled world requires.

Yet this more singular, problematic view ignores the multifaceted story that is museums, and fails to capture their complexity and the progressive changes afoot. In this chapter I recognize museums as problematic, but my purpose is to render visible popular education and cultural leadership strategies museums in Canada and Scotland that aim to overcome the trying disguises of convention by taking up critically, creatively, and courageously, some of society's most contentious issues. My intention therefore, is to use these examples place museums in a more composite light of challenge, creativity, and possibility in this "troubled world."

I begin this chapter by situating museums as "pedagogic contact zones," fraught with both difficulty and possibility, and then define how I understand and use the terms popular education and cultural leadership, paying particular attention to their intersections. I then tell three stories from Canada and Scotland of popular education and exhibitionary practices aimed at tackling issues of identity, stereotypes, and intolerance and stimulating critical dialogue and what Haiven and Khasnabish (2004) call the "radical imagination": the ability to reimagine the museum as a cultural leadership institution, and society, "not as [they] are but as [they] might otherwise be" (p. 3).

Museums as Pedagogic Contact Zones

In her studies of early colonial expeditions in Latin American, Pratt (1991) conceptualized these encounters as "contact zones." Contact zones are spaces where diverse cultures meet, clash, and struggle, "often as highly asymmetrical relations of [domination], such as colonialism ... or their aftermaths as they are [still] lived out in many parts of the world today" (p. 1). These zones are marked by differences of power, and are where knowledge and other cultural attributes were appropriated to enhance the privilege, status, and wealth of the colonizers. British feminist theorist McRobbie (2009) applies the contact zone to higher education. She positions university classrooms in Britain as "pedagogic contact zones," spaces where people from diverse backgrounds come together to be assimilated into the dominant structures of a society to directly benefit that society. In these zones, western ideologies and canons of knowledge, history, and/or art are privileged and adopted.

In a framework of "contact zones," large-scale public museums in countries such as Canada and the United Kingdom are for the most part colonial "imaginaries," collusions of bringing into being colonialism and domination made material through exhibitions, displays, artifacts, and practices that reflect rather than disrupt patterns of inequality and injustice (Marstine, 2006; Phillips, 2011). Leadership and power are exercised through an intentional construction of meaning in the mechanisms of selective storytelling and representation that mask or legitimize exploitation, appropriation, and control the discourses of both history and the present. As pedagogic contact zones, museums play roles as civilizing agents, fashioning social conformity, practicing assimilation and maintaining dichotomies such as "modern" and "traditional," the "west" and "the rest," and the "wealthy/worthy of telling" and "the not" (Perry & Cunningham, 1999; Phillips, 2011). Indeed, existing systems of classification privilege western canons of knowledge, the histories of the victorious, the aesthetics of one particular gender, and shape the parameters of what counts as knowledge, has merit and/or relevance (Hooper-Greenhill, 1992; Mayo, 2012). These attributes of social, cultural, and epistemological power were entangled in museum pedagogical strategies that have served to maintain the museums' authority, and enhance primarily, the lives of the already privileged and educated. Power and knowledge are always mutually implicated as the former involves the construction of truth, and latter has implications for who has power.

Yet Foucault (1980) reminded us, power was never located solely in one place or held by a single group. Pratt (1991) recognized colonial encounters as complex and contradictory, knots of conflict as well as collaborative interaction. Contact zones could be spaces of exchange, undertaken in a spirit of reciprocity. McRobbie (2009), too, acknowledges "pedagogic contact zones" as spaces of collective meaning making, with the potential for active critique, debate, knowledge cocreation, resistance, and a praxis of social and self-reflexivity.

This complexity has also been true of museums. As expressions of the spirit of enlightenment, public museums have shown an enthusiasm for equality of access to knowledge, art, and education, and have always provided a plethora of learning opportunities for adults (UNESCO, 1997). Since the 1800s, museum professionals have countered exclusionary and elitist trends, designing what Perry and Cunningham (1999, p. 239) called "revolutionary policies" to expand the museum's role in society beyond serving the elite and patronizing the masses. In 1927, Voaden positioned Canadian museums as places to challenge the emptiness of the "greed of industrial conservatism" by providing access to creativity and imagination (cited in Tippett, 1990, p. 11). Crucial adult education institutions such as the Workers' Education Association saw museums as places of pedagogical possibility, where workers could "learn to refuse to know their place [and thereby] disrupt class conformity" (Highmore, 2010, p. 95). It is this spirit of possibility, opportunity, and disruption I argue lies at the heart of popular education and cultural leadership.

Popular Education

The term popular education is commonly associated with liberation theology work in Latin America, the cultural literacy work of Paulo Freire in Brazil, and the arts-based and dialogic work of the Highlander Center in the southern United States. This means there is no singular definition of popular education, but rather multiple traditions worldwide with nomenclatures such as adult education, community cultural animation, and critical public pedagogy. Popular education therefore is best understood through its various positioning and purposes (Laginder, Nordvall, & Crowter, 2013). Martin (1999) argues that first and foremost, popular education is political in its orientation making it "intentional" in its practice. It offers a "clear analysis of the nature of inequality, exploitation and oppression" and is a primary player in the struggle "for a more just social and cultural order" (p. 5). Popular education understands learners/people as socially located, and works to render visible societal relations of power as ideological obfuscations that legitimize and maintain the status quo, disempowering people by limiting and circumscribing what they feel is possible to achieve or to change (Brookfield, 2006). Popular education is dependent upon institutions located in the intersections and intestacies between the state and social movements such as museums that "perform" pedagogically and thereby have a major impact on society (Crowther, Martin, & Shaw, 1999; Mayo, 2012).

As a knowledge-based practice, popular education begins with and draws on people's knowledge. But as Horton and Freire (1990) argued, knowledge from experience can run out and this has implications for "pedagogy." They dismissed therefore the notion that educators were mere "facilitators." Educators must in fact have an authority of knowledge – values, stated positions, and understandings of issues – and provide access to new resources, knowledge, and social and cultural interventions. By privileging people's knowledge and experiences yet opening doors to alternatives, individuals, and groups could better enhance their ability to assert their interests and be challenged to examine their own assumptions and claims to truth.

Central to popular education is creative practice. For Freire, education itself was an artistic practice. Intentional dialogic processes encouraged people to visualize emancipatory possibilities, reconfigure historical conditioning, and explore representations that blind them to reality (see Shor & Freire, 1987). Popular educators also employ various arts such as drawing, images, videos, poems, music, theater, and puppetry. They marry these with pedagogical processes to uncover, decode, confront, mock, imagine, and/or tell new stories (Barndt, 2011). Artists play key roles as educators and provocateurs in popular education, as they have for centuries responded to the upheavals and changes of their times, interpreting and representing these in visual, poetic, narrative, and performative ways that encourage thought beyond the restrictions of logic and language.

Cultural Leadership

Analogous to popular education, cultural leadership has no ubiquitous definition. However, Sutherland and Gosling (2010) best capture its essence, its connections to popular education and how I actually take up cultural leadership in my own teaching and research. For Sutherland and Gosling, cultural leadership is activity centered on

> encouraging engagement with various cultural activities, practices and artefacts in the belief that such engagement may have positive social benefits … Through advocacy for, and facilitation of, cultural engagement, cultural leaders are involved in projects that invite others to

situations outside everyday experience ... in attempts to emerge positive affordances from cultural interactions for world-dwelling. (pp. 6–7)

Cultural leadership is not a "designated position" but rather "comes from many different people [and is] practiced in many different ways" (British Council, n/d, n/p). Leadership is a dynamic process, in fact a "pedagogical" process, that provides people with access to new and unfamiliar experiences aimed at questioning the nature of culture and society, and the normative narratives and practices that mask vested interests and regimes of truth and power. The British Council refers to this act of leadership as risky or "living dangerously." Illeris (2006) picks up on this, calling for museum processes to be "dangerous [acts] of proposing alternative ways of seeing the world" (p. 16). Cultural leadership is thus a "performance," including the theatrical, the communicative, the ambiguous, experimentation, and interventions. Performance is a practice or exercise of power that juxtaposes incongruities, uses irony, creates disturbances, dislocates the familiar, and shapes new presences and ways of seeing and comprehending.

Central to cultural leadership is also creative practice, which can be seen as a response to Adler's (2006) suggestion that the "twenty-first century society yearns for a leadership of possibility, a leadership based more on hope, aspiration, and innovation than on the replication of historical patterns of constrained pragmatism" (p. 487). A key part of cultural practice, and the work of museums, is telling stories through visuals, objects, narratives, and even theater to engage their audiences. Museums as cultural leaders also use "storytellers" in the form of artists. Artists bring inspirational creativity and forms of improvisational skills that can help us "to create the kind of world that we all wish for" (p. 497).

Today, museum practitioners and artists are being called upon to play leadership roles in constructing the conditions for different kinds of encounters, encounters that seek to engage the public more critically and creativity, and to bring redress to the social, cultural, and material ravages of history and the ideological and political schisms of our time (Sandell & Nightingale, 2012). One of these roles is developing pedagogical and visual means to challenge deeply rooted institutional conventions, and reconstitute the museum as a site of popular struggle. I turn now to these contemporary popular education practices in public museums Canada and Scotland.

Reimagining and Decolonizing

> Art … is a vehicle for the expression and elucidation of
> real situations and events, within which one's political
> and social views are of necessity, exemplified.
>
> (Beyer, 2000, p. 98)

Canada is a contact zone with a colonial legacy and contemporary mind set of Eurocentrism ingrained in its structures, policies, institutions, and the social imagination. A result has been the oppression and marginalization of the Indigenous population, and museums have played a unique role on this stage. Through the glass of the "cabinet of curiosity," museums have whitewashed the brutality of colonization, and presented a one-dimensional face of Indigenous "culture" as static and frozen in time in a bygone era. Yet Indigenous peoples live in the modern world, yet try to honor and carry on traditions, and thereby continually struggle "to bridge and … to live between these two worlds" (Kenny, 2012, p. 4).

Exploring this complicity in maintaining this type of static "colonial imaginary," rendering visible the complexity of contemporary Indigenous identity, and making a commitment to disrupting ingrained, stereotypical notions in society, and gallery lay behind an extraordinary exhibition commissioned in 2014 by the Art Gallery of Greater Victoria (AGGV). This exhibition entitled *Urban Thunderbirds /Ravens in a Material World* was a multimedia display of Indigenous artworks that told new types of stories in imaginative ways, highlighted inhabiting dual cultural existences as paradox and irony, and asked provocative and difficult questions both of itself, as well as society. One specific example was a series of photographers by Kwakwaka'wakw artist Rande Cook, in which he had positioned himself in a traditionally painted mask against a diversity of "modern" backdrops. One particularly poignant and humorous image was of Cook standing in front of the Sistine Chapel, Vatican City. With a jauntily tilted head, the masked artist juxtaposes a representation of his identity against an altar adorned with gold and jewels plundered from Indigenous lands, and numerous other symbols of colonial complicity, power, and domination. Ironically, as the exhibition lets you know, during the photography shoot Cook was actually ejected from the chapel by security guards for being "disrespectful."

Other works in the exhibition challenge the visitor to query who has power and what power looks like in the "contact

zone"? One example is old video footage of an Indigenous
Elder performing a dance for tourists. At first glance it "feels"
like pure appropriation and one feels the shame and sadness.
But the artist asks us to consider how "the other" creates a
counter-dialogue to colonization through what Pratt (1992,
p. 35) called "pariodic, oppositional representations" that mimic
the conqueror's imaginings of Indigenous cultural practices. We
are equally asked to consider within contact zones that aimed to
obliterate traditional practices, what are acts of defiance, and
work toward cultural maintenance. How is cultural power both
exercised and contested? How is it masked and unmasked, both
figuratively and literally?

The entire exhibition is a collision of illusion and reality, of
humor and pathos, of past and present that troubles assurances
and assumptions, and poses questions with no definitive answers.
It provides a way to enter attentively, into the experience of
others and for thinking visually about relations of power. As the
curator noted, educational programming around the exhibitions
ensured that the visitors to the gallery understood that neither
they nor the gallery had "authority here; we have no knowledge.
It was a moment for us to stand back, to listen and to learn. We
are not in control, but we are now a conduit in the process of reconciliation and learning." The exhibition and the programming
work around it is an example of Freirean dialogic pedagogy, processes of reflection on the world that pose a problem to which
educators, learners/visitors, and even the museum itself, must all
mutually apply themselves.

Deconstructing "the Other"

Imagination is what, above all, makes empathy possible.
It is what enables us to cross the empty spaces between
ourselves and those we ... have called other.

(Maxine Green, 1995, p. 3)

For Said (1993), a deeply problematic social practice was what
he called "orientalism," which is today taken up as a discourse
of "othering." Othering is the practice of differentiation that
humans make to distance themselves from each other and create
distinctions composed of hierarchical values. A central component of "othering," as alluded to in the story above, is stereotyping or essentializing. Popular education calls for us to find ways

to deconstruct these often "blatant misrepresentations" with frequently "negative consequences on individuals and groups" (James & Shadd, 2001, p. 6).

In response to this problematic practice, and working within their new mandate to be a more engaged space for dialogue and debate around art and society, the AGGV hosted a Human Library (HL). The HL is a dialogic approach conceived by a group in Denmark who wanted to do something to challenge rising anti-Islamic sentiment (Kudo, Motohashi, Enomoto, Kataoka, & Yajima, 2011). Although the HL most often takes place in a library, the AGGV staff felt it aligned well with a temporary portraiture exhibition that aimed to illustrate the complexity of "identity." Essentially, portraits are about "nonfixed" identity, in essence, how people want themselves to be seen and how they are seen by others and artists.

The HL brought together living "Books," people from different walks of life in Victoria who had agreed to speak with "Readers," the general public, in one-to-one dialogue about their lives and/or work. The Books ranged from a graffiti artist to a Muslim woman artist, a Zen Buddhist Nun to a burlesque dancer, a community police officer to antipoverty and sex trade workers. The HL provided an opportunity to explore dialogically misconceptions and ignorance amongst people who seldom come into contact with or know each other, yet perpetuate problematic constructions and assumptions. The majority of "Readers" were members of AGGV but many had never before frequented the space (Clover & Dogus, 2014). As the evaluator of the event, I found the Readers to be very open about why they came. In particular, I found that they wanted to expand the limits of their own knowledge and come to better understand the members of their community.

The HL provided an interesting balance between two somewhat paradoxical attributes of popular education: to be a safe space for learning but equally, risk-taking or "danger." In the former, it was a nonjudgmental space – "ask me what you want" as the slogan; in the latter, it was a space of discomfort, of unfamiliar lives and stories which highlighted ignorance and bias, best articulated by this woman's comment after speaking with the young Muslim woman artist:

> I don't know, I expected her to be middle aged and dressed in black. Where did that come from I asked myself? It probably came from images of elderly Muslim women crying over dead bodies in places like Palestine

that you see all the time on television. So I guess I had that in my subconscious and that was kind of limiting, don't you think? When I told what I had expected she was kind. But the media has a lot to answer for and so do I.

(Clover & Dogus, 2014, p. 79)

This comment is an out-loud example of critical self and social/media reflection that is central to popular education and cultural leadership. Activities such as the HL work to incur what Lorde (1984) called the act of creative solidarity – understood as the possibility of new ways of feeling, and seeing the world around us.

Tackling Religious Intolerance

[The radical imagination] is the courage and intelligence to understand that the world can and must be changed.

(Haiven & Khasnabish, 2014, p. 3)

When an intolerant Catholic visitor at St. Mungo Museum for Religious Life in Glasgow smashed a Hindu idol, staff members decided to develop a program to tackle intentionally, religious prejudice in its many forms. They began by reshaping consciously their exhibitions to speak more openly to problems such as intolerance, war, genocide, or the place and role of women in the church (Carnegie, 2009). These exhibitions became the platforms for on-site workshops that brought together in conversation diverse religious-political groups of people who share timeless animosities such as Northern Ireland Protestants and Catholics, and Hindus with Muslims. Gray (in press), an adult educator at St. Mungo, argued that one had to have great pedagogical skill to take up issues such as sectarianism and racism as "they have the potential to be incredibly uncomfortable for people taking part and possibly even damaging if not carefully facilitated" (n/p). The educational process included both planned and unstructured activities. The planned or structured exercises asked each person to introduce themselves and their current views on the subject of religious pluralism, and the educators then took these statements and worked with people to explore levels of agreement about specific issues amongst participants as well as the degree of commitment they have to a particular and different opinion. The workshops were seen as spaces for "pedagogical struggle," for risk-taking discomfort. Educators often stayed a step back from the discussions, even when situation became quite uncomfortable. For this to work, however, the educators had to be very attentive to the discussion, listening actively, and only intervening when someone felt "the situation could be dangerous" (Gray, in press, n/p). Lopes and Thomas (2006) call this "dancing on live embers" and they argue it requires great courage as well as the educational skill to pull off successfully. Central to the process were the objects and displays themselves, used to trigger collective reactions and opinions that could be tested against the group for agreement or disagreement, claims to truth, blindness/intolerance, in order to generate empathy. Empathy is powerful because it is not "knowing" another's religion but rather, a sense of curiosity to question and to engage in conversation.

The popular education and cultural leadership strategies at St. Mungo are based on visual and conversational juxtaposing, using the power of imagery, language, ideas, and objects, in combination with pedagogical expertise to strengthen the communicative value of the exhibitions in what Amin (2002) calls a "politics of living of together" (p. 960). Further, the combination of the exhibitions and workshop aim to provide distinctive spaces where personal, religious, and political roles and relations can be renegotiated and reimagined beyond a divisionary and intolerant world.

Contributions to Popular Education and Cultural Leadership

> Without the radical imagination, we are left only with
> the residual dreams of the powerful.
>
> (Haiven & Khasnabish, 2014, pp. 3−4)

Public museums as contact zones carry the "residual dreams" of those with wealth, power, and status. Many remain stuck in time, prisoners of elitist roots and practices where knowledge, art, and history are presented as unequivocal statements of truth and authority. Through veils of impartiality and authority, they seem to deny their own complicity in whitewashing oppression, marginalization, conflict, and contradiction. But museums are not simply neutral, uncontested, and problematic spaces: they have always been in processes of change and their contributions have always been more complex than unidimensional (Marstine, 2006). This

has never been more true than today where museums face growing
pressure from professionals, scholars, and society to become more
socially responsive and responsible, to be places for critical discourse and thinking, and to take strides to recreate new histories
and stories that challenge both audiences and their own institutional imaginaries (Sandell & Nightingale, 2012).

Before I turn to some of the key elements of cultural leadership and popular education in museums as outlined in the stories
above, let me first recognize that activities such as these can be
characterized as isolated projects and therefore, unlikely to
achieve the widespread social change this troubled world, or the
museum itself requires. But one could say that with near impunity about any popular education workshop, popular theater
project, street puppet demonstration, or even a course in our
higher education institutions. Single acts may not always be the
stuff of instant, monumental change, but each progressive act is a
form of resistance against normative framings and attitudes in
the world, and as such, each is a contribution to the struggle for
justice and change.

Museums are powerful sites as they are first and foremost
pedagogical and leadership institutions that do not just reflect
cultural identity but rather, produce it through the practice of
framing. New exhibitionary framing practices can counter depo-
liticized, stunted, repetitive, and sanitized discourses of normative
Indigenous peoples or uncover uncomfortable aspects of religion.
Working with Indigenous artists to speak their own truths, or
reshaping religious stories around new issues, are "dangerous
acts" of leadership that reposition control and authority, and disrupt or and reorganize power. In so doing, educators plant seeds
for future institutional, social, and epistemological change.

Going further, through new insights and "theatrics," the
artists and educators engage in dialogic and visual rebelliousness,
something popular educators argue is critical to social change
(e.g., Crowther et al, 1999). Set against the steady state of the
status quo of society and the museum, the stories I have told
show how pedagogical practices can work to reposition the
world as if it might be otherwise, to stimulate what Haiven and
Khasnabish in their 2014 book call the radical imagination, and
what I will illustrate in this chapter as a creative coming together
of the rational and the nonrational, truth, and illusion, in a process of encounter with the unexpected, the unfamiliar. Radical
imaginative interventions are powerful not because they resolve,
have the answer or point the way but because they disrupt

familiar and entrenched modes of "knowing" and create an unease around that knowing. What the visitor/learner will do is equally unknown, but Arendt (1963) reminds us challenges never go unheeded, but compel different kinds of thought, reflection, and even sometimes, action.

Popular educators such as Shaw and Meade (2013) argue that in these times of fear-mongering and neoliberal individualism, we desperately need spaces for "authentic" dialogue and "really useful" knowledge. Authentic dialogue goes beyond sharing monologues, taking turns telling each other what we already know. Authentic dialogue is an exchange, sometimes risky, aimed directly at generating new understandings and empathy, through eye contact and deep listening. Key to empathy as noted above is curiosity about others, and the ability to ask questions, rather than simply feigning alliance or consensus. Authentic dialogue was a clear strategic objective of both St Mungo and the AGGV. These were "intentional" political pedagogical acts that brought together people with different world views, a search or quest for knowledge not in isolation, but with other knowledge seekers. Really useful knowledge is about a collective, mutually socially critical and mature cultural understanding of difference and diversity that in the cases presented above, arises from arts and object-based practices that evoke creativity, imagination, and informed critique.

What I have demonstrated in the stories I have told are what Newman (2006) calls "practices of discomfort." By engaging in practices of discomfort artists, educators, and museums create opportunities to move beyond stereotyping, ignorance, and entitlement. Discomfort is by its very nature controversial, dislocating, and most importantly, disruptive, making it invaluable to complicating, deconstructing, and questioning the ideologies and myths that separate groups, spark violence, hate, or intolerance. For Greene (1995, p. 109) "disruption has to do with consciousness and the awareness of possibility" and this has so much to do with educating other human beings. The amount of mettle this type of popular education and cultural leadership work takes in museums should never be under-estimated. To disrupt one's own institutional practices and defy convention is never easy; it takes both courage and skill on the part of educators and artists. Perhaps the popular education and culture leadership practices of museums such as St Mungo and the AGGV are just beginnings, and may be thwarted by the persistence of convention. But they reveal a promise for museums to be spaces where people might not only imagine, but also produce new ways of being and living together.

References

Adler, N. (2006). The arts and leadership: Now that we can do anything, what will we do? Retrieved from http://amle.aom.org/content/5/4/486.short. Accessed on April 12, 2008.

Amin, A. (2002) Ethnicity and the multicultural city: Living with diversity. *Environment and Planning A, 34*, 959–980.

Arendt, H. (1963). *On revolution*. New York, NY: Viking Press.

Barndt, D. (2011). *Community arts and popular education in the Americas*. Albany, NY: State University of New York Press.

Beyer, L. E. (2000). The arts and social possibility. In *The arts, popular culture and social change*. New York: Peter Lang.

British Council (2014). *Cultural leadership*. Retrieved from http://creativeconomy.britishcouncil.org/media/uploads/files/Cultural_Leadership_2.pdf. Accessed on March 15, 2017.

Brookfield, S. (2006). *The skillful teacher: On technique, trust and responsiveness in the classroom*. San Francisco, CA: Jossey-Bass.

Carnegie, E. (2009) Catalysts for change? Museums in a pluralistic society. *Journal of Management, Spirituality and Religion, 6*(2), 157–169.

Clover, D. E., & Dogus, F. (2014). In case of emergency, break convention: A case study of a Human Library project in an art gallery. *Canadian Journal for the Study of Adult Education, 26*(3), 75–91.

Crowther, J., Martin, I., & Shaw, M. (Eds.) (1999). *Popular education and social movements in Scotland*. Leicester: NAICE.

Foucault, M. (1980). *Power/knowledge*. New York, NY: Pantheon.

Gray, C. (2016). St Mungo Museum of Religious Life and art: A space to speak, discuss and be heard. In D. E. Clover, K. Sanford, L. Bell, & K. Johnson (Eds.), *Museums and adult education: Animating social and cultural change* (pp. 1526). Rotterdam: Sense Publishing.

Greene, M. (1995). *Releasing the imagination*. San Francisco: Jossey-Bass.

Haiven, M., & Khasnabish, A. (2014). *The radical imagination*. London: Zed Books.

Highmore, B. (2010). Out of place: Unprofessional Painting, Jacques Rancière and the distribution of the sensible. Retrieved from open.ac.uk. Accessed on August 9, 2015.

Hooper-Greenhill, E. (1992). *Museums and the shaping of knowledge*. London: Routledge.

Horton, M., & Freire, P. (1990). *We make the road by walking*. Philadelphia, PA: Temple University Press.

Illeris, H. (2006). Museums and galleries as performative sites for lifelong learning: Constructions, deconstructions and reconstructions of audience positions in museum and gallery education. *Museum and Society, 4*(1), 15–26.

James, C. E., & Shadd, A. (2001). *Taking about identity: Encounters in race, ethnicity and language*. Toronto: Between the Lines Publishing.

Janes, R. (2009). *Museums in a troubled world*. Milton Park: Routledge.

Kenny, C. (2012). Skilay: Portrait of a Haida artist and leader. In C. Kenny & T. Ngaroim Fraser (Eds.), *Living indigenous leadership: Native narratives on building strong communities* (pp. 84–96). Vancouver: UBC Press.

Kudo, K., Motohashi, Y., Enomoto, Y., Kataoka, & Yajima, Y. (2011). *Bridging differences through dialogue: preliminary findings of the outcomes of the Human Library in a university setting.* Retrieved from http://humanlibrary.org/paper-from-dokkyo-university-japan.html. Accessed on September 05, 2013.

Laginder, A., Nordvall, H., & Crowter, J. (2013). *Popular education, power and democracy.* Leicester: NIACE.

Lopes, T., & Thomas, B. (2006). *Dancing on live embers: Challenging racism in organizations.* Toronto: Between the Line Publishing.

Lorde, A. (1984). *Sister outsider: Essays and speeches.* Trumansburg, NY: The Crossing Press.

Marstine, J. (Ed.) (2006). *New museum theory and practice.* Oxford: Blackwell Publishing.

Martin, I. (1999). Introductory essay: Popular education and social movements in Scotland today. In J. Crowther, I. Martin, & M. Shaw (Eds.) *Popular education and social movements in Scotland.* Leicester: NAICE.

Mayo, P. (2012). Museums, cultural politics and adult learning. In L. English & P. Mayo, *Learning with adults.* Rotterdam: Sense Publishing.

McRobbie, A. (2009). *The aftermath of feminism: Gender, culture and social change.* London: Sage.

Newman, M. (2006). *Teaching defiance: Stories and strategies for activist educators.* San Francisco, CA: Jossey-Bass.

Perry, G., & Cunningham, C. (1999). *Academies, museums and canons of art.* London: The Open University.

Phillips, (2011). *Museum pieces: Toward the indigenization of Canadian museums.* Montreal: McGill/Queens University Press.

Pratt, M. L. (1992). Arts of the contact zone. *Profession*, 33–40.

Said, E. W. (1993). *Culture and imperialism.* New York, NY: Knopf.

Sandell, R., & Nightingale, E. (Eds.) (2012). *Museums, equality and social justice* (3rd ed.). London: Routledge.

Shaw, M., & Meade, R. (2013). Community development and the arts: Towards a more creative reciprocity. In P. Mayo (Ed.), *Learning with adults: A Reader* (pp. 195–204). Rotterdam: Sense Publishers.

Shor, I., & Freire, P. (1987). *A pedagogy for liberation: Dialogues on transforming education.* South Hadley, MA: Bergin & Garvey.

Sutherland, I., & Gosling, J. (2010).Cultural leadership: Mobilizing culture from affordances to dwelling. *The Journal of Arts Management, Law, and Society*, 40(1), 6–26. doi:10.1080/10632921003603984

Tippett, M. (1990). *Making culture: English-Canadian institutions and the arts before the Massey commission.* Toronto: University of Toronto Press.

UNESCO (1997). *Museums, libraries and cultural heritage: Democratising culture, creating knowledge and building bridges.* Hamburg: IEU.

Epilogue

In my part of the introduction to this book, I focused on the power of the arts to challenge existing worldviews and to create opportunities for real change. In this epilogue, I want to shift attention to implications for leadership. How might leaders, whether they have formal authority or not, take best advantage of the insights presented here?

First, a bit of backdrop. The gulf between those who practice grassroots leadership and those who theorize about leadership has been shrinking for some time. Much of this is due to changing images of who leaders are and what they should do. In the past half century, notions about the essence of leadership have shifted from a hierarchical view that leadership flows from a leadership *position* to a much more lateral view that leadership roles are available to everyone. James MacGregor Burns' *Leadership* (1978), which popularized "transformative leadership," was one of the first to describe the shift from a command-and-control vision to one that is more inclusive and participatory. Robert Greenleaf's notions about "servant leadership" (1977) held that leadership should at its core attend to matters of inequity and social injustice. A third seminal work, one that left solely hierarchical views of leadership behind forever, theoretically if not always in practice, was Ronald Heifetz' 1994 book, *Leadership Without Easy Answers*. In it, Heifetz introduced the notion of what he calls *adaptive work*, or the learning required when neither the problem nor its solution is clearly defined (a term cited in several of the chapters in this book). *Learning* is the key term in adaptive work. Because there are no easy answers or singular solutions in adaptive work, achieving agreement on a course of action means first that participants must recognize that their existing perspectives won't lead them to a resolution, and second that they must suspend assumptions, entertain fresh questions, and try on the perspectives of others. They must realize that a solution is not a matter of applying technical solutions more expertly, but rather one of framing problems differently. Thus, for Heifetz, the essence of leadership lies in creating space for important learning to occur. The arts as a means of creating space for learning and change is evident in virtually every chapter of this book.

A more recent example of the affinity between arts and leadership is Amanda Sinclair's book *Leadership for the Disillusioned: Moving Beyond Myths and Heroes to Leading that Liberates* (2007). Rejecting the notion that leadership is about controlling people, she defines leadership as "a relationship in which leaders inspire or mobilize others to extend their capacity to imagine, think, and act in positive new ways" (p. xvi). Sinclair is just one of many in recent years who have called for a shift in perspective about leadership: from hierarchical to lateral, from command-and-control to participatory, from "heroic" to team-oriented, and from mechanistic to organic.

Artists who work in the service of social change are there already, and always have been. They know that leadership roles are available to everyone; they know that leadership at its core should attend to matters of inequity and social injustice; they know that deep change requires that we suspend assumptions, entertain fresh questions, and try on the perspectives of others; and they know that real leaders mobilize others to extend their capacity to imagine, think, and act in positive new ways. They know this without ever having read Burns, Greenleaf, Heifetz, or Sinclair. As these authors uniformly recognize, the chapters in this book go far beyond merely reinforcing emerging leadership theory, however. They have done this in several ways.

First, they have shown that effective leaders must appeal to the extra-rational side in all of us. Artists know that they first have to create a *feeling* of disorientation. The cellist of Sarajevo (Chapter 1) did this with beautiful music in a war zone; Fela Kuti (Chapter 2) did this through provocative music and outrageous behavior; Václav Havel (Chapter 4) did this with absurdist theater; Banksy and other "tricksters" (Chapter 6) did this by creating mild disorder through street art; and JR (Chapter 7) does this through humor. Common to all of these, and the other artists profiled here, is the recognition of the power of dissonance as a precursor to change, what Clover in Chapter 18 calls "practices of discomfort."

Second, these chapters have shown that provocation, while necessary, is not sufficient, and can easily be counter-productive. The provocation must be modulated, producing a "productive zone of disequilibrium," as Heifetz et al. put it (2009, p. 29). Mwangi (Chapter 5) realized that his photographs of victims of injustice had to be selected carefully; practitioners of Theatre of the Oppressed and Theatre for Development (Chapters 13 and 14) learned that raising consciousness is effective only temporarily, and that organizers have to be careful about the kind and intensity of disorientation they want to create. Challenge must be balanced with support.

Third, leadership is a social experience, and art creates a collective "critical consciousness," a term coined by Paulo Freire, the person most cited in this book. Freire is most well known as an emancipatory educator, but these chapters reveal his importance to leadership. Freire is seemingly everywhere here. His theory that people undergo a shift in consciousness as they become aware of the limits that surround them, and require a "dialogic process" for this to happen (Chapter 8), highlights a critical role for the arts, namely providing a forum for participation in a safe "aesthetic space" (Chapter 12), and consolidation of energy (through music in Chapters 9 and 10). A similar dialogic process can be created through dance (Chapter 17): "Within an intercultural creative process, contrasting socio-political assumptions and values about movement can be placed under scrutiny."

Fourth, successful artists as leaders know that they cannot, as artists, go it alone. They must join forces with champions and supporters in other sectors. A striking example is the hard lesson learned in the ACT-UP movement (Chapter 11). As Jarc and Garwood note (Chapter 6), "In order to exert influence, the leader must find a balance between significant visibility and expert/referent power." The skateboard project (Chapter 15) would never have gotten off the ground, so to speak, had it not been for the Kennedy Center's investment in the artists' visions. And in the Tikondwe Teachers' Project (Chapter 16), the artists and teachers from outside that culture had to work to be accepted as influential people within the group dynamic. "The continued growth and success of the group depends on such leadership," the chapter authors write.

Fifth, while the arts might provide a catalyst for grassroots change, it is never predictable what that catalytic effect will be. This leads to potentially contradictory positions. On one side is the importance of persistence, illustrated most dramatically by the Sarajevo cellist (Chapter 1). On the other, as Hayden notes in his profile of Havel (Chapter 3), "one of the challenges of grassroots leadership is resisting the temptation to continue operating from one's initial diagnosis of the social situation that first compelled one to action." A quality that made the "Gap Fillers"

(Chapter 8) successful is that they considered their work as a continuous experiment: "when something doesn't work, the Gap
Fillers may improvise, or try something new, *but they never stop*
(italics added)." The key therefore is for artists as leaders is to
both persist and reflect, and never become victims of what John
Dewey (1933) called "dogmatic thinking," the sense that "facts"
are permanently settled and not up for reconsideration.

Sixth and finally, leadership through the arts not only trans-
forms, the art *itself* is transformed, and in fact must be transformed if it is to effect change. As Augusto Boal is quoted as
saying (Chapter 15), "the image of reality can be translated into
the reality of the image." Or as Ross notes in Chapter 16,
"Artistic leaders see invisible bridges, use questions to make them
visible and strong, and then lead us across." Examples of this are
Armand Gatti (Chapter 4) and practitioners of Theatre of the
Oppressed (Chapter 12) who, by inviting participants to speak
and perform in ways counter to their own beliefs, help create a
transformation of those words and actions into participants' own
repertoire.

The insights contained in this book are not new. They have
all been expressed before – but never so powerfully or compre-
hensively. The beauty of the arts for grassroots leadership is that
while they disturb, they can also encourage; while they create
conflict, they can also bring together; and while they may be eva-
nescent, they can also transcend time and space.

Jon F. Wergin
Editor

References

Burns, J. (1978). *Leadership*. New York, NY: Harper & Row.

Dewey, J. (1933). *How we think* (Rev. ed.). Boston, MA: D.C. Heath.

Greenleaf, R. (1977). *Servant leadership*. New York, NY: Paulist Press.

Heifetz, R. (1994). *Leadership without easy answers*. Cambridge, MA: Harvard University Press.

Heifetz, R., Grashow, A., & Linsky, M. (2009). *The practice of adaptive leader-ship*. Boston, MA: Harvard Business Press.

About the Authors

Denise Archuleta began her journey into the world of computer graphics at Sandia National Laboratories. Her artwork was published in *Art and the Computer* (Pruiett, 1984). The book, with an introduction by Carl Sagan, was second runner up in the Gesnigraphics Government Users Conference at the National Security Agency. She relocated to AT&T and found her way to Alamance Community College where she utilizes her experiences with the "real world" in teaching.

Greg Artzner and **Terry Leonino** are professional musicians with more than 40 years of experience. In addition to their work as concert performers and political activists they are distinguished artists in the field of music and history, well-known for researching and producing lecture-concert programs of music and history for schools, universities, festivals, special events, commemorations, the National Parks, and numerous museums, including programs and performances produced especially for the Smithsonian Institution.

Noora Baker is a performer, creator and a member of El-Funoun Dance Troupe since 1987, also a co-founder and member of CACTUS performance art collective since 2012. She is the Head of Training and Production at the Troupe, choreographing and directing different productions.

Liz Barber is an experienced teacher, literacy studies professor, and ethnographic researcher. She teaches in the Watson School of Education at the University of North Carolina Wilmington, and conducts service learning and participatory action research projects in schools in North Carolina and Domasi, Malawi. Her research focuses on writing, literacy, and leadership as these develop within cultures or communities of practice.

Ralph Bathurst lectures in leadership and management at Massey University's Albany Campus. His particular focus is on the arts and aesthetics of leadership, and his background as a musician and music educator informs his interest in translating ideas from the world of music into organizational behavior and leadership practice. He has published in a number of journals including *Leadership*, *Journal of Management Inquiry*, and *Administrative Sciences*; he is a contributor in *The Sage Handbook of Leadership* and is an associate editor of *Organizational Aesthetics* and *Corporate Governance*. Ralph is actively involved in the music world and is a member of the St Matthew's Chamber Orchestra, where he plays viola.

Marta D. Bennett (M.Div, Ed.D in Leadership), originally from the United States, has lived in Nairobi, Kenya, since 1994, where she teaches and serves as Head of Department, Leadership Studies, at International Leadership University, Kenya. Prior to ILU, she served at Seattle Pacific University in the United States, then Daystar University in Nairobi. Besides raising her adopted Kenyan sons and daughter, she enjoys reading, mentoring, community involvement and relishing the diversity of Africa.

Bonface Njeresa Beti is a peace educator who applies theatre-based interventions with communities to transform conflict. Since 2004 he has worked with Amani People's Theatre, and has used theatrical tools in conflict zones in Kenya, South Sudan, Somalia, Sierra Leone, Rwanda, and Canada. He spent his earlier life with Shangilia Mtoto Wa Africa street children's theatre in Nairobi. He has a BA in communication and is pursuing graduate studies in Peacebuilding at the University of Manitoba, Canada.

Kevin Bottomley serves as Lead Faculty Area Chair for Research and Dissertation in the School of Advanced Studies at the University of Phoenix. He teaches doctoral research methodology courses and serves as a dissertation committee chair. Kevin received his Ph.D. in Leadership Studies from North Carolina Agricultural and Technical State University. His current research focuses on sustainable leadership, decision-making, and the education system in Malawi.

Mecca Antonia Burns holds a master's degree in counseling psychology and is a registered drama therapist and board-certified drama therapy trainer. She is co-founder of Presence Center for Applied Theatre Arts in Charlottesville, Virginia, USA. Since 2007, she has been training groups in Theatre of the Oppressed in Uganda, Kenya, Senegal, Spain, and Romania. She contributed to the books *Transforming Leadership* and *Interactive and*

Improvisational Drama and the journal *African Conflict and Peacebuilding Review*.

Kennedy C. Chinyowa is the Director for the Centre for Creative Industries at Tshwane University of Technology, South Africa. The centre incorporates research and capacity building within the Creative Industries. He has taught at several universities including the university of Zimbabwe, Griffith University (Australia) and Wits University where he was Head of the Division of Dramatic Arts. He has won numerous research awards and has published widely in books and referred journals.

Darlene E. Clover is Professor of adult education, Faculty of Education, University of Victoria, Canada. Her areas of study and teaching include: women and leadership; feminist and arts-based adult education and research; and cultural leadership and learning in museums and art galleries. Darlene's most recent co-edited volumes include: *Women, adult education and leadership in Canada*. Toronto (2015, Thompson Educational Publishing); *Lifelong learning, the arts, and creative cultural engagement in the contemporary university: International perspectives* (2013, Manchester University Press); and *Adult education and museums: Animating social, cultural and institutional change* (2016, Sense Publishing).

David H. Davenport is an experienced teacher, artist and graphic designer. He is a Design Instructor in the Advertising and Graphic Design Department, Alamance Community College, Graham, North Carolina. David received his BFA from East Carolina University and MFA from the University of Maryland. He was awarded the Skowhegan Painting Scholarship and Yaddo Fellowship Award in painting.

Marsha Dwyer is a student and senior research assistant in an entomology lab at North Carolina Agricultural and Technical State University. She graduated from Alamance Community College in 2015 with a degree in Horticulture Technology. Upon completion of her education, Marsha hopes to fill a role as a college educator and work with international farming communities.

David Edelman is Associate Professor of Arts Management and Director of the Performing Arts Leadership and Management Program at Shenandoah University. He is the founder and co-editor of *The American Journal of Arts Management* and serves on the board of directors of the Association of Arts Administration

Educators. He has been a professional arts manager, AIDS activist, and fighter for LGBTQ social justice for much of his adult life.

Margot Edwards has a Management PhD from Massey University and explores leadership in the not-for-profit sector which had implications for the visual arts. Her current research agenda focuses on artists as leaders which, in particular, examines how artists are leading the social change towards environmental awareness and sustainability. She is part of a group of management scholars at Massey University who work in the area of organizational creativity.

Suzanne Epstein received her doctorate in education and leadership from Union University & Institute in Cincinnati, Ohio. Currently, her primary research interest is on the connection between leadership and communication. She worked and studied in France as a theater and radio artist where she began to follow the work of Gatti and other experimental theater and dance artists. Her work has appeared in theater, communication and leadership journals.

Susan (Susie) J. Erenrich is a social movement history documentarian. She uses the arts for social change to tell stories about transformational leadership, resilience and societal shifts as a result of mobilization efforts by ordinary citizens. She holds a Ph.D. in Leadership and Change from Antioch University, an M.S. in Conflict Analysis and Resolution from George Mason University, an M.A. in Performing Arts from American University, and a B.A. in Sociology from Kent State University. Susie is the founder/Executive Director of the Cultural Center for Social Change. In that role she has created projects for diverse populations, which have brought to life images of social movement history long forgotten while offering new and thoughtful perspectives on issues never fully addressed. This was accomplished through various artistic mediums. Susie has more than three decades of experience in nonprofit/arts administration, civic engagement, community service and community organizing. She also has diversified teaching experience at universities, public schools and community-based programs for at-risk, low-income populations; has edited and produced historical audio recordings and anthologies; and has extensive performance, choreography and production experience. She currently teaches at American University and New York University.

Tricia Garwood has been researching creativity and innovation and teaching corporate, educational and individual clients how to develop and apply creative and innovative techniques for over 25 years. Previously a consultant based out of Philadelphia, Tricia is currently a Manager of Leadership Programs specializing in creativity and innovation for the Walt Disney Company.

Joshua M. Hayden is Director of Executive Programs at Lipscomb University where he works with organizational leaders to create customized leadership development programs in downtown Nashville. He teaches leadership ethics in the College of Leadership and Public Service. Prior to Lipscomb, Josh was Assistant Professor of Leadership Studies at Cumberland University for six years. Josh's doctoral and master's degrees in higher education leadership and policy and organizational leadership are from Vanderbilt University and his undergraduate degree is from the University of Richmond Jepson School of Leadership Studies.

Nita Hungu is a musician and co-founder of Hue Music, a company that uses music to develop talent and leadership in vulnerable children and young creatives in Kenya, thereby promoting social change. Nita graduated from International Leadership University, Kenya, with a Masters in Organizational Leadership. She developed a curriculum based on her thesis *Enhancing Leadership Development through Music* from which she teaches and trains various organizations. She lives with her husband in Nairobi, Kenya.

Edin Ibrahimefendic is an attorney who works for the Institution of Human Rights Ombudsman of Bosnia and Herzegovina in Sarajevo. He focuses on the promotion and protection of human rights, rule of law, and good governance. He assists individuals who believe that their human rights have been violated find resolutions. During his career, he has collaborated with various international non-governmental organizations. His additional fields of interest include history and art, especially of post-conflict countries. He graduated from the Law Faculty of Sarajevo.

James Jarc is currently pursuing a Doctorate from Creighton University's Interdisciplinary Leadership program. He holds a Master's in Communication and Leadership from Gonzaga University. James teaches a variety of communication courses at the college level, and, when not in the classroom, provides organizational and communication consulting services to clients across the country.

Lucy Kapenuka hails from Mulunguzi Village, Traditional Authority Juma in Mulanje, Malawi. She attended Namulenga Primary in Mulanje, St. Mary's Girls Secondary, and graduated from Mzuzu Teachers Training College as a Professional Teacher in 1986. Formerly the Head Teacher at Domasi Demonstration Primary, she currently heads the Infant School at Malemia Primary. Lucy has co-authored several publications on topics in education. She is mother of two boys and two girls, and wife to Rex Kapenuka.

Ata Khatab is a dancer, choreographer and member of El-Funoun Dance Troupe since 1989, touring the Arab world and internationally. He is the artistic coordinator of the Troupe and a trainer for children and youth at the Popular Art Centre's dance school and outreach program.

Natalia Kostenko is Professor of Sociology and Head of the Department of the Sociology of Culture and Mass Communication at the Institute of Sociology of the National Academy of Sciences of Ukraine. The field of her scientific interest: media theory, communication research and cultural studies. Her last publications deal with the processes of culture dynamics in modern societies, media development trends, production and translation of meanings in multicultural society.

Alinane Misomali is pursuing his Bachelor of Education degree at Domasi College of Education, progressing towards his goal to become a teacher educator in Malawi. Previously he served as a Standard 5 and 6 grade teacher at Domasi Demonstration School. He is the author of *Vain Hope*, the first book in the Warm Heart H.O.P.E. project. His success has been an inspiration to many other Malawian teachers.

Anu M. Mitra has a Ph.D. from the University of Rochester, Rochester, New York. Since 1988, she has worked at the Union Institute & University in various administrative and teaching capacities. Since 2000, she has served as faculty in the Graduate College of the University. She has also taught at Yale University, Antioch College, Empire State College, and Sichuan University in China. Her areas of scholarly research are design thinking; visual culture and leadership development; social justice theory and practice; and arts-based practices in organizational settings.

Selloane Mokuku is an experienced theater maker, facilitator and academic. She is a former member of Marotholi Traveling theatre, a Drama For Life Alumni, ShakeXperience Programmes Manager and co-producer of award-winning theater production; Animal Farm. She coordinates use of arts to teach Science, English and mathematics. She is a DTech student at Tshwane University of Technology; South Africa. Her research interests are in arts education and community development.

Holly Near has been a strong voice for integrity, justice and peace for over four decades. Influenced by social change movements around the world, she writes and sings songs that look at the world through the lens of feminism, anti-racism and peace. Born in rural northern California, Holly Near has a powerful performance style that rings true whether from a stage like Carnegie Hall or from a make-shift platform in war-torn El Salvador.

Destenie Nock is a PhD student in Industrial Engineering at the University of Massachusetts Amherst. Her work focuses on the cost of integrating renewable resources to the power grid, in hopes of making it easier for developing nations to have a consistent reliable source of electricity. She hopes to continue to focus on increasing the ease of access to education for people in underdeveloped communities, as she progresses through her career.

Greg Chidi Obi, a Nigerian-American, is an assistant professor, and the coordinator/adviser for the Business Management Technology program (BMT) at Ohio University Chillicothe Campus. He is currently a Ph.D. candidate at Indiana Institute of Technology, Fort Wayne, IN, for studies in Global Leadership with a major in Organizational Management. The proud father of a son (Clive) holds an MBA from Purdue University, while his undergraduate studies were at IMT and ESUT in Enugu, Nigeria.

Maxwel Eliakim Okuto is Executive Director of Amani People's Theatre, based in Nairobi, Kenya, which uses a participatory multi-arts approach to conflict and peacebuilding. His background is in social sciences and he has many years of experience working throughout Kenya and internationally. He helps design and facilitate conflict transformation and peacebuilding projects with agencies in Kenya, Uganda, Rwanda, Sudan, Tanzania, Austria, Canada, Sweden, and the Netherlands.

Ann Potts is Associate Dean for Teacher Education and Outreach in the Watson College of Education, University of North Carolina Wilmington. Experiences in Europe, the Middle East and Africa inform her work with teachers on culturally responsive practice. Research involves teachers' situated understandings of language, literacy, and culture within school and community. She has published in *International Journal of Multicultural Education*, *International Journal of Learning*, and *International Journal of Teaching and Learning in Higher Education*.

Garth A. Ross is Vice President for Community Engagement at the John F. Kennedy Center for the Performing Arts in Washington, DC, where he has produced over 5,000 performances featuring artists from all 50 states and over 50 countries. He is responsible for the *Millennium Stage* daily, free performance series, as well as many other notable projects and festivals including *Joyful Sounds: Gospel Across America*, *Look Both Ways: Street Arts Across America*, *American Voices with Renee Fleming*, *One Mic: Hip Hop Culture Worldwide*, and *Finding a Line: Skateboarding, Music and Media*. Garth received his BA in English Literature and Music from Connecticut College, and is a Henry Crown Fellow of the Aspen Institute.

Nicholas Rowe has performed with dance companies internationally. He resided in the West Bank from 2000 to 2008, and is currently an associate professor in Dance Studies at the University of Auckland.

Mziwoxolo Sirayi is Executive Dean, Faculty of the Arts at Tshwane University of Technology, South Africa. He has received numerous accolades and published extensively. He was the first scholar to do research on pre-colonial indigenous drama in South Africa. Mpingana is one of the many community engagement projects he is passionately involved in. He is the Chair for the UNESCO Chair in cultural industry and sustainable development.

Justin Snyder is Department Head of Horticulture Technology at Alamance Community College in Graham, North Carolina. His courses focus on soils and sustainability. Justin is pursuing his Ph.D. in Leadership Studies from North Carolina Agricultural and Technical State University. His dissertation examines outcomes of the Warm Heart H.O.P.E. (Helping Others Prosper

Educationally) mother tongue literacy book project described in this chapter.

Randal Joy Thompson is a scholar-practitioner who has spent her career as a Foreign Service Officer in international development, working in countries in all regions of the world. She has advised governments and helped to change systems that impact women's health, child welfare, education, social science research, and program evaluation. Her research interests include leadership, organization development, and the commons. Dr. Thompson is President and CEO of Dream Connect Global, a social networking corporation, and its subsidiary, Excellence, Equity, and Empowerment.

Kateryna Tiahlo is Research Fellow at the Institute of Sociology of the National Academy of Sciences of Ukraine. Recently she was conferred PhD in sociology for studies in relations between Ukrainian modern belles-lettres and formation of the ethnic and national identity. She continues studying the problems of contemporary fiction and literary practices, up-to-date informal education methods, the "Theater of the Oppressed" in particular.

Jon F. Wergin has been Professor of Education Studies at Antioch University's Graduate School of Leadership & Change since 2003, following a 30-year career at Virginia Commonwealth University, where he won awards for both teaching (1996) and scholarship (1998). He was the founding director of the Forum on Faculty Roles and Rewards in the American Association for Higher Education in 1992, and continued an active association with AAHE until 2004, focusing his scholarship on leadership and change in higher education. He is the author or co-author of 18 books and monographs, 13 book chapters, and 64 scholarly papers, and has given invited addresses to more than 100 colleges, universities, and professional organizations on such topics as faculty development, evaluation research, professional education, curriculum development in higher education, evaluation and change in higher education, and department chair development. His most recent publication is "Differentiation and Integration: Managing the Paradox in Doctoral Education" (L. Alexandre, co-author), Emerald, 2016.

Chifundo Ziyaya comes from Mtogolo Village, Traditional Authority Malemia, in Zomba, Malawi. She attended Zomba Primary, Nkhamenya Girls' Secondary, and St. Joseph Teacher

Training College, and qualified as a T2 Teacher in 1993. At Domasi Demonstration Primary she heads the Child Feeding Program Committee, was a central planner of the mother tongue literacy seminar there, and has co-authored a journal article on this topic. Chifundo is mother of three and a wife to John Stone.

Index